T0383877

IT Governance and Information Security

Advances in Cybersecurity Management

Series Editors: Yassine Maleh and Ahmed A. Abd El-Latif

The *Advances in Cybersecurity Management* series is a knowledge resource for practitioners, scientists, and researchers working in the various fields of cybersecurity, hacking, digital forensics, cyber warfare, viruses, or critical infrastructure. It explores the complexity of the business environment and the rapidly changing risk landscape in which it must operate.

IT Governance and Information Security: Guides, Standards, and Frameworks
Yassine Maleh, Abdelkebir Sahid, Mamoun Alazab, Mustapha Belaissaoui

For more information about this series, please visit: https://www.routledge.com/Advances-in-Cybersecurity-Management/book-series/AICM

IT Governance and Information Security
Guides, Standards, and Frameworks

Yassine Maleh, Abdelkebir Sahid,
Mamoun Alazab, Mustapha Belaissaoui

CRC Press
Taylor & Francis Group
Boca Raton London New York

CRC Press is an imprint of the
Taylor & Francis Group, an **informa** business

First edition published 2022
by CRC Press
6000 Broken Sound Parkway NW, Suite 300, Boca Raton, FL 33487–2742

and by CRC Press
2 Park Square, Milton Park, Abingdon, Oxon, OX14 4RN

CRC Press is an imprint of Taylor & Francis Group, LLC

ISBN: 978-0-367-75324-5 (hbk)
ISBN: 978-0-367-75325-2 (pbk)
ISBN: 978-1-003-16199-8 (ebk)

DOI: 10.1201/9781003161998

Typeset in Times
by Apex CoVantage, LLC

For Adam, Lina, Walid and Sabrine . . .
Yassine Maleh

In loving memory of my dad
Abdelkebir Sahid

Mamoun Alazab would like to acknowledge the support from Charles Darwin University, and the Department of Corporate and Digital Development, Northern Territory Government of Australia.

This work was supported by the Ministry of Education of the Republic of Korea and the National Research Foundation of Korea (NRF-2021S1A5A2A03064391)

Contents

Detailed Contents

Preface

Implementing information technology (IT) governance is imperative for driving and evolving the information system (IS) in agreement with the stakeholders. This requirement has been seriously amplified in the era of digital transformation. Historically, the information system entered the company in stages, as services were provided, but today, it plays a key strategic role and must be managed in this way.

IT Governance (*IT-GOV*), which has emerged in the business and IT world, is a complex subject to demystify. Researchers and professionals from different perspectives have investigated this field. From a theoretical point of view, studies have been carried out on decision-making structures, affecting factors and characteristics of IT-GOV. Instead, professionals became interested in the technical mechanisms and tools of IT-GOV. More broadly, despite the wealth of research on the latter, there has been no study addressing IT-GOV as a whole, nor a holistic approach integrating governance, risk management, compliance, and agility into a single approach to manage IT services. To develop this approach, we have a plethora of methodologies and standards, which have been developed to ensure a good IT-GOV within organizations to optimize processes to achieve business objectives, including ISO 27001, ISO 38500, COBIT, ISO 27005, and ITIL or DevOps and SecOps. Organizations use various mechanisms to ensure that their security architecture is aligned with the organization's business objectives and complies with local standards, rules, and regulations for global IT and IT-GOV governance. Despite the different options available, there is a fundamental confusion about the various methods used by IT managers and between the different terminologies that have suddenly emerged (all at once) in the business world, including corporate-GOV (C-GOV) and IT-GOV, due to their lack of a Universal approach to governance.

This book discusses strategic information technology governance and information security: guides, practices, and maturity frameworks. There are many works which discuss the topic of IT governance. However, this book's main concept is to explore IT governance and information security through new approaches for IT governance maturity in a large organization. This book can examine IT governance and information security and provide IT staff, managers, and various IT professionals with frameworks and models to implement effective strategic IT governance.

The book's scope covers the maturity of IT governance and information security processes in the organization, which closely associates general management, business alignment, and IT departments.

On the other hand, and despite their importance, it does not cover the operational aspects of IT management, such as project development and the recurring production of services, as long as these are placed entirely under the responsibility of the IT department and therefore have less interaction with the rest of the organization.

These operational aspects are also dealt with, particularly in the 'general IT controls'. Our approach consists of addressing IT governance and information security through four main axes:

- IT governance guides and practices;
- IT Service Management as a key pillar for IT governance;
- Cloud computing as a key pillar for Agile IT Governance; and
- IT-GOV and maturity frameworks.

In the context of these trends, this book addresses significant issues in the field of IT governance and cybersecurity. For its value to be practically and scientifically realized, this book aims to provide a sampling of recent advances and ideas on research progress. It will present the state of the art and the state of the practice of how to address unique IT governance and information security challenges facing emerging technologies. This book is ideally designed for policymakers, students, researchers, academicians, and professionals looking for current research interested in exploring and implementing efficient IT governance and information security strategies.

Yassine Maleh
Abdelkebir Sahid
Mamoun Alazab
Mustapha Belaissaoui

About the Authors

Yassine Maleh (http://orcid.org/0000-0003-4704-5364) is an associate professor of cybersecurity and IT governance at Sultan Moulay Slimane University, Morocco. He is the founding chair of IEEE Consultant Network Morocco and founding president of the African Research Lab in Cybersecurity and Information Technology. He is a senior member of IEEE and a member of the International Association of Engineers IAENG and The Machine Intelligence Research Labs. Dr Maleh has made contributions in the fields of information security and privacy, Internet of things security, wireless and constrained network security. His research interests include information security and privacy, Internet of things, network security, information systems, and IT governance. He has published over 50 papers (book chapters, international journals, and conferences/workshops), eight edited books, and three authored books. He is the editor-in-chief of the *International Journal of Information Security and Privacy* (IJISP) and the *International Journal of Smart Security Technologies* (IJSST). He serves as an associate editor for IEEE Access (2019 Impact Factor 4.098) and the *International Journal of Digital Crime and Forensics* (IJDCF). He was also a guest editor of a special issue on *Recent Advances on Cyber Security and Privacy for Cloud-of-Things in the International Journal of Digital Crime and Forensics* (IJDCF), Volume 10, Issue 3, July–September 2019. He has served and continues to serve on executive and technical program committees and as a reviewer of numerous international conferences and journals such as *Elsevier Ad Hoc Networks*, *IEEE Network Magazine*, *IEEE Sensor Journal*, *ICT Express*, and *Springer Cluster Computing*. He was the Publicity chair of BCCA 2019 and the General Chair of the MLBDACP 19 symposium and ICI2C'21 Conference. He received the Publon Top 1% reviewer award for the years 2018 and 2019.

Abdelkebir Sahid (https://orcid.org/0000-0003-2952-5700) is a Ph.D. of the Hassan 1st University in Morocco, in Information Systems Management Agility, since 2014. Dr Sahid is Senior Lecturer ISDS (Information Systems and Decision Support) laboratory at Hassan 1st University since 2019. Dr Sahid has made contributions in the fields of Information Systems Strategic Agility. His research interests include Information Systems Agility, IT Management, and Governance. He has published over 30 papers (book chapters, international journals, and conferences/workshops) and is the author of two books: *Strategic IT Governance and Performance Frameworks in Large Organizations* by IGI-Global and *Strategic Information System Agility: From Theory to Practices* by Emerald. In addition, he has served and continues to serve as the reviewer of numerous international conferences and journals, such as the *Journal of Cases on Information Technology* (JCIT) and the *International Journal of End-User Computing and Development* (IJEUCD).

Mamoun Alazab (https://orcid.org/0000-0002-1928-3704) is the associate professor in the College of Engineering, IT and Environment at Charles Darwin University, Australia.

He received his Ph.D. degree in Computer Science from the Federation University of Australia, School of Science, Information Technology and Engineering. He is a cybersecurity researcher and a practitioner with industry and academic experience. Dr Alazab's research is multidisciplinary and focuses on cybersecurity and digital forensics of computer systems, including current and emerging issues in the cyber environment like cyber-physical systems and the Internet of things, by taking into consideration the unique challenges present in these environments, with a focus on cybercrime detection and prevention. He looks into the intersection use of machine learning as an essential tool for cybersecurity; for example, for detecting attacks, analyzing malicious code, or uncovering vulnerabilities in software. He has more than 100 research papers. He is the recipient of a short fellowship from the Japan Society for the Promotion of Science (JSPS) based on his nomination from the Australian Academy of Science. He delivered many invited and keynote speeches, 27 events in 2019 alone. He convened and chaired more than 50 conferences and workshops. He is the founding chair of the IEEE Northern Territory Subsection: (February 2019–current). He is a senior member of the IEEE; is the Cybersecurity Academic Ambassador for Oman's Information Technology Authority (ITA) is a member of the IEEE Computer Society's Technical Committee on Security and Privacy (TCSP), and has worked closely with government and industry on many projects, including IBM, Trend Micro, the Australian Federal Police (AFP), the Australian Communications and Media Authority (ACMA), Westpac, UNODC, and the Attorney General's Department.

Mustapha Belaissaoui is a professor of Computer Science at Hassan 1st University, Settat, Morocco, president of the Moroccan Association of Free Software (AMP2L), and head of Master Management Information System and Communication. He obtained his Ph.D. in Artificial Intelligence from Mohammed V University in Rabat. His research interests are combinatorial optimization, artificial intelligence, and information systems. He is the author and co-author of more than 70 papers including journals, conferences, chapters, and books, which appeared in refereed specialized journals and symposia.

Introduction

BOOK TOPIC

Every organization has an information system (IS) to support its activities, business, and exchanges with the outside world, whatever its size, purpose, means, or sector of activity. The IS is at the heart of any organization. It is the organization's nervous system; indeed it reflects its image. The organization's performance depends on the efficiency of its IS; in other words, the organization cannot function without IS. The services they provide are just as indispensable as the supply of water or electricity. Communication, which occupies a prominent place in our contemporary societies searching for ever-increasing productivity, requires the mastery of economic, social, and cultural information. The global explosion of the Internet has considerably changed the situation and given IS an inescapable dimension to the development of the global economy and society (Ali et al., 2015). All this makes IS governance, security, and agility a nationwide issue (Sahid et al., 2020). Thus, any organization must understand and be aware of the need to ensure the security of its IS by analyzing and managing the risks that weigh on its IT assets to ensure the continuity of operation of its services to ensure sustainability over time. The environment related to IT and communication is the target of many threats. The openness of networks and their increasing complexity involving actors with multiple profiles have increased the vulnerability of IS, which is manifested by the destruction, alteration, access, and disclosure of sensitive data to modify them or harm the proper functioning of IS or the reputation of organizations (Chatterjee et al., 2018). Organizations are subject to numerous attacks. The balance sheet has enough to worry executives and IT managers (Benaroch & Chernobai, 2017), in fact, according to a study by the consulting firm Price Waterhouse Coopers (PwC) published in October 2015 (PwC, n.d.), the number of computer attacks against companies has increased by 38% worldwide in 12 months.

Thus, a quantitative study conducted by OpinionWay on cybersecurity among 174 members of the Club des Experts de la Sécurité de l'Information et du Numérique (CESIN) revealed a lot of information on this subject; according to the report of this study, 80% had suffered at least one cyberattack in 2018. This is the headline figure of the study, 48% of these companies have suffered at least four cyberattacks over the past 12 months (CESIN, 2019). That's why some of the findings of this CESIN barometer prove to be much more worrying. Indeed, the cyberattacks encountered would be more and more harmful and influential on the business of companies. It would even be

DOI: 10.1201/9781003161998-1

59% of the affected companies that would have noticed a negative impact after having suffered a cyberattack.

To face IT risks, organizations multiply security layers by implementing firewalls, IDS/IPS, PKI architecture, NAC, access control, anti-virus, among others (Kumar & Kumar, 2014). This approach is fundamentally necessary (Eroğlu & Çakmak, 2016). It is even the first brick to be implemented to build a robust security program. However, this approach remains insufficient and reactive because of its purely technical aspect; it is due to its structures which consist of a technical and a functional part. To ensure the resilience of the Information management system, organizations are increasingly adopting proactive strategies, through the implementation of business continuity plans (BCPs) and disaster recovery plans (DRPs), or by using private or public clouds that allow outsourcing business applications to an external entity to solve security problems (attacks, viruses, intrusion, etc.) (Bahl & Wali, 2014). These approaches have given a lot of satisfaction over time. Still, the feedback from the giants in the field. Rocha Flores et al. (2014) show that economic changes and new technological trends influence the current vision of IS. The obvious problem is that all these approaches (both proactive and reactive) do not cover all aspects of the organization (functional, social, organizational, operational, managerial, etc.).

Hence, it is important to adopt a broader vision that includes risk management, agility, and IS governance (Nicho, 2017). In this sense, several methodologies and standards have emerged to ensure good governance and agility of the organization's IS to optimize processes to achieve business objectives and align them with IT while complying with the legislation in force. This broad spectrum of approach choices creates significant confusion among IT managers and between the different terminologies that have suddenly emerged in the business world, including IT governance, IS governance, organizational governance, information security management system (ISMS), and change management and IT agility.

Facing the problems generated by the use of IT is done, among other things, by the implementation of an information security management system (ISMS) to protect the fundamental pillars of information security, namely confidentiality, integrity, and availability (Nicho, 2017). To achieve this crucial objective, several reference systems, methods, and standards (COBIT, ITIL, ISO 27000, ISO38500, CMMI, COSO, etc.) can be used separately or at the same time to benefit from the set of complementary functionalities at some levels and redundant at others (Maleh et al., 2019). However, the use of these standards and references generates a considerable additional cost, not to mention the problems caused by redundancy and the mountains of documentation that go with it. At this point, it must be emphasized that there is no single leading practice model defined for IT-GOV because the security risk profile and the objectives and practices of each organization differ (even within the same sector). Therefore, it is important to recognize that any model must be customized or merged with others to fit the needs of each organization.

This book aims to study the impact and role of implementing IT governance practices on the business value derived from IT. This research looks at the gaps between business practices in IT governance and information security: best practices, guides, and maturity frameworks. Several surveys and case studies have been conducted in organizations, aiming to provide readers with a practical vision of IT governance and information security.

BOOK OVERVIEW

The threat to technology-based information assets is greater today than in the past. The evolution of technology has also been reflected in the tools and methods used by those who attempt to gain unauthorized access to data or disrupt business processes. Attacks are inevitable, regardless of the organization (Tashi & Ghernaouti-Hélie, 2007). But the sophistication and persistence of these attacks depend on the attractiveness of that organization as a target, primarily based on its role and assets. Today, the threats posed by some misguided individuals have been replaced by highly specialized international organized crime groups or foreign states that have the skills, personnel, and tools to conduct covert and sophisticated cyber-espionage attacks (Ula et al., 2011).

We live in a technology-driven world. It is not uncommon for organizations to look to technical security solutions first, without considering how these solutions will be implemented, maintained, and managed on a day-to-day basis. Too often, we see organizations implementing technical safeguards such as firewalls or intrusion detection, but not correctly implementing security policies or procedures. This results in inadequate practices that compromise security and expose assets to significant risk (von Solms & van Niekerk, 2013).

Security governance brings together all the basic elements of cyber defense and effective risk management. Without this governance, dangerous gaps persist and assets are inevitably compromised. In addition, the executive team is unaware of their organization's risk exposure, for which they will ultimately be held accountable.

Security cannot exist in a vacuum and must be part of an overall risk management strategy based on the organization's business objectives and values. Organizations need to know their risk tolerance or 'acceptable risk level'. This threshold may vary by asset class (Soomro et al., 2016). For example, an organization may tolerate a certain level of risk where the impact is considered minor but be very resistant to any risk that could damage its reputation. Governance is the mechanism by which these risk values are reflected in the direction and judgment that determine business plans, information architecture, security policies and procedures, and operating practices (Xue et al., 2008). However, there is no point in determining direction if there are no measures to ensure it is followed.

Compliance audits and reviews are the 'secret ingredients' that ensure security policies and processes are strictly adhered to, by the company's risk or security management strategy (Gwebu et al., 2020). They are also an integral component of all operations management programs, including ISO 27001, COBIT, Sarbanes Oxley, and ITIL. Without a compliance assurance process, it is impossible to ensure that risks are being managed as intended or to detect and correct potential problems when they are not.

BOOK OBJECTIVES

This book discusses IT governance and information security. Many books discuss the topics of IT governance. However, the main concept of this book is to explore IT governance and information security through best practices, standards, and maturity frameworks. This book contains three sections and eight chapters to explore this topic. This book can explore IT governance and information security characteristics and provide IT staff, managers, and different IT professionals' frameworks and models to implement an efficient IT governance and information security strategy in the organization.

This book describes many case studies from International viewpoints and collects a lot of literature and research from scientific databases. Hence, this book clearly illustrates the issues, problems, and trends related to the topic and promotes the readers' international viewpoints.

The overall objectives are as follows:

- To propose practical solutions for effective IT governance and information security, taking into account recent technological developments. To help decision-makers, managers, Information security professionals, and researchers design a new IT governance and information security paradigm taking into account the new opportunities associated with the digital era.
- To combine guides and practices so that readers of the few books (beginners or experts) find both a description of the concepts and context related to the IT governance and information security, as well as practical solutions and maturity frameworks for various IT application areas (Information System, IT service management, information security, etc.).

The books proposed in this sense will not give more details on the different standards and maturity frameworks of IT governance and information security. We will try to address this issue by bringing together academic and professional background to provide readers with a solid theoretical and practical basis for a good understanding of this subject.

THE BOOK'S ORGANIZATION

The book is organized into three sections and eight chapters. A brief description of each of the chapters follows:

The Introduction section provides the background for the book; introduces the research, including the problem being addressed, the motivation for the research, and the book organization.

Section 1: IT Governance: Definitions and Standards

Chapter 1, 'Information System and IT Governance Evolution', illustrates the evolution of information systems development based on three interdependent phases and provides a profound overview of current IT governance literature.

Chapter 2, 'IT Governance and Information Security: Guides and Standards', presents a comprehensive understanding of the current state of IT governance standards and best practices. It exploits a frame of reference inspired by the four 'words' framework that was initially introduced to characterize IT engineering problems.

Section 2: Maturity Frameworks for Information Technology Governance

Chapter 3, 'IT Governance in Organizations: A Maturity Framework based on COBIT 5', provides a deeper understanding of IT governance frameworks and their adoption, drawing on established information systems theories. A mixed two-stage approach using quantitative and qualitative studies is used to examine the feasibility of developing an IT governance assessment framework based on COBIT.

Chapter 4, 'IT Service Management as a key pillar for IT Governance: A Maturity Framework Based on ITILv4', proposes a practical maturity framework to improve ITSM/ITAM processes with the addition of two drivers: agility and security.

Chapter 5, 'Cloud Computing as a Key Pillar for Agile IT Governance', proposes a conceptual framework to improve IT agility, through cloud computing. One of the primary motivations of this research is the lack of fieldwork when considering how cloud computing improves information system's agility.

Section 3: Maturity Frameworks for Information Security Governance

Chapter 6, 'Information Security Governance: Best Practices in Organizations', aims to explore the engagement processes and the practices of organizations involved in a strategy of information security governance.

Chapter 7, 'Information Security Governance: A Maturity Framework Based on ISO/IEC 27001', aims to discuss information security governance and to address the weaknesses identified in the literature. Based on ISO/IEC 27001 framework and practices of information security management and governance described in Chapter 6, the authors propose a practical maturity framework for information security governance and management in organizations.

Chapter 8, 'Information Security Policy: A Maturity Framework Based on ISO/IEC 27002', aims to guide organizations in their approach to implementing an IT Security policy. The purpose is to present a practical model of IT security policy based on ISO/IEC 27002 through a case study.

The last section of this book will summarize the different contributions while highlighting the challenges and limits of current IT governance and information security strategies.

REFERENCES

Ali, S., Green, P., & Robb, A. (2015). Information technology investment governance: What is it and does it matter? *International Journal of Accounting Information Systems*, *18*, 1–25. https://doi.org/10.1016/j.accinf.2015.04.002

Bahl, S., & Wali, O. P. (2014). Perceived significance of information security governance to predict the information security service quality in software service industry: An empirical analysis.

Information Management & Computer Security, *22*(1), 2–23. https://doi.org/10.1108/IMCS-01-2013-0002

Benaroch, M., & Chernobai, A. (2017). Operational IT failures, IT value destruction, and board-level IT governance changes. *MIS Quarterly*, *41*(3), 729–762. https://doi.org/10.25300/MISQ/2017/41.3.04

CESIN. (2019). *Club des experts de la sécurité de l' information et du numérique baromètre de la cyber- sécurité des entreprises sommaire*. Barometre CESIN.

Chatterjee, S., Kar, A. K., & Gupta, M. P. (2018). Alignment of IT authority and citizens of proposed smart cities in India: System security and privacy perspective. *Global Journal of Flexible Systems Management*, *19*(1), 95–107. https://doi.org/10.1007/s40171-017-0173-5

Eroğlu, Ş., & Çakmak, T. (2016, January). Enterprise information systems within the context of information security: A risk assessment for a health organization in Turkey. *Procedia Computer Science*, *100*, 979–986. https://doi.org/10.1016/j.procs.2016.09.262

Gwebu, K. L., Wang, J., & Hu, M. Y. (2020). Information security policy noncompliance: An integrative social influence model. *Information Systems Journal*, *30*(2), 220–269. https://doi.org/10.1111/isj.12257

Kumar, G., & Kumar, K. (2014). Network security–an updated perspective. *Systems Science & Control Engineering: An Open Access Journal*, *2*(1), 325–334.

Maleh, Y., Sahid, A., & Belaissaoui, M. (2019). *Strategic IT governance and performance frameworks in large organizations*. IGI Global. https://doi.org/10.4018/978-1-5225-7826-0

Nicho, M. (2017). Managing information security risk using integrated governance risk and compliance. *Computer and Applications (ICCA), 2017 International Conference on*, 56–66. https://doi.org/10.1109/COMAPP.2017.8079741

PwC. (n.d.). *The Global State of Information Security® Survey 2017*, www.pwc.com, http://www.pwc.com/gx/en/issues/cybersecurity/information-security-survey.html.

Rocha Flores, W., Antonsen, E., & Ekstedt, M. (2014). Information security knowledge sharing in organizations: Investigating the effect of behavioral information security governance and national culture. *Computers & Security*, *43*, 90–110. https://doi.org/10.1016/j.cose.2014.03.004

Sahid, A., Maleh, Y., & Belaissaoui, M. (2020). *Strategic information system agility: From theory to practices*. Emerald Publishing Limited. https://doi.org/10.1108/978-1-80043-810-120211001

Soomro, Z. A., Shah, M. H., & Ahmed, J. (2016). Information security management needs more holistic approach: A literature review. *International Journal of Information Management*, *36*(2), 215–225. http://doi.org/10.1016/j.ijinfomgt.2015.11.009

Tashi, I., & Ghernaouti-Hélie, S. (2007). Security metrics to improve information security management. *Proceedings of the 6th Annual Security Conference*, 47-1–47-13.

Ula, M., Ismail, Z., & Sidek, Z. (2011). A framework for the governance of information security in banking system. *Journal of Information Assurance & Cybersecurity*, *23*(8), 1–12. https://doi.org/10.5171/2011.726196

von Solms, R., & van Niekerk, J. (2013). From information security to cyber security. *Computers & Security*, *38*, 97–102. http://doi.org/10.1016/j.cose.2013.04.004

Xue, Y., Liang, H., & Boulton, W. R. (2008). Information technology governance in information technology investment decision processes: The impact of investment characteristics, external environment, and internal context 1. *MIS Quarterly*, *32*(1), 67–96. www.jstor.org/stable/25148829

SECTION 1

IT Governance
Definitions and Standards

Information System and IT Governance Evolution

1

1.1 INTRODUCTION

The first generation of information systems was mainly considered as a strictly technical discipline. To automate existing manual processes, each application is considered a separate entity, and its use aims to increase organizational productivity and efficiency. As a result, the primary efforts of IT professionals have been to develop new methods for modeling organizational information; hence, database management was the 'killer application' (Chen, 1976; Halpin, 2001). Also, the possibility of networking and the advent of personal computers (instead of terminals) has provided the cornerstone for a new and broader use of information technology, which promotes a transition in the use of technology and its use. However, the second phase's conceptual challenge was to manage the information rather than merely collect it and store it in a central database (Aiken et al., 1991; Batra et al., 1988; Dennis et al., 1988; Drucker, 1995; Gallupe et al., 1988; Olson, 1985; Zwass, 1992). The designation of the services reflected this commitment to support management rather than office work: most IT services became management services and were coordinated by IT system managers (Couger et al., 1979).

However, during this period, most IS activities focused primarily on data management, with little attention to information management needs (Goodhue et al., 1988; Senn, 1978).

Since the 1980s to the early 1990s, research has focused more on identifying relevant information technology applications, which has led to new applications, supported through generic system types, in data-processing systems and management information system (MIS). CIOs realized that it is possible to effectively leverage the advanced information content of MIS applications in support of top management's decision-making processes. Thus, during the second phase, a new concept was developed, including decision support systems (Kasper, 1996), expert systems (Yoon et al., 1995), data warehousing

DOI: 10.1201/9781003161998- 3

(Chenoweth et al., 2006), intelligent system (Gregor & Benbasat, 1999), knowledge management systems (KMSs) (Alavi & Leidner, 2001), and executive information systems (Walls et al., 1992).

The management services were renamed information systems services, the primary objective of which was to make information accessible to all departments of the organization. Issues of inter-connectivity, scalability, and reliability of the information system have become essential. Also, enterprise resource planning (ERP) software is emerging with an exponential increase in installations in large organizations (Beatty & Smith, 1987; Hayes et al., 2001; Scheer & Habermann, 2000; Sharif et al., 2005).

In the third phase, the most critical change introduced was the emergence of global networks and the World Wide Web (WWW), which have overcome the traditional limitations of IT use.

Since then, applications have become an integral part of business strategies and created new opportunities to develop alliances and collaborations beyond organizational and national boundaries (Lyytinen & Rose, 2003; Walters, 2001).

Many researchers perceive Internet computing as a significant computer revolution that has changed previous computer concepts (Isakowitz et al., 1995), in different ways, mainly how a computer service is developed and compiled. A new concept marked this phase: the 'digital enterprise' (Bauer et al., 2001).

The Internet has enabled new digital relationships to be established through inter-organizational systems, taking advantage of e-commerce and e-business trends (Allen, 2003; Daniel & White, 2005; Shore, 2006), electronic markets (Albrecht et al., 2005; Bakos et al., 2005), new application services and CRM, other services (Currie et al., 2014; Ma et al., 2005; Susarla et al., 2006). The Internet has allowed the emergence of new business models that support organizational operations based on the degree of digitization of their products, services sold, business processes, or delivery agents (Oetzel, 2004; Turban, 2007).

Meanwhile, organizations have become aware of the strategic importance of information systems. While some initially considered IT as 'necessary evil', IT had emerged as a necessary part of staying in business, and most companies see it as an essential source of strategic opportunities, proactively trying to determine in what way it can help them gain a competitive advantage.

Strategic information systems have been developed to support strategy formulation and planning, particularly in uncertain and highly competitive environments (Buhalis, 2004; Newkirk & Lederer, 2006).

The third phase marks the technological development in terms of miniaturization of the devices and increasing processing capacity, which ultimately allowed them to be commercially exploited in line with their functions.

The manifestation of IT devices in physical space makes it possible to offer new applications and services that target a much larger and more diverse group of users. Traditionally, users had to be trained in the functionalities of the information system. This training process could be supplemented either formally or through repeated trial and error.

The vision of 'everyday computing' (Zaphiris et al., 2002) requires that information technologies can be used, literally by everyone, regardless of their knowledge and experience in computing. Wireless sensors can detect and process information about the individual and trigger the system response based on certain dynamic or predefined events.

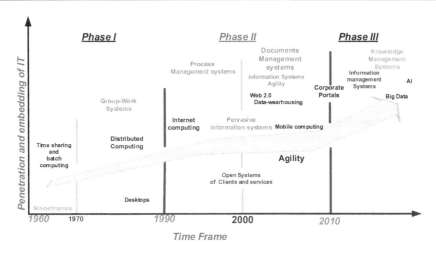

FIGURE 1.1   The evolution of information systems.

User-system interactions are extended beyond the desktop concept. Environmentally driven technologies (hand-gesture recognition) (Alewine et al., 2004; Sawhney & Schmandt, 2000) encourage more realistic communication with the new IS class. Figure 1.1 illustrates the evolution of information systems.

1.1.1 Information System Definition and Objective

Nowadays, organizations are more open to the outside world than ever before, forcing managers to seek the adequacy and coherence between external and internal factors and the content of the company's strategy. As such, information is the nerve center of war and development. The need to collect, process, and diffuse information and the need for increased coordination of activities inside and between companies are emerging sources of competitive advantage (Figure 1.2).

The information system must address these needs through new information technologies and the implementation of KMSs appropriate to the technologies acquired to put external knowledge to the company's benefit and facilitate the internal distribution of knowledge (Galliers, 2006). ICT-based KMSs accelerate information flows, remove non-value-added tasks, enhance process reliability and quality, support tacit and explicit knowledge, promote knowledge sharing across the organization, and facilitate decision-making (Halawi et al., 2005; Wickramasinghe, 2003). However, new information technologies do not always guarantee the efficiency of modern information systems, which require new critical success factors. Thus, the continuous and coherent evolution of information systems constitutes the major problem facing companies. Organizations are confronted with some issues, including the integration, interoperability, and agility of information systems in the context of their company strategy to ensure evolution in correlation with unpredictable internal and external changes.

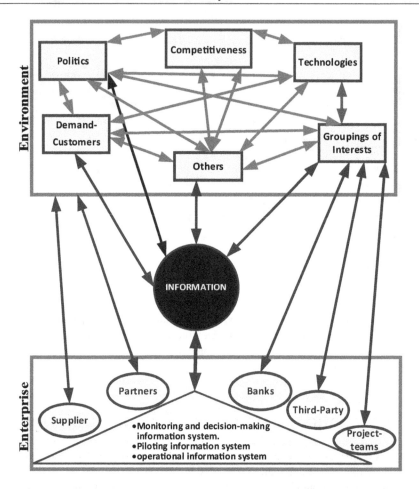

FIGURE 1.2   A systemic view of the company and the environment (Galliers, 2006).

1.1.2 Information System Concept

Regardless of its size, purpose, or means, any human organization has an information system to support its internal activities and its exchanges with the outside world, as shown in Figure 1.3. Today, the information system is at the heart of the functioning of any organization. It reflects its image through the data it handles, and its efficiency determines its performance. In this way, information systems are associated with the notion of organization.

The information system is the company's nervous system. As such, it is at the heart of its processes and an essential element of its strategy. On the other hand, the term system indicates a set of interacting elements and not a simple combination of its elements. In this context, Enterprise Information Systems constitute an interactive set of all informational

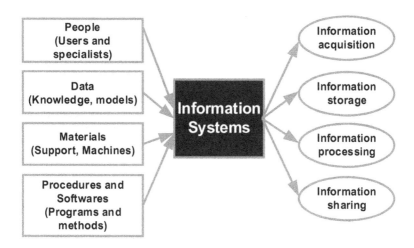

FIGURE 1.3 Information system structure.

situations, even more, the complex interplay of all the exchanges of information necessary for the company's proper functioning. It is at the heart of the quest for competitive advantage in improving the way the company operates and is a tool for serving its users and serving its strategy, where information is considered the vital raw material for its operations. In a company, the information system constitutes a network of dynamic and logical links that support the interactions between the organization's different elements.

Rather than being wiring that passes data between different locations, the information system represents an effective way of connecting people. It capitalizes on collective knowledge, actively structures the organization and management and ensures the availability of relevant information where and when needed while ensuring the company's responsiveness and its communication with the environment (markets, partners, etc.).

The objective of the information system is to allow the decision-maker to have information that will enable them to decide a suitable action at the right time (Dove, 1995; Wim Van Grembergen & De Haes, 2009; Zhang & Sharifi, 2000).

There are various definitions related to the information system: An information system consists, at least, of a person of a given psychological type who faces a problem in an organized context for which he needs evidence to arrive at a solution, where a presentation method makes the proof available. It determines the main variables of an MIS (Mason & Mitroff, 1973).

According to Dove (1995) (Wim Van Grembergen and De Haes (2009), and Zhang and Sharifi (2000), an Information system is an organized set of resources:

- People: users and developers;
- Data: knowledge, models;
- Equipment: computer machines and supports;
- Software and procedures: data-processing programs, allowing to execute the following functions: acquisition, processing, storage, and communication of information in various forms in an organization.

Information systems are systematically defined as follows:

According to Dove (1995), a company information system can be perceived as the company's subsystem, hence a system that embraces all components with informational-type interactions. This database aims to provide the information necessary for the company's operations at various levels.

Based on Le Moigne (1994), an organization is defined as the composition of three systems as shown in Figure 1.4.

The operating system responds to daily events coming from the environment, according to the defined rules. It is responsible for transforming primary resources or flows (input variables) of financial, personnel, material, or information types into finished products or services (output variables).

The decision-making or piloting system allows the initiation of the decision-making process while defining the objectives, the evaluation criteria, and the management rules in advance. It manages the company and stays focused on its goals.

The information system interconnects the two previous systems while acting as a coupler. It is the party responsible for collecting, processing, storing, and disseminating information. This can be seen as representing the operating system's activity and/or the control system. For this IT system view, the typology of information systems is based on

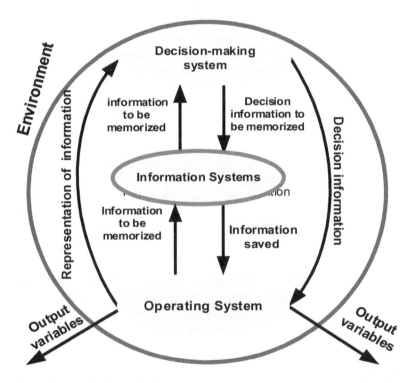

FIGURE 1.4   A systemic view of an IS.

the primary purpose: information systems supporting operations (transaction processing, industrial process control, etc.) and MISs supporting management (assistance with report production, decision support, etc.) (Dove, 1995; Van Grembergen & De Haes, 2009).

1.1.3 Concepts of Enterprise Application

An EIS can contain a multitude of computer applications. An enterprise application is a set of programs, or software, articulated between them, and used to automate or assist information processing tasks in a particular area within the company (Walls et al., 1992; Imache et al., 2012).

According to Hasselbring (2000), the main characteristics of an application are as follows:

- The application components it contains, which represent the coherency of the application's sub-assemblies (modules or software);
- The application field(s) (context of use) defines either structurally (a workstation, a department) or functionally (a management function: maintenance, orders);
- Functionality that refers to a set of tasks supported by the application;
- Data processing means the various forms of information used and produced by the application. The different human resources, software, and hardware used by the application.

Figure 1.5 presents a summary of these characteristics, using the UML notation.

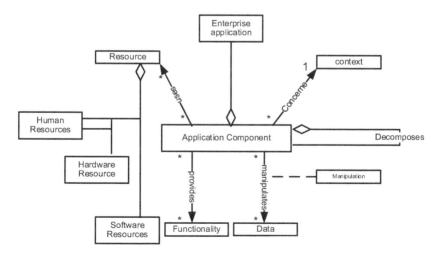

FIGURE 1.5 Concept of application.

1.1.4 Features of Enterprise Applications

The critical characteristics of enterprise applications are autonomy, distribution, and heterogeneity (Hasselbring, 2000; Roman et al., 2005).

The three attributes are mutually perpendicular to each other because they constitute the application's independent dimensions. Each of these characteristics can create specific problems to make different applications work together. The objective is to manage these dimensions to increase the capacity of applications. To these three dimensions, some authors such as Hasselbring (2000) have added another dimension called dynamism because applications can evolve according to the evolutions and changes that occur in their environment, as shown in Figure 1.6.

1.1.5 Autonomy

An organizational application is autonomous when it is possible to design and execute it independently. In the context of databases, Hasselbring (2000) proposes a classification of autonomy notion by defining several aspects of this concept:

- Design autonomy means that an application is independent of other applications in its intrinsic design (its data model, its processing model, etc.);
- Autonomy of communication means that an application can locally choose with which applications it can communicate;
- Runtime autonomy means the independence of the application to manage interactions with its external environment. The level of autonomy depends on the organizational changes implemented to this end.

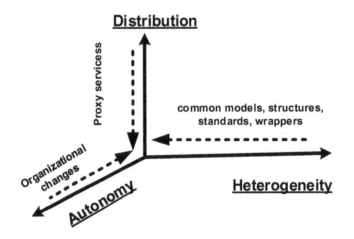

FIGURE 1.6 Dimensions of enterprise applications.

1.1.6 Distribution

The second characteristic of enterprise applications is distribution, which refers to the fact that applications are often physically distributed over the enterprise network. This is achieved by distributing the data and/or processing so that specific data and/or processing in the information system can be implemented at the local level.

Among the techniques most often used to enable application, distribution is based on the implementation of middlewares such as CORBA (Group, 1997), Java/RMI (Newcomer, 2002; Vaughan-Nichols, 2002), and MOM (Hohpe & Woolf, 2004).

1.1.7 Heterogeneity

The heterogeneity is an aspect inherent in that enterprise applications can be developed and deployed independently and according to different approaches and methodologies. There are several reasons why heterogeneity can occur at different levels, and three primary levels of heterogeneity can be distinguished as follows (Wiederhold, 1992):

- Technological heterogeneity that corresponds to the differences present in the necessary hardware and software used;
- Heterogeneity at the hardware level includes differences related to computers and networks used;
- Basic software heterogeneity (platform heterogeneity) includes differences associated with operating systems, database management systems, execution platforms, etc;
- Syntactic heterogeneity refers to the differences in data formats and application interfaces, the signature of functions that syntactic transformations can resolve.

This heterogeneity expresses that the symbolic name of a concept can be interpreted differently according to the applications considered. These semantic conflicts occur mainly when (1) the same symbolic name covers different concepts (in this case homonymy) or (2) several symbolic names cover the same concept (and in this case, synonymy).

Semantic problems are a fact in any company. Also, it becomes vital that these conflicts are identified and resolved as soon as possible, preferably during the upstream phases of the project. Many authors (Hasselbring, 2000; Roman et al., 2005) admit that the heterogeneity of applications is the real challenge in integration.

1.1.8 Dynamism

The dynamism of enterprise applications is another feature introduced by Sarkis (2001). Indeed, as current information systems are open and exposed to frequent changes in response to strategic, commercial, or technological changes affecting the company, the applications of these systems should evolve dynamically to cope with these changes. Dynamism is a dimension that is generally manifested in two ways:

- **The first aspect** concerns the dynamism in the behavior that an application can display autonomously according to its internal configuration;
- **The second aspect** concerns the changes that can occur within the application components of an application, such as modifying specific components, the arrival of new components, the deletion of specific components considered obsolete, and the temporary lack of the substitution of some components.

1.1.9 EIS and Company Strategy

The information system must remain an element that enables the company to carry out and succeed in its strategy while respecting the security, integrity, accuracy, and traceability of data and information. Thus, to make the IS a strategic tool for achieving its strategy, it must be adequately supported by a backbone that corresponds to this strategy. Before explaining the relationship between the information system and the company's strategy, we begin by defining the notion of strategy and alignment:

- What is an information system strategy?
- An information system strategy should define a target information system, its priorities, steps, and means necessary for its implementation, as shown in Figure 1.7.

What is the organizational strategy? Elaborating on the company's strategy means choosing the areas of activity in which the company intends to be present and allocate resources to maintain and develop. The strategy is divided into two levels: The group strategy that determines the company's business areas and the competitive strategy

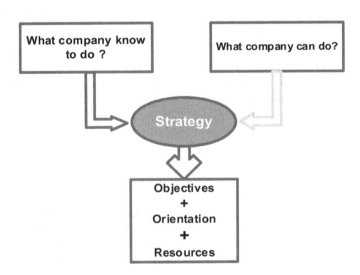

FIGURE 1.7 What is the strategy?

implemented in each of these business areas (Bruce, 1998; Conboy & Fitzgerald, 2004; Imache et al., 2012; Sharifi & Zhang, 1999).

- What does IS strategic alignment mean? The expression 'strategic IT alignment' means first that the IT corresponds to its strategy and provides the company's employees with the tools and means necessary for its implementation.

  According to Goldman and Nagel (1993), IT alignment is a managerial practice that aims to understand better, create, and strengthen the convergences and synchronizations of the information system with its objectives and trajectories rhythms and operations. Also, according to Anthony Byrd et al., (2006), strategic alignment is an approach to aligning the information system strategy with the company's business strategy(s). This approach aims to reinforce the use-value of the information system and make it an advantage for the company.

- What does IS strategic alignment mean? The expression 'strategic IT alignment' means first of all that the IT corresponds to the company's strategy and that it provides the company's employees with the tools and means necessary for its implementation.

According to Goldman and Nagel (1993), IT alignment is a managerial practice that aims to understand better, create, and strengthen the convergences and synchronizations of the information system with its objectives and trajectories rhythms and operations. According to Anthony Byrd et al. (2006), a strategic alignment is an approach to aligning the information system strategy with the company's business strategy(s). This approach aims to reinforce the use-value of the information system and make it an advantage for the company.

The fundamental challenge of strategic alignment is to make the information system an asset in the service of the company's strategy. The information system creates value and is a source of competitive advantage, provided that it is aligned with business needs through strategic alignment. The notion of strategic alignment is not specific to the information system: all the company's businesses and functions must be aligned with the company's strategy.

The relationship between the IS and strategy is described by IS ability to draw strategy's consequences (Xiaoying et al., 2008). However, for this to work, the strategy must be explicit. It is not enough to define an IS to say that you would like to do something: You have to specify how you intend to do it. It should be noted that reflection on the IS contributes to the quality of strategic expression, resulting in initial feedback from the IS on the strategy itself.

That we have defined, implemented, and aligned the IS with the strategy, including feedback. The process does not stop there because the implementation of the IS often opens up strategic opportunities for the company that did not exist earlier. It then appears that the IS, first placed at the service of an existing positioning, modifies the scope of what is possible and opens the prospect of a new positioning for managers. The IS has become a new type of asset, and information asset that the company can value under the same profitability constraint as its other assets.

An information system is generally considered a simple support resource for strategy. In contrast, it can be a strategic weapon capable of giving a sustainable competitive advantage to the organization successfully exploiting it (Swafford et al., 2008; Kumar & Stylianou, 2014).

1.1.10 Enterprise Information Systems Complexity

Over the past 70 years, information technologies have rapidly evolved and revolutionized the company's tools (high-level programming languages, databases, integrated software packages, Internet, Big Data, AI, etc.). However, decision-makers have difficulty obtaining appropriate information that will facilitate their decision-making, which remains a challenge.

The rapid evolution of the IT infrastructure leads to creating 'layers' in the IS that make it complicated and rigid by making interventions to develop it costly and risky. The complexity of information systems reduces their flexibility when flexibility, adaptability, interoperability, and agility are essential for their survival. The complexity of complicates monitoring progress and building qualified teams requires extensive outsourcing and increases the difficulty of overall control (Goldman & Nagel, 1993).

1.1.11 Complexity Factors

Information system's complexity is due to three factors: Heterogeneity, autonomy, and development, making it challenging to model and define the engineering methods of the information systems. The purpose is to manage these characteristics to increase the individual and collective capacity of the different EIS parts.

Heterogeneity: It is related to the multiplicity and diversity of the models used: various models from different points of view, different levels of abstraction (conceptual, physical, etc.), types of abstraction (data, transactions, etc.), usage categories (managers, users, etc.), domains (study, production, finance, etc.), etc. (Arteta & Giachetti, 2004);

Autonomy: A system is autonomous when it is disconnected and independent of other systems. Autonomy is driven by the fact that an information system is never isolated; it is embedded in its environment and consequently into another system with which it interacts through interfaces, technical devices, temporal or factual events, etc. This environment limits an IS's autonomy (time, material, human, and financial resource constraints, etc.) (Arteta & Giachetti, 2004).

Evolution and dynamism: Evolution and dynamism constitute the 'vital' aspect of an IS. The information system is scalable in response to changes in its environment (strategic, business, or technological changes that the company is undergoing) (Goldman & Nagel, 1993; Peterson, 2001; Singh et al., 2005), (Goldman & Nagel, 1993; Peterson, 2001).

Also, information system complexity increases with the heterogeneity and evolution and decreases with its autonomy (Goldman & Nagel, 1993).

1.1.12 Evolution of EIS's

Since 1960, the evolution of computer science has seen a significant expansion in computer program concepts.

Gradually, the information system concept was developed by extending a computer system concept through the translation of the strategic and organizational dimensions (Drucker, 1995; Keen, 1978; Mintzberg, 1973; Wiederhold, 1992). In the late 80s and early 90s, CIOs faced a situation where it was impossible to develop the system without rebuilding it. This context has led to high complexity, delays, and costs (Pinsonneault & Rivard, 1998; Willcocks, 2013).

During the 1990s, a logic of autonomy also emerged (Zviran, 1990). A company is composed of several subsystems with customer/supplier interactions – these developments enrich the information system with a considerable number of programs. Specific organizations then have an IS composed of a stack of applications. Evolutionary pressures often imposed on IS weaken it by lacking a coherent infrastructure (Robson, 1998).

Early in the 2000s, information systems became increasingly complex through outsourcing and the emergence of fusions (West & Hess, 2002). This has complicated the management and monitoring of EIS's evolution, mainly through inter-organizational integration, which has led to the emergence of the agility concept to address this need (West & Hess, 2002).

Also, the consequences of information technology (IT) extend beyond the company's borders, which requires redefining the network of relationships with partners, suppliers, customers, subcontractors, etc., to ensure inter-organizational integration that will improve its exchanges through the network.

IT affects the selection parameters of internal and external coordination structures. In particular, their use reduces communications time and costs and production costs. Generally, the impact depends mainly on the structure of the value chain and the characteristics of the business:

- Extension of the market's role in externalization: Common databases encourage supplier searches and the decision to outsource;
- Company-internal solution: Coordination within the company and possibly synergy allowing the production of services and/or products at a competitive cost.

Information technologies facilitate internal and external communication and, therefore, coordination internally and externally, regardless of the distance between the partners (Sharifi & Zhang, 1999; Zhang & Sharifi, 2000).

Industry 4.0 is being created in Germany around 2012 and is being exhibited to the general public by the Association of German Manufacturers of Production Machinery and Equipment. It is the digitization of industry in the broadest sense of the word. Digital technology is being integrated into product design and also into the associated means of production. The author states from the outset that this concept

> also integrates physical assets (machines, equipment, etc.), optimized and connected and keeping a constant link with the products they manufacture, to adapt in real-time to variations in customer demands and to respond to changes in end-consumer demand:

mass-produced but customized products, meeting their exact needs, offering a higher level of quality and giving rise to new services.

It is easy to conclude that many components enable the manufacturing company to be digitized from one end to the other.

Robotics are therefore used for not only manufacturing activities but also sometimes elsewhere. The Internet of Things (IoT) is also in place to ensure communication between heterogeneous objects.

The company may also have an ERP System and a Customer Relationship Management (CRM) to manage customer relations.

Dashboards are set up to monitor its main Key Performance Indicators (KPIs) constantly.

We also talk about mobility. Mobile devices are used in many of the company's processes.

The use of cloud-hosted services is also required for several activities. Gone are the days when the company had to have an infrastructure with several local servers.

The flexibility brought to new digital technologies allows us to put the customer back at the heart of the information system. It is a form of return to craftsmanship due to personalized services, combined with lower costs and quality made possible by automation. The whole relationship between the industry and its ecosystem is rethought. Thus, the digital factory makes it possible to imagine new products collaboratively due to new processes and materials in a close relationship with customers and suppliers. It also links R&D and design, operators, and support services.

Thus, company information systems benefit from rapid implementation, low costs, and better information circulation at all levels of the company. Specific products can be manufactured and customized much more efficiently than mass production. Machines, products, and systems can be configured, optimized, and controlled independently of each other. Small- and medium-sized enterprises (SMEs) are thus break free from the limitations of a small factory by taking advantage of processes and material flows more quickly and efficiently.

1.1.13 IT Governance

Despite IT Governance (ITG's) importance and the currency of the term since the late 1990s, academics working in the area continue to define the term in several ways (Webb et al., 2006). This lack of a comprehensive definition has possibly impeded in-depth research, further limiting the validity of cross-study comparisons of results (Simonsson & Johnson, 2006). It is thus necessary to clarify the concept of ITG through systematically classifying and drawing together various definitions of ITG in the hope of supporting active research. A variety of definitions of ITG are summarized in Table 1.1.

These diverse definitions may be classified into three perspectives. First, researchers seek to understand ITG as the location of decision-making rights and accountabilities within organizations. Peterson (2004) and Weill and Woodham (2002) define ITG as basically decision-making in the IT domain, focusing on the distribution of decision rights and accountabilities (or responsibilities) to effectively use IT resources.

TABLE 1.1   IT Governance Definitions

SOURCE	IT GOVERNANCE DEFINITION
(Rezaee & Reinstein, 1998)	At the conceptual core of IT, governance processes is an organizational model of decision-making, defined as identifying and solving problems.
(Sambamurthy & Zmud, 1999)	IT-related structures or architectures (and associated authority pattern) implemented to accomplish (IT Imperative) activities in response to an enterprise's environmental and strategic imperatives.
(Korac-Kakabadse & Kakabadse, 2001)	IS/ITG concentrates on the structure of company relationships and processes to develop, direct, and control IS/IT resources. These arrangements add value to organizations as they pursue enterprise goals. ITG aims to balance risk and return for IS/IT resources and their processes.
(Weill & Woodham, 2002)	ITG specifies decision rights and accountability frameworks encouraging the best use within firms of IT.
(ITGI, 2003)	ITG is the responsibility of the board of directors and executive management. It forms an integral part of enterprise governance and consists of the leadership and organizational structures and processes, which ensure that organizations keep and extend their strategy.
(Peterson, 2004)	ITG describes the distribution of IT decision-making rights and responsibilities among different enterprise stakeholders, defining the procedures and mechanisms for making and monitoring strategic IT decisions.
(Van Grembergen, 2004)	ITG refers to the organizational capacity exercised by the board, executive management, and IT management in formulating and implementing IT strategy, as this brings together business and IT.
(Brown et al., 2005)	Specifying the decision rights and accountability frameworks to encourage desirable behavior in using IT.
(Simonsson & Johnson, 2006)	ITG concerns IT decision-making, that is, preparation for, making, and implementing decisions regarding goals, processes, people, and technology on a tactical and strategic level.
(Webb et al., 2006)	ITG refers to the strategic alignment of IT with business, aiming to release maximum business value through the development and maintenance of effective IT accountability and performance and risk management.
(Verhoef, 2007)	IT governance is a structure of relationships and processes for controlling the IT role in the organization to achieve its business goals and add value to the organization.
(Ploesser et al., 2008)	IT governance is the organizational measurements exercised by the Board, executive management, and IT management to control the preparation and implementation of IT strategy.

(Continued)

TABLE 1.1   (Continued)

SOURCE	IT GOVERNANCE DEFINITION
(Brown et al., 2008)	Application of governance to an IT organization and its people, processes, and information to guide how those assets support the needs of the business.
(Van Grembergen & De Haes, 2009)	IT governance is the definition and implementation of processes, structures, and relational mechanisms in the organization that enable both business and IT to execute their responsibilities in support of business/IT alignment and creating business value from IT-enabled investments.
(Bart & Turel, 2010)	IT governance is intended to ensure that the organization and its board of directors or governing body are conscious of managing the organization's IT investment responsibly, efficiently, and effectively.
(Scholl et al., 2011)	Regimes of IT-related standards, agreements, methods, rules, and practices constrain, prescribe, and enable the implementation and use of ICTs to support government activity.
(Maes et al., 2012)	An integral part of corporate governance [that] addresses the definition and implementation of processes, structures, and relational mechanisms in the organization that enable both business and IT people to execute their responsibilities in support of business/IT alignment and the creation of business value from IT-enabled investments.
(Grant & Tan, 2013)	A dynamic, goal-directed, performance-driven, adaptive, and relational process seeks to bring congruence between organizational and IT strategies, structures, systems, processes, and practices to pursue valuable, risk-reduced, and measurable returns on IT investment.
(Aasi et al., 2014)	Preparation, development, and implementation of decisions on goals, processes, people, and technology at tactical and strategic levels.
(Elhasnaoui et al., 2015)	IT governance is the responsibility of the Board of Directors and senior management. It is an integral part of corporate governance and includes the leadership and organizational structures and processes that ensure its IT supports and expands its strategy and objectives.
(Valentine, 2016)	Governance of Enterprise Information and Technology supports the board and senior executives in fulfilling their duty of care responsibilities and is an integral part of board governance. IT governance includes the leadership, alignment, and oversight of enterprise technologies with its strategy, structure, systems, policies, and governance processes.
(Felix et al., 2017)	The positive effect on performance can be achieved through ITG governance mechanisms that are formally defined, operate with defined rules and standards widely disseminated, and are periodically monitored and improved.
(Maleh et al., 2019)	The clarification of decision-making rights and responsibilities as companies seek to leverage IT assets to business goals.

Second, researchers understand ITG as involving the strategic alignment between IT and business in order to achieve enterprises' full business value. Grembergen (2004) and Webb et al. (2006) define ITG as those activities maximizing business value through bringing about this strategic alignment. In achieving this goal, they emphasize the effective control of resources, performance management, and risk management.

Korac-Kakabadse, and Kakabadse (2001) describe IS/ITG as dealing with the structure of relationships and processes aiming to develop, direct, and control IS/IT resources such that IT adds value to the pursuit of its strategic objectives. The IT Governance Institute (ITGI, 2003) defines ITG as the responsibility of company executives and the board of directors, referring inclusively to the leadership, organizational processes, and structures to ensure that its IT supports the organization's goals and strategies. ITG concerns IT decision-making, that is, preparation for, making, and implementing decisions regarding goals, processes, people, and technology on a tactical and strategic level (Simonsson, & Johnson, 2006).

Verhoef (2007) presents an Architecture Theory Diagram (ATD) and a framework for defining IT governance based on an extensive literature study. Ploesser et al. (2008) defines IT Governance as the organizational measurements exercised by the Board, executive management, and IT management to control the preparation and implementation of IT strategy. IT governance aims to ensure that the organization and its board of directors or governing body are aware of managing the organization's IT investments responsibly, efficiently, and effectively (Bart & Turel, 2010). Scholl et al. (2011) define the ITG as a set of IT standards, agreements, methodologies, rules, and practices that limit, prescribe, and enable the implementation and use of ICTs to support government activity.

In recent works, Aasi et al. (2014) define IT governance as a phase of preparing, developing, and implementing decisions on objectives, processes, people, and technology at tactical and strategic levels. Elhasnaoui et al. (2015) describe IT governance as the responsibility of the Board of Directors and Executive Management. In her thesis, Valentine (2016) confirms that IT governance includes the leadership, alignment, and oversight of enterprise technologies with the organization's strategy, structure, systems, policies, and governance processes. IT governance seeks to facilitate data-driven decision-making and minimize risk throughout the enterprise. IT governance creates value by optimizing stakeholder engagement and strategic investments and in deriving returns. Felix et al. (2017) propose that the positive effect on performance can be achieved through ITG governance mechanisms that are formally defined, operate with defined rules and standards widely disseminated, and are periodically monitored and improved.

In short, IT governance can be commonly defined as the clarification of decision-making rights and responsibilities as companies seek to leverage IT assets to business goals (Maleh et al., 2019). This alignment is designed to allow organizations to achieve their goals by installing a systematic series of activities establishing structures and processes. Research suggests that organizations work on three levels in developing IT governance frameworks, designing 'structures', 'processes', and 'communication protocols or approaches' (Grembergen, 2004; Weill & Ross, 2004). Structures refer to organizational units and roles responsible for making IT decisions, such as committees, executive teams, and business/IT relationship managers. Processes involve the arrangement of formal decision-making and the design of forms of monitoring checking that daily behavior is consistent with firm IT policy. Monitoring also provides input to decision-making regarding investment proposals and evaluation processes, architecture exception processes, service-level agreements, chargeback, and specific metrics. Communication approaches include announcements, advocates, channels, and education efforts disseminating IT governance principles and policies. These may also inform workers of the outcomes of IT decision-making processes.

1.1.14 Urbanization

The dynamism of enterprise applications is another feature introduced by Singh et al. (2005). Indeed, since current information systems are open and subject to frequent changes in response to strategic, business, or technological changes affecting the company, the applications of these systems must then be able to evolve dynamically to cope with these changes.

1.1.14.1 The Metaphor of the City

Indeed, urban planning is generally based on geographical invariants. A city is structured into zones, districts, and blocks. Planning rules are then established and applied for each area. These divisions must be stable over time, and the city actor will consider them as invariant. Similarly, IS urbanization is based on the assumption that stable, functional blocks can be determined, at least for a long time, if not forever (Imache et al., 2012). Urbanization challenges are as follows:

- Cost-saving: Ways to eliminate redundancies and reduce costs without disrupting critical business processes;
- Providing more value: How to introduce new technology to bring more value to the business;
- Flexibility: Ability to design an architecture that facilitates the evolution of business processes;
- Cost-effective and efficient production: Whether new technology can be implemented at a lower cost without rebuilding the existing information system?
- Interoperability: How to integrate existing applications and data blocks and make them interoperable?
- Opening: How to build the foundations for applications that interact with the ecosystem (Internet, WEB, etc.);
- Ensure quality of service: The ways to manage and control the quality of the service offered.

Accordingly, urbanization provides an information system that is better adapted to serve the company's strategy and anticipate changes in the environment. Corporate information system managers want to satisfy the demands of technological solutions; however, they face several challenges: Costs, budgets, applications that are often not well known, resulting in difficulties in integrating new projects and evolving the information system. Management of these problems leads to dramatic failures. Organizations first wanted reliable and open information systems while maintaining a high level of security. The company's master plan is a strategic plan designed to steer the development of IT in the company by translating its strategy into IS-related actions (Byrd & Turner, 2000; Knapp et al., 2009), which has mostly met these expectations.

In addition to these two required qualities, agility is nowadays defined as a necessary and indispensable tool to face economic instability (Conboy, 2009; Dove, 1995; Knapp et al., 2009; Sharifi & Zhang, 1999).

Thus, IT agility becomes the primary objective of any IT department and must be a quality that any company must have within its reach to satisfy customer needs, competition, and rapid technological change (Goranson & Goranson, 1999). Currently, the company's roadmap does not address this issue; it replaces it with the concept of urbanization of the enterprise's information system.

To align the IS with the company's strategy, there needs to be sufficient flexibility. Nevertheless, it is difficult for the company to cope with increasing and random changes in the environment. In this way, when it comes to finding a new course for the company to face random and unexpected changes, the urbanization project of its information system becomes an adapted and essential compass. The urbanization process aims to simplify the vision of the EIS and promote its use as a factor of value creation and a source of innovation for the company to ensure its evolution and competitiveness (Sahid et al., 2020a).

The urbanization of the company will enable it to become a high-performance, efficient, and fulfilling environment. The organization will then become agile, in other words, react to external and internal constraints. According to Cumps et al. (2006), an urbanized company has an exceptional response capacity and structures that can be quickly mobilized.

Within the framework of the POIRE approach, the purpose of this phase is to improve the agility and characteristics of the EIS: coherence, flexibility, agility, proactivity, interoperability, adaptability, scalability, stability, and efficiency.

This will facilitate the management of unpredictable changes; while maintaining the EIS basis of good practices set that allows corporate governance alignment with new financial requirements and globalization legislation.

The information systems have several dimensions that can be analyzed with the typologies of the company (Izza & Imache, 2010) and a complexity that reflects the human organization they must serve.

Urbanization is necessary for two reasons: to manage and maintain an asset until it is effectively obsolete and to have an agile information system that can evolve quickly and effectively to meet changing needs (Sassone, 1988; Willcocks, 2013).

In this aim, we first define what the target information system should be, which will best serve the company's strategy and satisfy business processes, i.e., an aligned information system (Sassone, 1988). Then, establish construction rules to avoid inheriting old information system failures and anticipate changes, in other words, an agile information system (Stein et al., 2016), and finally, determine the path of the current IS to obtain the target, which requires a knowledge of the old IS, to define criteria to know when to start and when to finish.

Flexibility is essential to align EIS with the company's strategy. Nevertheless, there are difficulties for companies coping easily with increasing and random changes in their environment. Thus, urbanization has emerged as an essential and appropriate way to deal with random and unexpected changes.

The urbanization approach consists of simplifying the EIS's vision and promoting its use as a factor of value creation and innovation for a company to ensure its evolution and competitiveness (Sassone, 1988).

Urbanization will enable the company to become more efficient, more effective, and more rewarding. It makes it agile, which means it can react adequately to external and internal constraints.

1.1.14.2 *The Urbanization of Information System*

The complexity of information systems complicates company integration and can be compared to that of human cities or urban systems that are urbanized. As a result, the urbanization of information systems contributes to improving agility. Urbanization is the driving force behind a company's evolution, whose key to success is the effective use of information. It addresses the evolution of information systems by providing a framework for the system evolving in response to changes in the business environment (Trabelsi & Abid, 2013). The urbanization process has three main phases:

(1) Determine the business strategy required to satisfy the need;
(2) Definition of functional requirements and specific mapping;
(3) Identification of technological orientations.

As illustrated in Figure 1.8, Izza and Imache (2010) propose an urbanization approach. Urbanization contributes to the various dimensions of the EIS.

The design of the EIS, considering their interactions, and the alignment process will be implemented according to the governance guidelines defined by the company's strategy. Thus, the approach to urbanization and alignment is first from top to bottom (analysis and strategic design). It will increase EIS flexibility and alignment from bottom to top (execution and validation), enhancing its agility.

Through the urbanization process, the architecture of the EIS can be structured more efficiently. In this regard, the rules of urbanization and rules of good practice are used, which lead to a digressive decomposition of the overall EIS dimensions: **Zone**, **Neighborhood**, and **Block**.

- **Zone:** An area forms a homogeneous family of neighborhoods with the same construction rules and linkage;
- **Neighborhood:** An information system neighborhood is a fraction of an area that is a fraction of a processed information system. A neighborhood corresponds to what is called a subsystem. A neighborhood forms a homogeneous family of blocks that obey the same rules of construction and coupling;
- **Block:** A block is a set of homogeneous data and processing. The block is the basic unit of urban planning. A block forms a similar data and processing family, following the same construction, and coupling rules.

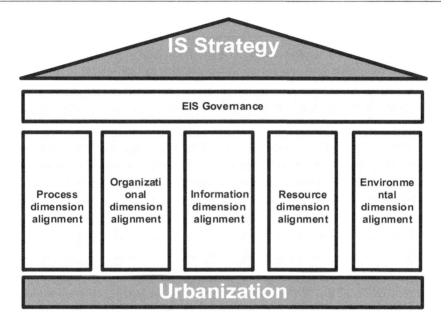

FIGURE 1.8   EIS urbanization and alignment.

1.1.15 Flexibility

The significance of IT organizational infrastructure capacity as a critical component of the organization's survival and competitiveness continues to grow. Sharing IT infrastructure is considered the basis for shared IT capabilities to develop IT applications and support business processes (Chung et al., 2003; Darke et al., 1998). IT infrastructures are generally the foundation of shared IT capabilities that enable the development of IT applications and support business processes (Lim, 2014). According to Zhu (2004), IT infrastructure is a set of IT organizational resources and capabilities shared across the organization and form the foundation on which IT applications are developed and business processes are supported. IT infrastructure capabilities are usually provided by IT/IS (service) organizational functions, and may also include public or outsourced facilities used by organizations (Chin et al., 2003). The main reason for developing IT infrastructure capabilities is to support similarities among different applications or uses, through facilitating information sharing across organizations for cross-functional integration (Broadbent & Weill, 1997).

Literature defines flexibility as the ability to react to environmental change in information systems, organizational theory, strategic management, or operational management (Lee & Xia, 2005). However, many researchers have characterized IT flexibility as the organizational capacity to support various information technologies and services based on four dimensions: compatibility, connectivity, modularity, and IT staff flexibility.

Compatibility is the ability to share any information between any technological components. Connectivity is the ability of technology to interact with other technological components. In other words, connect each person, functional area, and application in organizations.

Modularity means that software applications facilitate management by a processed routine in separate modules. It also allows the company to quickly create or modify software applications to support product development changes. IT staff flexibility refers to working collaboratively in cross-functional teams embracing various technology types (Byrd & Turner, 2000).

Halevi and Weill (1994) found that IT flexibility is linked to the efficiency and implementation of IT/IS (i.e., business transaction processing systems, information management systems, decision support systems, network management). Other research indicates that IT flexibility is essential in determining IS/IT effectiveness or operational performance. IT capabilities are usually provided by IT/IS organizational functions (department); they may also include public or external use by organizations. One of the main reasons for developing IT infrastructure capabilities is to support commonalities between different applications or uses by facilitating information sharing between organizations and cross-functional integration (Izza & Imache, 2010; Maas, 1998; Weill & Ross, 2004).

Generally, literature confuses agility with flexibility. However, agility is a combination of speed and flexibility. Agility means the ability to respond to unexpected environmental changes, while flexibility refers to responses to risk situations or anticipated unforeseen events (e.g., scenario planning) (Adams et al., 2009; Izza & Imache, 2010).

Mårtensson notes that it is important to not confuse agility, or agile information systems, with flexibility or flexible IT systems. The two concepts are related but different. Indeed, the researcher also considers that agility involves using flexibility and proposes a curve that illustrates, at the conceptual level, the relationship between agility and flexibility/complexity.

1.1.16 Agility

In IS research, the concept of agility is often associated with terms such as flexibility, dynamic, and organic. As previously mentioned, the concepts of flexibility and agility have been linked to the broader challenge of combining complex IT systems with unexpected, and sometimes surprising, changes in user needs, business processes, corporate structure, strategy, and markets.

Early in the 1990s, the concept of agility was introduced into IS research (Bamber et al., 2000; Ciborra, 2009; Markus & Benjamin, 1996; Sharifi & Zhang, 1999; Sharp et al., 1999; Zhang & Sharifi, 2000) after agile methods success in computer development. In 2000, the IS search focused on other attributes of explanatory agility (IS) through IT, development methods (IS), and (IS) outsourcing practices. Also, in the literature, we deduced a lack of a unique definition of the agility concept. The agility research in (IS) agility was devised on several streams. Table 1.2 highlights the main IS agility research streams.

This section briefly describes research related to the agility of the IS in four well-established research areas: IT infrastructure, IS development, IS organization, and IS personnel.

1.1.16.1 IS Organizational Design

Various researchers have also recognized the role of IS organizational structures and governance mechanisms for internal functions and IS outsourcing relationships. Clark et al.

TABLE 1.2   Agility Research Streams

IS AGILITY RESEARCH STREAMS	*AUTHORS*
IS design and governance	(Rockart et al., 1996a) (Prager, 1996) (Clark et al., 1997) (Boar, 1998) (Truex et al., 1999) (Tan & Sia, 2006) (Gerth & Rothman, 2007) (Sia et al., 2008) (Stettina & Kroon, 2013)
Strategic IS management	(Lacity et al., 1996) (Sia et al., 2008) (Schmidt & Buxmann, 2011) (Tiwana et al., 2010) (Joachim et al., 2013) (Alaceva & Rusu, 2015; Kale et al., 2018; Kaur et al., 2017)
Competencies and skills of IS professionals	(Markus & Benjamin, 1996) (Butler & Gray, 2006) (McCann et al., 2009) (Chamanifard et al., 2015; Lengnick-Hall et al., 2011; Saha et al., 2019)
IS development	(Baskerville & Pries-Heje, 2004) (Lee & Xia, 2005) (Holmqvist & Pessi, 2006) (Lyytinen & Rose, 2003) (Conboy, 2009) (Sarker & Sarker, 2009) (Zheng et al., 2011) (Hong et al., 2011) (Ramesh et al., 2012) (Wang et al., 2012) (McAvoy et al., 2013) (Moy, 2018; Shein et al., 2018)
Methods of software development	(Overby et al., 2006) (Börjesson et al., 2006) (Dybå & Dingsøyr, 2008) (Tanriverdi et al., 2010) (Stettina & Kroon, 2013) (Hobbs & Petit, 2017) (Saha et al., 2019)
Design of IT infrastructure	(Allen & Boynton, 1991) (Duncan, 1995) (Byrd & Turner, 2000) (Benamati & Lederer, 2001) (Wenzler, 2005) (Overby et al., 2006)

(*Continued*)

TABLE 1.2   (Continued)

IS AGILITY RESEARCH STREAMS	AUTHORS
	(Dybå & Dingsøyr, 2008)
	(Kim et al., 2008)
	(Fink & Neuman, 2009)
	(Tan et al., 2009)
	(Tanriverdi et al., 2010)
	(Schmidt & Buxmann, 2011)
	(Schapiro & Henry, 2012)
	(Celen & Djurdjanovic, 2012)
	(Joachim et al., 2013)
	(Li et al, 2014)
	(Murphy et al., 2018)
	(Morton et al., 2018)
Business agility and the value of IS applications	(Broadbent et al., 1999)
	(Rockart et al., 1996b)
	(Lee & Xia, 2005)
	(Gerth & Rothman, 2007)
	(Gerth & Rothman, 2007)
	(Gebauer & Schober, 2008)
	(Fink & Neuman, 2009)
	(Tanriverdi et al., 2010)
	(Bhatt et al., 2010)
	(Chiang et al., 2018)
	(Queiroz et al., 2018)
	(Benlian et al., 2018)
	(Ashrafi et al., 2019)
	(Sahid et al., 2020b)

1997) define change readiness as the ability of information systems (IS) organization to provide strategic IT applications in short development cycles using a highly skilled internal IT workforce.

IS organization requirements have been addressed in several conceptual documents. One of the primary antecedents of a flexible IS organization is a partnership relationship between the IS organization and the company. IT departments are advised to adopt a matrix organizational structure that manages technical knowledge as a competence center while simultaneously supporting customer-focused development and service processes. Often referred to as a center of excellence structure (Clark et al., 1997; Gerth & Rothman, 2007), it distinguishes technical and control tasks from business development tasks. Generally, an IT organization should aim to become an emerging organization and create virtual teams to promote close collaboration with business units (Prager, 1996).

1.1.16.2 Competencies and Skills of IS Professionals

IT staff skills and abilities were recognized as essential elements of information system flexibility and adaptability, IT infrastructures, and agile IT development. However, two studies in our sample reveal that to approach the capabilities of IS professionals more broadly than in the field of IT infrastructure alone or information systems development ISD. The starting point for these documents is that IS professionals will need change agent capabilities (Markus & Benjamin, 1996). In their documents, researchers argue (Butler & Gray, 2006) that organizational structures and the standardization of work roles and practices can prevent professionals from taking on a more effective change agent role or acting cautiously in the following areas unexpected situations.

1.1.16.3 IS Development

In information systems development (ISD), research related to agility has focused on agile methods. Conceptual research helped to define the key variables of the research. Lee & Xia (2005) developed measurement scales for the two central components of ISD flexibility: response effectiveness and the effectiveness of the response. Later, based on an exhaustive review of the use of the concepts of flexibility, agility, and leanness in business studies, Conboy (2009) defines the agility of an ISD method as follows.

The continuous readiness of an ISD method is to create a change quickly or inherently, to adopt it proactively or reactively, and to learn from the change while contributing to the perceived value of the client (economy, quality, and simplicity), through its common components and its relationship to its environment (Conboy, 2009).

Several case studies then attempted to identify a history of flexibility or agility in IST. A central book is that companies should follow the so-called agile ISD methods (Baskerville & Pries-Heje, 2004; Sarker & Sarker, 2009).

However, it was acknowledged that adopting such methods is a slow learning process (Berger & Beynon-Davies, 2009; Cao et al., 2009; Wang et al., 2012). Many other variables, such as the organizational context, the various attributes of the project, and collective and individual consciousness, define the ability of project teams to effectively deploy agile principles (Cao et al., 2009; Kalle & Rose, 2003; Ramesh et al., 2011; Zheng et al., 2011).

1.1.16.4 Design of IT Infrastructure

Research on IT infrastructure flexibility has benefited from early conceptual work by (Duncan, 1995) and then by (Byrd & Turner, 2000). Although Duncan does not provide a precise definition, the following description provides a starting point for understanding the flexibility of the IT infrastructure.

Infrastructure flexibility determines ISD's ability to respond quickly and cost-effectively to system demands, which evolve as business practices or strategies change. Ideally, flexible infrastructure would be an infrastructure designed to evolve itself with emerging technologies and support the ongoing restructuring of related activities and processes (Duncan, 1995).

Subsequently, Byrd & Turner (2000) developed an instrument to measure computer flexibility. The instrument was based on the assumption that the flexibility of the IT infrastructure has eight dimensions: four in the technical base (IT connectivity, application functionality, IT compatibility, data transparency) and four in the human component (technology management; business knowledge; management knowledge technical knowledge).

New technological trends can be both a means (Fink & Neumann, 2009) and a challenge (Benamati & Lederer, 2001) for the flexibility of IT infrastructures.

1.2 SUMMARY

The company's master plan, a strategic plan designed to pilot IT development in the company, by translating its strategy into actions relating to the information system, has mostly satisfied these needs. However, today, agility has become a necessary quality, especially in a constantly unstable economic environment, making it necessary, even indispensable.

IT agility has become the primary purpose of any information systems department; more than that, it is a quality that any company must have to meet the customers' needs, face competitiveness challenges and rapid technological evolution.

Faced with the various transformations and needs of the internal and/or external environment, it is essential to structure the EIS to facilitate its evolution and modify its positioning, structure, and skills, all in harmony with the strategic evolution of its company, while ensuring overall consistency in terms of permanent IT governance with the global strategy, interoperability, integration, autonomy, flexibility. In other words, the EIS must be agile.

REFERENCES

Aasi, P., Rusu, L., & Han, S. (2014). Culture influence on IT governance: What we have learned? *International Journal of IT/Business Alignment and Governance (IJITBAG)*, 5(1), 34–49.

Adams, D. A., Nelson, R. R., Todd, P. A., Ahmi, A., Kent, S., Al-Ansi, A. A., Ismail, N. A., Bin, A. S., A. K., Banker, R. D., Chang, H., Kao, Y., Bedard, J. C., Jackson, C., Ettredge, M. L., Johnstone, K. M., Bierstaker, J. L., Burnaby, P., Thibodeau, J., Bierstaker, J. L., . . . Willborn, W. W. (2009). Factors affecting the adoption of open systems: An exploratory study. *MIS Quarterly*, 16(2), 1521–1552. https://doi.org/10.1108/02686900510606092

Aiken, M. W., Liu Sheng, O. R., & Vogel, D. R. (1991). Integrating expert systems with group decision support systems. *ACM Transactions on Information Systems (TOIS)*, 9(1), 75–95.

Alaceva, C., & Rusu, L. (2015). Barriers in achieving business/IT alignment in a large Swedish company: What we have learned? *Computers in Human Behavior*, 51, 715–728. https://doi.org/10.1016/j.chb.2014.12.007

Alavi, M., & Leidner, D. E. (2001). Knowledge management and knowledge management systems: Conceptual foundations and research issues. *MIS Quarterly*, 107–136.

Albrecht, C. C., Dean, D. L., & Hansen, J. V. (2005). Marketplace and technology standards for B2B e-commerce: Progress, challenges, and the state of the art. *Information & Management*, 42(6), 865–875.

Alewine, N., Ruback, H., & Deligne, S. (2004). Pervasive speech recognition. *IEEE Pervasive Computing*, 3(4), 78–81.

Allen, J. P. (2003). The evolution of new mobile applications: A sociotechnical perspective. *International Journal of Electronic Commerce*, 8(1), 23–36.

Allen, B. R., & Boynton, A. C. (1991). Information architecture: in search of efficient flexibility. *MIS Quarterly*, 435–445.

Anthony Byrd, T., Lewis, B. R., & Bryan, R. W. (2006). The leveraging influence of strategic alignment on IT investment: An empirical examination. *Information and Management*, 43(3), 308–321. https://doi.org/10.1016/j.im.2005.07.002

Arteta, B. M., & Giachetti, R. E. (2004). A measure of agility as the complexity of the enterprise system. *Robotics and Computer-Integrated Manufacturing*, *20*(6 special issue), 495–503. https://doi.org/10.1016/J.rcim.2004.05.008

Ashrafi, A., Ravasan, A. Z., Trkman, P., & Afshari, S. (2019). The role of business analytics capabilities in bolstering firms' agility and performance. *International Journal of Information Management*, *47*, 1–15.

Bakos, Y., Lucas, Jr, H. C., Oh, W., Simon, G., Viswanathan, S., & Weber, B. W. (2005). The impact of e-commerce on competition in the retail brokerage industry. *Information Systems Research*, *16*(4), 352–371.

Bamber, C. J., Sharp, J. M., & Hides, M. T. (2000). Developing management systems towards integrated manufacturing: A case study perspective. *Integrated Manufacturing Systems*, *11*(7), 454–461.

Bart, C., & Turel, O. (2010). IT and the board of directors: An empirical investigation into the "governance questions" Canadian board members ask about IT. *Journal of Information Systems*, *24*(2), 147–172. https://doi.org/10.2308/jis.2010.24.2.147

Baskerville, R., & Pries-Heje, J. (2004). Short cycle time systems development. *Information Systems Journal*, *14*(3), 237–264.

Batra, D., Hoffer, J. A., & Bostrom, R. P. (1988). A comparison of user performance between the relational and the extended entity relationship models in the discovery phase of database design. *International Conference on Information Systems (ICIS)*, *43*.

Bauer, M. J., Poirier, C. C., Lapide, L., & Bermudez, J. (2001). *E-business: The strategic impact on supply chain and logistics*. Council of Logistics Management.

Beatty, S. E., & Smith, S. M. (1987). External search effort: An investigation across several product categories. *Journal of Consumer Research*, *14*(1), 83–95.

Benamati, J., & Lederer, A. L. (2001). Coping with rapid changes in IT. *Communications of the ACM*, *44*(8), 83–88.

Benlian, A., Kettingaer, W. J., Sunyaev, A., Winkler, T. J., & Editors, G. (2018). The transformative value of cloud computing: A decoupling, platformization, and recombination theoretical framework. *Journal of Management Information Systems*, *35*(3), 719–739.

Berger, H., & Beynon-Davies, P. (2009). The utility of rapid application development in large-scale, complex projects. *Information Systems Journal*, *19*(6), 549–570.

Bhatt, G., Emdad, A., Roberts, N., & Grover, V. (2010). Building and leveraging information in dynamic environments: The role of IT infrastructure flexibility as enabler of organizational responsiveness and competitive advantage. *Information & Management*, *47*(7–8), 341–349.

Boar, B. H. (1998). *Constructing blueprints for enterprise IT architectures*. John Wiley & Sons, Inc.

Börjesson, A., Martinsson, F., & Timmerås, M. (2006). Agile improvement practices in software organizations. *European Journal of Information Systems*, *15*(2), 169–182.

Broadbent, M., & Weill, P. (1997). Management by maxim: How business and IT managers can create IT infrastructures. *Sloan Management Review*, *38*, 77–92.

Broadbent, M., Weill, P., & St. Clair, D. (1999). The implications of information technology infrastructure for business process redesign. *MIS Quarterly*, 159–182.

Brown, A. E., Grant, G. G., & Sprott, E. (2005). Framing the frameworks: A review of IT governance research. *Communications of the Association for Information Systems*, *15*, 696–712.

Brown, W. A., Laird, R., Gee, C., & Mitra, T. (2008). *SOA governance: Achieving and sustaining business and IT agility*. Pearson Education.

Bruce, K. (1998). Can you align IT with business strategy? *Strategy & Leadership*, *26*(5), 16–20. https://doi.org/10.1108/eb054620

Buhalis, D. (2004). eAirlines: Strategic and tactical use of ICTs in the airline industry. *Information & Management*, *41*(7), 805–825.

Butler, B. S., & Gray, P. H. (2006). Reliability, mindfulness, and information systems. *MIS Quarterly*, 211–224.

Byrd, T. A., & Turner, D. E. (2000). Measuring the flexibility of information technology infrastructure: Exploratory analysis of a construct. *Journal of Management Information Systems*, *17*(1), 167–208. https://doi.org/10.1080/07421222.2000.11045632

Cao, L., Mohan, K., Xu, P., & Ramesh, B. (2009). A framework for adapting agile development methodologies. *European Journal of Information Systems*, *18*(4), 332–343.

Celen, M., & Djurdjanovic, D. (2012). Operation-dependent maintenance scheduling in flexible manufacturing systems. *CIRP Journal of Manufacturing Science and Technology*, *5*(4), 296–308.

Chamanifard, R., Nikpour, A., Chamanifard, S., & Nobarieidishe, S. (2015). Impact of organizational agility dimensions on employee's organizational commitment in foreign exchange offices of Tejarat Bank, Iran. *European Online Journal of Natural and Social Science*, *4*(1), 199–207.

Chen, H. S. (1976). Positron lifetime study on the structure of an electron irradiated metallic glass. *Physica Status Solidi A*, *34*(2), K127–K129.

Chenoweth, T., Corral, K., & Demirkan, H. (2006). Seven key interventions for data warehouse success. *Communications of the ACM*, *49*(1), 114–119.

Chiang, R. H. L., Grover, V., Liang, T. P., & Zhang, D. (2018). *Special issue: Strategic value of big data and business analytics*. Taylor & Francis.

Chin, W. W., Marcolin, B. L., & Newsted, P. R. (2003). A partial least squares latent variable modeling approach for measuring interaction effects: Results from a Monte Carlo simulation study and an electronic-mail emotion/ adoption study. *Information Systems Research*, *14*(2), 189–217. https://doi.org/10.1287/isre.14.2.189.16018

Chung, S. H., Rainer, Jr, R. K., & Lewis, B. R. (2003). The impact of information technology infrastructure flexibility on strategic alignment and application implementations. *Communications of the Association for Information Systems*, *11*(1), 11.

Ciborra, C. U. (2009). From thinking to tinkering: The grassroots of strategic information systems. *Bricolage, Care and Information*, 206–220. https://doi.org/10.1057/9780230250611_10

Clark, C. E., Cavanaugh, N. C., Brown, C. V., & Sambamurthy, V. (1997). Building change-readiness capabilities in the IS organization: Insights from the Bell Atlantic experience. *MIS Quarterly*, 425–455.

Conboy, K. (2009). Agility from first principles: Reconstructing the concept of agility in information systems development. *Information Systems Research*, *20*(3), 329–354. https://doi.org/10.1287/isre.1090.0236

Conboy, K., & Fitzgerald, B. (2004). Toward a conceptual framework of agile methods: A study of agility in different disciplines. *Proceedings of the 2004 ACM Workshop on Interdisciplinary Software Engineering Research*, 37–44. https://doi.org/10.1145/1029997.1030005

Couger, J. D., Zawacki, R. A., & Oppermann, E. B. (1979). Motivation levels of MIS managers versus those of their employees. *MIS Quarterly*, 47–56.

Cumps, B., Viaene, S., Dedene, G., & Vandenbulcke, J. (2006). An empirical study on business/ ICT alignment in European organisations. *Proceedings of the Annual Hawaii International Conference on System Sciences*, *8*(C), 1–10. https://doi.org/10.1109/HICSS.2006.53

Currie, A. R., Mcconnell, A., Parr, G. P., McClean, S. I., & Khan, K. (2014). Truesource: A true performance for hierarchical cloud monitoring. *Proceedings of the 2014 IEEE/ACM 7th International Conference on Utility and Cloud Computing*, 980–985. https://doi.org/10.1109/UCC.2014.161

Daniel, E. M., & White, A. (2005). The future of inter-organisational system linkages: Findings of an international Delphi study. *European Journal of Information Systems*, *14*(2), 188–203.

Darke, P., Shanks, G., & Broadbent, M. (1998). Successfully completing case study research: Combining rigour, relevance and pragmatism. *Information Systems Journal*, *8*(4), 273–289. https://doi.org/10.1046/j.1365-2575.1998.00040.x

Dennis, A. R., George, J. F., Jessup, L. M., Nunamaker, Jr, J. F., & Vogel, D. R. (1988). Information technology to support electronic meetings. *MIS Quarterly*, 591–624.

Dove, R. (1995). *Rick Dove agility forum best agile practice reference base – 1994: Challenge models and benchmarks Rick Dove, director strategic analysis, agility forum, Bethlehem, PA*. 4th Annual Agility Conference.

Drucker, P. F. (1995). The new productivity challenge. *Quality in Higher Education*, *37*, 45–53.

Duncan, N. B. (1995). Capturing flexibility of information technology infrastructure: A study of resource characteristics and their measure. *Journal of Management Information Systems*, *12*(2), 37–57. www.jstor.org/stable/40398165

Dybå, T., & Dingsøyr, T. (2008). Empirical studies of agile software development: A systematic review. *Information and Software Technology*, *50*(9–10), 833–859.

Elhasnaoui, S., Medromi, H., Chakir, A., & Sayouti, A. (2015). A new IT governance architecture based on multi agents system to support project management. *2015 International Conference on Electrical and Information Technologies (ICEIT)*, 43–46. https://doi.org/10.1109/EITech.2015.7162957

Felix, R., Rauschnabel, P. A., & Hinsch, C. (2017). Elements of strategic social media marketing: A holistic framework. *Journal of Business Research*, *70*, 118–126. https://doi.org/10.1016/j.jbusres.2016.05.001

Fink, L., & Neumann, S. (2009). Taking the high road to web services implementation: An exploratory investigation of the organizational impacts. *ACM SIGMIS Database: The DATABASE for Advances in Information Systems*, *40*(3), 84–108.

Galliers, R. D. (2006). Strategizing for agility: Confronting information. *Agile Information Systems*, *1*.

Gallupe, R. B., DeSanctis, G., & Dickson, G. W. (1988). Computer-based support for group problem-finding: An experimental investigation. *MIS Quarterly*, 277–296.

Gebauer, J., & Lee, F. (2008). Enterprise system flexibility and implementation strategies: Aligning theory with evidence from a case study. *Information Systems Management*, *25*(1), 71–82.

Gerth, A. B., & Rothman, S. (2007). The future IS organization in a flat world. *Information Systems Management*, *24*(2), 103–111.

Goldman, S. L., & Nagel, R. N. (1993). Management, technology and agility: The emergence of a new era in manufacturing. *International Journal of Technology Management*, *8*, 18–38. https://doi.org/10.1504/IJTM.1993.025758

Goodhue, D. L., Quillard, J. A., & Rockart, J. F. (1988). Managing the data resource: A contingency perspective. *MIS Quarterly*, 373–392.

Goranson, H. T., & Goranson, T. (1999). *The agile virtual enterprise: Cases, metrics, tools*. Greenwood Publishing Group.

Grant, G., & Tan, F. B. (2013). Governing IT in inter-organizational relationships: Issues and future research. *European Journal of Information Systems*, *22*(5), 493–497. https://doi.org/10.1057/ejis.2013.21

Gregor, S., & Benbasat, I. (1999). Explanations from intelligent systems: Theoretical foundations and implications for practice. *MIS Quarterly*, 497–530.

Grembergen, W. V. (2004). *Strategies for information technology governance*. IGI Global.

Group, O. M. (1997, February). *The common object request broker: Architecture and specification, revision 2.0*. O. M. Group.

Halawi, L. A., Aronson, J. E., & McCarthy, R. V. (2005). Resource-based view of knowledge management for competitive advantage. *The Electronic Journal of Knowledge Management*, *3*(2), 75.

Halevi, G., & Weill, R. (1994). *Principles of process planning: A logical approach*. Springer Science & Business Media.

Halpin, Terry A. (2001). Microsoft's new database modeling tool: Part 1. *Journal of Conceptual Modeling*, *20*, 1–11.

Hasselbring, W. (2000). Information system integration. *Communications of the ACM*, *43*(6), 32–38. https://doi.org/10.1145/336460.336472

Hayes, D. C., Hunton, J. E., & Reck, J. L. (2001). Market reaction to ERP implementation announcements. *Journal of Information Systems*, *15*(1), 3–18.

Hobbs, B., & Petit, Y. (2017). Agile methods on large projects in large organizations. *Project Management Journal*, *48*(3), 3–19.

Hohpe, G., & Woolf, B. (2004). *Enterprise integration patterns: Designing, building, and deploying messaging solutions.* Addison-Wesley Professional.

Holmqvist, M., & Pessi, K. (2006). Agility through scenario development and continuous implementation: A global aftermarket logistics case. *European Journal of Information Systems, 15*(2), 146–158.

Hong, W., Thong, J. Y., Chasalow, L. C., & Dhillon, G. (2011). User acceptance of agile information systems: A model and empirical test. *Journal of Management Information Systems, 28*(1), 235–272.

Imache, R., Izza, S., & Ahmed-Nacer, M. (2012). An enterprise information system agility assessment model. *Computer Science and Information Systems, 9*(1), 107–133. https://doi.org/10.2298/CSIS101110041I

Isakowitz, T., Stohr, E. A., & Balasubramanian, P. (1995). RMM: A methodology for structured hypermedia design. *Communications of the ACM, 38*(8), 34–44.

ITGI. (2003). *Board briefing on IT governance.* ITGI.

Izza, S., & Imache, R. (2010). An approach to achieve IT agility by combining SOA with ITSM. *International Journal of Information Technology and Management, 9*(4), 423–445.

Joachim, N., Beimborn, D., & Weitzel, T. (2013). The influence of SOA governance mechanisms on IT flexibility and service reuse. *The Journal of Strategic Information Systems, 22*(1), 86–101.

Kale, E., Aknar, A., & Başar, Ö. (2018). Absorptive capacity and firm performance: The mediating role of strategic agility. *International Journal of Hospitality Management, 78.*

Kalle, L., & Rose, M. G. (2003). Disruptive information system innovation: The case of internet computing. *Information Systems Journal, 13*(4), 301–330. https://doi.org/10.1046/j.1365-2575.2003.00155.x

Kasper, G. M. (1996). A theory of decision support system design for user calibration. *Information Systems Research, 7*(2), 215–232.

Kaur, S. P., Kumar, J., & Kumar, R. (2017). The relationship between flexibility of manufacturing system components, competitiveness of SMEs and business performance: A study of manufacturing SMEs in Northern India. *Global Journal of Flexible Systems Management, 18*(2), 123–137. https://doi.org/10.1007/s40171-016-0149-x

Keen, P. G. W. (1978). *Decision support systems; an organizational perspective.* Addison-Wesley.

Kim, Y. T., Park, D. G., Kang, J., & Seo, K. S. (2008, October). Development of patch type sensor module for real-time monitoring of heart rate and agility index. In *SENSORS, 2008 IEEE* (pp. 1151–1154). IEEE.

Knapp, K., Morris, R., Marshall, T. E., & Byrd, T. (2009). Information security policy: An organizational-level process model. *Computers & Security, 28.* https://doi.org/10.1016/j.cose.2009.07.001

Korac-Kakabadse, N., & Kakabadse, A. (2001). IS/IT governance: Need for an integrated model. *Corporate Governance: The International Journal of Business in Society, 1*(4), 9–11. https://doi.org/10.1108/EUM0000000005974

Kumar, R. L., & Stylianou, A. C. (2014). A process model for analyzing and managing flexibility in information systems. *European Journal of Information Systems, 23*(2), 151–184. https://doi.org/10.1057/ejis.2012.53

Lacity, M. C., Willcocks, L. P., & Feeny, D. F. (1996). The value of selective IT sourcing. *Sloan Management Review, 37,* 13–25.

Lee, G., & Xia, W. (2005). The ability of information systems development project teams to respond to business and technology changes: A study of flexibility measures. *European Journal of Information Systems, 14*(1), 75–92.

Le Moigne, J. L. (1994). *La théorie du système général: Théorie de la modélisation.* Jeanlouis le moigne-ae mcx.

Lengnick-Hall, C. A., Beck, T. E., & Lengnick-Hall, M. L. (2011). Developing a capacity for organizational resilience through strategic human resource management. *Human Resource Management Review, 21*(3), 243–255. https://doi.org/10.1016/j.hrmr.2010.07.001

Li, Y., Jia, X., Chen, Y., & Yin, C. (2014, August). Frequency agility MIMO-SAR imaging and anti-deception jamming performance. In *2014 XXXIth URSI General Assembly and Scientific Symposium (URSI GASS)* (pp. 1–4). IEEE.

Lim, S. (2014). Impact of information technology infrastructure flexibility on the competitive advantage of small and medium sized-enterprises. *Journal of Business & Management*, *3*(1), 1–12. https://doi.org/10.12735/jbm.v3i1p1

Lyytinen, K., & Rose, G. M. (2003). The disruptive nature of information technology innovations: The case of internet computing in systems development organizations. *MIS Quarterly*, 557–596.

Ma, Q., Pearson, J. M., & Tadisina, S. (2005). An exploratory study into factors of service quality for application service providers. *Information & Management*, *42*(8), 1067–1080.

Maas, J. (1998). Leveraging the new infrastructure: How market leaders capitalize on information technology. *MIT Sloan Management Review*, *40*(1), 104.

Maes, K., De Haes, S., & Van Grembergen, W. (2012). IT value management as a vehicle to unleash the business value from IT enabled investments. *International Journal of IT/Business Alignment and Governance*, *3*(1), 47–62. https://doi.org/10.4018/jitbag.2012010103

Maleh, Y., Sahid, A., & Belaissaoui, M. (2019). *Strategic IT governance and performance frameworks in large organizations*. IGI Global. https://doi.org/10.4018/978-1-5225-7826-0

Markus, M. L., & Benjamin, R. I. (1996). Change agentry-the next IS frontier. *MIS Quarterly*, 385–407.

Mason, R. O., & Mitroff, I. I. (1973). A program for research on management information systems. *Management Science*, *19*(5), 475–487. https://doi.org/10.1287/mnsc.19.5.475

McAvoy, J., Nagle, T., & Sammon, D. (2013). Using mindfulness to examine ISD agility. *Information Systems Journal*, *23*(2), 155–172.

McCann, J., Selsky, J., & Lee, J. (2009). Building agility, resilience and performance in turbulent environments. *People & Strategy*, *32*(3), 44–51.

Mintzberg, H. (1973). *The nature of managerial work*. Harper & Row.

Morton, J., Stacey, P., & Mohn, M. (2018). Building and maintaining strategic agility: An agenda and framework for executive IT leaders. *California Management Review*, *61*(1), 94–113.

Moy, B. (2018). PROGame: A process framework for serious game development for motor rehabilitation therapy. *PloS One*, 1–18.

Murphy, K., Lyytinen, K., & Somers, T. (2018). A socio-technical model for project-based executive IT governance. *Proceedings of the 51st Hawaii International Conference on System Sciences | 2018 A*, *9*, 4825–4834.

Newcomer, E. (2002). *Understanding web services: XML, WSDL, SOAP, and UDDI*. Addison-Wesley Professional.

Newkirk, H. E., & Lederer, A. L. (2006). The effectiveness of strategic information systems planning under environmental uncertainty. *Information & Management*, *43*(4), 481–501.

Oetzel, J. M. (2004). Differentiation advantages in the on-line brokerage industry. *International Journal of Electronic Commerce*, *9*(1), 105–126.

Olson, M. H. (1985). *Management information systems: Conceptual foundations, structure, and development*. McGraw-Hill.

Overby, E., Bharadwaj, A., & Sambamurthy, V. (2006). Enterprise agility and the enabling role of information technology. *European Journal of Information Systems*, *15*(2), 120–131.

Peterson, R. R. (2001). Configurations and coordination for global information technology governance: Complex designs in a transnational European context. *Proceedings of the Hawaii International Conference on System Sciences*, *C*, 217. https://doi.org/10.1109/HICSS.2001.927133

Peterson, R. R. (2004). Crafting information technology governance. *Information Systems Management*, *21*(4), 7–22.

Pinsonneault, A., & Rivard, S. (1998). Information technology and the nature of managerial work: From the productivity paradox to the Icarus paradox? *MIS Quarterly*, 287–311.

Ploesser, K., Recker, J., & Rosemann, M. (2008). Towards a classification and lifecycle of business process change: A classification and lifecycle of process change strategies. *BPMDS'08: Business Process Life-Cycle: Design, Deployment, Operation & Evaluation*, 10–18.

Prager, K. P. (1996). Managing for flexibility: The new role of the aligned IT organization. *Information Systems Management*, *13*(4), 41–46.

Queiroz, M., Tallon, P. P., Sharma, R., & Coltman, T. (2018). The role of IT application orchestration capability in improving agility and performance. *Journal of Strategic Information Systems*, *27*(1), 4–21. https://doi.org/10.1016/j.jsis.2017.10.002

Ramesh, B., Mohan, K., & Cao, L. (2012). Ambidexterity in agile distributed development: An empirical investigation. *Information Systems Research*, *23*(2), 323–339.

Ramesh, J. V., Singh, S. K., & Sharma, M. (2011). Development of private cloud for educational institution using Aneka grid container. *Proceedings of the International Conference & Workshop on Emerging Trends in Technology*, 244–247. https://doi.org/10.1145/1980022.1980078

Rezaee, Z., & Reinstein, A. (1998). The impact of emerging information technology on auditing. *Managerial Auditing Journal*, *13*(8), 465–471. https://doi.org/10.1108/02686909810236271

Robson, W. (1998). Strategic management and information systems: An integrated approach. *Systems Research and Behavioral Science*, *15*(4), 347–350.

Rockart, J. F., Earl, M. J., & Ross, J. W. (1996a). Eight imperatives for the new IT organization. *Inventing the Organizations of the 21st Century*, *38*(1), 43.

Rockart, J. F., Earl, M. J., & Ross, J. W. (1996b). *The new IT organization: Eight imperatives* [Sloan School of Management, No. 292, Massachusetts Institute of Technology (MIT)], 1–31.

Roman, D., Keller, U., Lausen, H., De Bruijn, J., Lara, R., Stollberg, M., Polleres, A., Feier, C., Bussler, C., & Fensel, D. (2005). Web service modeling ontology. *Applied Ontology*, *1*(1), 77–106.

Saha, N., Gregar, A., Van der Heijden, B. I. J. M., & Sáha, P. (2019). The influence of SHRM and organizational agility: Do they really boost organizational performance? In *Handbook of research on contemporary approaches in management and organizational strategy* (pp. 62–83). IGI Global.

Sahid, A., Maleh, Y., & Belaissaoui, M. (2020a). Information system evolution. In *Strategic information system agility: From theory to practices* (pp. 29–66). Emerald Publishing Limited. https://doi.org/10.1108/978-1-80043-810-120211004

Sahid, A., Maleh, Y., & Belaissaoui, M. (2020b). Strategic information system agility: From theory to practices. In *Strategic information system agility: From theory to practices*. Emerald Publishing Limited. https://doi.org/10.1108/978-1-80043-810-120211001

Sambamurthy, V., & Zmud, R. (1999). Arrangements for information technology governance: A theory of multiple contingencies. *Management Information Systems Quarterly*, *23*(2), 261–290. https://doi.org/10.2307/249754

Sarker, S., & Sarker, S. (2009). Exploring agility in distributed information systems development teams: An interpretive study in an offshoring context. *Information Systems Research*, *20*(3), 440–461.

Sarkis, J. (2001). Benchmarking for agility. *Benchmarking: An International Journal*, *8*(2), 88–107.

Sassone, P. G. (1988). A survey of cost-benefit methodologies for information systems. *Project Appraisal*, *3*(2), 73–84.

Sawhney, N., & Schmandt, C. (2000). Nomadic radio: Speech and audio interaction for contextual messaging in nomadic environments. *ACM Transactions on Computer-Human Interaction (TOCHI)*, *7*(3), 353–383.

Schapiro, S. B., & Henry, M. H. (2012, March). Engineering agile systems through architectural modularity. In *2012 IEEE International Systems Conference SysCon 2012* (pp. 1–6). IEEE.

Scheer, A. W., & Habermann, F. (2000). Enterprise resource planning: Making ERP a success. *Communications of the ACM*, *43*(4), 57–61.

Schmidt, C., & Buxmann, P. (2011). Outcomes and success factors of enterprise IT architecture management: Empirical insight from the international financial services industry. *European Journal of Information Systems*, *20*(2), 168–185.

Scholl, H. J., Kubicek, H., & Cimander, R. (2011). Interoperability, enterprise architectures, and IT governance in government. *Lecture Notes in Computer Science (Including Subseries Lecture Notes in Artificial Intelligence and Lecture Notes in Bioinformatics), 6846*, 345–354. https://doi.org/10.1007/978-3-642-22878-0_29

Senn, J. A. (1978). Essential principles of information systems development. *MIS Quarterly*, 17–26.

Sharif, A. M., Irani, Z., & Love, P. E. D. (2005). Integrating ERP using EAI: A model for post hoc evaluation. *European Journal of Information Systems, 14*(2), 162–174.

Sharifi, H., & Zhang, Z. (1999). Methodology for achieving agility in manufacturing organisations: An introduction. *International Journal of Production Economics, 62*(1), 7–22. https://doi.org/10.1016/S0925-5273(98)00217-5

Sharp, J. M., Bamber, C. J., Desia, S., & Irani, Z. (1999, March 9). *An empirical analysis of lean & agile manufacturing.* Proceedings of the IMechE Conference on Lean & Agile for the Next Millennium.

Shein, C., Robinson, H. E., & Gutierrez, H. (2018). Agility in the archives: Translating agile methods to archival project management. *RBM: A Journal of Rare Books, Manuscripts, and Cultural Heritage, 19*(2), 94.

Shore, B. (2006). Enterprise integration across the globally disbursed service organization. *Communications of the ACM, 49*(6), 102–106.

Sia, S. K., Koh, C., & Tan, C. X. (2008). Strategic maneuvers for outsourcing flexibility: An empirical assessment. *Decision Sciences, 39*(3), 407–443.

Simonsson, M., & Johnson, P. (2006). Defining IT governance-a consolidation of literature. *The 18th Conference on Advanced Information Systems Engineering, 6.*

Singh, M. P., Huhns, M. N., & Huhns, M. N. (2005). *Service-oriented computing: Semantics, processes, agents.* John Wiley & Sons.

Stein, M. K., Galliers, R. D., & Whitley, E. A. (2016). Twenty years of the European information systems academy at ECIS: Emergent trends and research topics. *European Journal of Information Systems, 25*(1), 1–15. https://doi.org/10.1057/ejis.2014.25

Stettina, C. J., & Kroon, E. (2013, June). Is there an agile handover? An empirical study of documentation and project handover practices across agile software teams. In *2013 International Conference on Engineering, Technology and Innovation (ICE) & IEEE International Technology Management Conference* (pp. 1–12). IEEE.

Susarla, A., Barua, A., & Whinston, A. B. (2006). Understanding the "service" component of application service provision: An empirical analysis of satisfaction with ASP services. In *Information systems outsourcing* (pp. 481–521). Springer.

Swafford, P. M., Ghosh, S., & Murthy, N. (2008). Achieving supply chain agility through IT integration and flexibility. *International Journal of Production Economics, 116*(2), 288–297. https://doi.org/10.1016/j.ijpe.2008.09.002

Tan, B., Pan, S. L., Lu, X., & Huang, L. (2009). Leveraging digital business ecosystems for enterprise agility: The tri-logic development strategy of Alibaba. com. *ICIS 2009 Proceedings, 16*(4), 248–280.

Tan, C., & Sia, S. K. (2006). Managing flexibility in outsourcing. *Journal of the Association for Information Systems, 7*(4), 10.

Tanriverdi, H., Rai, A., & Venkatraman, N. (2010). Research commentary—reframing the dominant quests of information systems strategy research for complex adaptive business systems. *Information Systems Research, 21*(4), 822–834.

Tiwana, A., Konsynski, B., & Bush, A. A. (2010). Research commentary—Platform evolution: Coevolution of platform architecture, governance, and environmental dynamics. *Information Systems Research, 21*(4), 675–687.

Trabelsi, L., & Abid, I. H. (2013). Urbanization of information systems as a trigger for enhancing agility: A state in the tunisian firms. *European Journal of Business and Management, 5*(5), 63–77.

Truex, D. P., Baskerville, R., & Klein, H. (1999). Growing systems in emergent organizations. *Communications of the ACM, 42*(8), 117–123.

Turban, E. (2007). *Information technology for management: Transforming organizations in the digital economy*. John Wiley & Sons, Inc.

Valentine, E. L. H. (2016, January). *Enterprise technology governance: New information and technology core competencies for boards of directors* [Doctoral dissertation, Queensland University of Technology], 1–295. https://doi.org/10.13140/RG.2.2.34027.95529

Van Grembergen, W., & De Haes, S. (2009a). *Enterprise governance of information technology: Achieving strategic alignment and value*. Springer Science & Business Media.

Van Grembergen, W., & De Haes, S. (2009b). *The IT balanced scorecard as a framework for enterprise governance of IT BT – enterprise governance of information technology: Achieving strategic alignment and value* (S. De Haes & W. Van Grembergen, Eds., pp. 111–136). Springer. https://doi.org/10.1007/978-0-387-84882-2_4

Vaughan-Nichols, S. J. (2002). Web services: Beyond the hype. *Computer, 35*(2), 18–21.

Verhoef, C. (2007). Quantifying the effects of IT-governance rules. *Science of Computer Programming, 67*(2–3), 247–277. https://doi.org/10.1016/j.scico.2007.01.010

Walls, J. G., Widmeyer, G. R., & El Sawy, O. A. (1992). Building an information system design theory for vigilant EIS. *Information Systems Research, 3*(1), 36–59.

Walters, G. J. (2001). Privacy and security: An ethical analysis. *ACM SIGCAS Computers and Society, 31*(2), 8–23.

Wang, X., Conboy, K., & Pikkarainen, M. (2012). Assimilation of agile practices in use. *Information Systems Journal, 22*(6), 435–455.

Webb, P., Pollard, C., & Ridley, G. (2006). Attempting to define IT governance: Wisdom or folly? *Proceedings of the Annual Hawaii International Conference on System Sciences, 8*(C), 1–10. https://doi.org/10.1109/HICSS.2006.68

Weill, P., & Ross, J. W. (2004). How top performers manage IT decisions rights for superior results. *IT Governance, Harvard Business School Press Boston, Massachusetts*, 1–10. https://doi.org/10.2139/ssrn.664612

Weill, P., & Woodham, R. (2002). Don't just lead, govern: Implementing effective IT governance. *CISR Working Paper, 17*. https://doi.org/10.2139/ssrn.317319

Wenzler, I. (2005). Development of an asset management strategy for a network utility company: Lessons from a dynamic business simulation approach. *Simulation Gaming, 36*(1), 75–90.

West, L. A., & Hess, T. J. (2002). Metadata as a knowledge management tool: Supporting intelligent agent and end user access to spatial data. *Decision Support Systems, 32*(3), 247–264.

Wickramasinghe, N. (2003). Do we practise what we preach? Are knowledge management systems in practice truly reflective of knowledge management systems in theory? *Business Process Management Journal, 9*(3), 295–316.

Wiederhold, G. (1992). Mediators in the architecture of future information systems. *Computer, 25*(3), 38–49.

Willcocks, L. (2013). *Information management: The evaluation of information systems investments*. Springer. https://doi.org/10.1007/978-1-4899-3208-2

Xiaoying, D., Qianqian, L., & Dezhi, Y. (2008). Business performance, business strategy, and information system strategic alignment: An empirical study on Chinese firms. *Tsinghua Science and Technology, 13*(3), 348–354. https://doi.org/10.1016/S1007-0214(08)70056-7

Yoon, Y., Guimaraes, T., & O'Neal, Q. (1995). Exploring the factors associated with expert systems success. *MIS Quarterly*, 83–106.

Zaphiris, P., Shneiderman, B., & Norman, K. L. (2002). Expandable indexes vs. sequential menus for searching hierarchies on the World Wide Web. *Behaviour & Information Technology, 21*(3), 201–207.

Zhang, Z., & Sharifi, H. (2000). A methodology for achieving agility in manufacturing organizations. *International Journal of Operations & Production Management, 20*(4), 496–512. https://doi.org/10.1108/01443570010314818

Zheng, Y., Venters, W., & Cornford, T. (2011). Collective agility, paradox and organizational improvisation: the development of a particle physics grid. *Information Systems Journal, 21*(4), 303–333.

Zhu, K. (2004). The complementarity of information technology infrastructure and e-commerce capability: A resource-based assessment of their business value. *Journal of Management Information Systems, 21*(1), 167–202. https://doi.org/10.1080/07421222.2004.11045794

Zviran, M. (1990). Relationships between organizational and information systems objectives: Some empirical evidence. *Journal of Management Information Systems, 7*(1), 65–84.

Zwass, V. (1992). *Management information systems.* William C. Brown Publishers.

IT Governance and Information Security

Guides and Standards

2

2.1 INTRODUCTION

As information and communication technology develops, an increasing number of companies recognize the potential value of IT resources in delivering their firm's strategic vision. IT is no longer a supporting tool for business, but a fundamental component of company strategy in roles such as operations, internal audit, compliance, and decision support. A recent survey conducted by the IT Governance Institute (ITGI) with CEO/CIOs drawn from 22 countries shows that 87% of respondents agree that IT plays a vital role in achieving company goals in the broadest sense (Simonsson & Johnson, 2006).

In recent years, leading international organizations have focused attention on effective corporate governance to improve the performance of firms' IT assets. These efforts have intensified in the wake of large-scale frauds such as Enron and WorldCom in the United States and shareholders' dissatisfaction with companies. Multinationals and others have devised corporate governance structures to clarify and monitor the respective roles and responsibilities of shareholders, management, and employees. These structures have emphasized the importance of IT assets and IT governance (ITG) structure, aiming to minimize financial risks on IT investment by providing transparency, accountability, and management processes. These criteria entail the effective allocation of IT resources in clear structures and decision-making procedures for IT management. At this juncture, it has become imperative to redefine effective ITG, seeking to understand governance's role in aligning organizations' information assets with their strategic goals (Webb et al., 2006). This alignment contributes to creating value in companies by suggesting optimal amounts of risk for companies to design their management structures and proactively respond to new business circumstances.

DOI: 10.1201/9781003161998-4

IT governance consists of structures, processes, and operational mechanisms that work together to ensure that IT investments and business objectives are aligned (De Haes & Van Grembergen, 2005). The cornerstone of IT governance is to provide decision-makers an acceptable level of assurance that an organization's strategic objectives are not jeopardized by IT failures (Benaroch & Chernobai, 2017). A conventional or, rather, inevitable approach for attaining a level of assurance includes evaluating the IT governance system in place. The evaluation was born of the need to assess the degree of conformation with standard practice by utilizing methodologies and frameworks (Vlietland et al., 2016). This in particular means that, by engaging in IT governance evaluation, organizations can periodically measure IT governance performance using well-proven worldwide frameworks or methods such as Control Objectives for Information and Related Technology (COBIT), IT Infrastructure Library ITIL, or the International Standards Organization's ISO 38500, to name few.

A range of research in literature examines IT governance structures and mechanisms (De Haes & Van Grembergen, 2005; Guldentops et al., 2002; McKay et al., 2003; Peterson et al., 2002; Wim van Grembergen & de Haes, 2009) explores factors inflecting adoption and implementation of IT governance systems (Aasi et al., 2014; Reich & Benbasat, 2000), and the use of codified frameworks and their impact on IT governance (El-Mekawy et al., 2015; Guldentops, 2002; Wim van Grembergen & de Haes, 2009; Weber, 2014). The literature also indicates that, while there is the widespread use of governance frameworks, more research is needed to investigate how these frameworks could be modified to fit a specific circumstance or context (Maleh et al., 2018). Aspects involving user behavior in IT governance, although they have long been acknowledged (Grunwel & Sahama, 2016; Herath & Rao, 2009), have received far less attention from academics (Smits & Hillegersberg, 2015).

Several IT governance frameworks can guide the implementation of an IT governance program. Although frameworks and guidelines such as CobiT, ITIL, ValIT, and ISO 38500 (Prieto-Diaz, 1991) have been widely adopted, there is no absolute standard IT governance framework; the combination that works best for an organization depends on business factors, corporate culture, IT maturity, and staffing capacity. The level of implementation of these frameworks will also vary by organization (Maleh et al., 2019).

This chapter presents the state of the art of research on the practice of information technology (IT) governance through an analysis of the various proposed standards. This analysis was conducted on the basis of a meta-model of four words. This chapter is organized as follows. The first part describes the proposed reference framework for IT governance. Five recognized approaches are then evaluated under this framework. Finally, this chapter highlights the gaps in current approaches, our positioning concerning the literature, and its contribution to IT governance.

2.2 RESEARCH METHODOLOGY

This section proposes a meta-model to evaluate IT governance ITG approaches. This model is built around facets capturing a specific dimension of information governance. The principle of facets was introduced in Jarke et al. (1992) for software engineering. This framework is not intended to describe governance activities but to organize governance approaches along structuring analytical lines that seem relevant to us.

The framework is structured around four poles or 'words'. The 'four words\ framework has been used in various engineering disciplines: IS engineering (Jarke & Pohl, 1993), requirements engineering (Rolland, 1998), process engineering (Nurcan & Rolland, 2003), and change engineering (Nehan & Deneckere, 2007). This framework has been used for IT governance engineering and component-based situational method engineering (Prieto-Diaz, 1991).

Facets supplement it according to the approach introduced in 'Information Security Governance: Guidance for Boards of Directors and Executive Management Guidance for Boards of Directors and Executive Management' (2006). The aim is to allow a more flexible and precise classification of software components and is based on the enumeration of component descriptors, their association with a lexicon of terms (thesaurus), and a graph of facets. The initial framework of the four words has been adapted by facets that are descriptive elements. Each facet can take a predefined value by a 'value domain':

- A simple value domain refers to a predefined primitive value type. This is the case of an integer or real value;
- An overall value domain (SET{a; b; . . .}) refers to a structured type. For example, a vector with n dimensions is typically structured on n elements;
- A listed value domain (Enum{a, b, . . .}) refers to a listed type. Thus, a mention for a diploma is from a listed field and can take its value among the values defined on Enum{'Fairly Good', 'Good', 'Very Good'}.

The meta-model in Figure 2.1 defines the proposed framework.

The reference framework is obtained by instantiating the metamodel described in Figure 2.1. The governance literature allows us to define the values taken by the attributes of the metamodel classes. The framework is presented in Figure 2.2 and comprises the following four words:

- The word 'subject'. It presents IS governance as the object of analysis and identifies its intrinsic characteristics. Governance is described as an organizational structure for decision-making concerned with the simultaneous evolution of IT projects, business processes, and IT processes;

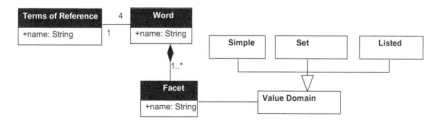

FIGURE 2.1 The proposed meta-model to evaluate IT governance frameworks.

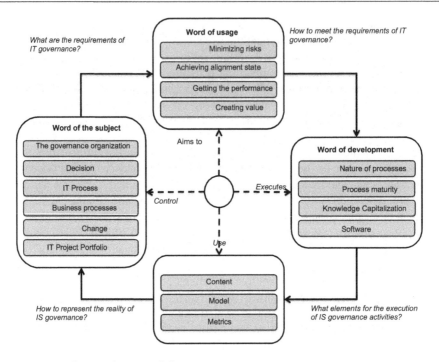

FIGURE 2.2   Reference framework for IT governance.

- The word 'use' is the purpose of ITG. It concerns the objectives of its users. In governance, CIOs make decisions to limit risk, create value, and achieve a certain performance level;
- The word 'system' contains all the valuable information about the activities of the ITG. It is the informational basis for decision-making. It contains the elements for measuring ITG objectives and all the documents and models helpful in sharing knowledge related to ITG;
- The word 'development' consists of the processes of ITG. Their execution achieves the objectives of ITG and relies on the manipulation of the information elements of the ITG system.

The words are in relation to each other (Claudepierre & Nurcan, 2007): The word *subject* defines a framework for identifying and justifying the purposes of the word of use. The word *system* is the support for the representation of the reality of the word subject. The word system word is built to facilitate the processes described in the word *development* word. Finally, the word system supports the achievement of the objectives presented in the word *use*.

The IT governance managers are thus positioned at the center of the four words: they control the governance environment and its mechanisms (subject word), sets a set of objectives to be achieved (use word), executes processes to achieve them (development word), and uses documents, models, and metrics (system word).

2.2.1 The Word of the IT Governance Subject

The word 'subject' answers the question 'What is IT governance?'. It is a faceted description of the intrinsic nature of governance. This word has six facets: GOVERNANCE ORGANIZATION, DECISION, IT PROCESS, BUSINESS PROCESS, CHANGE, and IT PROJECT PORTFOLIO. All of these facets make it possible to situate IT governance as a set of organized activities for decision-making dedicated to the choices to be made for IT project evolutions, their impacts on business processes and IT processes. Table 2.1 lists all the facets and their values for the subject's word.

- *ORGANIZATION OF GOVERNANCE*

Weill and Ross (2004) propose to analyze the management behavior of information systems by comparing it to the archetypes of state governance. They thus describe the organization around decision-making. Centralized decision-making responsibility is then compared to a monarchy, and collaborative decision-making is compared to participatory democracy between two groups (business and IS). This decision-making structure is organized around a typology of decisions, and the study shows that investment decisions in new technologies are the responsibility of the business departments.

In contrast, more technical decisions concerning the architecture and infrastructure of the system are the responsibility of the IT department. De Haes (2005) agrees with this idea that an organization of Information systems is structured for decision-making around a committee where roles and responsibilities are distributed.

The ORGANIZATION OF GOVERNANCE facet captures this aspect. A centralized GOVERNANCE ORGANIZATION reflects a structure where responsibility for decisions is assigned to a single person. For example, the CIO can be solely responsible for IT decisions without consulting business managers. A decentralized governance structure represents an organization where the decision results from an exchange and constitutes a consensus among several stakeholders. A hybrid structure makes it possible to adopt a centralized mode of responsibility for certain decisions and decentralized for others.

- *DECISION*

TABLE 2.1 List of Facets of the Word 'Subject'

FACET	*VALUE*
GOVERNANCE ORGANIZATION	*Enum{centralized, decentralized, hybrid}*
DECISION	*Enum{IT architecture, IT infrastructure, project planification}*
IT PROCESS	*Enum{documented, piloted, evolutive}*
BUSINESS PROCESS	*Enum{productive, administrative, ad-hoc, collaborative}*
CHANGE	*Enum{ad-hoc, evolutive, corrective}*
IT PROJECT PORTFOLIO	*SET{classification mode: Enum{monocriteria, multi-criteria}; transformation mode: Enum{creation, maintenance, evolution}}*

Weill and Ross (2005) propose a model structuring the decision-making process in terms of information systems governance. This study presents five types or areas of governance decisions:

- Information Technology Principles: These are decisions about the strategic role played by information technology.
- Architecture: This field refers to technological choices to satisfy the company's organizational needs. Business processes guide the decision here for a properly urbanized IS.
- Infrastructure: These are the decisions regarding the supporting technological infrastructure. It refers to the equipment and its ability to implement them or identify outsourcing solutions depending on the criticality of strategic objectives.
- Business applications: This area concerns application needs, internal developments, and outsourcing for business functionalities.

It appears that the significant decisions to be made in relation to IS governance focus on the provision of IS services and the mode of deployment of applications. Application architecture is an important decision-making aspect. This architecture could not exist without a technical support infrastructure. Finally, IS developments are ensured by a set of projects that need to be planned. The DECISION facet representing the typology of possible decisions relating to IS architecture, IS infrastructure, or project planning, as shown in Table 2.1.

- *IT PROCESS*

IT governance is based on a set of processes that make it possible to control that the objectives assigned to the IS are well-considered and to react if necessary. Grembergen (2004) proposes to consider the IT processes essential for IT management around a control process (reporting) and an active process for decision-making. It joins the idea developed earlier in Luftman et al. (1999), which advocates six steps for business/SI alignment. They mainly concern the following: identifying objectives, understanding alignment links, analysis (in- fine, measurement, and control) and prioritization of gaps, specification and choice of actions to be taken. The IT PROCESSES are thus linked to obtaining IS quality through a control mechanism whose foundations are based on the PDCA's generic Deming approach (Plan, Do, Check, Act) (Moen & Norman, 2006).

The values associated with this facet measure the degree of control of these processes based on the principle that an IT PROCESS is documented. Identifying metrics, indicators, and control rules enables decisions to be made on the audit process: The process is then steered. An evolutionary process is a process under control whose evolution has been considered and representative of mature governance, as listed in Table 2.1.

- *BUSINESS PROCESSES*

Davenport (1993) defines a business process as

> a structured and measured framework of activities designed to produce a specific output for a customer or market. This involves focusing on how work is done within an organization, rather than focusing on the product. Therefore, a process is a precise order of activities across time and space, with a clearly defined beginning and end, inputs and outputs: a structure for action.

There are several business processes: Two approaches characterize this notion (Alonso et al., 1997; Rummler & Brache, 2012). The first structure defines processes in terms of their direct/indirect contribution to value creation. The approach (Rummler & Brache, 2012) distinguishes primary processes, which are in direct contact with the customer and directly generate value, from supporting processes.

The BUSINESS PROCESS captures these aspects. The typology of Alonso et al. (1997) is used to characterize the values of the business process facet as shown in Table 2.1.

- *CHANGE*

CHANGE management refers to the management of the organization's transformation processes and its business or IT processes. Ploesser et al. (2008) propose a typology of change processes:

- Change by substitution: The temporary replacement of one business process by another, structurally different business processes, and usually responding to an unforeseen event such as an emergency;
- Adaptive change: The temporary adaptation of the structure of a business process in response to a planned and temporary event, without erasing the structural identity of the process;
- Change by evolution: The changes made in the business process are permanent. They considerably modify the structural composition of the process or its type.

The classification of Ploesser et al. (2008) is taken on the typology of business process changes and adapts it to propose the values of the change facet. Changes can be as follows: (i) ad hoc, this is the case for unwanted changes; (ii) evolutionary, when an improvement is envisaged; and (iii) corrective, when processes are adapted to execution.

In the context of IT governance, changes occur in business processes and IT processes or IT development and maintenance projects. The CHANGE facet captures this aspect and takes its values from an enumerated domain that includes ad hoc, evolutive, and corrective values, as shown in Table 2.1.

- *IT PROJECT PORTFOLIO*

The information system is the object of IT governance. The latter is continuously transformed to meet the support and IT services needs of the company's players. IS project portfolio management is defined as an identified practice in IT governance. Its objective is to prioritize IT transformation projects according to a set of criteria. For Reyck et al. (2005), classifying projects according to their order of urgency concerning these criteria is a question. Two ways of classifying projects are identified: single-criteria or multi-criteria.

The IT PROJECT PORTFOLIO facet is complex. It makes it possible to characterize the classification mode of IT projects and the mode of IT transformation.

2.2.2 The Word of IT Governance Usage

The word 'usage' answers the question, 'What are the objectives of IT governance, what is its purpose?'. It is a faceted characterization of governance objectives. This word has four facets: MINIMIZING RISKS, ATTENDING THE STATE OF ALIGNMENT, GETTING PERFORMANCE, and CREATING VALUE. All facets associated with this word helps to highlight the objectives of ITG. The remainder of this section defines each facet that is summarized in Table 2.2.

Thus, whether it is a question of managing projects, business processes, or ensuring the satisfaction of IT users in terms of security, information must always be provided at the lowest cost, on time, and with the expected quality.

In conclusion, the analysis and synthesis of the objectives granted to ITG lead to the following proposal:

- *MINIMIZING RISKS*

Risk management is strongly linked to IS project portfolio management. For each project, it is essential to measure the impact of risks on cost, quality, and deadlines. It is a question of managing projects, business processes or ensuring the satisfaction of IT users in terms of security. The information must always be provided at the lowest cost, on time, and with the expected quality.

The MINIMIZE RISKS facet captures the types of risks related to information needs. It takes its value in an enumerated area, including extra cost, non-quality, and delay as shown in Table 2.2.

- *ACHIEVING ALIGNMENT STATE*

The primary objective of an IS is to satisfy the need for support from the actors of an organization. The IS can also be used as a competitive advantage. The strategic alignment

TABLE 2.2   List of facets of the word usage

FACET	VALUE
MINIMIZING RISK	Enum{extra cost, non-quality, delay}
ACHIEVING ALIGNMENT STATE	Enum{IT evolution, business evolution, co-evolution}
GETTING THE PERFORMANCE	Enum{ad-hoc, process maturity}
CREATING VALUE	Enum{IT asset, business asset, IT usage}

model (SAM) developed by Henderson and Venkatraman (1999) distinguishes between the external information perspective (IT strategy) and its internal objective (IT infrastructure and process infrastructure), recognizing the potential of IT to support both the organization's business and its strategy. The model is based on two types of alignment: strategic adjustment and functional adjustment. Alignment thus consists of making business, and IT strategies evolve in coherence on the one hand and business and IT services.

The facet ACHIEVING ALIGNMENT STATE takes its values on a listed domain including the values IT evolution, business evolution, and co-evolution, as shown in Table 2.2.

- *GETTING THE PERFORMANCE*

Performance is at the heart of the concerns of CIOs. This results from mastering the business and IS processes (Ravichandran et al., 2005). In addition, the application of process-oriented methods such as COBIT or CMMi is relevant. These frameworks propose a predefined set of objectives to be achieved and metrics to measure process maturity.

Two strategies are identified for achieving governance performance: an ad hoc strategy and a strategy guided by process maturity. This aspect is captured through the GETTING PERFORMANCE facet, which can take the ad hoc or mature values of the processes, as shown in Table 2.2.

- *CREATING VALUE*

In the literature, two main types of value are addressed when dealing with IS. The financial value of the human, material, and energy resources used (heritage value) from the value in use. Governance deals with alignment; it is therefore also relevant to analyze value creation both at IS level (IT assets) and at the organizational level (business assets). The use-value (use of the IS) is linked to the efficient use of the system by its users (Grover & Kohli, 2012).

The facet CREATING VALUE captures the elements of value concerned: IT assets, business assets, and IT usage.

2.2.3 The Word of the IT Governance System

The word of the ITG system answers the question, 'What information is useful for ITG activities?'. It is a faceted characterization of information media for IS governance. This word has three facets: CONTENT, MODEL, and METRIC. All the facets selected to highlight the useful elements for IT Asset Management's decision-making activities in terms of value creation objectives, risk control, alignment, and performance achievement. Table 2.3 lists all the facets and their values for the system word.

In conclusion, the analysis and synthesis of the elements of the ITG system lead to the following proposal:

- *CONTENT*

TABLE 2.3   List of facets of the word system

FACETTE	VALEUR
CONTENT	Enum{document name}
MODEL	Enum{process, object, decision, evolution}
METRICS	Enum{risk, performance, value, alignment}

IT governance activities are based on information media, most often documents. A document summarizes valuable information for decision-making. A non-exhaustive list is provided as follows:

- Documents for alignment: strategic plan and IS/business process mapping;
- Documents for management: hierarchical organization chart, RACI of the members of the management committees, activity reports, and description of the programs;
- Resource management documents: incident reporting, architecture, and infrastructure model;
- Risk management documents: risk mapping, emergency plan, and restoration procedure;
- Performance management documents: dashboards;
- Value management documents: budget, investment plan, and invoices;
- Maturity management documents: best practices.

The CONTENT facet highlights the need for an IT governance system to manage a set of documents. It is characterized by the unique document name value as listed in Table 2.3.

- *MODEL*

Models allow the representation of a domain and are the support for analysis and reasoning. They respect a particular paradigm, that is, a way of seeing, of representing a particular subject. ITG activities require the representation of four topics:

- Processes: Process models are used to describe the business and IS processes. In computing, there are several languages for process modeling: The UML (Unified Modelling Language) standard (Booch et al., 1999) makes it possible to represent processes in the activity diagram. BPMN (Business Process Modeling Notation) (Briol, 2008) is a standard maintained by the OMG (Object Management Group). It allows representing the sequence of activities, their distribution to actors, and the events inherent to a process.
- Objects: Object models are used to represent object classes. UML is based on object principles and provides class and object diagrams with specific notations. This paradigm is used in many computer applications, including object databases, operating systems, and object programming languages such as C++, C#, or Java.

- Decisions: Decision models must allow a decision-maker to act as prescribed by specific theories of choice. In the ideal case of a specifiable problem, this consists of visualization of a decision tree, making it possible to make an optimal choice according to the desired criteria (for example, minimization of risk).
- Evolutions: The MAP model (Rolland, 1998) was also proposed for IS and process re-engineering. It is based on the concepts of intention, which represents the projection of the need for evolution that one wishes to have for the future IS, and of the strategy that is the way to achieve these intentions.

The MODEL facet characterizes the types of models considered by a governance approach. It is based on a listed value area containing values: process, object, decision, and evolution. This facet reflects the ability of the governance system to represent business and IT processes, decisions, projects, and their evolution.

- *METRIC*

IT governance activities are based on metrics that enable decision-makers to assess the current situation concerning the objectives to be achieved. The metrics are thus the dimensions of 'What?' measurement (the IS, its projects, processes, and resources) and the 'Why?' (Performance, value, risk, and alignment objectives).

The METRIC facet captures this aspect and is based on a listed value domain, including risk, performance, value, and alignment.

2.2.4 The Word of IT Governance Development

The development word of ITG is a word that is related to the other three words of the framework. It captures the characteristics of IT governance deployment. It refers to the description of IT management processes, how decision-making roles are distributed, the organization of the IT management committee, the way changes and innovations in the IT project portfolio are managed, and the IT development processes and business processes. The development word adapts to the nature of ITG described by the subject word and its objectives described in the word of usage. ITG processes must enable performance in achieving value, risk, performance, and alignment objectives. These processes are collaborative for decision-making. Therefore, it is essential to consider how IT management actors share their knowledge and manipulate information through dedicated reporting and modeling tools. These ITG-specific processes use elements of the system word, such as the content aspects, models, and metrics described in that word.

The development word comprises four facets: PROCESS NATURE, PROCESS MATURITY, KNOWLEDGE CAPITALIZATION, and SOFTWARE. All facets and their values are presented in Table 2.4.

In conclusion, the analysis and synthesis of the ITG development processes lead to the following proposal.

- *NATURE OF PROCESSES*

TABLE 2.4   List of Facets of the word Development

FACETTE	VALEUR
NATURE OF PROCESSES	Enum{ad-hoc, systematic}
PROCESS MATURITY	SET{level; Objective}
KNOWLEDGE CAPITALIZATION	Enum{socialization, externalization, internalization, combination}
SOFTWARE	Enum{ISI, CAGE}

A process is a set of activities that, from one or more inputs, produces one or more outcomes representing value to an internal or external client (Hammer et al., 1993). Referring to Hammer's definition of processes, the IS development process is a set of activities coordinated and executed by a system engineer to produce the governance of IS. The result is a decision support and assistance system (DIS) whose use and utility must be measured.

Two approaches are distinguished to building decision support systems. (i) A collaborative approach in which the engineer progressively defines the steps of the process 'the fly'. The process is ad hoc. (ii) The development of the system can follow a set of activities known in advance. For each system creation or maintenance project, the engineer will follow predefined steps.

- *PROCESS MATURITY*

The MATURITY level of the development process has a strong impact on the performance of ISG activities. Thus, highly mature IS management processes will generate more efficient documentation and feedback for decision-making and orientation of IS management objectives and projects.

Several maturity models exist. The most proven and used by IT professionals is the CMMI (Capability Maturity Model Integrated) maintained by the Software Engineering Institute. The CMMI does not evaluate the maturity of IS management processes but that of IS development processes. However, there is a relationship with ISG because at a high level of maturity (CMMI levels 3, 4, and 5), IS processes and projects must be managed, associated with performance objectives, and must evolve.

- *CAPITALIZATION OF KNOWLEDGE*

The knowledge-sharing mechanisms manipulated during ISG activities allow their CAPITALIZATION. Internalization is a process of appropriating explicit knowledge into tacit knowledge.

These aspects are captured through the KNOWLEDGE CAPITALIZATION facet defined on a domain, including socialization, outsourcing, internalization, and combination values.

- *SOFTWARE*

The SOFTWARE facet captures IT media dedicated to ISG. Current approaches emphasize the need to produce indicators for ISG and present them to decision-makers in dashboards. However, none deals in an integrated way with the provision of support applications to ISG. The SOFTWARE facet captures these aspects. It takes ISI (Information System Intelligence) as its value when an approach deals with application elements dedicated to decision-making for information systems. It takes its CAGE value (Computer-aided Governance Engineering) when an approach deals with application elements to support governance engineering activities.

2.3 IT GOVERNANCE STANDARDS

Governance, whatever the level at which it operates (management control, project portfolio, data administration, COBIT alignment, CMMI, ITSM by ITIL, etc.) must be situated with a trajectory of the evolution of the information system toward its progressive overhaul. The renovation of information systems tends toward the addition of devices that promote agility. It is necessary to modify systems more quickly and more reliably to consider business and technical developments (Valentine, 2016).

To achieve quality objectives and ensure the continuous improvement of the enterprise information system, the company must be managed according to a governance framework based on good practices and standards combined with agile practices.

A comprehensive enterprise information system program should include IT governance. IT governance is the primary means by which stakeholders can ensure that IT investments create business value and contribute to business objectives. This strategic alignment of IT with business is both challenging and essential. IT governance programs go further and aim to improve IT performance and deliver optimal business value while meeting regulatory compliance requirements (Benaroch & Chernobai, 2017).

While the CIO is generally responsible for implementing IT governance, the CEO and Board of Directors must receive reports and updates to fulfill their IT governance responsibilities and ensure that the program is working well and delivering business benefits (Turel & Bart, 2014).

Several IT governance frameworks can guide the implementation of an IT governance program. Although frameworks and guidelines such as CobiT, ITIL, ValIT, and ISO 38500 (Simonsson & Johnson, 2006) have widely adopted, there is no comprehensive standard IT governance framework; the combination that works best for an organization depends on business factors, corporate culture, IT maturity, and staffing capacity. The level of implementation of these frameworks will also vary by organization.

IT governance is a relatively new term, first coming into general use in the late 1990s (Magnusson, 2010). Until about 2009, definitions of IT governance primarily focused on creating the correct settings for the effective internal management of technological infrastructure and IT department (Ali et al., 2009; Weill & Ross, 2005; Xue et al., 2008). IT departments were expected to deal with many different issues, including rapid technological change over a brief period. 'Boards needed little or no understanding of technical issues because the technology was simply a tool to implement a strategy' (Carter &

Lorsch, 2003). The role of IT governance originally had an internal and primarily operational focus. From around 2003, however, a growing range of scholars began to consider IT governance as deserving board attention (Cater-Steel, 2009). Perhaps awareness of the need to distinguish between governance and management arose because 'new technologies are themselves creating strategic choice for businesses worldwide' (Carter & Lorsch, 2003). Others brought the integration of corporate governance and ITG closer, suggesting IT governance involving boards needed to be integral to overall enterprise or corporate governance (De Haes et al., 2013).

Every company or organization is structured around its missions to achieve the objectives it has set itself. Its activity defines its orientations. It gathers and coordinates a set of means to carry them out and defines itself as a system, 'that is to say, as a set of interacting elements, grouped within a piloted structure, having a communication system to facilitate the circulation of information, to respond to needs and achieve specific objectives'.

Some researchers have sought to develop a more comprehensive ITG framework by combining a variety of existing definitions and approaches. In general, frameworks designate the structure of a set of objects within a given domain, besides describing the relationships among those objects (Brown et al., 2005). The organizing effect of frameworks is especially useful during the early stages of research in a domain in delineating a research area, providing a foundation for the description of knowledge, and uncovering or highlighting opportunities for more specific theory development and testing within the domain in question (Dibbern et al., 2004).

Having uncovered some of the IT governance concepts and challenges, including the lack of a mutually agreed definition of IT governance, it is now helpful to discuss the mechanisms that lead to realizing the anticipated benefits of IT governance. In general, IT governance can be deployed using a mixture of structures, processes, and relational mechanisms (Ali et al., 2009; Weill & Ross, 2004). By integrating the work of A. E. Brown et al. (2005), Cadete and da Silva (2017), Grembergen (2004), Nugroho (2014), Peterson (2004), Tallon et al. (2013), Weill and Ross (2005) developed a conceptual model that describes a comprehensive view of the core elements of IT governance as depicted in Figure 2.3. The model is considered well matured as it covers the contingency, multidimensionality, and dynamic nature of IT governance in addition to incorporating the significant elements (structure and processes) and the four objectives (IT value delivery and strategic alignment, and performance and risk management) that drive IT governance (Grant et al., 2007).

Similarly, each dimension of the model (structures, processes, and relational mechanisms) consists of the necessary mechanisms for implementing IT governance, as presented in Table 2.5 (Wim van Grembergen & de Haes, 2009). Even though several mechanisms exist within this model, the decision to implement is influenced by the context and contingencies within the organization and the interacting environment (Nfuka & Rusu, 2011).

In recent years, many organizations have implemented IT governance mechanisms based on a single IT governance framework or a combination of frameworks. In general, frameworks can be categorized into groups, namely, business-oriented frameworks, such as the Committee of Sponsoring Organizations of the Treadway Commission (COSO), technology-focused frameworks (e.g., ITIL), and frameworks that aim at aligning business and technology goals (e.g., COBIT) (Warland & Ridley, 2005). Predominantly, IT governance frameworks enable executives and practitioners alike to make decisions, direct as

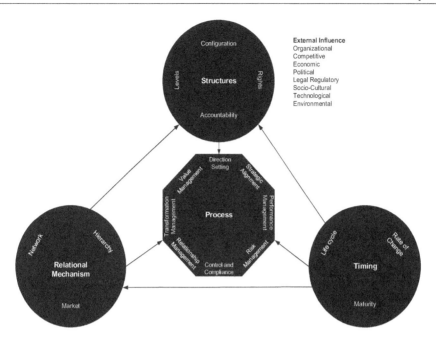

FIGURE 2.3   Extended IT governance model.

TABLE 2.5   The dimension of the IT governance model

DIMENSION	*DEFINITION*
Structures	This dimension is concerned with the planning and organizational elements outlined in the high-level governance strategy of organizations. Four main governance structures are included, namely, rights, accountability, configuration, and levels.
Processes	Processes refer to the tools used for the control and evaluation of IT governance. There are eight core elements in the processes dimension, as displayed in Figure 2.3, that organizations should enact for effective IT governance. Processes are fundamental elements of IT governance frameworks.
Relational mechanisms	Relational mechanisms refer to the internal and external relationship management required to ensure the successful implementation of IT governance. Three relational mechanisms are identified, namely: network, hierarchy, and market.
Timing	The timing dimension addresses the temporal aspects of IT governance implementation: maturity, life cycle, and rate of change.
External influences	Different external influences shape the mix of mechanisms used by organizations and should be considered when implementing IT governance. The external influences include organizational, competitive, economic, political, legal, or regulatory, sociocultural, technological, and environmental factors.

well as evaluate and monitor governance-related activities using a standard and unified approach. Adopting appropriate IT governance frameworks assists executives in better understanding the critical role they play in governing IT (Marrone & Kolbe, 2011). For instance, executives' commitment, strategic objectives, and resource allocation influence the adoption and selection of a particular framework (Benaroch & Chernobai, 2017; Murphy et al., 2018). From an evaluation perspective, many organizations use frameworks or integrate multiple governance frameworks to improve their compliance with specific regulatory requirements (i.e., SOX), while also enhancing the internal controls environments (Nianxin et al., 2011).

Some of the general frameworks within the IT governance sphere include COSO, ITIL, ISO 38500, and COBIT (Brown et al., 2005). The ISO standard addresses the corporate governance of IT and is concerned with governing management processes and decision-making. On the other hand, ITIL is a framework that focuses mainly on IT service management, enabling IT departments to apply strong systematic execution of operations with stringent controls (Marrone et al., 2014). COBIT is generally accepted as a standard and as a common framework for IT governance that, in comparison with COSO, provides more guidance regarding control over IT (Dahlberg & Kivijärvi, 2006; Steven De Haes et al., 2013; Oliver & Lainhart, 2012).

Despite their established usefulness, Otto (2010) suggests that IT governance frameworks cannot be considered merely off-the-shelf solutions. They cannot be implemented without any customization due to organizational structure, business objectives, and company size. Raghupathi (2007) highlights an urgent need for IT governance models and frameworks that can be expanded and transformed from generic frameworks into something more relevant and applicable to businesses and organizations. The COBIT framework (Neto et al., n.d.) states that frameworks, best practices, and standards are useful only if they are adopted and adapted effectively. Accordingly, Dahlberg and Lahdelma (2007), Simonsson and Johnson (2006), Webb et al. (2006) draw attention to the very little academic research that guides how to turn theories on IT governance frameworks and structures into practice.

No real framework thoroughly covers IT governance. From standards, the information system is approached according to very different facets: production service and management (Library for Information Technology Infrastructure – ITIL), project development and organization (Integrated Maturity Level Model – CMMI, Guide to the body of knowledge – ITIL), project management (ITIL), project management (ITIL), and project management (ITIL).

In project management PMBOK, technology, and process management (Information control objectives and associated technologies – CobiT and ISO 38500) and security (ISO 27000).

Each standard tends to extend its field of competence so that it may overlap or duplicate each other. Therefore, the key is integration and adaptation by choosing to build a practical approach and implementing some parts of the standards rather than implementing everything. Van Grembergen and De Haes (2009) define the governance objectives through three questions: How are decisions made? About the information system? How to improve and gain acceptance of the making of these decisions? How to ensure that these decisions will be made implementations appropriately? Thus, the implementation of governance must allow the ascent of understandable performance indicators used by management to assess the proper functioning of IT services, in response to the strategic business needs (Beloglazov et al., 2014). The most common IT governance standards are presented later.

2.3.1 COBIT

The Information Systems Audit and Control Association (ISACA) and the ITGI founded COBIT in 1992. The first edition of COBIT was published in 1996, and the fifth and latest editions were published in April 2012. The framework has grown to be, and still is, one of the most significant global frameworks for IT governance (Omari et al., 2012). COBIT was initially built as an IT audit guideline (ISACA, 2012) because the framework contained a comprehensive set of guidelines to improve audit and compliance, provided detailed guidance on governance practices, and offered auditors several customized checklists for various aspects of controls assessment (Hiererra, 2012). These aspects make COBIT a perfect framework for establishing control over IT, facilitating performance measurement of IT processes, and allowing executives to bridge the gap between control requirements, technical issues, and business risks (Brustbauer, 2016). Also, COBIT has significant business value in terms of increased compliance, corporate risk reduction, and proper accountability and is proven to be a useful tool to establish a baseline for process maturity (Nianxin et al., 2011). Moreover, the framework is growing to be universally applicable due to its full implementation as an IT governance framework (Ribeiro & Gomes, 2009; Wim van Grembergen & de Haes, 2009).

From an IT governance perspective, the primary objective of COBIT is to enable value creation by ensuring benefits are realized, risk-reduced, and resources optimized. It is also proclaimed to provide business stakeholders with an IT governance model that improves the management of risks associated with IT and leverages a top–down structure to ensure systematic management of the detailed processes to achieve proper IT governance (Von Solms, 2005). The COBIT framework is considered to be a generic, comprehensive, independent, and large body of knowledge designed to measure the maturity of IT processes within organizations of all sizes, whether commercial, not-for-profit, or in the public sector (Elhasnaoui et al., 2015; Nianxin et al., 2011).

The COBIT framework has been steadily achieving worldwide recognition as the most effective and reliable tool for implementing and auditing IT governance and assessing IT capability. It is regarded as the leading standard to adopt for organizations striving to comply with Sarbanes–Oxley (SOX) regulations in the United States. It is also considered a trusted standard that has been adopted globally, as it provides extensive sets of predefined processes that can be continually revised and customized to support different organizational objectives. Whether for private or public industries, governments, or accounting and auditing firms (Cadete & da Silva, 2017; Guldentops, 2002; Maes et al., 2013; Wim van Grembergen & de Haes, 2009; Warland & Ridley, 2005; Wood, 2010), COBIT is viewed as an exhaustive framework that encompasses a complete lifecycle of IT investment (Steven De Haes et al., 2013) and supplies IT metrics to measure the achievement of goals (Williams et al., 2013).

It is also defined as the best framework to balance organizational IT goals, business objectives, and risks (Warland & Ridley, 2005). This is achieved by making use of (Kaplan Norton, 1996) Balanced Scorecard (BSC) dimensions – Financial, Customer, Internal; and Learning and Growth – to introduce goals cascade mechanism that translates and links stakeholders' needs to specific enterprise goals, IT-related goals, and enabler goals (COBIT processes). A set of 17 enterprise goals has been developed and mapped to 17 IT-related goals and sequentially to the COBIT processes (ISACA, 2012). In addition to providing a set of IT governance processes, COBIT also facilitates the appropriate implementation and effective management of these processes through establishing clear roles and responsibilities using a detailed Responsible, Accountable, Consulted, and Informed (RACI) matrix (Simonsson et al., 2007).

In the COBIT framework, the IT governance focus area is divided into five subareas as shown in Figure 2.4: strategic alignment, value delivery, resource management, risk management, and performance management. These five areas consist of topics that executive management needs to address in governing IT within their enterprises (ITGI, 2007). A description of each ITG subareas is shown in Figure 2.5.

The fifth version of COBIT is built on five basic principles: Meeting Stakeholder Needs; Covering the Enterprise End-to-End; Applying a Single, Integrated Framework; Enabling

FIGURE 2.4   COBIT IT governance areas.

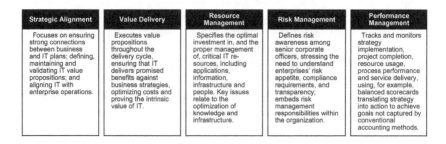

Strategic Alignment	Value Delivery	Resource Management	Risk Management	Performance Management
Focuses on ensuring strong connections between business and IT plans; defining, maintaining and validating IT value propositions; and aligning IT with enterprise operations.	Executes value propositions throughout the delivery cycle, ensuring that IT delivers promised benefits against business strategies, optimizing costs and proving the intrinsic value of IT.	Specifies the optimal investment in, and the proper management of, critical IT resources, including applications, information, infrastructure and people. Key issues relate to the optimization of knowledge and infrastructure.	Defines risk awareness among senior corporate officers, stressing the need to understand enterprises' risk appetite, compliance requirements, and transparency; embeds risk management responsibilities within the organization.	Tracks and monitors strategy implementation, project completion, resource usage, process performance and service delivery, using, for example, balanced scorecards translating strategy into action to achieve goals not captured by conventional accounting methods.

FIGURE 2.5   IT governance focus areas in COBIT.

a Holistic Approach, and Separating Governance from Management. Furthermore, the COBIT 5 Process Reference Model (PRM) divides IT into five domains:

- Evaluate, Direct and Monitor (EDM);
- Align, Plan and Organize (APO);
- Build, Acquire and Implement (BAI);
- Deliver, Service and Support (DSS);
- Monitor, Evaluate and Assess (MEA)

The COBIT 5 domains are broken into 37 high-level IT processes, and over 300 detailed IT controls covering IT management and governance (ISACA, 2012). Another distinctive feature within COBIT lies in its ability to identify seven categories of enablers (or factors):

- Principles, policies, and frameworks;
- Processes;
- Organizational structures;
- Culture, ethics, and behavior;
- Information;
- Services, infrastructure, and applications;
- Availability.

Thus, it is considered the most appropriate framework to facilitate the alignment between business and IT goals (Oliver & Lainhart, 2012).

COBIT 5 transformed into a more business-oriented framework by establishing one integrated framework that consisted of different models (e.g., Val IT, Risk IT). This amalgamation was mainly due to the recognized need to provide a comprehensive basis for options, not only for users and auditors but also for senior managers and business process owners to cover all aspects of business and functional IT responsibilities leading to effective IT governance and management outcomes. Moreover, COBIT 5 has been aligned with the ISO/IEC 15504 Process Capability Model (PCM) (ISACA, 2012). From an IT governance evaluation perspective, the shift from the Capability Maturity Model (CMM) or the more recent Capability Maturity Model Integration (CMMI) developed by the Software Engineering Institute (SEI) to the new PCM has revolutionized COBIT, giving it a cutting edge in assessing capability at the process level instead of assessing maturity at the enterprise level (ITGI, 2007). This new approach is more consistent and repeatable, but it is also verifiable and can demonstrate traceability against objective evidence gathered during the evaluation process (Basson et al., 2012). The PCM has been used extensively by financial institutions in Europe to conduct internal control audits to assess the need for improvement. It adds to the advantages organizations should expect from implementing COBIT as the partnership between the framework and the PCM delivers a measurement scale to quantitatively evaluate the existence, adequacy, effectiveness, and compatibility of IT governance processes.

Recently, COBIT 2019 was published in November 2018. It contains several new, amended, and updated elements (Steuperaert, 2019).

Practical information and technology governance is essential to the business success of any organization. This new version further cements COBIT's continued role as an essential driver of business innovation and transformation.

COBIT 2019 (Steven De Haes et al., 2020) is an evolution of the previous version of ISACA's governance framework. Building on the foundation of COBIT 5, it incorporates the latest developments affecting business information and technology.

COBIT 2019 offers greater flexibility and openness to improve the timeliness of COBIT. The reflections on the significant changes brought by COBIT 2019 are as follows:

- The introduction of new concepts such as focus areas and design factors allows the company to propose good practices to adopt a governance system to its needs;
- Updating the alignment with standards, frameworks, and best practices improves the relevance of COBIT;
- An open-source model will allow the global governance community to contribute to future updates by providing feedback, sharing applications, and proposing improvements to the framework and derivatives in real-time. In this way, new COBIT developments can be published on a cyclical basis;
- New guidelines and tools support the development of an optimal governance system. It makes COBIT 2019 more prescriptive;
- COBIT 2019 reference model with now 40 governance management objectives (processes) instead of 37 processes in COBIT 5;
- Enabler Guidance: It has been removed to simplify COBIT;
- The COBIT Principles for the Governance System and the Governance Framework have been renamed and changed;
- The IT Related Goals have been renamed Alignment Goals;
- The process guide is now structured in 'Governance/Management Goals', the process guide (only) part of it, supplemented by other governance components.

COBIT 2019 introduces three new governance and management objectives:

- APO14 – Managed Data;
- BAI11 – Managed Projects;
- MEA04 – Managed Assurance.

COBIT 2019 now explicitly integrates DevOps. DevOps illustrates both a component variant and a focus area. It is a current topic in the market and certainly requires specific guidance.

DevOps includes several generic governance and management objectives of the central COBIT model and many process variants and organizational structures related to development, operations, and monitoring. DevOps also requires establishing a specific culture and attitude of openness, sharing skills, and taking teams out of their comfort zone. Similarly, DevOps requires a certain level of automation (services, infrastructure, and applications). DevOps is an area of interest, prioritized among the first and under development.

A focus area describes a governance topic, area, or problem addressed by a set of governance and management objectives and their components.

Focus areas may contain a combination of generic governance components and variants.

The four areas of interest currently prioritized and in the process of being published are as follows:

- Small and medium enterprises;
- Cybersecurity;
- Risks;
- DevOps.

The number of areas of interest is practically unlimited. That is what makes COBIT open. The addition of new areas of interest will occur at the request or with the input of experts and practitioners.

2.3.2 LIBRARY (ITIL)

ITIL is a framework of best practices, based on a process-based approach, to improve the delivery of high-quality IT services at a low cost. Before its creation, agencies and private sector contractors independently created their own IT management practices and duplicated efforts. The content of ITIL is independent of tools, vendors, or industry in which the service is executed and can be applied to organizations of any size. However, it is not intended to be applied as-is; organizations are motivated to adapt it to meet their own business needs.

According to ITIL, service management is a set of specialized organizational capabilities for providing value to customers in services. The act of transforming resources into valuable services is at the core of service management. Without these capabilities, a service organization is merely a bundle of resources that by itself has relatively low intrinsic value for customers. However, ITIL considers service management as more than just a set of capabilities. It is also a professional practice supported by an extensive body of knowledge, experience, and skills.

ITIL also defines the distinction between functions and processes. Functions are specialized organizations with certain types of work and responsible for specific outcomes. Such organizations are self-contained, with all the necessary capabilities and resources available for their performance and outcomes. For example, the Service Desk is a function of the role's primary point of contact when there is a service disruption. On the other hand, processes can be assumed as closed-loop systems, providing changes and transformations toward a specific goal and using feedback for self-reinforcing and self-corrective actions. Processes are measurable, have specific results delivered to customers, and respond to specific events. For example, event management is a process responsible for monitoring all the events throughout the IT infrastructure.

Up to version 2, the ITIL focus was on processes, but since its version 3, the focus changed to business value. This change occurred to strengthen the relationship between the organization's business needs and operational IT processes. Version 3 also recognizes the value and applicability of other standards, such as COBIT and CMMI. The ITIL v3 structure comprises two components: the ITIL Core, which provides best practices applicable to organizations of all sizes and types, and the ITIL Complementary Guidance, which comprises a complementary set of publications with guidance specific to industry sectors, operating models, and technology architectures.

The focus on Change Management Advisory Boards (CABs) in previous ITIL versions has led to a misperception of ITIL as not being agile or hindering rapid deployment. However, ITIL was never designed to be implemented in such a way that the IT department would evaluate or finetune all changes.

To reinforce this and help organizations develop flexible service management strategies, ITIL 4 now incorporates agile and DevOps practices into the framework. ITIL 4 encourages collaboration and communication within the organization and guides how to implement change quickly (Woo et al., 2020).

2.3.3 Structure of ITIL v4

ITIL 4 comprises the following subdivisions:

- Key concepts (key concepts) of service management;
- The four dimensions of service management;
- Service value system (SVS), whose guiding principles are detailed later;
- Management practices.

A brief explanation for each of these four subdivisions is as follows:

- **Key concepts: value, cocreation, outcomes**

ITIL Foundation introduces some key concepts that are important for a good understanding of the framework. These concepts include standard terms such as service providers, stakeholders, and risks. Nevertheless, new concepts are also emerging.

ITIL 4 does not focus on service delivery, as was the case in version 3, but rather on value creation. It is not up to the service provider alone to provide this value. Instead, it is a co-creation, the result of a partnership with the customer. This version does not aim at respecting processes, but rather at pursuing objectives: outcomes and improved customer experience as one of the main objectives.

- **The four dimensions of service management**

Where v3 focused primarily on how the 26 IT processes can be arranged, ITIL 4 goes further. The new version's spirit also involves taking into account the four dimensions of service management for each service designed or delivered:

- Organizations and individuals;
- Information technology;
- Partners and suppliers;
- Value flows and processes.

- **Service Value System and Service Value Chain**

With a value-oriented perspective, we will no longer speak of 'process models' but instead of 'value systems' or 'value chains'.

The value chain (ITIL Service Value Chain, SVC) is an overview of all the activities you can do to generate value, as shown in Figure 2.6. These activities are Plan, Improve, Engage, Design & Transition, Obtain/build, Deliver & support. It is unnecessary to perform all these activities for each service, and there is no set order. Fixing a bug and replacing a server farm involve different activities.

This value chain (SVC) is part of a more extensive value system (Service Value System, SVS). ITIL SVS describes all the factors that influence the value chain, as shown in Figure 2.7. These are referred to as guiding principles, governance, and the improvements that the organization performs.

- **The Guiding Principles**

The guiding principles introduced in ITIL Practitioner take on a prominent role in version 4. The nine Practitioner Principles have been revised to seven principles:

- Focus on Value: Everything the organization does must, in some way, provide value to customers or other stakeholders;
- Start Where You Are: When an organization wants to improve something, it should not eliminate all current methods but keep the good things and change what does not work;

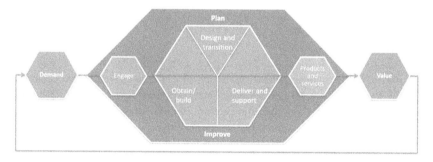

FIGURE 2.6   ITIL Service Value Chain.

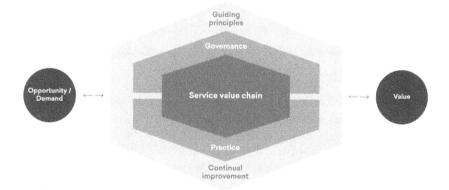

FIGURE 2.7   ITIL Service Value System.

- Progress Iteratively with Feedback: The organization should implement improvement processes in small steps, even if they are large projects. Immediately evaluate each step and start over where necessary;
- Collaborate and Promote Visibility: The organization must work closely with other parties such as customers and suppliers to promote its visibility;
- Think and work Holistically: Do not think of the IT organization as an island, but as part of a network where the sum of all parts creates value for customers;
- Keep It Simple and Practical: The organization must ensure that its work and processes remain as simple as possible and remove any steps that do not provide value;
- Optimize and Automate: Whenever possible, optimize or automate tasks, unless it means higher costs or a more lacking customer experience;
- The underlying ITIL Service Management processes remain – but are now called 'practices';
- The underlying processes from Release 3, such as Incident Management, Service Level Management, and Capacity Management, remain fundamentally unchanged. However, the 26 processes of v3 are replaced by the 34 practices of ITIL 4.

Why practices? Because ITIL 4 describes how a process works and, for example, for each of the practices, looks in more detail at the skills the team needs, how they can work with the suppliers, and the technology used to do this.

- **One Response to Agile, Lean, and DevOps?**

ITIL itself has become more agile. This can be seen mainly in the seven guiding principles. The emphasis on value generation, improvement in small steps, the importance of process simplicity, etc., are all part of this. There is a clear perception of agile thinking. These agile ITIL guidelines also facilitate collaboration with agile teams. To demonstrate that version 4 is adapted to the agile philosophy, Axelos recently published a case study of Spotify, which is known to be one of the most agile companies.

However, this version does not provide a complete answer to the agile, lean, and DevOps aspects. Admittedly, Foundation mentions the terms agile and DevOps. There are few concrete solutions on the possibilities of combining ITIL with more agile methods. Example: how should a helpdesk comply with strict service level agreements collaborate with an agile back office team? How do IT Ops and DevOps work best together?

2.3.4 CMMI

The CMMI (Capability Maturity Model Integrated) is a model for assessing the level of maturity of an organization's systems, product, and/or software development. Its objective is to control engineering processes, and consequently, the quality of the products and services resulting from these processes. It provides a reference for best practices in software development.

The CMMI is an extension of the CMM (Capability Maturity Model), presented by the SEI (Software Engineering Institute) in the 1980s.

At the US Department of Defense (DoD) request, the SEI developed a set of criteria to determine whether a project would be completed on time, budget, and specifications.

In 2001, the SEI created a new version of the CMM, incorporating all the advances of other models that had emerged to fill specific gaps in the CMM. The latest version of the CMMI (version 2.0) was released in 2018. It allows the model to be applied to hardware, software, and services in all industries.

CMMI proposes a set of objectives to guarantee the quality of projects (Ramírez-Mora et al., 2020). It is accompanied by a repository of good practices expected to achieve these objectives. CMMI provides a framework for the definition of the organization's key processes, including project management (planning, resource management, risk management, etc.), engineering (requirements management, technical solutions, product integration, etc.), and support (configuration management, quality assurance, measurement, and analysis, etc.). It is a tool to help define and improve processes.

The need to implement a CMMI model in an organization arises when the company detects recurring problems such as late deliveries, budget overruns, customer dissatisfaction, and lack of management visibility.

CMMI, therefore, aims to:

- Improve the quality of the delivered product and the productivity of the project;
- Increase customer satisfaction by better meeting their requirements;
- Reduce costs and meet deadlines;
- Give better visibility to management and allow better risk management.

The good practices recommended by the model are grouped into 25 key processes (Process Area), themselves grouped into five levels of maturity/capacity:

2.3.4.1 Level 1: Initial

Every organization defaults to level 1. Project management is not defined within the organization. Effectiveness relies on the skills and motivation of individuals. No control is carried out.

The project can succeed but with cost and time overruns. Success factors are not identified, and the project does not build on experience.

2.3.4.2 Level 2: Managed

Project management is defined at the organization level and is applied by default to all projects. All projects meet the CMMI level 2 model's objectives with the processes proposed by the organization or by default with processes defined at the project level. The project builds on what has been done previously, thanks to better discipline. Successes are repeatable.

2.3.4.3 Level 3: Defined

Project management processes are extended to the entire organization through standards, procedures, tools, and methods also defined at the organizational level. The entire organization has a discipline that is applied consistently. The organization monitors and manages the improvement of these processes.

2.3.4.4 Level 4: Quantitatively Managed

The success of projects is quantified. The causes of deviations can be analyzed. Process performance is predictable in terms of quantity and quality.

2.3.4.5 Level 5: Optimizing

It is referred to as the stage of continuous process improvement incrementally and innovatively. Developments are anticipated. Processes are constantly challenged to stay in line with the objectives.

The latest version of CMMI is written in non-technical language, making it more user-friendly and comfortable to implement. Organizations can explore CMMI online and configure it according to their specific goals for performance improvement and organizational success. Tools such as Visure Requirements improve maturity by monitoring and tracking requirements and helping to standardize and harmonize the application of business processes.

2.3.5 Committee of Sponsoring Organizations of the Treadway Commission (COSO)

The U.S. Congress convened the Committee of Sponsoring Organizations of the Treadway Commission (commonly referred to as COSO) in response to well-publicized financial irregularities in the late 1980s. COSO formulated an internal control framework designed to help organizations reduce the risk of asset loss, ensure the reliability of financial statements and compliance with laws and regulations, and promote efficiency. COSO is recognized by many public and professional bodies as a standard for evaluating internal control and the risk environment (Chiu & Wang, 2019). Under the COSO framework, the effectiveness of an internal control system is measured by its capacity to provide reasonable assurance to management and the board of directors of their bank's achievement of its objectives in three categories:

- Effectiveness and efficiency of operations;
- Reliability of financial reporting;
- Compliance with applicable laws and regulations.

The emphasis on behavior in the COSO model recognizes reality, namely that policies specify what management wants to happen, what happens, and which rules are obeyed, bent, or ignored, which is determined by corporate culture. The COSO 'internal control model' consists of five interrelated components inherent in managing the organization. The components are linked and serve as criteria for determining whether or not the system is active. The COSO components include control environment, risk assessment, control activities, monitoring and learning, and information and communication. COSO is indeed a framework that allows to manage risks at all levels of the company, and not only for its IS component. COSO divides the enterprise risk management

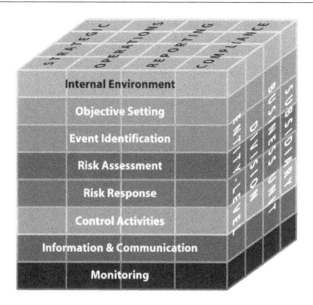

FIGURE 2.8   The ERM model proposed by COSO.

(ERM) framework into eight interrelated components, as shown in Figure 2.8, including the following:

- **Internal environment:** Internal environment describes the work environment and risk preferences of an organization and sets the framework for how risk is viewed and addressed by its management and employees. The internal environment includes risk management philosophy, risk appetite, integrity, and ethical values, and the environment in which they operate;
- **Objective setting:** Objectives must be set up-front. The risk management function should ensure that corporate management has a process to set the objectives. The chosen objectives support and align with the entity's mission and consistent with its risk appetite;
- **Event identification:** Internal and external events affecting the achievement of an entity's objectives must be identified, distinguishing between risks and opportunities. Opportunities are channeled back to management's strategy or objective-setting processes;
- **Risk assessment:** Risks are analyzed, considering the likelihood of occurrence and impact, as a basis for determining how they should be managed. Risks are assessed on an inherent and continuing basis;
- **Risk response:** Management selects risk responses – avoiding, accepting, reducing, or sharing risk – developing a set of actions to align risks with the entity's risk tolerances and risk appetite;
- **Control activities:** Policies and procedures should be established and implemented to help ensure the risk responses are effectively carried out;

- **Information and communication:** Relevant information is identified, captured, and communicated in a form and timeframe that enable people to carry out their responsibilities. Effective communication also occurs in a broader sense – flowing down, across, and up the entity;
- **Monitoring:** The entirety of enterprise risk management must be monitored, and modifications made as necessary.

2.3.6 PMBOOK

Project Management Body of Knowledge (PMBOOK), whose origins date back to 1983 with a first publication by the global non-profit organization Project Management Institute (PMI), aims to standardize project management approach and procedures. The first PMBOOK was published in 1996 and recognized as an official ANSI standard since 1999. This standard has a solid support; in 2015, there were 476,000 members in 204 countries. PMBOK defines a set of 47 processes grouped around these five parent processes: 1 – Start-up, 2 – Planning, 3 – Execution, 4 – Monitoring and Control, and 5 – Closing. Each process details input transformation mechanisms (planning, design documents) into outputs (documents, products). PMBOK is complementary to the CMMI continuous improvement approach.

2.3.7 ISO/IEC 27001:2005 (Revised by ISO/IEC 27001:2013)

ISO 27000 is a suite of good practices grouped into standards that deal with information security. Written from 2005, it is constantly evolving. The ISO 27000 version published in 2009 is a short 38-page introductory document defining the family of standards and terms. The only standard leading to certification is ISO 27001, which defines a set of requirements and control points to protect IT assets against any loss, theft, intrusion, or alteration of the IT system. ISO 207002 is a good practice guide listing measures for implementing or maintaining an Information Security Management System (ISMS) (ISO, 2013). Good practices are applied IS security rules to guarantee the protection of its infrastructure.

The international standard is not tailored to any specific industry. Thus, many organizations may seek certification of their ISMS. Over 7,300 organizations worldwide have already been certified compliant with ISO/IEC 27001 or equivalent national variants. Even though certification is not compulsory, it is increasingly being demanded by some business partnerships. In terms of marketing, the certificate gives assurance to business partners of the organization's status regarding information security without the necessity of conducting their security reviews. Getting certified under ISO/IEC 27001 is a means of assuring that the organization has implemented a system for managing information security and maintains and continuously improves the system. Practical uses of the standard include the following (ISO, 2013):

- Use within organizations to formulate security requirements and objectives;
- Use within organizations as a way to ensure that security risks are cost-effectively managed;

- Use within organizations to ensure compliance with laws and regulations;
- Use within an organization as a process framework for the implementation and management of controls to ensure that the specific security objectives of an organization are met;
- Definition of new information security management processes;
- Identification and clarification of existing information security management processes;
- Use by the management of organizations to determine the status of information security management activities;
- Use by the internal and external auditors of organizations to determine the degree of compliance with the policies, directives, and standards adopted by an organization;
- Use by organizations to provide relevant information about information security policies, directives, standards, and procedures to trading partners and other organizations with whom they interact for operational or commercial reasons;
- Implementation of business-enabling information security;
- Use by organizations to provide relevant information about information security to customers.

Structure of ISO/IEC 27001:2005

The 34-page document is structured into nine sections and has three appendices. The highlight of each section is described here:

- **Introduction**: Asserts the standard uses a process approach;
- **Scope**: It specifies generic ISMS requirements suitable for organizations of any type, size, or nature;
- **Normative references**: The standard recommends the essential use of ISO/IEC 27002:2005.
- **Terms and definitions**: A brief, formalized glossary.
- **Information security management system**: The details of the standard based on the Plan-Do-Check-Act cycle, where Plan = define requirements, assess risks, decide which controls are applicable; Do = implement and operate the ISMS; Check = monitor and review the ISMS; Act = maintain and continuously improve the ISMS. Also specifies certain specific documents that are required and must be controlled and states that records must be generated and controlled to prove the operation of the ISMS (e.g., certification audit purposes);
- **Management responsibility**: Management must demonstrate their commitment to the ISMS, principally allocating adequate resources to implement and operate it;
- **Internal ISMS audits**: The organization must conduct periodic internal audits to ensure the ISMS incorporates adequate controls which operate effectively;
- **Management review of the ISMS**: Management must review the suitability, adequacy, and effectiveness of the ISMS at least once a year, assessing opportunities for improvement and the need for changes;

- *ISMS improvements*: The organization must continually improve the ISMS by assessing and, where necessary, making changes to ensure its suitability and effectiveness, addressing nonconformance (noncompliance), and where possible preventing recurrent issues;
- *Annex A*: Control objectives and controls – little more than a list of titles of the control sections in ISO/IEC 27002, down to the second level of numbering (e.g., 9.1, 9.2), 133 in total;
- *Annex B*: OECD principles and this International Standard: a table briefly showing which parts of this standard satisfy seven key principles laid out in the OECD Guidelines for the Security of Information Systems and Networks;
- *Annex C*: Correspondence between ISO 9001:2000, ISO 14001:2004, and this International Standard – the standard shares the same basic structure of other management systems standards, meaning that an organization that implements anyone should be familiar with concepts such as PDCA, records, and audits.

2.4 ISO/IEC 27002:2005 (REVISED BY ISO/IEC 27002:2013)

ISO/IEC 27002:2005 is another generic standard applied to health information systems to ensure security. It establishes general principles and guidelines for effective initialization, implementation, maintenance, and improvement of information security management. The objectives outlined therein provide general guidance on the commonly accepted goals of information security management. Thus, any organization seeking to adopt a comprehensive information security management program or improve its existing information security practices can use the standard. The ISO standard asserts that information can be protected using a wide variety of controls. Such controls include hardware and software functions, procedures, policies, processes, and organizational structures. Organizations, including healthcare organizations, must develop, implement, monitor, evaluate and improve these security controls.

2.5 ISO/IEC 27002:2005 (REVISED BY ISO/IEC 27002:2021)

The typical lifespan of an ISO standard is 5 years. After this period, it is decided whether the norm can stay valid, needs revision, or retracts. In 2018, it was decided that ISO 27002:2013 should be revised. The draft is currently under review and is expected to be published by the end of 2021.

As Annex A of ISO 27001 is based on ISO 27002, it is expected that this standard will soon follow, after which it will be possible to certify against the new standard.

ISO 27002:2013 contains 114 controls, divided over 14 chapters. This is going to be restructured. ISO 27002:2021 will contain 93 controls, divided over four chapters:

- Chapter 5 Organizational (37 controls);
- Chapter 6 People (8 controls);
- Chapter 7 Physical (14 controls);
- Chapter 8 Technological (34 controls).

2.5.1 NIST

The NIST-National Institute of Standards and Technology Framework for Improving Critical Infrastructure Cybersecurity, commonly referred to as the NIST Cybersecurity Framework (CSF), provides private sector organizations with a structure to assess and improve their ability to prevent, detect, and respond to cyber incidents.

The Framework uses operational factors to guide cybersecurity activities and considers cybersecurity as part of an organization's risk management processes. Many organizations are adopting this framework to help manage their cybersecurity risks. Figure 2.9 shows the three components of NIST-CSF.

The three parts of the Framework are as follows:

2.5.2 Core Framework

The Core Framework is a set of cybersecurity activities, desired outcomes, and applicable benchmarks common to all critical infrastructure sectors. It consists of five concurrent and continuous functions: Identity, Protect, Detect, Respond, and Recover. Figure 2.10 presents NIST Core Framework.

Core	Implementation Tiers	Profile
Contains an array of activities, outcomes, and references, organized into five functions (Identify, Protect, Detect, Respond, Recover), 22 categories, and 98 subcategories, with detailed approaches to aspects of cyber security.	The four tiers (Partial, Informed, Repeatable, Adaptive) can be used by any organization as references to clarify for itself and its partners the organization's visions on cyber security risk and the degree of sophistication of the management approach.	a list of outcomes that an organization can choose from the categories and subcategories, based on its business needs and individual risk assessments (Current Profile), as means to support prioritization and measurement of progress toward a desirable risk level.

FIGURE 2.9   The three components of NIST-CSF.

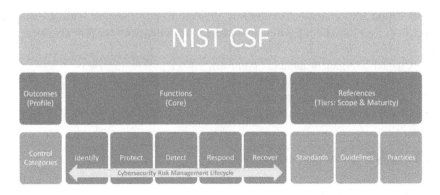

FIGURE 2.10   Core framework.

2.5.3 Implementation Tiers

Implementation tiers describe the extent to which an organization's cybersecurity risk management practices exhibit the characteristics defined in the Framework, ranging from partial (tier 1) to adaptive (tier 4).

2.5.4 Framework Profile

Framework profile represents the categories and subcategories of core functions prioritized by an organization based on business needs. It can be used to measure the organization's progress toward the target profile.

2.5.5 Comparison and Analysis

The six different governance approaches reviewed each cover specific IS properties. IS governance is a large-scale project that requires prior evaluation to avoid failure during its implementation.

IT governance concerns mid-sized and larger companies. Initiating and undertaking governance work is complex, time-consuming, and costly. It requires ongoing stakeholder investment and the establishment of teams to implement the governance project. The cost of implementation can be high: training of the persons concerned in the company, use of an external consultant, and certification of the standard. Governance does not solve all problems. As we have seen, each of the approaches is dedicated to specific subjects. Because of its implementation cost, a return on investment is even less guaranteed.

Governance concerns the discipline of management information technology explicitly. This thesis is concerned with the alignment between trades and software architectures. One of the governance subjects would seem to respond to our concern. Indeed, governance addresses the notion of alignment. Table 2.6 compares the different IT governance

TABLE 2.6 IT Governance Standards Comparison According to the Four Words

THE FRAME OF THE FOUR WORDS	FACET	IT GOVERNANCE STANDARDS AND MODELS					
		COBIT	COSO	ITIL	CMMI	PMBOOK	ISO 27000
Subject	GOVERNANCE ORGANIZATION	*	*	–	–	*	*
	DECISION	–	–	Infrastructure	–	Plan. project	–
	IT PROCESS	*	*	*	*	*	*
	BUSINESS PROCESS	–	*	*	–	*	*
	CHANGE	*	–	Evolutive	*	*	*
	IT PROJECT PORTFOLIO	–	–	*	Clas.: Multi-criteria Transfo.: *	Clas.: Multi-criteria Transfo.: *	–
Usage	MINIMIZE RISKS	*	*	Quality	*	*	*
	REACH ALIGNMENT STATUS	–	–	IT Evolution	–	IT Evolution, Business evolution	–
	GETTING PERFORMANCE	–	–	–	Process Maturity	Process Maturity	
	CREATE VALUE	–	Business Asset	IT Asset, usage	IT Asset	IT Asset, Business Asset	–
System	CONTENT	document	Document	document	document	document	document
	MODELE	Process, object	Process, object	Process, object	Process, object	Process, object, decision	Process, object

(Continued)

TABLE 2.6 (Continued)

THE FRAME OF THE FOUR WORDS	FACET	IT GOVERNANCE STANDARDS AND MODELS					
		COBIT	COSO	ITIL	CMMI	PMBOOK	ISO 27000
	METRICS	Risk, performance, value	Risk	Alignment, performance	Performance	Risk, Performance, Value	Business goals, information assets, measurement
Development	NATURE PROCESS	systematic	Systematic	systematic	systematic	systematic	systematic
	MATURITY PROCESS	*	–	–	*	*	*
	CAPITALIZATION OF KNOWLEDGE	externalization	Externalization	externalization	externalization	externalization	externalization
	SOFTWARE	*	*	*	*	*	*

*Fully covered facet – Uncovered facet

standards (CobiT, COSO, ITIL, CMMI, PMBOK) according to the four words described in Chapter 1.

This overview of the leading IT governance methods has enabled us to fully understand what governance means and the role of each of them: security, quality, supply, services, standardization, project management, and costs. The application of different good governance practices influences the operational aspects of IT transformation and facilitates its management and control. Knowing the governance function for the IT also means avoiding confusing it with the enterprise architecture, which is also concerned with the IT.

Most IT governance frameworks are designed to help you determine how your IT department is functioning overall, what key metrics management needs, and what return IT is giving back to the business from its investments.

Where COBIT and COSO are used mainly for risk, ITIL helps to streamline service and operations. Although CMMI was initially intended for software engineering, it now involves processes in hardware development, service delivery, and purchasing. As previously mentioned, FAIR is squarely for assessing operational and cybersecurity risks.

Though COBIT is one of the most popular frameworks used by publicly traded companies in the United States to comply with the Sarbanes-Oxley Act, the purpose is for IT management and compliance. It helps strengthen the security of healthcare systems, but security is not the primary goal of COBIT. This standard may not be suitable for small healthcare organizations that want to improve the security of their system.

ISO/IEC 27002:2005 can be applied to the organization of any size concerned with the information security of their systems. An organization can use this standard as a guide to managing its information security program. Organizations can seek certification for their Information Security Management System to comply with ISO/IEC 270001: 2005.

When reviewing frameworks, consider your corporate culture. Does a particular framework or model seem like a natural fit for your organization? Does it resonate with your stakeholders? That framework is probably the best choice. However, you don't have to choose only one framework. For example, COBIT and ITIL complement one another in that COBIT often explains why something is done or needed where ITIL provides the 'how'. Some organizations have used COBIT and COSO, along with the ISO 27001 standard (for managing information security).

2.6 SUMMARY

This chapter proposed a faceted framework for the analysis of IT governance. This framework considers four perspectives, called words of the subject, use, system, and development of ITG. Facets and their values detail these four perspectives. This framework has been applied to five known IT governance standards. This application exercise revealed that none of the current approaches covers all facets of the framework. The approaches do not have an overall vision of ITG but piecemeal visions. The emphasis is on collections of good practices that are updated regularly. This work on state of the art has highlighted the need for research on the globality of ITG. This chapter aimed to provide a comprehensive understanding of ITG.

Chapter 3 will discuss the practices of organizations in terms of IT governance. It will present an evaluation of ITG through a case study in the Middle East and North African Large Organizations.

REFERENCES

Aasi, P., Rusu, L., & Han, S. (2014). Culture influence on IT governance: What we have learned? *International Journal of IT/Business Alignment and Governance (IJITBAG)*, *5*(1), 34–49.

Ali, S., Green, P., & Parent, M. (2009). The role of a culture of compliance in information technology governance. *GRCIS'09: Governance, Risk and Compliance*, *459*, 1–14.

Alonso, G., Agrawal, D., El Abbadi, A., & Mohan, C. (1997). Functionality and limitations of current workflow management systems. *IEEE Expert*, *12*(5), 105–111.

Basson, G., Walker, A., McBride, T., & Oakley, R. (2012). ISO/IEC 15504 measurement applied to COBIT process maturity. *Benchmarking: An International Journal*, *19*(2), 159–176. https://doi.org/10.1108/14635771211224518

Beloglazov, A., Banerjee, D., Hartman, A., & Buyya, R. (2014). Improving productivity in design and development of information technology (IT) service delivery simulation models. *Journal of Service Research*, *18*(1), 75–89. https://doi.org/10.1177/1094670514541002

Benaroch, M., & Chernobai, A. (2017). Operational IT failures, IT value destruction, and board-level IT governance changes. *MIS Quarterly*, *41*(3), 729–762. https://doi.org/10.25300/MISQ/2017/41.3.04

Booch, G., Rumbaugh, J., & Jacobson, I. (1999). *The unified modeling language user guide*. Rational Software Corporation.

Briol, P. (2008). *BPMN, the business process modeling notation pocket handbook*. LuLu.com.

Brown, A. E., Grant, G. G., & Sprott, E. (2005). Framing the frameworks: A review of IT governance research. *Communications of the Association for Information Systems*, *15*, 696–712.

Brustbauer, J. (2016). Enterprise risk management in SMEs: Towards a structural model. *International Small Business Journal*, *34*(1), 70–85. https://doi.org/10.1177/0266242614542853

Cadete, G. R., & da Silva, M. M. (2017). *Assessing IT governance processes using a COBIT5 model BT – information systems* (M. Themistocleous & V. Morabito, Eds., pp. 447–460). Springer International Publishing.

Carter, C. B., & Lorsch, J. W. (2003). *Back to the drawing board: Designing corporate boards for a complex world*. Harvard Business Press.

Cater-Steel, A. (2009). IT service departments struggle to adopt a service-oriented philosophy. *International Journal of Information Systems in the Service Sector (IJISSS)*, *1*(2), 69–77.

Chiu, T., & Wang, T. (David). (2019). The COSO framework in emerging technology environments: An effective in-class exercise on internal control. *Journal of Emerging Technologies in Accounting*, *16*(2), 89–98. https://doi.org/10.2308/jeta-52500

Claudepierre, B., & Nurcan, S. (2007). A framework for analysing IT governance approaches. *ICEIS 2007–9th International Conference on Enterprise Information Systems, Proceedings*, 512–516. www.scopus.com/inward/record.url?eid=2-s2.0-70349560477&partnerID=40&md5=2b2b4447a92d4202094243103e916a44

Dahlberg, T., & Kivijärvi, H. (2006). An integrated framework for IT governance and the development and validation of an assessment instrument. *39th Hawaii International Conference on System Sciences*, *C*, 1–10. https://doi.org/10.1109/HICSS.2006.57

Dahlberg, T., & Lahdelma, P. (2007). IT governance maturity and IT outsourcing degree: An exploratory study. *Proceedings of the Annual Hawaii International Conference on System Sciences*, 1–10. https://doi.org/10.1109/HICSS.2007.306

Davenport, T. H. (1993). *Process innovation: Reengineering work through information technology.* Harvard Business Press.

De Haes, S., & Van Grembergen, W. (2005, January). IT governance structures, processes and relational mechanisms: Achieving IT/business alignment in a major Belgian financial group. In *Proceedings of the 38th Annual Hawaii International Conference on System Sciences* (pp. 237b). IEEE.

De Haes, S., Van Grembergen, W., & Debreceny, R. S. (2013). COBIT 5 and enterprise governance of information technology: Building blocks and research opportunities. *Journal of Information Systems, 27*(1), 307–324. https://doi.org/10.2308/isys-50422

De Haes, S., Van Grembergen, W., Joshi, A., & Huygh, T. (2020). *COBIT as a framework for enterprise governance of IT BT – enterprise governance of information technology: Achieving alignment and value in digital organizations* (S. De Haes, W. Van Grembergen, A. Joshi, & T. Huygh, Eds., pp. 125–162). Springer International Publishing. https://doi.org/10.1007/978-3-030-25918-1_5

Dibbern, J., Goles, T., Hirschheim, R., & Jayatilaka, B. (2004). Information systems outsourcing: A survey and analysis of the literature. *ACM SIGMIS Database: The DATABASE for Advances in Information Systems, 35*(4), 6–102.

Elhasnaoui, S., Medromi, H., Chakir, A., & Sayouti, A. (2015). A new IT governance architecture based on multi agents system to support project management. *2015 International Conference on Electrical and Information Technologies (ICEIT),* 43–46. https://doi.org/10.1109/EITech.2015.7162957

El-Mekawy, M., Rusu, L., & Perjons, E. (2015). An evaluation framework for comparing business-IT alignment models: A tool for supporting collaborative learning in organizations. *Computers in Human Behavior, 51,* 1229–1247. https://doi.org/10.1016/j.chb.2014.12.016

Grant, G., Brown, A., Uruthirapathy, A., Mcknight, S., & Grant, G. G. (2007). Association for information systems ais electronic library (AISeL) an extended model of IT governance: A conceptual proposal. *AMCIS 2007 Proceedings, 215.* http://aisel.aisnet.org/amcis2007/215

Grembergen, W. V. (2004). *Strategies for information technology governance.* IGI Global.

Grover, V., & Kohli, R. (2012). Cocreating IT value: New capabilities and metrics for multifirm environments. *MIS Quarterly, 36*(1), 225–232.

Grunwel, D., & Sahama, T. (2016, February). Delegation of access in an information accountability framework for eHealth. *Proceedings of the Australasian Computer Science Week Multiconference on – ACSW'16,* 1–8. https://doi.org/10.1145/2843043.2843383

Guldentops, E. (2002). *Governing information technology through COBIT BT – integrity, internal control and security in information systems: Connecting governance and technology* (pp. 115–159). Springer. https://doi.org/10.1007/978-0-387-35583-2_8

Guldentops, E., Van Grembergen, W., & De Haes, S. (2002). Control and governance maturity survey: Establishing a reference benchmark and a self assessment tool. *Information Systems Control Journal, 6,* 32–35.

Hammer, M., Champy, J., & Le Seac'h, M. (1993). *Le reengineering* (Vol. 93). Dunod.

Henderson, J. C., & Venkatraman, H. (1999). Strategic alignment : Leveraging information technology for transforming organizations. *IBM Systems Journal, 32*(1), 472–484.

Herath, T., & Rao, H. R. (2009). Encouraging information security behaviors in organizations: Role of penalties, pressures and perceived effectiveness. *Decision Support Systems, 47*(2), 154–165. http://doi.org/10.1016/j.dss.2009.02.005

Hiererra, S. E. (2012). *Assessment of IT governance using COBIT 4.1 framework methodology: Case study university IS development in IT directorate* [Master's thesis, BINUS University].

Information Security Governance: Guidance for Boards of Directors and Executive Management Guidance for Boards of Directors and Executive Management. (2006). *IT Governance Institute,* 1–52. www.itgi.org

ISACA. (2012). COBIT 5: *A business framework for the governance and management of enterprise IT.* Information Systems Audit and Control Association.

ISO. (2013). *ISO home: Standards.* ISO Website. Retrieved March 24, 2013, from www.Iso.Org/Iso/Home/Standards.Htm

ITGI. (2007). *COBIT mapping overview of international IT guidance* (2nd ed.). IT Governance Institute.

Jarke, M., Mylopoulos, J., Schmidt, J. W., & Vassiliou, Y. (1992). DAIDA: An environment for evolving information systems. *ACM Transactions on Information Systems (TOIS), 10*(1), 1–50.

Jarke, M., & Pohl, K. (1993). Establishing visions in context: Towards a model of requirements processes. *International Conference on Information Systems (ICIS),* 23–24.

Kaplan, R. S., & Norton, D. P. (1996). *The balanced scorecard: Translating strategy into action.* Harvard Business Press.

Luftman, J., Papp, R., & Brier, T. (1999). Enablers and inhibitors of business-IT alignment. *Commun. AIS, 1*(3es). http://dl.acm.org/citation.cfm?id=374122.374123

Maes, K., De Haes, S., & Van Grembergen, W. (2013). Investigating a process approach on business cases: An exploratory case study at Barco. *International Journal of IT/Business Alignment and Governance (IJITBAG), 4*(2), 37–53.

Magnusson, J. (2010). *Unpackaging IT governance.* BAS Publishing.

Maleh, Y., Sahid, A., & Belaissaoui, M. (2019). *Strategic IT governance and performance frameworks in large organizations.* IGI Global. https://doi.org/10.4018/978-1-5225-7826-0

Maleh, Y., Zaydi, M., Sahid, A., & Ezzati, A. (2018). Building a maturity framework for information security governance through an empirical study in organizations. In Y. Maleh (Ed.), *Security and privacy management, techniques, and protocols* (pp. 96–127). IGI Global. https://doi.org/10.4018/978-1-5225-5583-4.ch004

Marrone, M., Gacenga, F., Cater-Steel, A., & Kolbe, L. (2014). IT service management: A cross-national study of ITIL adoption. *Communications of the Association for Information Systems, 34*(1), 865–892.

Marrone, M., & Kolbe, L. M. (2011). Uncovering ITIL claims: IT executives' perception on benefits and business-IT alignment. *Information Systems and E-Business Management, 9*(3), 363–380. https://doi.org/10.1007/s10257-010-0131-7

McKay, J., Marshall, P., & Smith, L. (2003, July). Steps towards effective IT governance: Strategic IT planning, evaluation and benefits management. *Pacific Asia Conference on Information Systems,* 956–970. www.pacis-net.org/file/2003/papers/is-strategy/214.pdf

Moen, R., & Norman, C. (2006). *Evolution of the PDCA cycle.* API Organization.

Murphy, K., Lyytinen, K., & Somers, T. (2018). A socio-technical model for project-based executive IT governance. *Proceedings of the 51st Hawaii International Conference on System Sciences | 2018 A, 9,* 4825–4834.

Nehan, Y. R., & Deneckere, R. (2007). Component-based situational methods: A framework for understanding SME. *IFIP International Federation for Information Processing, 244,* 161–175. https://doi.org/10.1007/978-0-387-73947-2_14

Neto, J. S., CGEIT, C., Assessor, C. C., & de Luca Ribeiro, C. H. (n.d.). Is COBIT 5 process implementation a wicked problem? *COBIT Focus, 2,* 8–10.

Nfuka, E. N., & Rusu, L. (2011). The effect of critical success factors on IT governance performance. *Industrial Management & Data Systems, 111*(9), 1418–1448. https://doi.org/10.1108/02635571111182773

Nianxin, W., Xue, Y., Liang, H., & Ge, S. (2011). The road to business-IT alignment: A case study of two Chinese companies. *Communications of AIS, 28,* 415–436. http://content.ebscohost.com/ContentServer.asp?T=P&P=AN&K=70400209&S=R&D=buh&EbscoContent=dGJyMNLe80Sep7A4yOvqOLCmr0qeprJSsai4TLSWxWXS&ContentCustomer=dGJyMPGnr0m0r7JJuePfgeyx44Dt6fIA%5Cnwww.redi-bw.de/db/ebsco.php/search.ebscohost.com/login.aspx?d

Nugroho, H. (2014). Conceptual model of it governance for higher education based on Cobit 5 framework. *Journal of Theoretical & Applied Information Technology, 60*(2).

Nurcan, S., & Rolland, C. (2003). A multi-method for defining the organizational change. *Information and Software Technology, 45*(2), 61–82. https://doi.org/10.1016/S0950-5849(02)00162-3

Oliver, D., & Lainhart, J. (2012). COBIT 5: Adding value through effective geit. *EDPACS: The EDP Audit, Control, and Security*, *46*(3), 1–12. https://doi.org/10.1080/07366981.2012.706472

Omari, L. Al, Barnes, P. H., & Pitman, G. (2012). *An exploratory study into audit challenges in IT governance: A Delphi approach*. Symposium on IT Governance, Management and Audit. https://eprints.qut.edu.au/53110/

Otto, B. (2010). IT governance and organizational transformation: Findings from an action research study. *Americas Conference on Information Systems*, *421*.

Peterson, R. (2004). Crafting information technology governance. *Information Systems Management*, *21*(4), 7–22.

Peterson, R., Parker, M., Ribbers, P., Peterson, R. R., & Parker, M. M. (2002). Information technology governance processes under environmental dynamism: Investigating competing theories of decision making and knowledge sharing. *ICIS 2002 Proceedings*, 562–575.

Ploesser, K., Recker, J., & Rosemann, M. (2008). Towards a classification and lifecycle of business process change: A classification and lifecycle of process change strategies. *BPMDS'08: Business Process Life-Cycle: Design, Deployment, Operation & Evaluation*, 10–18.

Prieto-Diaz, R. (1991). Implementing faceted classification for software reuse. *Communications of the ACM*, *34*(5), 88–97. https://doi.org/10.1145/103167.103176

Raghupathi, W. (2007). Corporate governance of IT: A framework for development. *Communications of the ACM*, *50*(8), 94–99. https://doi.org/10.1145/1278201.1278212

Ramírez-Mora, S. L., Oktaba, H., & Patlán Pérez, J. (2020). Group maturity, team efficiency, and team effectiveness in software development: A case study in a CMMI-DEV level 5 organization. *Journal of Software: Evolution and Process*, *32*(4), e2232. https://doi.org/10.1002/smr.2232

Ravichandran, T., Lertwongsatien, C., & Lertwongsatien, C. (2005). Effect of information systems resources and capabilities on firm performance: A resource-based perspective. *Journal of Management Information Systems*, *21*(4), 237–276. https://doi.org/10.1080/07421222.2005.11045820

Reich, B. H., & Benbasat, I. (2000). Factors that influence the social dimension of alignment between business and information technology objectives. *MIS Quarterly*, *24*(1), 81–113. https://doi.org/10.2307/3250980

Reyck, B. De, Grushka-Cockayne, Y., Lockett, M., Calderini, S. R., Moura, M., & Sloper, A. (2005). The impact of project portfolio management on information technology projects. *International Journal of Project Management*, *23*(7), 524–537. https://doi.org/10.1016/j.ijproman.2005.02.003

Ribeiro, J., & Gomes, R. (2009, September). IT governance using COBIT implemented in a high public educational institution – a case study. *Proceedings of the 3rd International Conference on European Computing Conference*, 41–52. wseas.us/e-library/conferences/2009/georgia/CCI/CCI04.pdf

Rolland, C. (1998). A comprehensive view of process engineering. *International Conference on Advanced Information Systems Engineering*, 1–24.

Rummler, G. A., & Brache, A. P. (2012). *Improving performance: How to manage the white space on the organization chart*. John Wiley & Sons.

Simonsson, M., & Johnson, P. (2006, December). *Assessment of IT governance – a prioritization of COBIT*. Proceedings of the Conference on Systems Engineering Research. http://sse.stevens.edu/fileadmin/cser/2006/papers/151-Simonsson-AssessmentofITGovernance.pdf

Simonsson, M., Johnson, P., & Wijkström, H. (2007). Model-based IT governance maturity assessments with COBIT. *ECIS: Educational Collaborative for International Schools*, 1276–1287.

Smits, D., & Hillegersberg, J. V. (2015). IT governance maturity: Developing a maturity model using the Delphi method. *2015 48th Hawaii International Conference on System Sciences*, 4534–4543. https://doi.org/10.1109/HICSS.2015.541

Steuperaert, D. (2019). COBIT 2019: A significant update. *EDPACS*, *59*(1), 14–18. https://doi.org/10.1080/07366981.2019.1578474

Tallon, P. P., Ramirez, R. V., & Short, J. E. (2013). The information artifact in IT governance: Toward a theory of information governance. *Journal of Management Information Systems, 30*(3), 141–178.

Turel, O., & Bart, C. (2014). Board-level IT governance and organizational performance. *European Journal of Information Systems, 23*(2), 223–239.

Valentine, E. L. H. (2016, January). *Enterprise technology governance: New information and technology core competencies for boards of directors* [Doctoral dissertation, Queensland University of Technology], 1–295. https://doi.org/10.13140/RG.2.2.34027.95529

Van Grembergen, W., & De Haes, S. (2009a). *Enterprise governance of information technology: Achieving strategic alignment and value.* Springer Science & Business Media.

van Grembergen, W., & De Haes, S. (2009b). *COBIT as a framework for enterprise governance of IT BT – enterprise governance of information technology: Achieving strategic alignment and value* (Steven De Haes & W. Van Grembergen, Eds., pp. 137–164). Springer. https://doi.org/10.1007/978-0-387-84882-2_5

Vlietland, J., van Solingen, R., & van Vliet, H. (2016). Aligning codependent scrum teams to enable fast business value delivery: A governance framework and set of intervention actions. *Journal of Systems and Software, 113*, 418–429. https://doi.org/10.1016/j.jss.2015.11.010

Von Solms, B. (2005). Information security governance: COBIT or ISO 17799 or both? *Computers and Security, 24*(2), 99–104. https://doi.org/10.1016/j.cose.2005.02.002

Warland, C., & Ridley, G. (2005). Awareness of IT control frameworks in an Australian state government: A qualitative case study. *Proceedings of the 38th Annual Hawaii International Conference on System Sciences, C*, 236b. https://doi.org/10.1109/HICSS.2005.116

Webb, P., Pollard, C., & Ridley, G. (2006). Attempting to define IT governance: Wisdom or folly? *Proceedings of the Annual Hawaii International Conference on System Sciences, 8*(C), 1–10. https://doi.org/10.1109/HICSS.2006.68

Weber, L. (2014). *Addressing the incremental risks associated with adopting a bring your own device program by using the COBIT 5 framework to identify keycontrols* [Doctoral dissertation, Stellenbosch University].

Weill, P., & Ross, J. W. (2004). *How top performers manage IT decisions rights for superior results* (pp. 1–10). IT Governance, Harvard Business School Press. https://doi.org/10.2139/ssrn.664612

Weill, P., & Ross, J. W. (2005). A matrixed approach to designing IT governance. *MIT Sloan Management Review, 46*(2), 26–34. https://doi.org/10.1177/0275074007310556

Williams, S. P., Hardy, C. A., & Holgate, J. A. (2013). Information security governance practices in critical infrastructure organizations: A socio-technical and institutional logic perspective. *Electronic Markets, 23*(4), 341–354. https://doi.org/10.1007/s12525-013-0137-3

Woo, H., Lee, S., Huh, J. H., & Jeong, S. (2020). Impact of ITSM military service quality and value on service trust. *Journal of Multimedia Information System, 7*(1), 55–72. https://doi.org/10.33851/JMIS.2020.7.1.55

Wood, D. J. (2010). *Assessing IT governance maturity: The case of San Marcos, Texas.* [Master's thesis, Texas State University].

Xue, Y., Liang, H., & Boulton, W. R. (2008). Information technology governance in information technology investment decision processes: The impact of investment characteristics, external environment, and internal context. *MIS Quarterly*, 67–96.

SECTION 2

Maturity Frameworks for Information Technology Governance

IT Governance in Organizations

A Maturity Framework Based on COBIT 5

3

3.1 INTRODUCTION

Strategic information technology (IT) has become an indispensable element for success in the contemporary business world. The dependency on IT by many organizations today to support, sustain and drive organizational growth increases (Posthumus & von Solms, 2004). Business and IT alignment are considered one of the main issues in managing its IS (information system). However, alignment is described as an object that can never be achieved entirely and must be adjusted frequently within the organization (Baker & Jones, 2008). To maximize alignment facilitators and minimize inhibitors, various frameworks are developed for IT Governance (ITG), which is an important concept for IT organizations in enterprises (Joshi et al., 2018).

Many professionals and researchers believe that Information System Governance is a complex subject. The words that immediately come to mind are 'Arid, Boring, Wave, Unrealistic'. This is mainly due to the intensive use of jargon such as 'strategic alignment, organizational transformation, value creation, synergy creation', complicated vision and mission statements, which the average person finds difficult to understand (Peterson, 2001). The result is that IT governance is as poorly adopted as corporate governance because of the lack of understanding of its role within an organization (Luna-Reyes et al., 2020).

The purpose of this chapter is to determine how to effectively adopt frameworks, best practices, and standards as organizations face significant challenges in meeting their IT governance obligations. Despite the potentially costly consequences of IT and business alignment failure, there is little direct guidance to organizations on providing, demonstrating, and maintaining adequate IT governance (Renaud et al., 2016).

A key aspect of this problem is twofold. The finding is that there is a lack of theoretical knowledge on examining the adoption and adaptation of IT governance frameworks.

DOI: 10.1201/9781003161998- 6

Although IT governance has gained popularity, there is little academic research on the subject (Marrone & Kolbe, 2011). On the other hand, IT governance concerns are very present in professional journals and reports, which advocate the need to deploy frameworks and standards to address governance challenges. Thus, several different models and standards have been developed for IT governance, of which COBIT is most often used. Research shows that efforts devoted to these models and standards can help create value, improve productivity, optimize resources, increase compliance, reduce costs, and improve lead times (Beloglazov et al., 2014).

The adoption of best practice frameworks by IT departments aims to provide IT services to business entities more effectively and efficiently according to their demand. When IT begins its journey to better support business, a chain of events will begin requiring adopting standards and best practices that meet business service needs (Peterson et al., 2002). Furthermore, it takes significant time to fully implement a framework the size of COBIT in its entirety. Such timeframes mean that the COBIT framework is often considered an expensive approach for many organizations, as significant resources need to be allocated over an extensive period. The substantial investment required leads to many organizations being reluctant to embark on a long path of IT governance implementation. Despite the importance of IT governance frameworks, little empirical research has been carried out on developing ways to implement, maintain effectively, and evaluate IT governance programs (Bermejo et al., 2014).

Significant focus has been placed on the development of IT governance standards and models. This suggests that the current challenges of IT governance are not the absence of standards or models, but rather the absence of an effective and practical strategy for successfully assessing IT governance. In particular, there is little research in the literature that analyzes COBIT or uses COBIT as a tool for implementing research programs (Aprilinda et al., 2019). To facilitate effective IT governance implementation, the maturity of organizations should be measured by using IT governance evaluation methods (De Haes & Van Grembergen, 2005). These evaluation methods are often based on a more or less comprehensive set of criteria and provide a way of scoring the capability of IT governance processes (Cadete & da Silva, 2017). However, organizations generally adopt ad hoc methods instead of standard methods to assess IT governance. Therefore, IT governance assessment methodologies need to be adjusted according to their applicability in a specific area and sector (Tonelli et al., 2017). Therefore, it is necessary to contextualize COBIT before it can be applied appropriately to assess IT governance in any industry. This can reduce the time and cost of assessing IT governance and provide more contextualized methods (Omari et al., 2012).

The major challenges of IT governance are the lack of practical methods to contextualize or adapt evaluation frameworks, particularly in specific contexts, and the lack of understanding of the adoption of the framework, particularly the factors that influence its adoption (Maleh et al., 2019). Therefore, this chapter aims to determine the main areas of adoption of IT governance, based on the COBIT, to provide a practical and efficient framework to evaluate IT governance in medium and large organizations (Rizal et al., 2020).

The remaining sections of this chapter present the background and the literature review in the next section. Section 3.2 describes the theoretical framework. An overview of the research methodology will be presented in Section 3.3 and the chapter's contribution in Section 3.4. The proposed case study will be described in Section 3.5. Section 3.6 provides the chapter summary.

3.2 BACKGROUND AND LITERATURE REVIEW

IT governance is considered a complex system as it includes several critical aspects, namely, leadership, organization and decision rights, scalable processes, and enabling technologies (Selig, 2008). Early conceptualizations of IT governance, often considered a subset of corporate governance (De Haes et al., 2013; Posthumus et al., 2010), recognized the role of IT governance in ensuring a valuable contribution from the organization's IT to its overall business strategy. More specifically, the role of IT governance is to 'ensure that the organization's IT sustains and extends the organization's strategies and objectives' (ITGI, 2003).

Several highly respected organizations and authors have attempted to define IT governance (Simonsson & Johnson, 2006). Still, there is no commonly accepted universal definition of IT governance at the date of this chapter. IT governance can be defined as the process of controlling an organization's IT resources (Hunton et al., 2004). The International Standard for ICT Corporate Governance extends this definition to indicate that IT governance is the system by which the current and future use of ICT is directed and controlled. This involves assessing and guiding ICT use plans to support the organization and monitoring ICT use to achieve the plans. It includes the strategy and policies for using ICT within an organization.

As a result, IT governance has become a standard component of most organizations' governance, oversight, and control landscapes (Schubert, 2004). As with most social phenomena, the increasing importance of IT governance has given rise to several industry frameworks, tools, best practices, and maturity models, offering a prescriptive and deterministic approach to establishing effective IT governance. Nonetheless, the significant role of frameworks has been established as a practical approach to IT governance (Guldentops, 2002; Webb et al., 2006) by way of providing guidance to organizations and offering an advantage as compliance with these standards allows the enterprise to demonstrate they are following best practices and complying with regulatory rules (Brown et al., 2005a). For example, prominent meta-frameworks such as ISO 38500 and ITIL provide a comprehensive suite of best practices for standardizing, monitoring, and controlling IT activities (Wallhoff, 2004). However, guidance on IT governance can perhaps be better found through the Information Systems Audit and Control Association (ISACA) and its related professional organization, the IT Governance Institute (ITGI) (Moeller, 2011).

COBIT is a set of best practices developed by ITGI and is widely accepted as the main IT governance framework for establishing control over the IT environment, facilitating performance measurement of IT processes, and allowing executives to bridge the gap between control requirements, technical issues, and business risks (van Wyk & Rudman, 2019).

Given the varied and significant organizational pressures to ensure proper oversight and control of IT, it is interesting to note that the considerable academic and practitioner focus on COBIT as a de facto framework for IT governance over the last two decades (Brown et al., 2005b; De Haes et al., 2013; Guldentops, 2002; Webb et al., 2006). Many organizations continue to struggle with fundamental governance practices, such as selecting, implementing, managing, and evaluating IT governance processes (Heier et al., 2007; McKay et al., 2003).

From an anecdotal perspective, COBIT's size and multifaceted and complex structure make implementing a framework of this magnitude in its entirety too medium and large task (De Haes et al., 2013; Warland & Ridley, 2005). This is also echoed by statements that view the COBIT framework as too extensive to be applied entirely and proposed to move to a less complex approach to defining and establishing selective controls. Prominent researchers in the domain, (De Haes & Van Grembergen, 2005; Peterson, 2004; Webb et al., 2006; Weill & Ross, 2005) all put forth converging definitions of IT governance that recognizes the importance of all three structural, process, and relational mechanisms. Although the value of user involvement in various aspects of IT governance has long been recognized (Grembergen, 2004; Posthumus et al., 2010), human behavior aspects of IT governance has received far less attention from academics (El-Mekawy et al., 2015; Lengnick-Hall et al., 2011).

The importance of IT governance and the relevance of frameworks provide the context for this study, which also focuses on the factors underlying the adoption of IT governance frameworks. In particular, the intentions and opinions of the adopters are explored to shed light on the factors influencing adoption intent.

Several studies have endeavored to tailor and adapt the COBIT framework for a specific organizational context. For example, a study by Nugroho (2014) examined COBIT 5 as an IT governance tool in higher education institutions in Indonesia. The author concluded that each organization must consider its specific situation to define its own set of governance processes as it sees fit, as long as all necessary governance and management objectives are covered. Similarly, Hiererra (2012) conducted a focused evaluation using eight high-level control objectives from COBIT to determine the IT governance maturity of the information systems (ISs) department within a single university in Indonesia. Along the same line, a study by Wood (2010) adopted a case study design based on nine of the COBIT high-level control objectives as a modified framework to evaluate the IT governance maturity of the city of San Marcos in the United States. Similarly, the implementation of COBIT as an IT governance framework was examined in an educational institution in Portugal by Gomes and Ribeiro and Gomes (2009) and two Australian institutions of higher education by Bhattacharjya and Chang (2010).

In a similar effort to derive an abbreviated list of IT processes for creating an integrated IT governance framework in the Malaysian Ministry of Education, Azizi Ismail (2008) noted that the focus on IT governance domains differs the organization. For example, the Plan and Organize domain was the main focus at the ministerial level, whereas the Monitor and Evaluate domain was given the highest emphasis at the school's level. Their study determined 20 high-level control objectives that were considered to be most important in one organization. Similarly, Braga (2015) recommended adopting COBIT for private sector organizations in Argentina. The author utilized the framework's goals cascade mechanism to pick a specific set of primary and secondary processes that relate to two IT-related goals: compliance with external regulations and laws and security of information, processing infrastructure, and applications.

In the same vein, Al-Khazrajy (2011) indicated that COBIT helps in conducting IT governance evaluations at low cost with better value, as it can be tailored to fit certain organizational needs. However, none of these studies provided empirical evidence of the validity of their selection or practical methods for utilizing COBIT by auditors. As a result, it is proposed that tailoring the COBIT framework to conduct IT governance evaluation that is relevant to a specific organizational context is possible.

Afterward, Warland and Ridley (2005) conducted a study to establish a reference benchmark of maturity levels of control over IT processes in the Australian financial sector by adopting a self-assessment tool based on the study's selection of 15 controls from COBIT by Guldentops (2002) to elicit the level of control over IT processes. The authors then compared the Australian benchmark with the international benchmark established by Guldentops (2002) and concluded that the Australian financial sector had a better performance for IT control over the 15 most important IT processes. Subsequently, a study by Nfuka and Rusu (2010) also used the previously selected 15 processes from the COBIT framework to evaluate IT governance maturity in five Tanzanian public organizations and compared the results with those of previous studies (Guldentops, 2002; Warland & Ridley, 2005).

They concluded that when the maturity levels in the studied environment were compared with those in the public sector in Australia and internationally in a range of nations, the maturity pattern appeared to be relatively lower in Tanzania as a developing country. As observed in the previous studies, the authors agreed on three points. First of all, only a limited number of empirical research studies exist that focus on the evaluation of IT governance using COBIT in the public sector environments worldwide. Second, the authors noted the similarity between the rankings of the leading IT processes, which suggests that the priority placed on these specific IT processes is medium and largely consistent.

This also indicates a consistency in the nature of the IT governance practices and maturity within the public sector worldwide. Third, none of the studies provided a justification or a mechanism for the selection of the leading (or most important) 15 IT processes from the COBIT framework. Another project was undertaken by the IT working group at the European Organization of Supreme Audit Institutions (EUROSAI) to design a self-assessment tool for evaluating IT governance based on the COBIT framework. Similar to the previous studies, a list of 16 key control objectives was identified as the most important to Supreme Audit Institutions (Huissoud, 2005). In the same way, a study was undertaken by Webb et al. (2006) in Australia to identify and assess a set of control objectives to be used as an IT evaluation instrument by the Tasmanian Audit Office within public organizations. The authors produced an abbreviated list of 17 high-level control objectives from the COBIT framework that were considered to be important to Tasmanian organizations.

3.3 THEORETICAL FRAMEWORK

The COBIT framework recognizes the importance of effectively assessing IT governance to organizations by articulating that a basic need for every enterprise is to understand the status of its own IT systems and to decide what level of management and control the enterprise should provide ('Information Security Governance: Guidance for Boards of Directors and Executive Management Guidance for Boards of Directors and Executive Management', 2006). It also notes that the assessment of process capability based on the COBIT maturity models is a key part of IT governance implementation as shown in Figure 3.1.

Although obtaining an objective view of an organization's own IT performance level through maturity models has been described as a challenging undertaking, COBIT enables the measurement of IT capability as a portfolio by assessing individual IT processes' maturity (Chen et al., 2008). Evaluating IT governance can be based on the Process Capability Model (PCM) or the generic maturity model (in previous versions of COBIT), with selected or all 37 IT processes ('Information Security Governance: Guidance for Boards of Directors and Executive Management Guidance for Boards of Directors and Executive Management', 2006). For example, De Haes et al. (2013) undertook a medium and large field study to evaluate the maturity of IT processes.

The authors used all 34 processes in COBIT 4 as a foundation to evaluate process capability by interacting with process owners at 52 organizations in several countries. The authors applied an extensive survey instrument, which found that the mean level of process maturity is rather low, with higher process maturity being observed in more operational processes. However, the authors concluded that exploiting the COBIT framework in its entirety was too generic and may not have directly correlated to the capabilities of any particular organization. On the other hand, Weber (2014) developed an evaluation framework based on a selection of processes to be used in South African organizations. The author concluded that using a selection of processes from COBIT 5 produced an acceptable and fit-for-purpose framework to use in evaluating ITG.

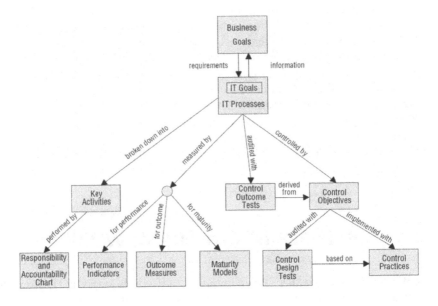

FIGURE 3.1 COBIT governance model.

The PCM utilized in COBIT provides a structured approach for IT capability assessment through evaluating processes capability against a consistent and well-established scale (Oliver & Lainhart, 2012). The evaluation is performed through metrics that assess a unique set of key goal indicators (KGIs) and key performance indicators (KPIs) for each IT process. KGIs are lead indicators that aim to identify and measure the application of processes. On the other hand, KPIs are lag indicators that assess the achievement of process goals. KPIs and KGIs are often associated with Balanced Scorecards (BSC). They are important in measuring the relationship between IT processes and business goals which is critical to the success of ITG. For all 37 IT processes, a set of IT-related goals (i.e., to define what IT objectives are achieved by the process), process goals (i.e., to define what IT must deliver to support objectives), and activities (i.e., to assess actual performance) is provided.

According to ISACA (2012), there are six levels of capability that a process can achieve in COBIT as shown in Figure 3.1:

- Incomplete (level 0): The process is not implemented or fails to achieve its objective. This level has no process attributes;
- Performed (level 1): The process is implemented and achieves its objective. This level has only one process attribute: process performance;
- Managed (level 2): The previously described performed process is now implemented using a managed approach and its outcomes are appropriately established. This level has two process attributes: performance management and work product management;
- Established (level 3): The previously described managed process is now implemented using a defined process capable of achieving its process outcomes. This level has two process attributes: process definition and process deployment;
- Predictable (level 4): The previously described established process now operates within a defined boundary that allows the achievement of the process's outcomes. This level has two process attributes: process management and process control;
- Optimizing (level 5): The process is continuously improved to enable it to achieve relevant, current, and projected goals. This level has two process attributes: process innovation and process optimization.

Furthermore, each capability level can be achieved only when the level below has been fully achieved as shown in Table 3.1. For example, a process capability level 4 (predictable) requires the process management and process control attributes to be medium and primarily achieved, on top of full achievement of the attributes for a process capability level 3 (established).

The COBIT framework was selected for use in this research. It was explicitly derived to guide IT governance and is used extensively throughout the public and private sectors for this purpose. It is important to note that in many previous studies, the decision to utilize all or a collection of IT processes from COBIT was based on the opinion of the researchers. As a result, no consistency for selecting specific IT processes was provided for a given context, which also makes it difficult to compare results. Consequently, the following section explores previous studies that have attempted to adapt the COBIT framework to evaluate IT governance.

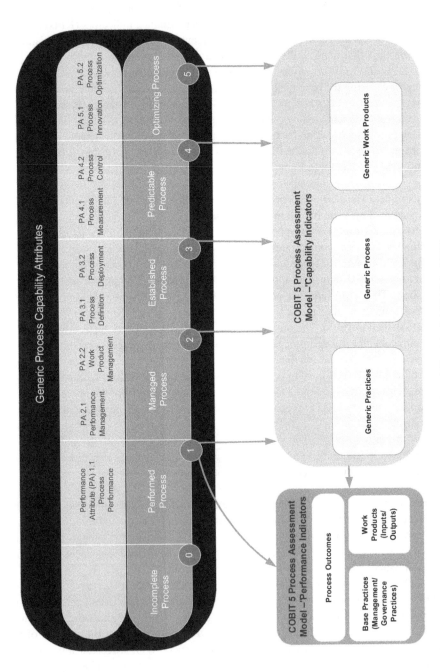

FIGURE 3.2   Summary of the COBIT 5 Process Capability Model (ISACA, 2012).

TABLE 3.1   COBIT 5 Process Capability Levels (ISACA, 2013)

Process Capability Level	DOES PROCESS EXIST?	Process Attribute								
		PA 1.1	PA 2.1	PA 2.2	PA 3.1	PA 3.2	PA 4.1	PA 4.2	PA 5.1	PA 5.2
Level 5 (Optimized)	Yes	L or F	L or F	L or F	L or F	L or F	L or F	L or F	L or F	L or F
Level 4 (Predictable)	Yes	L or F	L or F	L or F	L or F	L or F	L or F	L or F		
Level 3 (Established)	Yes	L or F	L or F	L or F	L or F	L or F				
Level 2 (Managed)	Yes	L or F	L or F	L or F						
Level 1 (Performed)	Yes	L or F								
Level 0 (Incomplete)	NO									

Rating scale: N: Note achieved (0–15%)   P: Partially Achieved (15%–50%)   L: Medium and largely Achieved (15%–50%)   F: Fully Achieved (15%–50%)

3.4 RESEARCH METHODOLOGY

Despite its prevalence in practice, little academic literature has been published on adapting and adopting best practice frameworks and models for assessing IT governance. It is necessary to understand whether theoretical constructions of information systems (IS) can help understand the adoption of the IT governance framework and how these factors can guide developers and proponents of contextualized frameworks. More formally, the overarching research question for this research is: How can best practice frameworks be adapted and adopted to assess IT governance in medium and large organizations across all sectors? The secondary research questions are as follows:

- **Question 1.** Which pertinent process can be adapted to conduct IT governance assessments in medium and large organizations?
- **Question 2.** How can medium and large organizations assess IT governance using appropriate best practice frameworks?

A mixed approach was adopted because this conception is linked to the research paradigm of 'realism' chosen for this research. As critical realism, research methods were chosen on the basis of the nature of the research problem (McEvoy & Richards, 2006). Therefore, a mixed approach, which combines quantitative and qualitative methods, is considered the most effective strategy for this research (Perry et al., 1997). By applying both approaches at different stages of the research program, the researcher collected data on the same questions from different sources, which could be triangulated together. This approach also reduces the weaknesses associated with using a single method (Charles & Tashakkori, 2009). In addition, a mixed approach is considered most appropriate for exploring the research question 'How to adapt and adopt best practice frameworks to assess IT governance in medium and large organizations', as the implementation of multiple methods across several steps or research activities helps answer this type of general question (Morse & Niehaus, 2009). From a theoretical perspective, a mixed approach gave this research the best chance to discover the theoretical mechanisms underlying the contextualization and adoption of IT governance frameworks (Charles & Tashakkori, 2009). A combination of quantitative and qualitative methods has been designed to lead to a thicker and deeper understanding of the research question (Creswell & Creswell, 2017). As the research progressed, the design of mixed methods developed so that the results of the first phase, including three research activities or studies, contributed to the development of a more in-depth study of the drivers of innovation adoption and IT governance frameworks in the second phase (Charles & Tashakkori, 2009). In addition, the mixed approach allowed this research to develop from the literature on IT governance and innovation adoption theories, and thus, this research is considered from a unified position. Therefore, this research can combine the strengths of quantitative research with those of qualitative research to deepen understanding of a complex phenomenon.

Several apparent gaps emerge from previous research concerning the challenges of assessing IT governance, particularly appropriate governance frameworks, or the lack of governance frameworks in medium and large organizations. There is also a gap in the study of the methodological adaptation of the COBIT framework to the specific needs of individual organizations or sectors. Therefore, this research seeks to address the gaps identified in the area of IT governance by answering the primary research question: 'How can best practice frameworks be adapted and adopted to assess IT governance in financial sector organizations'?

The primary research questions are as follows:

- Research activity 1. Which is the best process that can be adapted to conduct IT governance assessments in medium and large organizations? This question aims to address one of the key IT governance assessment challenges identified. While there may be several ways to do this, as an intervention in this research, IT governance frameworks, particularly COBIT, have been taken into account because of the need highlighted in the literature to focus on contextualization (or adaptation) important research area. To make optimal use of scarce medium and large organizations' resources effectively and efficiently.
- Research activity 2. How can medium and large organizations evaluate IT governance using adapted best-practice frameworks? A method with guidelines in the form of an evaluation framework for IT governance was tested. The research activity evaluated IT governance in medium and large organizations in terms of the capability levels of their IT processes.

Embarking on a research project requires the investigator to understand the research process and associated activities. The research methodology and approach must be carefully planned and formulated to successfully answer the research questions and successfully solve the research problem. To explore whether the COBIT framework can be adapted and adopted to evaluate IT governance in the Middle East and North Africa MENA Port organizations from different sectors, the researchers employed a two-stage mixed-methods approach that evolved.

Generally, two research approaches are often employed by social science research studies, including information systems (IS), namely, quantitative and qualitative. Typically, researchers choose one or both of these two approaches (also known as mixed methods) depending on the problem definition (Punch, 2013). Although research studies can be generally classified as having a more qualitative or quantitative focus in nature, the distinction between the two methods has become less clear. It can usually be more accurately described as representing different ends on a continuum (Creswell & Creswell, 2017). This study adopted a mixed-methods approach because it is a suitable fit within the realism paradigm and provides the depth dictated by the nature of the research problem. This approach assisted in attaining a better understanding of the research problem and leverage the most appropriate tools for the research questions. In addition, using a mixed-methods approach provided an opportunity to minimize flaws associated with using qualitative methods (e.g., lack of generalizability) and quantitative methods (e.g., lack of context understanding) individually, as embracing a blend of qualitative and quantitative approaches will draw from the strengths and mitigate the weaknesses of both.

Similarly, Charles and Tashakkori (2009) suggest that linkages between qualitative and quantitative methods will reduce bias in the results and mutually strengthen the findings from both approaches. The mixed-methods approach was essential in understanding the evaluation of IT governance processes, customized IT governance frameworks, and the factors impacting the adoption of information systems-related innovation in the financial sector environment. Published mixed-methods studies (De Haes & Van Grembergen, 2006; Hiererra, 2012; McEvoy & Richards, 2006; McGuire, 2016) suggest that social researchers use mixed-methods approaches for one or more of the following purposes: providing a complete picture, improving accuracy, compensating for strengths and weaknesses, and, more importantly, developing robust analysis (Denscombe, 2014).

In the first research activity, a quantitative survey is used to developing an evaluation framework for IT governance in medium and large organizations. An online questionnaire was developed to gather respondents' perceptions of the importance of each of the 37 high-level IT processes from the COBIT framework. Given the findings from the previous research activities, the second research activity was designed to evaluate IT governance processes using the adapted framework by applying a case study research in a medium and large organization in Morocco. The case study was selected for a number of reasons. (i) According to Hancock and Algozzine (2016), case study research emphasizes studies in natural settings. It allows for a greater understanding of the context in which a phenomenon exists by collecting rich data from which to conclude. IT governance is a phenomenon that occurs within the context of the organization and is the unit of analysis. (ii) Case studies allow the exploration of the individual participant's viewpoint and various groupings of participants (Cronin, 2014). The use of multiple sources of data from the perspective of various stakeholders was required to ensure an accurate evaluation of IT governance processes. (iii) Case study research is suitable for dynamic organizations investigating emergent and rapidly evolving phenomena. The examined company is considered a dynamic organization, with IT governance being an emergent and rapidly evolving phenomenon. (iv) Case studies can investigate and describe the processes and underlying meaning of current events by collecting and integrating quantitative survey data, facilitating a holistic understanding of the phenomenon being studied (Lewis, 2015). This research could have utilized a number of data collection techniques based on applied research methods, including interviews, survey questionnaires, and documents review (Hyett et al., 2014). Although the choice of using one or a combination of these techniques depends on the goal of the research activity, initial discussions with potential participants from the MENA Port organizations revealed that they opposed participating in interviews and would prefer to respond to anonymous questionnaires instead. As a result, the two research activities utilized questionnaires as a main data collection technique. In this research, it was applied to research activities 1 and 2 to analyze data obtained from the questionnaires. This mainly involved measures related to relative location, such as rankings, and those related to the center, such as means. Structural equation modeling is better known as a data analysis tool for testing and estimating causal relationships in quantitative research studies.

3.5 EXPLORING IT GOVERNANCE IN MENA MEDIUM AND LARGE ORGANIZATIONS

The authors have carefully identified 20 medium and large Port organizations in the MENA region (Morocco, Algeria, Tunisia, UAE, Saudi Arabia, and Kuwait) that are either fully or partially implemented COBIT. Since this research is exploratory, it used a qualitative research method using the 10 organizations as case studies to identify the best practices for implementing COBIT. The above approach enabled us to inquire and ask questions to capture the contributor's rich knowledge, experience, and views.

A semi-structured interview was conducted with the organization's IT service managers. Due to the business sensitivity of the information and comments, the real business names of the organizations can't be revealed. The ten organizations are referred to throughout the research discussion as cases A–E. Table 3.1 presents each organization in terms of nature, size, COBIT version, knowledge and experience of COBIT within the staff, the phase of COBIT implementation, and the motivation of COBIT implementation. COBIT professionals in these organizations were interviewed and questioned. The interview questionnaire comprises two main parts: part 1 contains questions about the organization's demographics (i.e., nature, size, the number of IT employees) and part 2 covers questions about the best practice in implementing each process of the COBIT. Although questions of part b are used as a guide throughout the interviews we did not depend on these questions, other developed inquiries and thoughts during the interviews were also discussed.

Subsequently, an online questionnaire was developed consisting of asking participants to rate the 37 high-level IT processes and 210 practices from the COBIT 5 framework according to their importance to the MENA Port organizations on a five-point Likert-type scale.

3.5.1 Data Collection

The targeted population included participants at different levels (c-suite, managers and senior IT, audit and business officers) who have knowledge of IT governance within the MENA Port organizations. Support was gained from the aforementioned groups to e-mail a personal invitation to potential participants containing a link to the online questionnaire and an information research sheet (for the right of usage ISACA, the questionnaire was not included).

The selected organizations invited to participate were advised that the origin and details of individual respondents would not be directly identified in any publication or other materials arising from the research. This was considered an important factor in the success of the research, as obtaining the CIOs' permission conveyed top management support for the study. The participating organization returned this information and the persons nominated by the organization were e-mailed a personal invitation outlining the research study, its motivation, and information about the interview process. Data collection processes were designed to evaluate the levels of IT governance processes in MENA Port organizations using COBIT 5. Initially, a semi-structured, open-ended data collection instrument and interview protocol were developed for this research activity. However, on contacting nominated respondents to arrange a suitable time and place for the interview, everyone indicated that they were, although keen to assist, uncomfortable with participating in a face-to-face interview and would prefer to respond to an anonymous questionnaire instead. As a result, the researcher decided to utilize an online questionnaire as a data collection instrument. A questionnaire was considered an appropriate method to collect perceptions of capability levels from respondents within the organizations. A principal

TABLE 3.2 Summary of Key Attributes of MENA Organizations Cases

ORGANIZATIONS	A	B	C	D	E	F	G	H	I	G
No. of employees	1125	3500	2400	7000	12000	8920	5245	2400	1700	22500
No. of IT employees	80	280	190	220	420	240	115	44	35	360
Government (Gov.)/ Multinational (multi.)	Gov.	Multi.	Gov.	Gov.	Gov.	Multi.	Multi.	Gov.	Gov.	Multi.
COBIT Version	V4	V5	V4	V4	v V5	V5	V5	V5	V4	V5
Knowledge of COBIT with IT staff/Familiarity	30%	70%	45%	25%	60%	50%	60%	70%	34%	65%
Certified COBIT staff	5%	15%	5%	0%	10%	15%	20%	5%	0%	10%
Stage of COBIT Implementation (Fully (F), largely (L), Partially (P))	P	L	F	P	L	L	F	P	P	L

advantage of this technique was the ability to cost-effectively collect data in a timely fashion from a significant number of organizations. The data were collected from more than one person for a given process, the between-person variation was typically within one level of maturity. Data are, of course, self-reported and subject to bias.

The data were collected from ten different companies that had established proper information governance through COBIT. Follow-up e-mails were sent to encourage non-respondents to participate and a total number of 160 responses were received. However, only 122 complete surveys were included as only completed surveys were considered in the final analysis. The response rate at 80 valid responses was 66%, which is considered above average for academic research and representative of the whole population (Baruch & Holtom, 2008). The release of COBIT 5 in April 2012, shortly before starting data collection, might explain the good response rate for this research, suggesting it was recognized as credible and relevant to the public sector. The demographic data derived from the first section of the questionnaire comprised an organizational type, respondent's position level, familiarity with IT processes, and familiarity with the organization's business goals. This provides a context for the data obtained from the second section of the questionnaire, rating the high-level COBIT IT processes. Table 3.2 shows the summary of key attributes of medium and large organizations cases.

3.5.2 Data Analysis

This research aims to present a conceptual framework that shows how information governance through COBIT 5 arises in organizations. The data were collected using a Likert scale and questionnaires. The items for each construct are adopted from previous studies and each question relates to an item (Bergner et al., 2013; Pat & Piattini, 2011). To estimate the extent of non-respondent bias, it was not possible to compare respondents' with non-respondents' answers. This is because the survey was anonymous and we had access only to names and e-mail addresses of participants, unlinked to their responses, and not those who chose not to participate. As a result, a non-response bias test was undertaken by comparing early respondents with late respondents instead (Lewis-Beck et al., 2003).

Overall, given the preliminary nature of this study, the non-response bias test, and response rates reported in information systems (IS) research, the 80 responses can be considered a reasonable sample.

3.6 Results

To produce a ranked list of high-level IT processes, ratings from the second section of the questionnaire were analyzed to provide a total score, average, and standard deviation for each of the 37 high-level IT processes. Data were sorted in descending order based on the mean values. In the case of matching means, IT processes were then sorted in descending order based on the total values. The ranked list is presented in Table 3.3.

TABLE 3.3 Rating for COBIT 5 High-Level IT Processes as Perceived by MENA Port Organizations

DOMAIN	PROCESS ID	PROCESS	MEAN	T STAT	P
Evaluate, Direct and Monitor	EDM01	Ensure Governance Framework Setting and Maintenance	4.86	1.05	0.23
Evaluate, Direct and Monitor	EDM02	Ensure Benefits Delivery	5.13	1.76	0.09
Evaluate, Direct and Monitor	EDM03	Ensure Risk Optimization	5.21	0.85	0.19
Evaluate, Direct and Monitor	EDM04	Ensure Resource Optimization	4.91	0.52	0.37
Evaluate, Direct and Monitor	EDM05	Ensure Stakeholder Transparency	4.39	0.61	0.37
Align, Plan and Organize	APO01	Manage the IT Management Framework	4.61	2.21	0.09
Align, Plan and Organize	APO02	Manage Strategy	4.96	0.87	0.22
Align, Plan and Organize	APO03	Manage Enterprise Architecture	4.40	0.39	0.29
Align, Plan and Organize	APO04	Manage Innovation	3.89	1.92	0.02
Align, Plan and Organize	APO05	Manage Portfolio	4.13	1.35	0.08

(Continued)

TABLE 3.3   (Continued)

DOMAIN	PROCESS ID	PROCESS	MEAN	T STAT	P
Align, Plan and Organize	APO06	Manage Budget and Costs	4.84	1.35	0.09
Align, Plan and Organize	APO07	Manage Human Resources	4.17	2.07	0.08
Align, Plan and Organize	APO08	Manage Relationships	3.78	0.65	0.41
Align, Plan and Organize	APO09	Manage Service Agreements	3.84	0.24	0.47
Align, Plan and Organize	APO10	Manage Suppliers	3.92	1.54	0.06
Align, Plan and Organize	APO11	Manage Quality	4.54	0.96	0.21
Align, Plan and Organize	APO12	Manage Risk	5.02	1.86	0.05
Align, Plan and Organize	APO13	Manage Security	5.25	1.15	0.13
Build, Acquire and Implement	BAI01	Manage Programs and Projects	4.34	0.85	0.37
Build, Acquire and Implement	BAI02	Manage Requirements Definition	3.91	1.03	0.15
Build, Acquire and Implement	BAI03	Manage Solutions Identification and Build	4.05	1.86	0.12
Build, Acquire and Implement	BAI04	Manage Availability and Capacity	4.51	1.13	0.05
Build, Acquire and Implement	BAI05	Manage Organizational Change Enablement	4.05	1.94	0.08
Build, Acquire and Implement	BAI06	Manage Changes	4.85	0.85	0.27
Build, Acquire and Implement	BAI07	Manage Change Acceptance and Transitioning	4.03	0.78	0.31
Build, Acquire and Implement	BAI08	Manage Knowledge	3.98	1.05	0.19
Build, Acquire and Implement	BAI09	Manage Assets	4.63	1.56	0.31

DOMAIN	PROCESS ID	PROCESS	MEAN	T STAT	P
Build, Acquire and Implement	BAI10	Manage Configuration	4.05	0.87	0.19
Deliver, Service and Support	DSS01	Manage Operations	4.65	0.65	0.27
Deliver, Service and Support	DSS02	Manage Service Requests and Incidents	5.12	1.04	0.06
Deliver, Service and Support	DSS03	Manage Problems	4.86	1.12	0.09
Deliver, Service and Support	DSS04	Manage Continuity	5.12	1.31	0.08
Deliver, Service and Support	DSS05	Manage Security Services	5.26	0.76	0.06
Deliver, Service and Support	DSS06	Manage Business Process Controls	4.03	1.76	0.17
Monitor, Evaluate, and Assess	MEA01	Monitor, Evaluate, and Assess Performance and Conformance	4.65	0.47	0.37
Monitor, Evaluate, and Assess	MEA02	Monitor, Evaluate, and Assess the System of Internal Control	4.37	0.83	0.21
Monitor, Evaluate, and Assess	MEA03	Monitor, Evaluate, and Assess Compliance with External Requirements	4.56	0.56	0.37

As part of the statistical analysis employed by this research, the ratings were subjected to the paired sample Student's t-test to identify significant differences between high-level IT processes. The test commenced from the top of the list, the highest-ranked high-level IT processes at $P < .05$ and 56 degrees of freedom and continued until a group or tier was identified through detecting a significant difference. The test then recommenced using the first high-level IT processes in the next grouping as the point of comparison until the list of 37 high-level IT processes were exhausted, and five groupings, or tiers, were identified.

Five groups of high-level IT processes were identified through the statistical analysis of the perceived ratings, presenting several points at which an adapted ITG framework could be formed. Previous research by Guldentops (2002) identified a list of 15 important control objectives, while the study by Huissoud (2005) classified 16 as being most important. The Australian study by Warland and Ridley (2005) derived an abbreviated list of 17 important control objectives, as perceived by the Tasmanian public sector. Based on these sources, it was proposed that the initial ITG framework for the MENA port organizations would be created using the first two tiers to give a size of 16 high-level IT processes as displayed in Table 3.4.

The high-level IT processes identified as being most important were drawn from four of the five broad domains in the COBIT 5 framework, namely:

TABLE 3.4   Top High-Level IT Processes for MENA Port Organizations

DOMAIN	PROCESS ID	PROCESS
Deliver, Service, and Support	DSS05	Manage Security Services
Deliver, Service, and Support	DSS02	Manage Service Requests and Incidents
Align, Plan and Organize	APO13	Manage Security
Evaluate, Direct and Monitor	EDM03	Ensure Risk Optimization
Evaluate, Direct and Monitor	EDM02	Ensure Benefits Delivery
Deliver, Service and Support	DSS04	Manage Continuity
Align, Plan and Organize	APO12	Manage Risk
Align, Plan and Organize	APO02	Manage Strategy
Evaluate, Direct and Monitor	EDM04	Ensure Resource Optimization
Evaluate, Direct and Monitor	EDM01	Ensure Governance Framework Setting and Maintenance
Deliver, Service and Support	DSS03	Manage Problems
Build, Acquire, and Implement	BAI06	Manage Changes
Align, Plan and Organize	APO06	Manage Budget and Costs
Deliver, Service and Support	DSS01	Manage Operations
Monitor, Evaluate and Assess	MEA01	Monitor, Evaluate, and Assess Performance and Conformance
Build, Acquire and Implement	BAI09	Manage Assets

- Evaluate, Direct, and Monitor (EDM);
- Align, Plan and Organize (APO);
- Build, Acquire and Implement (BAI);
- Deliver, Service and Support (DSS);
- Monitor, Evaluate and Assess (MEA).

With the Monitoring domain seen as irrelevant and more focus given to the APO and DSS domains. This indicates a focus on early-cycle activities of IT governance instead of those concentrating on monitoring and evaluating. The abbreviated list initially derived contained 15 high-level IT processes. The high-level IT process is most important, DSS05 Manage Security Services, was the same as that identified by prior national and international studies.

The high-level IT processes common to at least four of the previous studies investigated as being important in other contexts and the initial list derived from this study were as follows:

- Manage Security Services;
- Manage Service Requests and Incidents;
- Manage Security;
- Ensure Risk Optimization;
- Ensure Benefits Delivery;
- Manage Continuity;

- Manage Risk;
- Manage Strategy;
- Ensure Resource Optimization;
- Ensure Governance Framework Setting and Maintenance;
- Manage Problems;
- Manage Changes;
- Manage Budget and Costs;
- Manage Operations;
- Monitor, Evaluate and Assess Performance and Conformance;
- Manage Assets.

Given the similarities found between these research results and previous studies, the consistencies between the results supported the suggestion that the importance of some high-level IT processes is independent of geographical context. Given the difference in the organizational setting between previous studies examined, the results also demonstrated clear evidence that the importance of some high-level IT processes is also independent of the organizational type. As a result, this chapter concludes that an adapted ITGEF within the Australian financial sector can be derived from the COBIT framework based on the ten high-level IT processes identified to be both enduring and relevant across geographical and organizational contexts as presented in Table 3.4.

3.7 CASE STUDY

In order to gain a detailed understanding of the process for evaluating IT governance using the adapted IT Governance Framework based on the COBIT model, previously unexplored in the MENA port organizations, exploratory case study research was deemed appropriate.

Specifically, this research activity applied case study research considering that 'where only limited theoretical knowledge exists on a particular phenomenon, an inductive research strategy can be a valuable starting point' (Siggelkow, 2007). An inductive, case study strategy was adopted as it facilitates the identification of practical insights into IT governance evaluation frameworks. It also allows 'replication logic', whereby multiple cases are treated as a series of experiments, with each case serving to confirm, or not, the inferences drawn from previous cases. This approach also matches the research's paradigm (i.e., realism) and adds credibility to the study (Tsang & Kwan, 1999). In addition, the use of case study research permits a flexible and thorough approach by employing a variety of data sources and research methods (Denscombe, 2014). Table 3.5 presented the selected top high-level IT processes for MENA port organizations.

In the evaluation of IT governance using the COBIT framework, organizations make assertions about how these IT governance processes are met. This is verified by internal or external auditors or by conducting self-assessments. The COBIT framework utilizes capability levels to assess IT processes on a scale from 0 (non-existent) to 5 (optimized).

TABLE 3.5   Top High-Level IT Processes for MENA Port Organizations

DOMAIN	PROCESS ID	PROCESS	PRACTICE ID	PRACTICE NAME
Evaluate, Direct and Monitor	EDM01	Ensure Governance Framework Setting and Maintenance	EDM01.01	Evaluate the governance system.
			EDM01.02	Direct the governance system.
			EDM01.03	Monitor the governance system.
			DSS02.02	Record, classify and prioritize requests and incidents.
			DSS02.03	Verify, approve and fulfill service requests.
			DSS02.04	Investigate, diagnose and allocate incidents.
			DSS02.05	Resolve and recover from incidents.
			DSS02.06	Close service requests and incidents.
Evaluate, Direct and Monitor	EDM02	Ensure Benefits Delivery	EDM02.01	Evaluate value optimization.
			EDM02.02	Direct value optimization.
			EDM02.03	Monitor value optimization.
Evaluate, Direct and Monitor	EDM03	Ensure Risk Optimization	EDM03.01	Evaluate risk management.
			EDM03.02	Direct risk management.
			EDM03.03	Monitor risk management.
Evaluate, Direct and Monitor	EDM04	Ensure Resource Optimization	EDM04.01	Evaluate resource management.
			EDM04.02	Direct resource management.
			EDM04.03	Monitor resource management.

DOMAIN	PROCESS ID	PROCESS	PRACTICE ID	PRACTICE NAME
			APO02.01	Understand enterprise direction.
			APO02.02	Assess the current environment, capabilities, and performance.
			APO02.03	Define the target IT capabilities.
			APO02.04	Conduct a gap analysis.
			APO02.05	Define the strategic plan and roadmap.
			APO02.06	Communicate the IT strategy and direction.
			APO02.01	Understand enterprise direction.
Align, Plan and Organize	APO02	Manage Strategy	APO02.02	Assess the current environment, capabilities, and performance.
			APO02.03	Define the target IT capabilities.
			APO02.04	Conduct a gap analysis.
			APO02.05	Define the strategic plan and roadmap.
			APO02.06	Communicate the IT strategy and direction.
			APO06.01	Manage finance and accounting.
			APO06.02	Prioritize resource allocation.
Align, Plan and Organize	APO06	Manage Budget and Costs	APO06.03	Create and maintain budgets.
			APO06.04	Model and allocate costs.
			APO06.05	Manage costs.
			APO12.01	Collect data.

(Continued)

TABLE 3.5   (Continued)

DOMAIN	PROCESS ID	PROCESS	PRACTICE ID	PRACTICE NAME
			APO12.02	Analyze risk.
			APO12.03	Maintain a risk profile.
			APO12.04	Articulate risk.
Align, Plan and Organize	APO12	Manage Risk	APO12.05	Define a risk management action portfolio.
			APO12.06	Respond to risk.
			APO13.01	Establish and maintain an ISMS.
Align, Plan and Organize	APO13	Manage Security	APO13.02	Define and manage an information security risk treatment plan.
			APO13.03	Monitor and review the ISMS.
			BAI06.01	Evaluate, prioritize and authorize change requests.
Build, Acquire and Implement	BAI06	Manage Changes	BAI06.02	Manage emergency changes.
			BAI06.03	Track and report change status.
			BAI06.04	Close and document the changes.
			BAI09.01	Identify and record current assets.
			BAI09.02	Manage critical assets.
Build, Acquire and Implement	BAI09	Manage Assets	BAI09.03	Manage the asset lifecycle.
			BAI09.04	Optimize asset costs.
			BAI09.05	Manage licenses.
			DSS01.01	Perform operational procedures.
Deliver, Service and Support	DSS01	Manage Operations	DSS01.02	Manage outsourced IT services.

DOMAIN	PROCESS ID	PROCESS	PRACTICE ID	PRACTICE NAME
			DSS01.03	Monitor IT infrastructure.
			DSS01.04	Manage the environment.
			DSS01.05	Manage facilities.
				Define incident and service request classification schemes.
Deliver, Service and Support	DSS02	Manage Service Requests and Incidents	DSS02.01	Define incident and service request classification schemes.
				Define incident and service request classification schemes.
				Define incident and service request classification schemes.
				Define incident and service request classification schemes.
				Define incident and service request classification schemes.
			DSS03.01	Identify and classify problems.
			DSS03.02	Investigate and diagnose problems.
			DSS03.03	Raise known errors.
Deliver, Service and Support	DSS03	Manage Problems	DSS03.04	Resolve and close problems.

(Continued)

TABLE 3.5   (Continued)

DOMAIN	PROCESS ID	PROCESS	PRACTICE ID	PRACTICE NAME
			DSS03.05	Perform proactive problem management.
			DSS04.01	Define the business continuity policy, objectives, and scope.
			DSS04.02	Maintain a continuity strategy.
			DSS04.03	Develop and implement a business continuity response.
			DSS04.04	Exercise, test, and review the BCP.
Deliver, Service and Support	DSS04	Manage Continuity	DSS04.05	Review, maintain and improve the continuity plan.
			DSS04.06	Conduct continuity plan training.
			DSS04.07	Manage backup arrangements.
			DSS04.08	Conduct post-resumption review.
			DSS05.01	Protect against malware.
			DSS05.02	Manage network and connectivity security.
			DSS05.03	Manage endpoint security.
			DSS05.04	Manage user identity and logical access.
Deliver, Service and Support	DSS05	Manage Security Services	DSS05.05	Manage physical access to IT assets.
			DSS05.06	Manage sensitive documents and output devices.

DOMAIN	PROCESS ID	PROCESS	PRACTICE ID	PRACTICE NAME
			DSS05.07	Monitor the infrastructure for security-related events.
			MEA01.01	Establish a monitoring approach.
Monitor, Evaluate, and Assess	MEA01	Monitor, Evaluate, and Assess Performance and Conformance	MEA01.02	Set performance and conformance targets.
			MEA01.03	Collect and process performance and conformance data.
			MEA01.04	Analyze and report performance.
			MEA01.05	Ensure the implementation of corrective actions.

Case selection involved three key decisions. First, a single sector was chosen to eliminate possible confounds that might arise from investigating multiple sectors. The research involved a large Port agency in Morocco, which were selected for a number of reasons:

The agency is highly dependent on IT to support its core functions. IT governance is likely to be a significant concern to these organizations and the study, therefore, more relevant. The agency is generally more supportive of research studies and consequently likely to assist in this study.

3.7.1 Data Collection

A case study was conducted as a pilot project to identify relevant ITG practices in the organization. The capability maturity framework is implemented at a leading port sector organization in Morocco. The organization manages more than 30 ports and sites with more than 12,000 employees. The Information System department has 40 employees with different profiles. The purpose is to study IT governance practices. Figure 3.3 shows the ITG framework architecture proposed for eventual implementation in the organization.

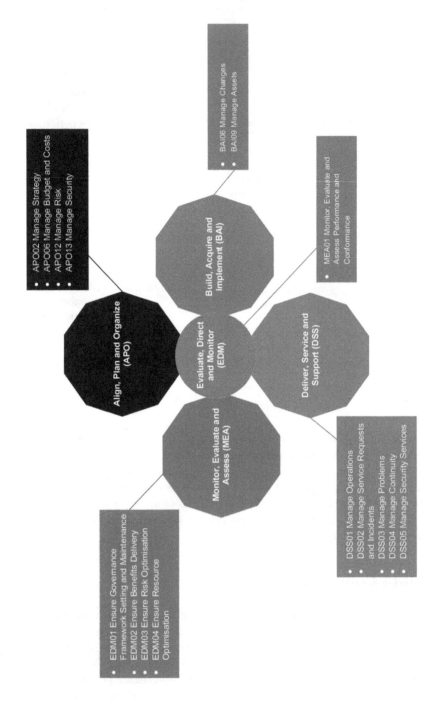

FIGURE 3.3   The resultant conceptual framework for IT governance.

The respondents were asked to self-evaluate IT governance processes in their organizations based on the ITG framework, which contained 16 high-level IT processes. This approach was consistent with that of the original study (Gerke & Ridley, 2009). The guidelines provided through the 'Process Assessment Model (PAM): Using COBIT 5' contained nine process capability levels to evaluate the IT governance processes of an organization as described. Taking one IT process at a time, the questionnaire introduces the processing purpose and key practices from the PAM so that respondents could simply choose the process capability level for each of the nine attributes for that process.

However, face-to-face interviews have been scheduled with IT staff to assess IT governance within the organization. For each organization, a maximum of 100 data points was collected, representing achievement levels for ten attributes (nine process attributes + level zero criteria question), for the 16 processes. When calculating the overall capability level for one process, the highest full or medium and large achievement level of the nine attributes associated with that process was taken. Similarly, a simple average of responses was calculated when more than one score was given. The capability levels for the 16 most critical IT processes reported a mean for each process.

This research activity also prepared and analyzed a list of possible process work products (WP) according to the evaluated IT processes (ISACA, 2013). The WPs included strategic and operational plans, structures, processes, policies, frameworks, service level agreements, performance reports, and so forth. The nominated WPs were included in the data collection instrument to elicit well-informed responses from respondents. For instance, in the process, APO02 Manage Strategy, respondents were instructed to consider a strategic IT plan as a work product of that process if it was the organization's practice. In other words, this allowed the triangulation of different data sources, thus adding to the credibility of the evaluated IT governance processes. The researcher could not validate the responses by inspection of each IT process WP listed or through other techniques. Therefore, based on the researcher's experience in the field, only two WPs were chosen and included in the questionnaire for each IT process to indicate capability levels. The number of level 0 and level 1 responses received indicates the respondents seemed candid in the information they provided.

In the last section of the questionnaire, respondents were asked to rate the importance of 17 enterprise goals and 17 IT-related goals of IT governance of their respective organizations. This will assist in building a mapping between enterprise goals, IT-related goals, and IT governance processes similar to the goals cascade established by the COBIT 5 framework (ISACA, 2012b).

Before distributing the final version of the self-evaluation instrument, a web-based pilot was created. This pilot was posted online and two senior IT auditors were asked to complete it for a real-life situation. Based on their comments and suggestions, the instrument was made more user-friendly and accessible. Data collection for this research activity was performed in the period January–March 2018.

After data collection, a draft case report for each organization was sent back to respondents within that organization for review and confirmation.

The results for the position level of the respondents are presented in Table 3.6. From the 20 responses received, 15% (3 respondents) specified executive officer, 20% (4 respondents) specified officer, 30% (6 respondents) specified IT manager, 15% (3 respondents) specified Senior, and 20% (4 respondents) specified Auditor.

TABLE 3.6   Position Level of Respondents within the Public Sector

Executive Officer	3	15%
Officer	4	20%
IT Manager	6	30%
Senior Manager	3	15%
Auditor	4	20%

3.7.2 Data Analysis

The data collected from the questionnaire were analyzed using Microsoft Excel to establish the capability level of selected IT governance processes. MS Excel was selected as an exploratory data analysis tool because of the combination of its simplicity and its capability to calculate and present the results in tables and graphs. Specifically, respondents' scores (from 'not achieved' to 'fully achieved') for each attribute description of the evaluated IT process were incorporated into an Excel worksheet (see Table 3.7 as an example). This was carried out for each capability level's key practices and statements (from 0 to 5). Eventually, the capability level of each IT process was obtained. This was carried out for all ten IT processes in each studied organization.

All data collected analyzed each case study individually, across the case studies, and collectively for all case studies combined. The evaluation of the IT governance processes from this analysis is discussed further in the following section.

This study opted to distinguish between the utilization of maturity and capability levels as these terms were found to be used loosely in previous studies. Often considered similar concepts, *organizational maturity* applies to an organization's overall maturity and is concerned with evaluating a set of process areas. In contrast, process capability relates to evaluating a set of sub-processes and generic practices for a process area that can improve the organization's processes associated with that area (Huang & Han, 2006). A maturity level results from aggregating the capability levels of all capability areas and demonstrates the extent to which an organization has developed its capabilities (Forstner et al., 2014).

3.7.3 Assessing Capability Maturity

The analysis of the average maturity level across the studied organization involved calculating the average of each IT process capability level across these organizations. The averages provided the range within which the maturity levels of all assessed IT processes were calculated. The overall capability ratings of each IT process as evaluated by the respondents are presented in Table 3.8. The table also displays the means for the individual processes of each organization as well as the overall mean for each IT process.

The organization's analysis of the organization's maturity levels was carried out using the obtained capability level for each IT process from each organization's point of view. Different from the previous one, the capability levels of IT processes were compared at the level of individual organizations. Such comparisons provided the relative evaluation of the processes in each organization and led to the individual organizations' maturity levels for the adapted ITG framework based on the COBIT 5.

TABLE 3.7 Example of Detailed IT Governance Process Capability Evaluation

PROCESS NAME	LEVEL 0	LEVEL 1	LEVEL 2		LEVEL 3		LEVEL 4		LEVEL 5	
DSS05	Y/N	PA1.1	PA2.1	PA2.2	PA3.1	PA3.2	PA4.1	PA4.2	PA5.1	PA5.2
Rating by criteria	Y	F	F	L	P	N				
Capability level achieved			2							

Rating scale:

N: Not Achieved (0–15%)	P: Partially Achieved (15% – 50%)	L: Medium and largely Achieved (50% – 85%)	F: Fully Achieved (85% – 100%)

TABLE 3.8 Summary of capability levels for the ten most important IT processes (in order of priority) for Moroccan organization

DOMAIN	PROCESS ID	PROCESS	MEAN	CAPABILITY MATURITY
Deliver, Service and Support	DSS05	Manage Security Services	2.2	2
Deliver, Service and Support	DSS02	Manage Service Requests and Incidents	3.8	4
Align, Plan and Organize	APO13	Manage Security	2.7	3
Evaluate, Direct and Monitor	EDM03	Ensure Risk Optimization	1.7	2
Evaluate, Direct and Monitor	EDM02	Ensure Benefits Delivery	1.5	1
Deliver, Service and Support	DSS04	Manage Continuity	1.7	2
Align, Plan and Organize	APO12	Manage Risk	2.7	3
Align, Plan and Organize	APO02	Manage Strategy	1.5	1
Evaluate, Direct and Monitor	EDM04	Ensure Resource Optimization	2.0	2
Evaluate, Direct and Monitor	EDM01	Ensure Governance Framework Setting and Maintenance	1.4	1
Deliver, Service and Support	DSS03	Manage Problems	2.3	2
Build, Acquire and Implement	BAI06	Manage Changes	2.0	2

(Continued)

TABLE 3.8   (Continued)

DOMAIN	PROCESS ID	PROCESS	MEAN	CAPABILITY MATURITY
Align, Plan and Organize	APO06	Manage Budget and Costs	2.0	2
Deliver, Service and Support	DSS01	Manage Operations	2.1	2
Monitor, Evaluate, and Assess	MEA01	Monitor, Evaluate, and Assess Performance and Conformance	1.8	2
Build, Acquire and Implement	BAI09	Manage Assets	2.6	3
Organizational maturity level			**2.2**	**2**

3.7.4 Capability Level Analysis

Figure 3.4 provides a box plot of the average capability level by the IT process. The mean capability level for all ten COBIT 5 processes is at level 2 (managed process) but with a significant variation (SD = 0.89), strikingly clear from the whiskers in the box plots. There are outliers at the lowest and highest levels of capability for each of these processes. As shown in Figure 3.4 there are clear differences between the 16 most important processes. The average level of process capability scores is relatively low within the organization, with most processes having a mean capability level score between 1 (19%) and 2 (56%) on a scale from 0 to 5. Only 19% of the processes had a mean capability level of 3, while just 6% had a mean capability level of 4.

3.7.5 Maturity Level Analysis

From a domain perspective, the Deliver, Service and Support (DSS) and Build, Align, Plan and Organize (APO) domains are perceived to have higher capability levels than the other three domains. Most of the processes in these domains are in the top quartile (DSS02 Manage Service Requests and Incidents), (APO13 Manage Security), (APO12 Manage risk), (BAI09 Manage Assets), (DSS03 Manage Problems), (DSS05 Manage Security services), (DSS01 Manage Operations), (APO06 Manage Budget and Costs), except (DSS04 Manage Continuity processes) and (APO02 Manage Strategy) from those two domains were in the lowest quartile of processes. An even more distinct result applies to the Evaluate, Direct, and Monitor (EDM) domain, with four processes (EDM01 Ensure Governance Framework Setting and Maintenance (EDM02 Ensure Benefits Delivery), (EDM03 Ensure Risk Optimization), and (EDM04 Ensure Resource Optimization) being in the lowest quartile of capability. The more prosaic process has a relatively higher level of capability (EDM04 Ensure Resource Optimization). The Build, Acquire and Implement

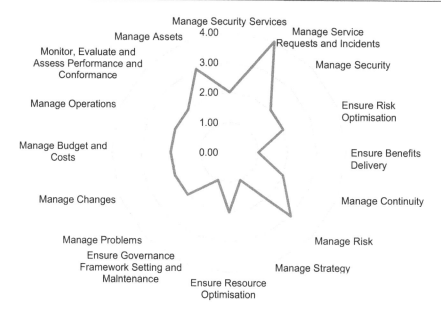

FIGURE 3.4   Range and distribution of capability level scores for the IT processes in the organization.

(BAI) domain was represented by two processes (BAI06 Manage Change) and (BAI09 Manage Asset), which were in the lowest quartile of processes. The domain Monitor, Evaluate and Assess (MEA) was only represented by one process (MEA01 Monitor, Evaluate and Assess Performance and Conformance), which was in the top quartile of processes. considered of high importance by the organization.

3.7.6 Goals Cascade

The COBIT goals cascade mechanism translates and links stakeholders' needs into specific enterprise goals, IT-related goals, and COBIT IT processes. The questionnaire asked respondents to rate the importance for each of the 17 enterprise goals and 17 IT-related goals from the COBIT 5 framework according to their importance to the organization a five-point Likert-type scale. The focus of this undertaking is not on enterprise goals or IT-related goals themselves, but rather to confirm, through the COBIT 5 goals cascade the importance of the adapted ITG framework for the MENA port organizations. The results were analyzed to produce a ranked list of enterprise goals and IT-related goals and provide a total score and average for each enterprise's goals and IT-related goals. The enterprise goals and IT-related goals ranked list are presented in Tables 3.9 and Table 3.10, respectively.

As part of the statistical analysis employed by this research activity, the ratings were subjected to the paired sample Student's *t*-test to identify significant differences between enterprise and IT-related goals. The test commenced from the top of the list, the

TABLE 3.9   Rating for Enterprise Goals as Perceived by the Organization

BALANCED SCORECARD	ENTERPRISE BUSINESS GOAL	MEAN
	1. Stakeholder value of business investments	4.48
	2. Portfolio of competitive products and services	3.96
Financial	3. Managed business risk (safeguarding of assets)	4.40
	4. Compliance with external laws and regulations	4.32
	5. Financial transparency	4.16
	6. Customer-oriented service culture	4.64
	7. Business service continuity and availability	4.32
Customer	8. Agile responses to a changing business environment	4.28
	9. nformation-based strategic decision making	4.16
	10. Optimization of service delivery costs	4.40
	11. Optimization of business process functionality	4.28
	12. Optimization of business process costs	4.36
Internal	13. Managed business change programs	3.96
	14. Operational and staff productivity	4.28
	15. Compliance with internal policies	4.20
	16. Skilled and motivated people	4.40
Learning	17. Product and business innovation culture	4.32

TABLE 3.10   Rating for IT-Related Goals as Perceived by the Organization

PROCESS ID	IT-RELATED GOALS	MEAN
ITRG 01	Alignment of IT and business strategy	4.60
ITRG 02	IT compliance and support for business compliance with external laws and regulations	4.40
ITRG 03	The commitment of executive management for making IT-related decisions	4.68
ITRG 04	Managed IT-related business risk	4.52
ITRG 05	Realized benefits from IT-enabled investments and services portfolio	4.56
ITRG 06	Transparency of IT costs, benefits, and risk	4.28
ITRG 07	Delivery of IT services in line with business requirements	4.44
ITRG 08	Adequate use of applications, information and technology solutions	4.16
ITRG 09	IT agility	4.32
ITRG 10	Security of information, processing infrastructure, and applications	4.40
ITRG 11	Optimization of IT assets, resources, and capabilities	4.36
ITRG 12	Enablement and support of business processes by integrating applications and technology into business processes	4.16
ITRG 13	Delivery of programs delivering benefits, on time, on budget, and meeting requirements and quality standards	4.44

PROCESS ID	IT-RELATED GOALS	MEAN
ITRG 14	Availability of reliable and useful information for decision making	4.32
ITRG 15	IT compliance with internal policies	4.00
ITRG 16	Competent and motivated business and IT personnel	4.32
ITRG 17	Knowledge, expertise, and initiatives for business innovation	4.36

highest-ranked enterprise goal and the highest-ranked IT-related goal both at $p < .05$ and 24 degrees of freedom and continued until a group, or tier, was identified through detecting a significant difference. The test then recommenced using the first goal in the next grouping as the point of comparison until the list of 17 business enterprises goals, and 17 IT-related goals were exhausted and three groupings, or tiers, were identified for each category.

Three groups of enterprise and IT-related goals were identified through the statistical analysis of the perceived ratings, presenting several points at which a priority list for each category could be formed. However, as no previous research could be found in the literature to compare against, and considering that the second tier in both lists contained at least 14 out of 17 goals, it was proposed that the perceived priority list of enterprise and IT-related goals for the MENA port organizations consist of those controls in the first tier only. The priority list for the enterprise goals was made of six goals, whereas the same list for IT-related goals consisted of four.

The purpose of the mapping table in Table 3.10 is to demonstrate how enterprise goals are supported, or translate into, IT-related goals. Subsequently, Table 3.11 contains the mapping table between the IT-related goals and how these are supported by IT processes, as part of the goals cascade (ISACA, 2012). The results revealed that the required IT processes, a total of 28 IT processes, to support the perceived important IT-related goals for the MENA port organizations include the entire ITG framework total of 16 IT processes, as perceived by the same sector. This validates the conceptual model for IT governance evaluation in organizations. This also allowed the triangulation of different data sources, thus adding to the credibility of the adapted ITG framework.

3.7.7 Discussion

The majority of recent IT governance research on the international scale has focused on accountability, decision-making requirements, structures and mechanisms, and factors reflecting localized contexts for adoption and implementation. However, a significant yet understudied aspect of IT governance is the capability of organizations to meet the ever-increasing resources and budget challenges by employing effective IT processes. Measuring IT process capability is considered important to ensure successful governance over IT. Nonetheless, very little empirical data on the level of process capabilities in the medium and large organizations context exists. To overcome this clear gap in the research literature, this research activity endeavored to seek support for and refine the ITG framework adapted from the COBIT model within selected state organizations and compare the evaluation results with those obtained by other studies.

TABLE 3.11 Mapping Enterprise Goals to IT-Related Goals

BUSINESS GOALS

IT GOALS	CUSTOMER-ORIENTED SERVICE CULTURE	STAKEHOLDER VALUE OF BUSINESS INVESTMENTS	MANAGED BUSINESS RISK (SAFEGUARDING OF ASSETS)	OPTIMIZATION OF SERVICE DELIVERY COSTS	SKILLED AND MOTIVATED PEOPLE	OPTIMIZATION OF BUSINESS PROCESS COSTS	COMPLIANCE WITH EXTERNAL LAWS AND REGULATIONS	BUSINESS SERVICE CONTINUITY AND AVAILABILITY	PRODUCT AND BUSINESS INNOVATION CULTURE	AGILE RESPONSES TO A CHANGING BUSINESS ENVIRONMENT	OPTIMIZATION OF BUSINESS PROCESS FUNCTIONALITY	OPERATIONAL AND STAFF PRODUCTIVITY	COMPLIANCE WITH INTERNAL POLICIES	FINANCIAL TRANSPARENCY	INFORMATION-BASED STRATEGIC DECISION MAKING	PORTFOLIO OF COMPETITIVE PRODUCTS AND SERVICES	MANAGED BUSINESS CHANGE PROGRAMS
The commitment of executive management for making IT-related decisions																	
Alignment of IT and business strategy																	
Realized benefits from IT-enabled investments and services portfolio																	
Managed IT-related business risk																	
Delivery of IT services in line with business requirements																	
Delivery of programs delivering benefits, on time, on budget, and meeting requirements and quality standards																	
IT compliance and support for business compliance with external laws and regulations																	

Legend: Most pertinent / Pertinent

Security of information, processing infrastructure, and applications

Optimization of IT assets, resources, and capabilities

Knowledge, expertise, and initiatives for business innovation

IT agility

Availability of reliable and useful information for decision making

Competent and motivated business and IT personnel

Transparency of IT costs, benefits and risk

Adequate use of applications, information, and technology solutions

Enablement and support of business processes by integrating applications and technology into business processes

IT compliance with internal policies

Least Pertinent

The adapted ITG framework contains six IT processes from COBIT used by previous studies to evaluate IT processes. These were as follows:

- DSS05 Manage Security Services;
- APO13 Manage Security;
- EDM03 Ensure Risk Optimization;
- EDM02 Ensure Benefits Delivery
- DSS02 Manage Service Requests and Incidents;
- DSS04 Manage Continuity.

The remaining ten IT processes:

- DSS04 Manage Continuity;
- APO12 Manage Risk;
- APO02 Manage Strategy;
- EDM04 Ensure Resource Optimization;
- EDM01 Ensure Governance Framework Setting and Maintenance;
- DSS03 Manage Problems;
- BAI06 Manage Changes;
- APO06 Manage Budget and Costs;
- DSS01 Manage Operations;
- MEA01 Monitor, Evaluate and Assess Performance and Conformance;
- BAI09 Manage Assets.

The proposed framework was considered appropriate by many methods, including triangulation and the perceived relevance of the evaluation program. The trial of the ITG framework showed that it contained few evaluation measures that were not relevant to other jurisdictions in MENA or international organizations, which suggests that its development was appropriate. The results of this study show that

- The overall level of process capability in the MENA port organizations is relatively modest;
- Undertaking IT governance evaluation based on COBIT 5 is significantly more rigorous than earlier versions of the framework;
- There is considerable inter-process variability in capability levels as some processes that were expected to have a relatively high capability level were relatively underdeveloped;
- There is a similar inter-organizational variation in process capability and maturity level within the MENA port organizations, which appears to be linked to the organizational size.

The results demonstrated that medium and larger organizations tend to have higher IT governance maturity than smaller organizations. Therefore, when studying organizations with approximately 10,000 employees, IT governance maturity levels of between 2.5 and 3 should be expected. Insufficient literature exists to determine whether that maturity level is sufficient or not.

In retrospect, it seems highly impractical for organizations to achieve capability level 5 in all process areas. So, what is the ideal capability level these organizations need to achieve for each process area? It appears that organizations can very well be successful with a capability level 2 or 3 for most process areas. Depending on business objectives or the type of services being offered, organizations can aim for specific process areas to be at a higher capability level. In other cases, there would be no incentive or a justified business case for trying to achieve a higher capability level for a given process area. The results suggest that the adapted version of the COBIT 5 model was fit for evaluating IT governance and was contextualized to the needs of organizations. Accordingly, this study adds credibility to the practitioner reports that it is possible to implement COBIT to produce a practical ITG framework that reflects the needs of individual organizations or sectors.

3.8 SUMMARY

The primary objective of this research was to explore how best-practice frameworks, such as the COBIT model, can be adapted to conduct evaluations of IT governance within medium and large organizations and to explore further the factors that influence the acceptance and adoption of the adapted framework. Four sub-research questions were answered and a research model was proposed and supported to address the primary objective of the research.

The research findings reinforce the important role of frameworks in IT governance evaluation. Employing an approach based on innovation adoption theory enables the understanding of the factors related to acceptance of IT governance frameworks, providing practitioners with additional knowledge and thus enabling a better understanding, and hence influencing, the adoption of IT governance frameworks.

In conclusion, considering the limitations identified, it is recommended that this research is extended to other organizations in both the private and public sectors. In addition, it is recommended that the research model is further developed to improve the quality of the findings and that more exploratory research is conducted on the relationship paths specified in the model.

The next section, it proposes three chapters to address the IT agility axis in large organizations. The first chapter of this section discusses the different models and frameworks of agility. The second focuses on IT service management agility through a case study. The third chapter deals with the cloud-computing axis as a pillar of IT agility in organizations.

REFERENCES

Al-Khazrajy, M. (2011). *Risk based assessment of IT control frameworks: A case study.* [Master of philosophy thesis, Auckland University of Technology].

Aprilinda, Y., Puspa, A. K., & Affandy, F. N. (2019). The use of ISO and COBIT for IT governance audit. *Journal of Physics: Conference Series, 1381*, 12028. https://doi.org/10.1088/1742-6596/1381/1/012028

Azizi Ismail, N. (2008). Information technology governance, funding and structure: A case analysis of a public university in Malaysia. *Campus-Wide Information Systems, 25*(3), 145–160. https://doi.org/10.1108/10650740810886321

Baker, Jeff, & Jones, Donald. (2008). A theoretical framework for sustained strategic alignment and an agenda for research. *All Sprouts Content, 222.* https://aisel.aisnet.org/sprouts_all/222

Baruch, Y., & Holtom, B. C. (2008). Survey response rate levels and trends in organizational research. *Human Relations, 61*(8), 1139–1160. https://doi.org/10.1177/0018726708094863

Beloglazov, A., Banerjee, D., Hartman, A., & Buyya, R. (2014). Improving productivity in design and development of information technology (IT) service delivery simulation models. *Journal of Service Research, 18*(1), 75–89. https://doi.org/10.1177/1094670514541002

Bergner, J., Witherspoon, C. L., Cockrell, C., & Stone, D. N. (2013). Antecedents of organizational knowledge sharing: A meta-analysis and critique. *Journal of Knowledge Management, 17*(2), 250–277. https://doi.org/10.1108/13673273131315204

Bermejo, P. H. de S., Tonelli, A. O., Zambalde, A. L., Santos, P. A. dos, & Zuppo, L. (2014). Evaluating IT governance practices and business and IT outcomes: A quantitative exploratory study in Brazilian companies. *Procedia Technology, 16*, 849–857. https://doi.org/10.1016/j.protcy.2014.10.035

Bhattacharjya, J., & Chang, V. (2010). Adoption and implementation of IT governance: Cases from Australian higher education. In *Strategic information systems: Concepts, methodologies, tools, and applications* (pp. 1308–1326). IGI Global.

Braga, G. (2015). COBIT 5 Applied to the Argentine digital accounting system. *COBIT Focus*, 1–4.

Brown, A. E., Grant, G. G., & Sprott, E. (2005a). Framing the frameworks: A review of IT governance research. *Communications of the Association for Information Systems, 15*, 696–712. https://doi.org/Article

Brown, A. E., Grant, G. G., & Sprott, E. (2005b, May). Framing the frameworks: A review of IT governance research. *Communications of the Association for Information Systems, 15*, 696–712. https://doi.org/Article

Cadete, G. R., & da Silva, M. M. (2017). *Assessing IT governance processes using a COBIT5 model BT – information systems* (M. Themistocleous & V. Morabito, Eds., pp. 447–460). Springer International Publishing.

Charles, T., & Tashakkori, A. (2009). *Foundations of mixed methods research: Integrating quantitative and qualitative approaches in the social and behavioral sciences*. Sage Publications.

Chen, R. S., Sun, C. M., Helms, M. M., & (Kenny) Jih, W. J. (2008). Aligning information technology and business strategy with a dynamic capabilities perspective: A longitudinal study of a Taiwanese semiconductor company. *International Journal of Information Management, 28*(5), 366–378. https://doi.org/10.1016/j.ijinfomgt.2008.01.015

Creswell, J. W., & Creswell, J. D. (2017). *Research design: Qualitative, quantitative, and mixed methods approaches*. Sage Publications.

Cronin, C. (2014). Using case study research as a rigorous form of inquiry. *Nurse Researcher, 21*(5), 19.

De Haes, S., & Van Grembergen, W. (2005). IT governance structures, processes and relational mechanisms: Achieving IT/business alignment in a major Belgian financial group. *Proceedings of the 38th Annual Hawaii International Conference on System Sciences*, 237b. https://doi.org/10.1109/HICSS.2005.362

De Haes, S., & Van Grembergen, W. (2006, February). Information technology governance best practices in Belgian organisations. *Proceedings of the Annual Hawaii International Conference on System Sciences*, 8. https://doi.org/10.1109/HICSS.2006.222

De Haes, S., Van Grembergen, W., & Debreceny, R. S. (2013). COBIT 5 and enterprise governance of information technology: Building blocks and research opportunities. *Journal of Information Systems, 27*(1), 307–324. https://doi.org/10.2308/isys-50422

Denscombe, M. (2014). *The good research guide: For small-scale social research projects* (5th ed.). McGraw-Hill Education.

El-Mekawy, M., Rusu, L., & Perjons, E. (2015). An evaluation framework for comparing business-IT alignment models: A tool for supporting collaborative learning in organizations. *Computers in Human Behavior*, *51*, 1229–1247. https://doi.org/10.1016/j.chb.2014.12.016

Forstner, E., Kamprath, N., & Röglinger, M. (2014). Capability development with process maturity models–Decision framework and economic analysis. *Journal of Decision Systems*, *23*(2), 127–150.

Gerke, L., & Ridley, G. (2009). Tailoring CobiT for public sector it audit: An australian case study. In *Information technology governance and service management: Frameworks and adaptations* (pp. 101–124). IGI Global.

Grembergen, W. V. (2004). *Strategies for information technology governance*. IGI Global.

Guldentops, E. (2002). *Governing information technology through CobiT BT – integrity, internal control and security in information systems: Connecting governance and technology* (pp. 115–159). Springer. https://doi.org/10.1007/978-0-387-35583-2_8

Hancock, D. R., & Algozzine, B. (2016). *Doing case study research: A practical guide for beginning researchers*. Teachers College Press.

Heier, H., Borgman, H. P., & Mervyn, G. M. (2007). *Examining the relationship between IT governance software and business value of IT: Evidence from four case studies*. Proceedings of the 40th Hawaii International Conference on System Sciences, Hawaii.

Hiererra, S. E. (2012). *Assessment of IT governance using COBIT 4.1 framework methodology: Case study university IS development in IT directorate* [Master's thesis, BINUS University].

Huang, S. J., & Han, W. M. (2006). Selection priority of process areas based on CMMI continuous representation. *Information & Management*, *43*(3), 297–307.

Huissoud, M. (2005). *IT self-assessment project, current results and next steps*. Presentation to EUROSAI IT Working Group, Cypress, 14.

Hunton, J. E., Bryant, S. M., & Bagranoff, N. A. (2004). *Core concepts of information technology auditing*. Wiley.

Hyett, N., Kenny, A., & Dickson-Swift, V. (2014). Methodology or method? A critical review of qualitative case study reports. *International Journal of Qualitative Studies on Health and Well-Being*, *9*(1), 23606. https://doi.org/10.3402/qhw.v9.23606

Information Security Governance: Guidance for Boards of Directors and Executive Management Guidance for Boards of Directors and Executive Management. (2006). *IT governance institute*, 1–52. www.itgi.org

ISACA. (2012). *COBIT 5: A business framework for the governance and management of enterprise IT*. Information Systems Audit and Control Association.

ISACA. (2013). *Self-assessment guide: Using COBIT 5*. Information Systems Audit and Control Association.

ITGI. (2003). *Board briefing on IT governance*. ITGI.

Joshi, A., Bollen, L., Hassink, H., De Haes, S., & Van Grembergen, W. (2018). Explaining IT governance disclosure through the constructs of IT governance maturity and IT strategic role. *Information and Management*, *55*(3), 368–380. https://doi.org/10.1016/j.im.2017.09.003

Lengnick-Hall, C. A., Beck, T. E., & Lengnick-Hall, M. L. (2011). Developing a capacity for organizational resilience through strategic human resource management. *Human Resource Management Review*, *21*(3), 243–255. https://doi.org/10.1016/j.hrmr.2010.07.001

Lewis, S. (2015). Qualitative inquiry and research design: choosing among five approaches. *Health Promotion Practice*, *16*(4), 473–475. https://doi.org/10.1177/1524839915580941

Lewis-Beck, M., Bryman, A. E., & Liao, T. F. (2003). *The Sage encyclopedia of social science research methods*. Sage Publications.

Luna-Reyes, L., Juiz, C., Gutierrez-Martinez, I., & Duhamel, F. B. (2020). Exploring the relationships between dynamic capabilities and IT governance. *Transforming Government: People, Process and Policy*, *14*(2), 149–169. https://doi.org/10.1108/TG-09-2019-0092

Maleh, Y., Sahid, A., & Belaissaoui, M. (2019). *Strategic IT governance and performance frameworks in large organizations*. IGI Global. https://doi.org/10.4018/978-1-5225-7826-0

Marrone, M., & Kolbe, L. M. (2011). Uncovering ITIL claims: IT executives' perception on benefits and business-IT alignment. *Information Systems and E-Business Management, 9*(3), 363–380. https://doi.org/10.1007/s10257-010-0131-7

McEvoy, P., & Richards, D. (2006). A critical realist rationale for using a combination of quantitative and qualitative methods. *Journal of Research in Nursing, 11*(1), 66–78. https://doi.org/10.1177/1744987106060192

McGuire, M. (2016, February). The impact of performance management on performance in public organizations: A meta-analysis. *Public Administration Review, 76*, 48–66. https://doi.org/10.1111/puar.12433.48

McKay, J., Marshall, P., & Smith, L. (2003, July). Steps towards effective IT governance: Strategic IT planning, evaluation and benefits management. *Pacific Asia Conference on Information Systems*, 956–970. www.pacis-net.org/file/2003/papers/is-strategy/214.pdf

Moeller, R. R. (2011). *COSO enterprise risk management: Establishing effective governance, risk, and compliance (GRC) processes* (2nd ed.). John Wiley & Sons.

Morse, J. M., & Niehaus, L. (2009). *Mixed method design: Principles and procedures* (4th ed.). Left Coast Press.

Nfuka, E., & Rusu, L. (2010). IT governance maturity in the public sector organizations in a developing country: The case of Tanzania. *AMCIS 2010 Proceedings, 2010*, 536. http://aisel.aisnet.org/ecis2010/128/

Nugroho, H. (2014). Conceptual model of IT governance for higher education based on COBIT 5 framework. *Journal of Theoretical and Applied Information Technology, 60*(2), 216–221. https://doi.org/ISSN:1992–8645

Oliver, D., & Lainhart, J. (2012). COBIT 5: Adding value through effective geit. *EDPACS, 46*(3), 1–12. https://doi.org/10.1080/07366981.2012.706472

Omari, L. Al, Barnes, P. H., & Pitman, G. (2012). *An exploratory study into audit challenges in IT governance: A Delphi approach*. Symposium on IT Governance, Management and Audit. https://eprints.qut.edu.au/53110/

Pat, J. D., & Piattini, M. (2011). Software process improvement and capability determination. *11th International Conference, SPICE, 155*, 143–155. https://doi.org/10.1007/978-3-642-21233-8

Perry, C., Alizadeh, Y., & Riege, A. (1997). Qualitative methods in entrepreneurship research. *Proceedings of the Annual Conference of the Small Enterprise Association Australia and New Zealand*, 547–567.

Peterson, R. R. (2001). Configurations and coordination for global information technology governance: Complex designs in a transnational European context. *Proceedings of the Hawaii International Conference on System Sciences, C*, 217. https://doi.org/10.1109/HICSS.2001.927133

Peterson, R. R. (2004). Crafting information technology governance. *Information Systems Management, 21*(4), 7–22.

Peterson, R. R., Parker, M., Ribbers, P., Peterson, R. R., & Parker, M. M. (2002). Information technology governance processes under environmental dynamism: Investigating competing theories of decision making and knowledge sharing. *ICIS 2002 Proceedings*, 562–575.

Posthumus, S., & Von Solms, R. (2004). A framework for the governance of information security. *Computers & Security, 23*(8), 638–646. http://doi.org/10.1016/j.cose.2004.10.006

Posthumus, S., Von Solms, R., & King, M. (2010). The board and IT governance: The what, who and how. *South African Journal of Business Management, 41*(3), 23–32. https://journals.co.za/content/busman/41/3/EJC22396

Punch, K. F. (2013). *Introduction to social research: Quantitative and qualitative approaches* (3rd ed.). Sage Publications.

Renaud, A., Walsh, I., & Kalika, M. (2016). Is SAM still alive? A bibliometric and interpretive mapping of the strategic alignment research field. *The Journal of Strategic Information Systems, 25*(2), 75–103. https://doi.org/10.1016/j.jsis.2016.01.002

Ribeiro, J., & Gomes, R. (2009, September). IT governance using COBIT implemented in a high public educational institution – a case study. *Proceedings of the 3rd International Conference on European Computing Conference*, 41–52. wseas.us/e-library/conferences/2009/georgia/CCI/CCI04.pdf

Rizal, R. A., Sarno, R., & Sungkono, K. R. (2020). COBIT 5 for analysing information technology governance maturity level on masterplan e-government. *2020 International Seminar on Application for Technology of Information and Communication (ISemantic)*, 517–522. https://doi.org/10.1109/iSemantic50169.2020.9234301

Schubert, K. D. (2004). *CIO survival guide: The roles and responsibilities of the chief information officer*. John Wiley & Sons.

Selig, G. J. (2008). *Implementing IT governance: A practical guide to global best practices in IT management*. Van Haren Publishing.

Siggelkow, N. (2007). Persuasion with case studies. *Academy of Management Journal*, *50*(1), 20–24. https://doi.org/10.5465/amj.2007.24160882

Simonsson, M., & Johnson, P. (2006). Defining IT governance-a consolidation of literature. *The 18th Conference on Advanced Information Systems Engineering*, 6.

Tonelli, A. O., de Souza Bermejo, P. H., Aparecida dos Santos, P., Zuppo, L., & Zambalde, A. L. (2017). IT governance in the public sector: A conceptual model. *Information Systems Frontiers*, *19*(3), 593–610. https://doi.org/10.1007/s10796-015-9614-x

Tsang, E. W., & Kwan, K. M. (1999). Replication and theory development in organizational science: A critical realist perspective. *Academy of Management Review*, *24*(4), 759–780.

van Wyk, J., & Rudman, R. (2019). COBIT 5 compliance: Best practices cognitive computing risk assessment and control checklist. *Meditari Accountancy Research*, *27*(5), 761–788. https://doi.org/10.1108/MEDAR-04-2018-0325

Wallhoff, J. (2004). *Combining ITIL with COBIT and ISO/IEC 17799:2000*. Scillani Information AB.

Warland, C., & Ridley, G. (2005). Awareness of IT control frameworks in an Australian state government: A qualitative case study. *Proceedings of the 38th Annual Hawaii International Conference on System Sciences*, *C*, 236b. https://doi.org/10.1109/HICSS.2005.116

Webb, P., Pollard, C., & Ridley, G. (2006). Attempting to define IT governance: Wisdom or folly? *Proceedings of the Annual Hawaii International Conference on System Sciences*, *8*(C), 1–10. https://doi.org/10.1109/HICSS.2006.68

Weber, L. (2014). *Addressing the incremental risks associated with adopting a bring your own device program by using the COBIT 5 framework to identify key controls* [Doctoral dissertation, Stellenbosch University].

Weill, P., & Ross, J. (2005). A matrixed approach to designing IT governance. *MIT Sloan Management Review*, *46*(2), 26–34. https://doi.org/10.1177/0275074007310556

Wood, D. J. (2010). *Assessing IT governance maturity: The case of San Marcos, Texas* [Master's thesis, Texas State University].

IT Service Management as a Key Pillar for IT Governance

4

A Maturity Framework Based on ITILv4

4.1 INTRODUCTION

In the age of digitization, the world is evolving at a constant pace. Organizations need to respond to changing conditions and often agility is the only guarantee of survival. Globalization means that there is more competition (Kumbakara, 2008). The life cycle of products is shorter than ever. A disturbing technology can change markets overnight. The company faces challenging challenges in maintaining security and compliance while achieving its business objectives, complying with current regulations, and managing staff and technology. We understand that the IT staff must react quickly to changing business needs while maintaining the existing infrastructure. We also know that the management objective so often quoted, 'Doing more with less', is not only a goal but is also a corporate commitment (Mesquida, 2012).

Most CIOs believe that IT management is simply about filling security gaps, collecting inventory, and automating application delivery, and they are not convinced that it is also necessary to be able to define and better manage the assets, processes, and services that determine resource allocation, cost control, compliance, performance measures, and service delivery.

With improved IT Service Management (ITSM) processes and the adoption of best practice guides and benchmarks such as ITIL (van Bon, 2007) and ISO 20000 (ISO/IEC

20000, 2010), compliance appears to be a need rather than a strategic choice to improve rapidly and easily decisions about IT and business processes. Get better agility, which allows the business to benefit from a faster Return On Investment (ROI) and a constant competitive advantage.

Recent developments in the field of IT governance and ITSM have led to the introduction of new technology and concepts such as service-oriented architecture (SOA), decision-making, and of course agility (Uebernickel, 2006).

Over the last decade, agility has been proposed primarily around methods, such as Scrum (Ken Schwaber, 2004) and Extreme Programming XP (Beck, 1999), for lifecycle management of software and IT developments. However, with the strategic changes that companies are currently experiencing, agility is more a strategic choice than a simple development method, affecting all business activities.

The management of IT services implies the adoption of an agile vision. Referential repositories such as ITIL define service design methods and processes. Agility adds a layer of flexibility and dynamism to this management (Sahid et al., 2021).

The IT department's responsibility for maintaining and securing the IT environment now includes all devices that employees use, but budgets and IT resources are limited. Agility is the right solution for IT departments to streamline IT processes and manage all aspects of end-user productivity. The objective is to reinforce the traditional IT services of the 'control and control' type, oriented peripheral by a complete integrated approach, oriented user. ITSM increases communication efficiency between business departments and provides a structure to plan, research, and implement IT services. The needs of ITSM in organizations can be changes in how they do business, communicate, and also develop and innovate, gain a market advantage (Brooks, 2006). In addition, ITSM allows companies to internally govern and follow the set global standards (Mior, 2008). To better understand the ITSM concept in the organization, reviewing the ITSM component would be helpful. ITSM components consist of Process, Technology, Manpower (people), Organization, and Security, which is recently added to organization construction to improve the system security (Park, 2008), (McNaughton, 2010).

At first glance, the Agile and ITIL principles seem to contradict each other because of the values they promote. However, these two standards share common values that should be put in synergy to get the most out of them. Version 4 of ITIL, published in February 2019 (Shekhar, 2020), will go in this direction by adopting ITSM best practices to agile operating methods.

In the literature and industry as well, there is no practical, concrete, and agile model for implementing IT services and assets management in organizations in the literature and even references such as ITIL, ISO 20000, and COBIT (Abdelkebir et al., 2017). This chapter proposes a global, practical, and agile framework to support ITSM and IT Asset Management (ITAM). The proposed framework surpasses the limitations of existing methods/referential and meets the needs of international standards in terms of flexibility and agility to improve and enhance ITSM/ITAM processes. This generic framework will help any type of organization implement an agile, secure, and optimal IT Service Center. We measure the proposed framework by adopting a continuous improvement process based on DevOps (DevOps is the concatenation of the first three letters of the word 'development' and the usual abbreviation 'ops' of the word 'operations') and the PDCA Deming cycle.

4.2 RELATED RESEARCH

During the last two decades, the ITSM-related frameworks have provided a better systematic approach to manage IT services in the fields of IT operation to continual improvement, implementation, and design (Marrone, 2011). For example, different studies have concentrated on adopting ITSM as a 'specific service-oriented best practice'. According to Winniford (2009), about 45% of US corporations are operating an ITSM while 15% are preparing its usage. ITSM is somehow the quality customer service that tries to ensure that customer needs and expectations are met at all times (Tan, 2009).

In 'ITIL: What It Is And What It Isn't', Hank (2006) examined the measuring techniques of successful companies when implementing the ITIL best practice. He describes Service Support and Service Delivery and explains its stress on an ITSM-ITIL best practice that it does not stand alone and it could be successful when applied to other practices. The authors define three significant tasks, which define appropriate goal setting through a Process Maturity Framework (PMF), rigorous auditing and reporting through a Quality Management System (QMS), and Project Management and a Continuous Service Improvement Program (CSIP), to support ITIL usage. Furthermore, he also provided more information about business-aligned IT processes and continuous improvement of the tactical and operational components, especially those focused on service quality by clients and users (Hank, 2006). Apart from the other works on improving the efficiency of the ITSM field, there is a real-life example of a case study, which is focusing on the IT framework, and Service Strategy process of Steel Manufacturing Enterprise (SMC), which is related to the subject area of this thesis. A manufacturing enterprise (Zhong, 2010) used the integration of COBIT and ITIL best practices to implement and improve the ITSM framework. They introduced an approach to the service strategy evaluation framework in SMC by providing indicators for different evaluation processes to improve the result from ITIL implementation and increase the improvements in changed IT processes. They use different approaches to find the problem of business–IT alignment in SMC. These approaches aim at minimizing the difficulty of business–IT alignment in importance within the IT community. The same article (Bartolini, 2006) has suggested an IT Management by Business Objectives (MBO) method, which is a particular method to ensure business strategic objectives–IT alignment, by defining a new system for decision support ITSM. It is closely related to the ITIL component at the operational level and tactical level of theoretical model. In 'E-government: ITIL oriented Service Management Case Study', Meziani (2010) developed service management self-assessment plans for the government agency to support continuous quality improvement of IT processes based on ITIL governance gap analysis methods concerning ITIL standards (Meziani and Saleh). Kumbakara (2008) argues that the practical issues are based on standards and the management of IT services delivered by external or outsourced service providers. Here, the author's purpose is to assist IT organizations to recognize the significance of having a mutual standard for managing IT services.

van Grembergen (2009) illustrated a set of best guides and practices (COBIT Framework) for IT management control and assurance of information technology, and categorized them around a logical framework based on 34 IT processes. Marrone (2011) studied the benefits of both operational and strategic ITSM. The research outcome indicates that as ITIL implementation increased the number of realized benefits, like the levels of maturity of the business–IT alignment. Wilcocks (2013) proposes different approaches to evaluate practice at strategic levels and during the pre-purchase phase of IS assessment. Ang (2014) introduces a comprehensive and new approach to the secular problem of where to place your money in ITAM. In recent works, Duane & Charlie (2016) explore the balance of the three fundamental aspects that make up asset management and will focus on implementing strategies to reduce the total ownership cost.

Recently, Sahid et al. (2018) proposed a practical agile framework to improve IT service and asset management ITSM/ITAM processes through a case study in the organization.

4.2.1 Agility in Literature

The concept of agility was first used in the literature of strategic management and industry at the beginning of the years (Meade, 1997; Vernadat, 1999; Yusuf et al., 1999; Richards, 1996; Goldman, 1995). Agility is introduced and proposed in the literature to argue that success in volatile industries requires a set of capacities different from those required for success in stable industries (Volberda, 1996; Volberda & Rutges, 1999). In such situations, the organization must be agile and capitalize and respond to opportunities generated by new market situations faster than their competitors (Goldman, 1995). The key question then is: how can an organization become agile? How can they create the required capabilities? Moreover, perhaps more broadly, what are precisely these capabilities? This subject was being addressed in several strategic management and organizational studies, rooting the theory that began well before introducing the agility concept. In IS research, the agility concept has been Introduced in early 1990 (Ciborra, 1992; Markus & Benjamin, 1996; Clark et al., 1997; Sharp et al., 1999; Zhang & Sharifi, 1999) after the success of agile methods in computer development. In research, the concepts of flexibility and agility have been associated with the broader challenge of combining complex computer systems with unexpected changes, sometimes surprising in user needs, business processes, company structure, strategy, markets, and society overall. At the beginning of the year 2000, the emphasis was on other attributes of IS, which explain agility through IT, development methods (IS), and IS outsourcing practices.

In the literature, we deduced that as a lack of a unique definition of the agility concept; The Agility Research in IS was being devised on several axes (Lee, et al., 2006; Fink & Neuman, 2009; Holmqvist & Pessi, 2006; Hong et al., 2011). However, there is a lack of research regarding agility in IT Management Systems. Although the IT function, in all its dimensions, gains in flexibility and reactivity. Beyond that, the IT system function is at stake. It must have the capability to accelerate its adaptation to business needs, market requirements, and the strategic alignment of the IS and the organization. Agility is the best solution to cope with different internal/external changes. DevOps is a set of best practices and change guidance that ensures development, assurance, and quality improvement and operations to better respond to customer needs effectively. Patrick Debois invented the word DevOps during the organization of the first DevOps days in Ghent, Belgium, in October 2009. To ensure competitiveness, the organization must accelerate the delivery of new functionalities and software features. This is the idea behind agile application/ software development processes that are now widely used by application delivery teams to reduce delivery cycle times. DevOps can be applied in the ITSM/ITAM field to benefit from it and ensure an efficient and flexible ITSM/ITAM in the organization.

In a recent work, Gene et al. (2016) argued that more than ever, effective technology management is essential for business competitiveness. The book does not focus on tools such as infrastructure, code, containers, or configuration management. These are people, culture, and processes. The book creates a language to describe DevOps and a common understanding. It is highly recommended, no matter if you have a professional or technical environment. The DevOps Handbook shows leaders/practitioners how to reproduce these incredible results, showing how to integrate IT operations, development, product management, quality assurance, and information security to raise your business and win in the market. DevOps helps the organization bring together key players (companies, applications, and ops), focusing on collaboration, automation, and monitoring, resulting in better application delivery speed with quality. The ways in which DevOps helps to generate business value are listed as follows:

- Obtain a competitive advantage. Accelerate the output of applications in production – faster response to business demand.
- Increase the efficiency of IT resources. Automate provisioning and deployment. Delete the manual processes.
- Enable better and faster decisions. Create an immediate feedback loop. Identify problems earlier in the process.
- Hang on to business requirements. Bring new applications and updates to the market quickly to create satisfied customers.

4.3 THE PROPOSED ITSM/ITAM FRAMEWORK

ITSM/ITAM increases communication efficiency between business departments and provides a structure to plan, research, and implement IT services. ITSM/ITAM in organizations can be changed in the ways they operate, communicate and do business, and develop and innovate and gain a market advantage (Brooks, 2006). In addition, ITSM/ITAM allows companies to internally govern and follow the set global standards (Mior, 2008).

Table 4.1 attempted to manage the challenge of the practical ITSM framework in IT corporations from two different views: the empirical findings and literature. With an analysis of this challenge, it will be feasible to suggest some points to address these issues.

We can confirm that there are many problems in having a successful ITSM/ITAM process. Conversely, as identified before, many reasonable efforts have been made to improve these issues. For better understanding the concept of these challenges, there are three possible approaches to improve ITSM/ITAM efficiency. These approaches are detailed here.

TABLE 4.1   ITSM Drawbacks

Interview/ Findings	▪ Lack of maintenance objects/situation. ▪ Lack of ITIL support. ▪ Lack of knowledge evaluation framework by employee and management team. ▪ Problems in metrics level. ▪ Weakness in System performance and QS.
Literature	▪ Lack of users training and knowledge. ▪ Lack of unit and cohesion structure between metrics. ▪ Insecurity and doubt about what to measure. ▪ Lack of communication among users and producers of a Performance Indicator (PI).

Many academic and industrial efforts have been made in many IT corporations to improve the Quality Measurements of business-IT alignment. Researchers such as Das (1991), Reich (2000), and Luftman (2003) used multidimensional scales to measure the business–IT alignment. The result from our interviews and collected metrics exposed some essential elements to improve the efficiency of ITSM. The ITSM meets the need to align the IT services delivery directly with the requirements of the business. Some of these concerns and issues are reflected in this organization to provide ITIL best practices and deliver a comprehensive and valuable ITSM framework.

ITIL–ITSM best practice is not a one-time process; it is an ongoing activity to control system performance. Continuous improvement is needed to remain relevant in the market (Porter, 1996). Through our case study, we came to know that the target groups of our research are almost employing the same methods but there is a small difference in ITSM measurement and process implementation. According to Brooks (2006), ITSM tools deal with many ITSM measurements and most of them will be attractive to people in the related departments with the same activities. Metrics are identified to show the development and performance of the system. Therefore, there are three types of metrics to improve the quality level of the evaluation framework like effectiveness, capabilities, and efficiency. These elements could be matched with any technology, process, or service that focuses on Operational Level (Service Support Domain), Tactical Level (Service Delivery Domain), and Strategic Level.

This chapter aims to identify the important aspects that propose a comprehensive framework for ITSM/ITAM efficiency. It was collected in a theoretical and empirical research study that generated answers to the sub-level research questions. We tried to extract a framework based on the literature review and various sources from the practical environment.

The framework proposed ITSM/ITAM exploits the best practices of ITIL and ISO 2000 and integrates new strategic axes such as agility and security to propose an efficient and agile ITSM/ITAM. It replaces the traditional IT services of the 'control and control' type, oriented peripherally by a complete integrated, user-oriented approach with the integration of four disciplines of IT management (Service management, Asset management,

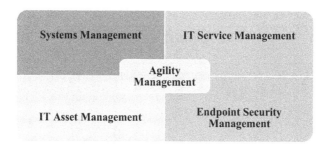

FIGURE 4.1   The proposed ITSM/ITAM model.

Agility Management, and Security Management). Figure 4.1 describes the architecture and component of the proposed ITSM/ITAM framework.

4.3.1 IT Service Management (ITSM)

Most ITSM organizations consider the Service Support process a difficult task. Difficulties are mainly due to the following reasons:

- IT organizations do not have a structured approach for measuring IT service and service management processes.
- Different tools exploited by IT Support Service Teams do not enable effective measurement.
- ITSM referential and standards do not provide practical guidelines and a road-map to measure the IT support process (Lahtela, 2010).
- Therefore, the IT organization needs a structured approach for measuring IT Service Support processes such as ITIL V2/V3 or other reliable sources to increase IT quality of services. So, implementations of the Service Support process are chosen as a priority to support continuous improvement in ITSM.

As illustrated in Table 4.2, the IT Service Support process includes five main steps (Wui-Gee, 2009).

The scope of the evaluation would cover only the key processes of the service operation and service transition. Data are collected through interviews, workshops, literature reviews, and site visits. Visits to the service desk and data center may be required. A list of questions is often used. A time-based assessment would aim to determine the level of maturity of each ITIL process. Other data to be collected include the availability of tools, competencies, the role, and responsibilities of the organization, availability, and quality of documentation, evidence of continuous improvement, measurement and reporting, dissemination, and the use of reports. Based on the answers to the questions collected, the scores are tabulated using a spreadsheet tool and presented. A time-based assessment can use the five-level ITSM maturity model to evaluate the individual process of ITSM as shown in Table 4.3.

TABLE 4.2   IT Service Support Process

SERVICE SUPPORT PROCESS	DESCRIPTION	EXAMPLE
Incident Management	Restores normal service operations as quickly as possible	'Virus Attack, Server crashes. Hardware alarm, Turn down and decline of system performance' (McNaughton, 2010)
Problem Management	It prevents incidents from happening and minimizes the impact of incidents that cannot be prevented	'All incidents that are not fixed basically with known errors' (McNaughton, 2010)
Change Management	Controls the lifecycle of all changes	
Release Management	Implements approved changes to IT services	'To provide a solution for the problems like a parameter, adjust, patch, configuration changes, upgrade of system version and server'
Configuration Management	Configuration management consists of managing the technical description of a system and its various components and managing all the changes made during the evolution of the system.	'Tracking, Reporting and controlling all equipment's' (McNaughton, 2010)

TABLE 4.3   ITSM Maturity Model

MATURITY LEVEL	DESCRIPTION
Level 1: Initial	Awareness of the existence of the problem and the need to study it. However, there are no standardized processes, but approaches and processes in this direction tend to be applied autonomously on a case-by-case basis. The global management approach is not organized.
Level 2: Reproducible	The organization makes significant efforts to develop and establish the management process for ITSM services. The notions of reactivity and the short term are generally there. At this level, the organization is a little more advanced in its management. Generally, the activities related to this process are not all coordinated and are irregular. Commitment to the process is evident in the allocation of resources. However, ITSM is not always formalized or compliant.
Level 3: Defined	Describes a formalized service management process in which the objective, activities, inputs, and outputs have been defined. The performance is consistent and can be repeated throughout the organization. The process is well implemented and managed as a whole satisfactorily. The management process is identified and documented but there is no recognition of its role within the IT organizations. However, the process has a manager, formal objectives, and dedicated resources. A report is put in place to capitalize on the experience.

MATURITY LEVEL	DESCRIPTION
Level 4: Managed	It is possible to monitor and measure ITSM compliance to standards and to act when processes do not seem to work correctly. The management of the services is constantly improving and corresponds to good practice. Automation and the use of tools are limited or partial.
Level 5: Optimized	ITSM has reached the level of best practice, following constant improvement and comparison with other similar contexts. The technology is an integrated way to automate workflows, providing tools that improve quality and efficiency and make the company quickly adaptable.

4.3.2 IT Asset Management (ITAM)

Today, in the challenging economic environment, knowing what assets you own, how they are used, and where they are physically and in a business context is essential.

Without this information, it is very difficult to plan and budget its IT resource requirements. Furthermore, without information on the nature of the possessions and their use, it is impossible to guarantee compliance with regulatory and contractual obligations.

Knowing and mastering this valuable information can help to solve many of the pressing problems that arise today, including:

- Provide decision-makers with detailed information on the allocation, cost, and forecast of assets;
- Reduce risk by avoiding penalties and expensive litigation due to regulatory or contractual non-compliance, especially in software licensing;
- Implement asset responsibility with management reporting to optimize the use of assets and protect against malicious use and/or theft;
- Reduce costs by eliminating unnecessary acquisitions if the property already exists;
- Proactively manage the warranty and support and maintenance contracts for optimal utility;
- Negotiate better contracts by properly managing assets and suppliers;
- Improve productivity by automating the flow of goods in your environment;
- Facilitate data-based internal compliance and accountability audits to improve processes continuously.

The ITAM maturity model is a proposed roadmap to help ITAM managers define a direction for their programs. For an organization that already has ITAM in place, but may be stuck in the phase of responding to software audits and not evolving beyond that, the proposed maturity model could be used as a roadmap for defining the following steps and expand the use of assets organizational data to help solve problems in other computer domains. Organizations often find it challenging to articulate the business case for the implementation of asset management. This implementation model helps in this effort by

TABLE 4.4   ITAM Maturity Model

Level 0: Unmanaged	Level 1: Initial	Level 2: Managed	Level 3: Optimized
▪ No Leadership	▪ Service Desk Leads	▪ IT Ops Leads	▪ Business/Board Leads
▪ No Tools	▪ Helpdesk Tools	▪ Change and Release Tracked	▪ Business Portfolio Mapped to Systems
▪ No Process	▪ Incident, Request Processes Only	▪ Configuration/Basic CMDB	▪ Supplier Performance
▪ No Standards	▪ Manual ITAM	▪ Basic Problem	▪ Financial
▪ No Visibility	▪ No Policy	▪ Knowledge DB	▪ Innovation
▪ Audit-driven	▪ No Standardization		▪ Risk
▪ Decentralized	▪ No Knowledge		

identifying the problems to be solved and their priority to evolve successfully to the next level of achievement. Progression from one level to another requires knowing what should be accomplished first to succeed in the next step. Sometimes an organization may ignore a step, but the overall result will be more effective if the progression occurs. In conjunction with process frameworks, questions on how to follow these steps can be answered. Keep in mind that the movement through the implementation model requires resources and dedicated efforts to get the benefits. One of the challenges encountered in proposing this model was an organization that identified the next steps of the ITAM/SAM program. These programs can be aligned with IT operations, and they are frequently aligned with IT procurement, procurement, vendor, and contract management. This creates an enigma, as it would be difficult to identify the steps for each role that might be interested in ITAM. Therefore, we have tried to do it at a high level. In addition, this model will not apply to businesses of all sizes. Small businesses may not have the staff or funds to invest in the advancement of their ITAM program. The achievement model begins by looking at the components of an effective ITAM discipline: governance, policies, processes, people, metrics, automation, and alignment with the business direction. Table 4.4 describes the ITAM achievement model.

4.3.3 IT Security Management

To manage and control the security management process to meet external/internal security requirements as it is found in SLAs, contracts, legislation and the company security policy (Meziani and Saleh), the ITSM/ITAM must offer an efficient but above all secure service.

The threat environment continues to evolve rapidly and the volume of unique malware is growing, increasingly being applied, and web-based. To complicate the puzzle,

TABLE 4.5   Reactive\Proactive Mature IT Security

Reactive organizations	Proactive organizations
Low-level security	Multiple point solutions
Multilayered security	Integrated security solution
Inefficient use of IT resources	Effective use of IT resources and alignment of IT processes
Manual methods to quarantine threats	Automatic ways to quarantine threats
IT Security manages all security processes	Security management processes are managed by IT operations, while IT security ensures surveillance and investigates threats

your users are different. They are more self-sufficient and, like water, they find the least resistant path to productivity. They bring things to the network and the information is just an application store and a credit card. The current approach to computer systems and security management must be more user-oriented.

Companies' efforts to improve security can motivate them to react and buy high-tech products that can make them more secure rather than more secure. The problem is that this proliferation of advanced attacks does not allow you to be more responsive. Taking a more proactive approach to security involves deploying multiple layers of integrated protection that stifle network violations. Table 4.5 indicates some of the trends of reactive organizations versus those that are more proactive or have more mature IT security:

The best approach is to ensure that your information security team members respond to new threats and your IT team members process mature systems. We propose a global model of maturity to achieve a practical ITSM framework, as shown in Table 4.6. The path to security maturity requires a diversified range of layered endpoint protection, management, and capabilities: defensive, integrated, and fully automated. The bottom line on endpoint security is that today's threat environment is simply too dynamic for any single-point solution to afford adequate protection. The only practical and survivable defensive strategy is to move to a more mature security model that incorporates multiple layers of protective technology.

4.3.4 Agility Management

To take advantage of the digital age, companies realize that they need to deliver strategic responses more quickly and efficiently. ITSM/ITAM teams are already focused on improving or constructing consistent, repeatable processes that reduce downtime and improve productivity (Robert et al., 2016). Effective initiatives within the ITSM/ITAM can extend the delivery and management of business services beyond the areas of computing. Service management teams become an advisory model for the company and your integrated, process-driven ITSM/ITAM enables agility that supports business strategy (Giudice et al., 2016).

TABLE 4.6 Security Maturity Model

MATURITY OF CAPABILITY BUILDING BLOCKS	LEVEL 1: INITIAL	LEVEL 2: BASIC	LEVEL 3: INTERMEDIATE	LEVEL 4: ADVANCED	LEVEL 5: OPTIMIZING
IT Service Security Management Business continuity planning IT Incident Management Communication and Training Security performance reporting	–Ad hoc definition of information security strategy, policies, and standards. –The physical environment and the security of the computer components are only locally addressed. –There is no explicit consideration of budget requirements for information security activities –No systematic management of security risks	–Maturity reflects the linking of a basic information security strategy to the business and IT strategies of the organization. It also involves developing and reviewing information security policies and standards, typically after significant incidents. –IT component and physical environment security guidelines are emerging.	–Maturity reflects a detailed information security strategy that is regularly aligned to business and IT strategies and risk appetite across IT and some other business units. –Information security policies and standards are developed and revised based on a defined process and regular feedback. –IT and some other business units have agreed-on IT component and physical environment security measures.	–Maturity is characterized by regular, enterprise-wide improvement in the alignment of the information security strategy, policies, and standards with business and IT strategies and compliance requirements. –IT component security measures on IT systems are implemented and tested enterprise-wide for threat detection and mitigation. Physical environment security is integrated with access controls and surveillance systems across the enterprise.	–Maturity reflects an information security strategy that is regularly aligned to business and IT strategies across the business ecosystem. –Information security policies and standards are periodically reviewed and revised based on input from the business ecosystem. –The management of IT component security is optimized across the security framework layers.

−Access rights and policies are best managed using informal procedures.	−There is some consideration of security budget requirements within IT, and requirements for high-level security features are specified for major software and hardware purchases.	−IT budget processes acknowledge and provide for the most important information security budget requests in IT and some other business units.	−Detailed security budget requirements are incorporated in enterprise-wide business planning and budgeting activities.	−Physical access and environmental controls are regularly improved. Security budget requirements are improved to provide adequate funding for current and future security purposes.
−IT security incidents and problems are managed on an ad hoc basis.	−A basic security risk-management process is established within IT based on perceived risk.	−The security risk-management process is proactive and jointly shared with corporate collaboration.	−A standardized security risk management process is aligned with the enterprise risk management process.	−The security risk-management process is agile and adaptable, and tools can be used to address the business ecosystem's requirements.
	−Access rights management is dependent on vendor-supplied solutions.	−Access rights are granted based on a formal and audited authorization process.	−Access rights are implemented and audited across the enterprise.	−Access rights and policies can deal effectively with the organization's restructuring assignments and acquisitions.

(Continued)

TABLE 4.6 (Continued)

MATURITY OF CAPABILITY BUILDING BLOCKS	LEVEL 1: INITIAL	LEVEL 2: BASIC	LEVEL 3: INTERMEDIATE	LEVEL 4: ADVANCED	LEVEL 5: OPTIMIZING
IT Asset Security Management Security budgeting Resource effectiveness Resource effectiveness Tools and resources Data identification and classifications Access rights management		–Processes or security management data throughout its life cycle are emerging. –Major security incidents are tracked and recorded within IT.	–Detailed processes for managing data security throughout its life cycle are implemented. –Security incidents are managed based on the urgency to restore services, as agreed on by IT and some other business units.	–Data is effectively preserved throughout its life cycle, and data availability is effectively managed to meet business, regulatory, and security requirements. –Recurring incidents are systematically addressed enterprise-wide through problem-management processes that are based on root cause analysis.	–Processes for managing data security throughout its life cycle are continuously improved. –Automated incident prediction systems are in place, and security incidents are effectively managed.

Vulnerability and Risk Management	Security threat profiling
	Security risk assessment
	Security risk prioritization
	Security risk monitoring
	Data identification and classifications
	Access rights management
	Compliance control
Compliance Management	Security assessment
	IT services, processes, and systems comply with enterprise policies

By agile, we do not just mean 'fast', but it is a significant element. Agility in ITSM/ITAM is more a measure of responsiveness, and not just, how fast IT technicians process tickets or changes in version. Instead, true agility includes the entire IT team that solves service demands while respecting optimized labor costs. In short, true ITSM/ITAM agility is achieved by implementing intelligent processes that work smarter and more efficiently (Sahid et al., 2021).

The implementation (or transition) of a DevOps development process (integration of development, operational teams, and processes) has proven to be a tool capable of reducing publication time. Automation Improved repetitive processes and a key element of Agile Development and Liberation. The DevOps approach is a philosophy, a way of thinking. It aims to establish closer and more effective collaboration between development and infrastructure teams by enabling faster deployments while reducing operational friction. It

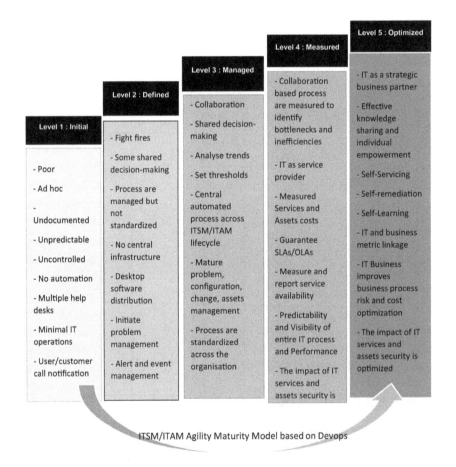

FIGURE 4.2 DevOps ITSM/ITAM maturity model for continuous organization's measure and improvement.

is a key element in implementing a continuous delivery process and translates into applying different cultural and technological concepts. Adopting DevOps requires changes in the way teams are structured, how responsibilities are shared, and the need to integrate and deliver services that enable teams to succeed.

To understand the DevOps maturity of the core development and IT operations processes, we propose a proven DevOps maturity model based on Hewlett Packard HP (Hewlet Packard HP, 2016) and IBM (Robert et al., 2016) return of experience of the adoption of DevOps model of agility in their business strategy to accelerate innovation and meet market demands. This model looks at DevOps from three viewpoints IT service, process, and assets; IT automation; and IT collaboration, and it spans a series of clearly defined states on the path to an optimized DevOps ITSM/ITAM environment. The DevOps maturity model described in Figure 4.2 represents a roadmap to achieve organization's maturity level in terms of ITSM/ITAM standardization, IT automation tools, IT collaboration approaches, and end IT user security management, along with insights into your opportunities for continuous IT service operations and organizational change improvement.

4.3.5 The Proposed Agile ITSM/ITAM Framework

In parallel with the development solutions and processes, ITSM/ITAM plays a key role in supporting DevOps practices and objectives such as incident management, application deployment, and performance management, to name a few than a few. The conception and implementation of the new agile ITSM/ITAM are a challenge. The proposed agile ITSM/ITAM is shown in Figure 4.3.

We conducted a study of the practices used by companies to manage the ITSM/ITAM service center. This study is based on a questionnaire drawn up in a sample of 10,000 IT professionals (Director, IT Manager, and IT practical).

The objective is to have a return experience concerning the IT services and assets management best methods and practices to measure the contribution of our proposed framework on the company's IS performance.

To meet the requirements of the proposed ITSM/ITAM Framework, all employees must feel concerned and involved. To this end, the quality department has undertaken a series of strategic actions. These actions are planned following an agile model based on DevOps. Inspired by the Deming wheel and DevOps, we organized the reports into four phases DDAO: Discover, Do, Act, and Optimize, as shown in Table 4.7. Our goal is to develop a quality approach for continuous IT improvement. We were starting with the auditing of all the functional and practical aspects of the management of the organization's services and the desired need, including implementing a roadmap for the desired organization's levels of maturity in terms of management of services, assets, and IT security. We define an agile approach based on the proposed model DevOps to guarantee a continuous improvement of the processes, services, security and organization, and contribution to the organization's business.

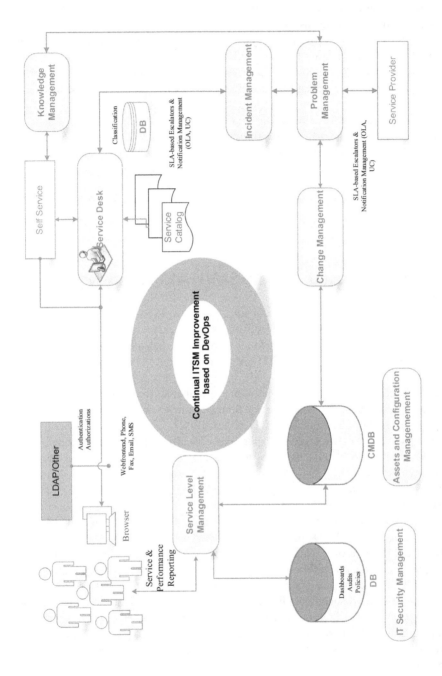

FIGURE 4.3 The proposed agile ITSM/ITAM framework.

TABLE 4.7   Continual Quality Improvement

DISCOVER	DO	ACT	OPTIMIZE
Vision and Strategy	Assessment	Organization	Performance Management
Auditing	Strategic Plan	Processes	Benchmarks
Key Performance Indicators	Roadmap	Tools And Technology	Continuous Improvement

4.4 USE CASE

4.4.1 Discover

This section presents the empirical study that concerns and identifies the measuring system of IT in the organization. During the empirical study, different possibilities in measuring and comparing the KPIs in different groups were found. In this section, we will present measuring operations and visualization of measurements and auditing IT services and security in the organization. IT managers described that different parts of ITIL are incorporated in the fields of IT Support, Service desk SLA's, Incident and problem management, and Deployment fields. The most important parameters to measures target Time Deliveries in different channels such as General Service management of core system functions, Business projects, Activities, Operational maintenance, and Admin. Another aspect that could be measured is Service improvement by providing surveys based every year (on process and maintenance object level) to improve and monitor the overall performance of the systems.

4.4.2 ITSM Audit Score

We conducted an audit of the organization's ITSM/ITAM and endpoint security practices. This audit was piloted based on the maturity models described in , to define the current levels of maturity and the desired level to be attained by the organization. Figure 4.4 shows the current ITSM maturity level. The maturity score of 1 indicates the initial level (ad hoc) and the score of 5 indicates the high score of maturity level (optimized).

As shown in Figure 4.4, the level of maturity of the organism in terms of ITSM is still at the initial and reproducible levels 1 and 2. Our objective is to set up service management and achieve level 4.

4.4.3 ITAM Audit Result

As the majority of the organization and companies are undertaking an ITAM program. The organization's ITAM audit is at the initial level (Table 4.3). Asset management is done manually, which negatively influences costs, increases risk, and weakens the quality of service. Our objective concerning this axis is to define an improvement strategy enabling the organization to automate and efficiently manage its IT assets to position the organization in the level of maturity 2 (managed).

FIGURE 4.4   ITSM maturity score.

FIGURE 4.5   IT Security audit score.

4.4.4 IT Security Audit Result

Based on the model of security maturity in Table 4.6. We audit the endpoint security of the organism that runs between the basic and intermediate levels. Our objective is to achieve an improved level of ITSM\ITAM security and to be a part of the overall governance of the organization's information security. The results of the audit are illustrated in Figure 4.5.

4.4.5 Do

4.4.5.1 The Practical Framework to Enhance ITSM/ITAM Efficiency

In section 4.4, we have proposed different feedbacks about the system performance without modifying the new solutions for the future model. To conclude the issue, we could say that organizations should take advantage of learning from the system performance and reduce the appropriate incident management because a successful approach and proper ITSM plan could make the difference between the organization's continued existence and sudden death. The suggested framework is a structured approach to increase ITSM efficiency and reduce incident management in new start-up companies. In this part, we discuss the axes of improvement referring to the results of the empirical study and interviews with the IT managers in the different axes of the IT disciplines (ITSM, ITAM, and security).

4.4.5.1.1 IT Service Management

In this part, we will discuss the improved points treated in terms of ITSM. The adoption of the proposed ITSM framework described in section 3.1 helps the organization increase ITSM maturity to level 4: managed as shown in Figure 4.6.

User expectations have changed and the IT department has to develop other ways of communicating with them. The goal is to provide ITSM with a tool to anticipate their requests, optimize productivity, reduce downtime, and have all the necessary ITSM processes, including incident management, problem management, changes, requests, self-service, SLA management, and others. The proposed solution fits easily into IT operations.

- Control of the support center with fundamental processes;
- Improved service and support performance, and reduced unforeseen costs and business risks;

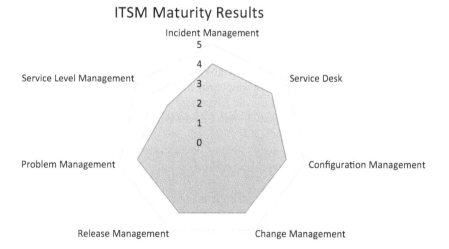

FIGURE 4.6 ITSM maturity score after implementation.

- Support center solution is easy to use and administer;
- IT administrators can easily configure, design, and modify the support center system. IT teams can configure it without coding to meet the changing needs of the enterprise and achieve faster profitability without disrupting users;
- Improved user satisfaction through the self-service portal: secure self-service functions, available anywhere and all the time enable endusers to log and resolve their own IT incidents, and display relevant information. The service catalog allows the end user to view and use the services for which they have rights, and automatically provides and maintains services, linking them to the policy and objectives of the IT department;
- Improved visibility of operations through reports and dashboards: Quickly evaluate your performance against the company's goals, for continuous improvement. Easily create or configure multilevel reports based on the metrics used to demonstrate ITSM value for the enterprise. Dashboards with cascading analysis functions to trend charts based on Key Performance Indicators (KPI) to provide context for decision-making and planning. The benefits of the adoption of the practical ITSM/ITAM framework are
- 95% success rate on SLAs;
- Reports meet auditor requirements;
- 50% reduction in end user calls;
- Data confirm cost-cutting decisions;
- Improved ITAM and cost control;
- Set up an agile approach to deal with the different changes in the SI;
- Improved the management of the security of IT services;
- Implemented a continuous improvement strategy DDAO (Discover, Do, Act, and Optimize).

4.4.5.1.2 IT Asset Management

After auditing and measuring the organization's practice in ITAM by applying the ITAM maturity achievement model. The organization is at the initial level of the ITAM program. They recognized the problems that need to be addressed systematically. Nevertheless, there is no asset management policy. The ITAM is manual. Our objective was to improve ITAM maturity in the organization by implementing the ITAM lifecycle and an open-source solution management based on the functionalities described in section 4.1. This global approach will help the company to move to the desired level of asset management, which is the level managed by

- Reducing operational expenses and control of audits.

The regularization of licenses is outdated. It is now possible to ensure that software licenses comply with audit requirements while avoiding unnecessary expenses. We have proposed an open-source solution that allows for the sharing of relevant information with auditors who facilitate the calculation of active software licenses and the identification of people who use particular software and license covers. The suite also improves the life-cycle of software and assets, licenses, and property rights. You can automatically recover unused software licenses, reducing costs and risks.

- Creating lifecycle processes around IT assets.

Go beyond software recovery, to track and manage all the assets in the organization. Import and automatically follow the warranty information at the time of purchase. Automate hardware reminders for assets such as batteries, ink or toner from printers, and other consumables. This improves your efficiency and centralizes control through automated responses to queries or events.

- Using discovery and inventory processes.

The implemented solution publishes analysis data and management reports on a tablet, smartphone, or another device with an Internet browser. Management and IT management teams get a complete view of the assets used and the company's compliance. By having the correct information at the right time, you have confidence in your data and decisions.

4.4.5.1.3 IT Security Management

Organized cybercrime has only one target: user data. Data protection against the most complex threats. After auditing this axis, it appears that this component is not supported in the ITSM process, and the management of security incidents is not supported. We proposed implementing a security management solution based on the model defined in section 4.3, to offer better visibility of risks, facilitate compliance with current regulations and improve your overall level of security. Figure 4.7 illustrates the results of the IT level of security maturity after implementation.

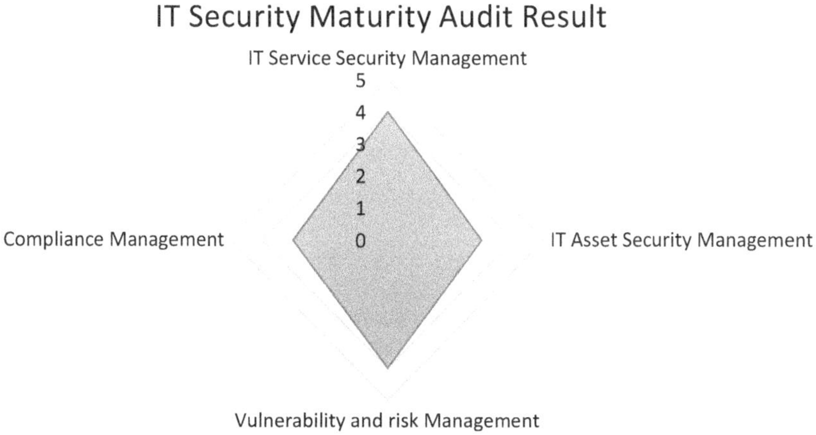

IT Security Maturity Audit Result

FIGURE 4.7   IT security maturity audit result after implementation.

4.4.6 Act

This step will evaluate the decisions and the approach taken. The quality department and management will study the results and judge the relevance of the decisions made. Moreover, this stage is required to reduce the gaps and dysfunctions deployed during each review or audit. Each year's planned management review takes into account the steps taken during the year or the last 6 months in trying to define opportunities for improvement. We exploit the DevOps approach to set up this step. DevOps brings fundamental changes to how application and execution teams interact and execute processes. It requires changes in technology, processes, and culture, and changes at this level can be difficult to resolve unless they are addressed systematically. We measure the organization's agility level using the proposed DevOps ITSM/ITAM Maturity model for continuous measurement and improvement. The organization's level of agility is initial; our objective is to orient the ACT part toward an agile approach to ensure delicate change management and consequently a continuous improvement by supporting people, process, and technology drivers. To create an agile IT service/assets center that delivers quicker resolutions, increase user satisfaction, and evolve with rapidly changing technologies, we suggest following the steps described in Figure 4.8.

The results obtained can be improved agile by adopting our agile approach based on DevOps. This approach will allow any organization to measure, control and manage IT services, asset, and endpoint security costs, and processes.

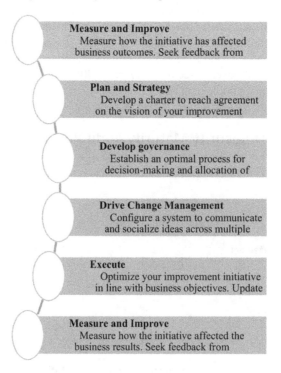

Measure and Improve
Measure how the initiative has affected business outcomes. Seek feedback from

Plan and Strategy
Develop a charter to reach agreement on the vision of your improvement

Develop governance
Establish an optimal process for decision-making and allocation of

Drive Change Management
Configure a system to communicate and socialize ideas across multiple

Execute
Optimize your improvement initiative in line with business objectives. Update

Measure and Improve
Measure how the initiative affected the business results. Seek feedback from

FIGURE 4.8   DevOps continues IT improvement.

4.4.7 Benefits of the Proposed Agile ITSM/ITAM after Implementation in the Organization

The suggested framework is a structured approach to increase ITSM efficiency and reduce incident management in new start-up companies. In this section, we discuss the axes of improvement referring to the results of the empirical study and interviews with the IT managers in different axes of the IT disciplines (ITSM, ITAM, and security). To measure the contribution of our proposed framework on the company's IS performance. This model has been implemented in the IT department of a port sector organization since 2019.

Because of the chapter-length limitations, we will not detail and discuss the audit of existing ITSM/ITAM in the organization and the improvement of IT management, asset, and security management after implementation of the proposed framework.

We highlight some benefits of implementing the proposed model in a port sector organization with more than 1,000 IT end-users. User expectations have changed and the IT department has to develop other ways of communicating with them. The goal is to provide ITSM with a tool to anticipate their requests, optimize productivity, reduce downtime, and have all the necessary ITSM processes, including incident management, problem management, changes, requests, self-service, SLA management, and others. The proposed solution fits easily into IT operations as it

- Continues to reduce variable costs by reducing the TCO per user;
- Involves the end-user in the incident management process (Self Servicing);
- SSO password management policy (fewer passwords);
- Increases the satisfaction rate of computer users by 75% to 90% for 2016, ensuring the quality of the services delivered through a survey quality system;
- Makes the profiles versatile (admin driver) internal or for client projects;
- Continues to improve the management of releases (business case, decision, planning, monitoring, deliverables, PIR, etc.);
- Continues to improve the configuration management process by operational practices (car inventory, life sheets, and ITSM tools);
- With the Quality Manager, continues to strengthen reporting;
- Makes the management system more efficient;
- Extends the scope of SLAs (backups, and ensure consistency between SLA with OLA/UC);
- Reviews the incident/problem relationship (status of the incident after opening a problem);
- Formalizes any type of structure to manage all goods, regardless of the type of goods, business applications or equipment, and so on;
- Provides decision-makers with detailed information on the allocation, cost, and forecast of assets;
- Reduces risk by avoiding penalties and expensive litigation due to regulatory or contractual non-compliance, especially in software licensing;
- Implements asset responsibility with management reporting to optimize assets and protect against malicious use and/or theft;

- Reduces costs by eliminating unnecessary acquisitions if the property already exists;
- Proactively manages the warranty and support and maintenance contracts for optimal utility;
- Negotiates better contracts by properly managing assets and suppliers;
- Improves productivity by automating the movement of goods in the business environment;
- Ensures that assets and services meet the baseline configuration for vulnerability patches, antivirus policies, and user security are well-addressed to meet compliance standards such as PCI and ISO 2700x;
- Facilitates data-based internal compliance and accountability audits to improve processes continuously.

4.5 SUMMARY

An efficient, agile, and practical approach to ITSM/ITAM is vital for IT organizations to increase the quality of services they provide, improve speed and agility of the service desk, and improve user experience, all reducing the cost run IT. This chapter aims to identify the important aspects of a practical agile framework for ITSM/ITAM efficiency. It was collected based on a theoretical and empirical research study that generated answers to the sub-level research questions, and a return of experience analysis of the best practices in organizations.

In a theoretical study, the concept and needs of ITSM in the organization are presented with applying different methods and improvement techniques, hence proving the most important of the ITIL-ITSM best practice model. This work aims to propose a global and practical ITSM/ITAM framework based on four aspects (ITSM, ITAM, Security Management, and Agility Management). The proposed framework was defined based on empirical study and was implemented in the large-scale organization (+900 employees). The result of adopting this framework gives a clear idea of its efficiency, making it reusable in any other organization. Additionally, performing ITSM is a costly task. Small changes in the framework process can lead to significant changes in the profit and management process within the organization, like maintaining and operating an information infrastructure. Thus, first, an organization needs to choose the comprehensive ITSM framework, which fulfills its required aims from a specific task. Second, it has a better performing quality in an ITSM model.

BIBLIOGRAPHY

Abdelkebir, S. A. H. I. D., Maleh, Y., & Belaissaoui, M. (2017, November). An agile framework for ITS management In organizations: A case study based on DevOps. In *Proceedings of the 2nd International Conference on Computing and Wireless Communication Systems*, ACM (pp. 1–8).

Ang, A. (2014). *Asset management: A systematic approach to factor investing*. Oxford University Press.

Bartolini, S. (2006). *IT service management driven by business objectives: An application to incident management*. IEEE/IFIP Network Operations and Management Symposium NOMS.

Beck, K. (1999). *Extreme programming explained: Embrace change*. Addison-Wesley.

Brooks, P. (2006). *Metrics for IT service management*. Van Haren Publishing.

Ciborra, C. (1992). From thinking to tinkering: The grassroots of IT and strategy. *Information Society*, *8*, 297–309.

Clark, C., Cavanaugh, N., Brown, C., & V, S. (1997). Building change-readiness capabilities in the IS organization: Insights from the bell Atlantic experience. *MIS Quarterly*, *21*(4), 425–455.

Das, Z. (1991). Integrating the content and process of strategic MIS planning with competitive strategy. *Decision Sciences*, 953–984.

Duane, L., & Charlie, S. (2016). *Reducing the cost of test through strategic asset management*. IEEE Autotestcon.

Fink, L., & Neuman, S. (2009). Exploring the perceived business value of the flexibility enabled by information technology infrastructure. *Information & Management*, *46*(2), 90–99.

Gene, K., Jez, H., Patrick, D., & John, W. (2016). *The DevOps handbook: How to create world-class agility, reliability, and security in technology organizations*. IT Revolution Press.

Giudice, D. L., Christopher, M. A., Amy, H., & Ian, M. (2016, March 30). *Agile and DevOps adoption drives digital business success*. Forrester Research. Transforming IT Organizations into Service Providers. www.hp.com/hps/itsm

Goldman, S. N. (1995). *Agile competitors and virtual organizations: Strategies for enriching the customer*. Van Nostrand Reinhold.

Gupta, P. (2008). *Automating ITSM incident management process*. International Conference on Autonomic Computing.

Hank, M. (2006). *ITIL: What it is and what it isn't*. Business Communications Review.

Hewlet Packard HP. (2016). *HP devops*. www.hpe.com;https://saas.hpe.com/fr-fr/software/devops-solutions

Holmqvist, M., & Pessi, K. (2006). Agility through scenario development and continuous implementation: A global aftermarket logistics case. *European Journal of Information Systems*, *15*, 146–158.

Hong, W., Thong, J. Y., Chasalow, L. C., & Dhillon, G. (2011). User acceptance of agile information systems: A model and empirical test. *Journal of Management Information Systems*, *28*(1), 235.

ISO/IEC 20000. (2010). *ISO/IEC 20000 information Technology*. ISO/IEC 20000.

Jurison, J. (1996). Toward more effective management of information technology benefits. *The Journal of Strategic Information Systems*, *5*(4), 263–274.

Kumbakara, N. (2008). Managed IT services: The role of IT standards. *Information Management & Computer Security*, 336–359.

Lahtela, J. (2010). *Implementing an ITIL-based IT service management measurement system*. Fourth International Conference on Digital Society.

LANDESK. (2010). Achieving security maturity [white paper]. *LANDESK*. http://landesk.avocent.com/WorkArea/downloadasset.aspx?id=5232

Lee, O., Banerjee, P., Lim, K., Kumar, K., Hillegersberg, V., & Wei, K. J. (2006). Agility in globally distributed system development. *Communications of the ACM*, *49*(10), 49–54.

Luftman, J. (2003). Assessing IT-business alignment. *Information Systems Management*, 9–15.

Markus, M., & Benjamin, R. (1996). Change agentry –the next IS frontier. *MIS Quarterly*, *20*(4), 385–407.

Marrone, K. (2011). Uncovering ITIL claims: IT executives' perception on benefits and business-IT alignment. *Information Systems and e-Business Management*, 363–380.

McNaughton, R. (2010). Designing an evaluation framework for IT service management. *Information & Management*, 219–225.

Meade, L. M. (1997). Method for analyzing agility alternatives for business processes. In G. L. Curry (Ed.), *Industrial engineering research – conference proceedings* (pp. 960–965). IIE.

Mesquida, A. L. (2012). *IT service management process improvement based on ISO/IEC 15504: A systematic review*. Information and Software Technology.

Meziani, S. (2010). *e-government: ITIL-based service management case study*. The 12th International Conference on Information Integration and Web-Based Applications &Services.

Mior. (2008). *The importance of ITSM: Malaysian business*. New Straits Times Press.

Park, K. (2008). *The study on the maturity measurement method of security management for ITSM*. Proceedings of the 2008 International Conference on Convergence and Hybrid Information.

Porter, M. (1996). What is strategy. *Harvard Business Review, 74*(6).

Reich, B. (2000). Factors that influence the social dimension of alignment between business and information technology objectives. *MIS Quarterly*, 81–113.

Richards, C. (1996). Agile manufacturing: Beyond lean. *Production & Inventory Management, Second Quarter*, 60–64.

Robert, H., Isabell, S., Kiess, O., Ingo, B., Sacha, M., & Bradley, L. (2016, June 28). *IT service management for DevOps*. IBM.www.ibm.com/developerworks/community/files/form/anony mous/api/library/42529e82-173a-4f45-805b-93d9eb35ffa6/document/19b71c8c-1675-4727- a3ab-b259ba1d49e6/media/ITSM%20Reference%20Architecture%20-%20DevOps%20 -%20Whitepaper.pdf

Sahid, A., & Belaissaoui, M. (2021). Strategic agility for IT service management: A case study. In *Strategic information system agility: From theory to practices*. Emerald Publishing Limited.

Sahid, A., Maleh, Y., & Belaissaoui, M. (2018). A practical agile framework for IT service and asset management ITSM/ITAM through a Case Study. *Journal of Cases on Information Technology (JCIT), 20*(4), 71–92.

Schwaber, K. (2004). *Agile project management with scrum*. Microsoft Press.

Sharp, J., Irani, Z., & Desai, S. (1999). Working towards agile manufacturing in the UK industry. *International Journal of Production Economics, 62*, 155–169.

Shekhar, G. (2020, October). Instructor led training and Certification-ITIL V4 Foundation. In *Proceedings of the 21st Annual Conference on Information Technology Education* (pp. 355).

Silva Molina, L. F. (2005). *How to identify and measure the level of alignment between IT and business governance*. Proceedings of the PICMET.

Tan, C.S. (2009). Implementing IT service management: A case study focussing on critical success factors. *Journal of Computer Information Systems*, 1–12.

Uebernickel, B.S. Z. (2006). *Service-engineering: A process model for the development of IS services*. Proceedings of the European and Mediterranean Conference on Information Systems (EMCIS).

van Bon, E. (2007). *Foundations of IT service management based on ITIL v3*. Van Haren Publishing.

van Grembergen, H. (2009). *COBIT as a framework for enterprise governance of IT*. Springer.

Vernadat, F. (1999). Research agenda for agile manufacturing. *International Journal of Agile, 1*(1), 37–40.

Volberda, H. (1996). Towards the flexible form: How to remain vital in hypercompetitive environments. *Organization Science, 7*(4), 359–387.

Volberda, H., & Rutges, A. (1999). FARSYS: A knowledge-based system for managing strategic change. *Decision Support Systems, 26*, 99–123.

Wilcocks, L. (2013). *Information management: The evaluation of information systems investments*. Springer Science Business Media.

Winniford, C. (2009). Confusion in the ranks: IT service management practice and terminology. *Information Systems Management*, 153–163.

Wui-Gee, A. (2009). *Implementing it service management: A case study focussing on critical success factors*. International Association for Computer Information Systems.

Yusuf, Y., Sarhadi, M., & Gunasekaran, A. (1999). Agile manufacturing: The drivers, concepts and attributes. *International Journal of Production Economics, 62*, 33–43.

Zhang, Z., & Sharifi, H. (1999). A methodology for achieving agility in manufacturing organizations: An introduction. *International Journal of Production Economics, 62*, 7–22.

Zhong, X. (2010). *An ITIL based ITSM practice: A case study of steel manufacturing enterprise*. 7th International Conference on Service Systems and Service Management.

Cloud Computing as a Key Pillar for Agile IT Governance

5

5.1 INTRODUCTION

In the world of development and innovation, the emerging concepts of Cloud Computing are increasingly used by software development companies to accelerate the pace of production.

In software development, agile methodology is an increasingly common approach used for effective project management. Agile project management is iterative and aims to continuously incorporate user adjustments in each iteration of the development project (Zhang et al., 2020).

Agile mode allows development in a continuous software production cycle. Cloud Computing provides tools and infrastructure to the teams that carry out these agile developments, to guarantee security and facilitate the integration, automation, and deployment processes.

Cloud computing blends two fundamental IT trends: IT efficiency, where IT performance is used effectively, and market agility, where IT becomes a strategic weapon with fast implementation, batch parallelism, and intensive processing (Lynn et al., 2018).

Previous research offers tentative empirical proof that agility and one of the variables shaping decision-making are linked to the implementation of cloud computing technologies and their role in increasing the agility of information systems (Yang et al., 2013).

Based on these studies, our chapter seeks to theorize and empirically validate the factors that influence the cloud-computing technology decision by responding to the following research questions:

- What are the reasons behind the use of cloud computing and why?
- How will cloud-based use boost IT governance through agility?

DOI: 10.1201/9781003161998- 8

To address these questions, we build on the literature on the Technology Acceptance Model (TAM) and Diffusion of Innovation (DOI) and suggest a web-based implementation paradigm and structure to enhance IT agility through cloud computing technologies. The next segment discusses the literature on factors affecting cloud adoption to create a theoretical model for implementing cloud technologies. The second section explains the empiric experiments that evaluate the proposed model.

5.2 LITERATURE REVIEW

This literature review synthesizes current cloud studies from an operational perspective. This incorporates the results using the defined framework. We organized the deductions according to the following four aspects: the properties of cloud computing, the features of implementation, governance mechanisms, and the effect on the agility of the information system. We noticed that research encouraging or discouraging cloud technology use and the study on cloud computing agility is rare. It can be because cloud computing is a recent and relatively new research topic (Adamson et al., 2017).

Although this concept is not fully modern, there is no standardized or traditional description of cloud computing. This has grown with recent technologies in virtualization, cloud computing, and Internet-based content delivery. The 'cloud' term refers to the universal development and connectivity of computing services by Internet technologies. Through cloud applications, businesses and customers can conveniently access large amounts of computing performance at a marginal cost, allowing organizations to reduce the overall cost of information technology. Cloud computing thus brings competitive and financial benefits that companies should certainly not ignore (Chemjor & Lagat, 2017).

Cloud computing reflects the convergence of IT performance and market agility. IT performance results from scalable hardware and software resources, improved work efficiency and coordination between firms, and high availability of services. In their study, Noor et al. (2018) enhanced work performance and collaboration between companies and readily accessible resources. The business agility in cloud infrastructure is the capacity to rapidly implement computational resources, rising initial capital spending, and adapting quickly to evolving customer demands. Cloud Computing removes the traditional boundaries between companies.

Cloud technology delivers its commitments through minimized complexity and limitless scalability to on-demand capability and CapEx cost savings (Nasir, 2017), cloud technology delivers its commitments. While there are still unanswered questions about cloud computing, regardless of how cloud computing performs on its commitments, the organizations cannot risk stability, efficiency, and flexibility to move to the cloud. In addition, agility is a critical element in cloud computing, this ability to respond to change reliably in times of uncertainty has become a necessity. This is why we have continued this work to analyze how cloud computing will increase the information system agility, and provide a model to adopt the cloud technology while getting the maximum benefit from this technology.

5.3 THEORETICAL FOUNDATION

Tornatzky et al. (1990) outlined the technological, organizational, and environmental (TOE) framework to understand the innovation process in an enterprise context. It addresses three factors that influence the adoption of an innovation: technology, organization, and the environment. Technology context means the internal and external technologies pertinent to the organization and those that could be adopted. Organizational context relates to company descriptive characteristics (i.e., size, organizational structure, level of centralization), resources (human and insufficient resources), and communication process (formal and informal) among employees. Concerning the environment, this context includes environmental market elements, competitors, and the regulatory framework.

Several studies have examined technical and operational issues related to cloud computing, involving topics such as selecting cloud computing services in terms of cost and risk, secure storage audit protocol and computing in the cloud, cost of cloud computing ownership models and security issues, privacy risks, and information loss.

Trigueros-Preciado et al. (2013) surveyed 94 Spanish small- and medium-sized businesses and found that knowledge of cloud computing was poor among companies and that companies did not know much about cloud computing.

Our analysis of academic sources revealed few research chapters that examined the implementation of cloud computing from an operational point of view, as given in Table 5.1.

In their study, Abdollahzadehgan et al. (2013) used DOI and TOE platforms to research the implementation of cloud computing in Taiwan's high-tech industry, they often found cloud adoption rather than a continuous cycle as a complex, dependent variable. However, their approach was not robust, as it did not consider core drivers such as cost savings and security issues essential to the company's cloud infrastructure adoption.

Nkhoma et al. (2013) used secondary data from the survey of a large services company to study the drivers and barriers to cloud computing adoption. Wu et al. (2013) investigated whether the information processing requirements and capacity affect the firm's intention to adopt cloud computing; they used the DOI theory and information processing view (IPV) to conduct their study in the supply chain domain.

The review of published journal articles indicates that most studies empirically evaluate the direct effects of innovation, contextual factors, or conduct analysis using qualitative methods or secondary data on the adoption of cloud computing. In addition, we founded that no study has taken a holistic approach to validate the direct and indirect effects of the innovation characteristics and the underlying technology, organization, and environmental contexts empirically. The study by Yang & Tate (2012) indicates that research on cloud computing is skewed mostly toward technological issues. They highlight the lack of cumulative research to address cloud computing's social, organizational, and environmental perspectives. This study addresses this crucial research gap by developing an integrative research model that combines the theoretical perspectives of the diffusion of innovation and the technology, organization, and environmental contexts. Table 5.1 discusses cloud computing studies in the literature.

TABLE 5.1   Cloud Computing Studies

AUTHOR	IT ADOPTION (DEPENDENT VARIABLE)	CONSTRUCTS/ FACTORS (INDEPENDENT VARIABLES)	METHODS	DATA AND CONTEXT
(Low et al., 2011)	Cloud computing	Technology (relative advantage, complexity, compatibility)	Factor analysis (FA), logistic regression	An e-mail survey of 111 firms belonging to the high tech
(Lin & Chen, 2012)	Cloud computing	Relative advantage, compatibility, complexity, Trial-ability, observability	Semi-structured qualitative interview	19 IT professionals, Taiwan
(Wu et al., 2013)	Cloud computing	Business process complexity, entrepreneurial culture, compatibility, application functionality	Confirmatory factor analysis, multiple regression analysis	An e-mail survey of N=289 firms in manufacturing and retail
(Trigueros-Preciado et al., 2013)	Cloud adoption	Barriers and benefits	Qualitative and quantitative methodology	Survey N=94 SMEs in Spain
(Hemlata et al., 2015)	Cloud adoption	Relative advantage, compatibility, complexity, organizational readiness, top management commitment, and training and education	Exploratory, confirmatory factor analysis, and structural equation modeling	A questionnaire was used to collect the data from 280 companies in IT, manufacturing and finance sectors in India
(Kshetri, 2013)	Cloud adoption	Regulative, normative, cognitive	Conceptual	Survey of CloudVendors in China N=7
(Sharma et al., 2017)	Cloud adoption	IT service cost, time to market, and organization size	qualitative and quantitative	Experts from 13 organizations (including 8 cloud service providers (CSPs) and 5 cloud service users (CSUs))

AUTHOR	IT ADOPTION (DEPENDENT VARIABLE)	CONSTRUCTS/ FACTORS (INDEPENDENT VARIABLES)	METHODS	DATA AND CONTEXT
(Senarathna, I., Wilkin, C., Warren, M., Yeoh & Salzman, 2018)	Cloud adoption	Relative advantage, quality of service and awareness, security, privacy and flexibility	Quantitative methodology	Survey of 149 Australian SMEs
(Butt et al., 2019)	Agile cloud adoption	Cost-effectiveness, security, and privacy	Excel sheet, questionnaires	A total of seven IT industries and many professionals from software industries related to cloud-agile adoption
(Skafi et al., 2020)	Cloud adoption	Complexity, security, top management support, and prior IT experience	Confirmatory factor analysis and logistic regression	Data collected from 139 respondents working in SMEs in Lebanon

5.4 COMBINING DOI AND TOE

To evaluate the integrative search paradigm principles, we analyzed through browsing databases, such as EBSCO Academic Research, ProQuest, Emerald, Springer, Science Direct, Taylor & Françis, and Google Scholar. The relevant studies were clustered together to classify the most common variables identified in the reviewed cloud adoption literature. Finally, we analyzed each factor to assess its contribution to cloud computing adoption.

Numerous studies suggest an approach incorporating more than one theoretical approach to consider implementing emerging new technologies (Wu et al., 2013). Thus, to clarify the operational decisions relevant to the implementation of technical innovation, the analysis context must be global and the variables tailored to the scope of innovation. Widely used in numerous IT integration reports, the TOE approach has provided ongoing methodological support.

In addition, the importance of context integration (TOE) to support DOI theory is recognized. Implicitly, technology is the same (Rogers, 2003). The DOI has the same internal and external organizational features as the TDE sense. The two hypotheses do have significant variations. The TOE does not define the function of individual characteristics (e.g., managerial support). At this point, DOI suggests that the company requires executive support.

Similarly, the DOI lacks environmental effects. Due to various DOI's limitations, TOE offers further insight into IT adoption across technology, organizational, and environmental contexts. The two hypotheses complement each other greatly.

Of the five DOI characteristics, cloud adoption has three innovation features: relative benefit, difficulty, and accessibility. For IT research studies, creativity and observational ability are not commonly used. Thus, following general knowledge and device analysis guidelines, these two attributes are overlooked, as they are not applicable to cloud computing technology. Rogers (2003) states that 'the nature of innovation determines the type of relative benefit that is important to the adopter' and that the relative benefit of innovation can be 'expressed in terms of economic profitability, social prestige or other means'. Our study postulates that cloud computing can lead to an economic advantage in terms of the cost reduction that it is capable of achieving IS agility (Yang et al., 2013).

Similarly, security issues will reduce the relative benefits of cloud computing. They also provide two additional characteristics: cost savings and stability as antecedents to cloud computing's relative advantage. They assess if cloud computing can be fairly advantageous in saving costs, enhancing agility to meet change, finding new opportunities, and staying competitive. Table 5.2 lists factors affecting cloud adoption.

TABLE 5.2 Summary of the Factors Studied Influencing Cloud Adoption

SOURCES	MODEL/THEORY	AGILITY	SECURITY, PRIVACY, AND TRUST	COST-SAVING	TOP MANAGEMENT SUPPORT	COMPETITIVE PRESSURE	FIRM SIZE	TECHNOLOGICAL READINESS	RELATIVE ADVANTAGE	COMPETENCE AND AWARENESS	COMPATIBILITY	COMPLEXITY	DATA SOVEREIGNTY
(Zhu, Dong, et al., 2006)	TOE and Others	*	*				*	*			*	*	
(Alam, 2009)	DOI and TOE				*		*				*	*	
(Tsai et al., 2010)	DOI			*	*						*		
(Low et al., 2011)	DOI and TOE	*			*	*				*	*	*	
(Lin & Chen, 2012)	DOI	*									*	*	
(Klein, 2012)	TOE					*					*	*	
(Abdollahzadehgan et al., 2013)	TOE					*	*	*			*		
(Oliveira et al., 2014)	DOI and TOE			*	*		*			*	*	*	

SOURCES	MODEL/ THEORY	FACTORS											
		AGILITY	SECURITY, PRIVACY, AND TRUST	COST-SAVING	TOP MANAGEMENT SUPPORT	COMPETITIVE PRESSURE	FIRM SIZE	TECHNOLOGICAL READINESS	RELATIVE ADVANTAGE	COMPETENCE AND AWARENESS	COMPATIBILITY	COMPLEXITY	DATA SOVEREIGNTY
(Amini et al., 2015)	DOI and TOE		*	*	*			*	*		*		*
(Senarathna, 2016)	DOI and TOE	*	*										
(Chemjor et al., 2017)	TOE			*			*				*	*	
(Sandu & Gide, 2018)	TOE				*			*	*				*
(Amron et al., 2019)	DOI and TOE		*	*	*	*	*		*	*	*	*	*

5.5 RESEARCH MODEL AND HYPOTHESES

Using DOI and TOE models, we examine organizations' decision-making regarding cloud computing. Top management support and firm size are common organizational consider-ations. Two variables, competitive pressure and regulatory security, determine the degree to which the environmental context will influence the cloud's decision system adoption, as shown in Figure 5.1.

By integrating the innovation features of cloud computing with the TOE system's techno-logical, organizational, and environmental dimensions, we respond to a researcher's request to develop a holistic model for understanding the spread of IT innovation. Linking this case study to our literature review mentioned in Table 5.2, we identify key features of cloud adop-tion in terms of technological, organizational, environmental, and innovation influences.

5.6 THE INNOVATION CHARACTERISTICS

- **Agility**

Cloud computing's most significant advantage is that it contributes to an organization's agility. Using cloud computing, enterprise systems are transformed to give companies

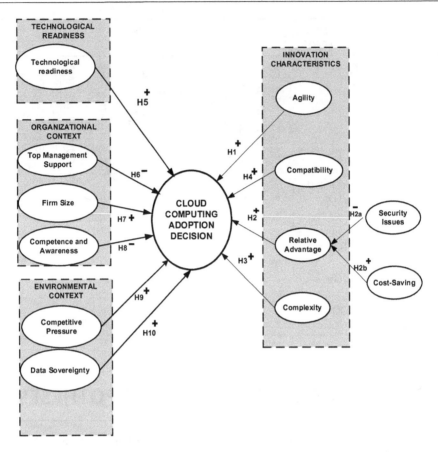

FIGURE 5.1   The proposed model for cloud adoption in organizations.

greater flexibility in service use, more efficiency, and higher productivity (Kunio, 2010). According to Sitaram & Manjunath (2012), agility and creativity are considered key growth engines of cloud computing. Companies willing to reconfigure cloud computing will be more adaptable to evolving external markets, and better equipped to leverage new opportunities by exploiting scalability and agility of cloud computing (Sahid et al., 2020).

Thus, **H1**. Agility can positively influence the relative benefits of cloud computing.

- **Relative Advantage**

Relative advantage is defined as how innovation is considered more advantageous than a substituted definition (Rogers, 2003). Unambiguous and straightforward competitive success (e.g., increased revenue) and operational efficiency (e.g., cost savings) improvements are driven to incorporate (TRISHA et al., 2004). If technology advantages (in this case cloud computing) outweigh existing processes and procedures (IFINEDO, 2011), the advantages will positively affect its implementation.

Therefore, **H2**. The relative advantage will have a positive influence on cloud computing adoption.

- **Security, privacy, and trust**

The term 'breach of security' applies to an incident where a corporation or government agency loses classified information, personal data, or other confidential information (Bishop, 2002). Cloud computing is a combination of resources in a shared multi-user network. This raises security threats (Schneiderman, 2011), as companies become unsure about future security risks (Benlian & Hess, 2011). Often, the lack of established security policies and identity management requirements means companies would be hesitant to implement a cloud-based solution. Cloud migration introduces new layers of complexity to data protection, significantly affecting the company's decision to embrace innovation.

Hence, **H2a.** The security and privacy issues will have a negative impact in terms of cloud computing's relative advantage.

- **Cost Savings**

Cloud computing technology provides innovation opportunities, decreases IT spending, and lowers overall computing costs. In selecting cloud storage, an organization will reduce the time spent on system maintenance and routine updates. Cloud computing also lowers network costs, electricity usage, and maintenance costs (Mazhelis & Tyrväinen, 2012).

Hence **H2b**. Cost savings would positively influence the relative benefits of cloud computing.

- **Complexity**

Complexity is the stage where creativity is considered difficult to understand. The better the technology incorporates into company processes, the greater the probability of adoption. Cloud systems will quickly pool resources to meet workloads. Moving to a cloud system, however, may be a problem for organizations lacking technological knowledge and IT specialists.

Hence, **H3**. Complexity will have a negative influence on cloud adoption.

- **Compatibility**

Compatibility is the degree to which innovation suits the prospective adopter's core principles, past experiences, and current needs. Compatibility is a primary determinant of creativity (Azadegan & Teich, 2010). For example, if cloud adoption aims to take advantage of low-security applications' scalability benefits, moving resources into cloud infrastructure makes economic sense.

So, **H4.** Compatibility can positively affect cloud adoption.

5.7 TECHNOLOGICAL READINESS

The technology background relates to the organization's technical features for technology adoption. This covers both institutional and individual human capital. Structural aspects refer to the company's platform or technological infrastructure that cloud-computing services can complement or replace. Unique human resources are people inside the company who have the expertise and skills to incorporate cloud computing together they improve an organization's technological readiness (Cervone, 2010)

Hence, **H5.** Technological readiness will positively influence cloud-computing adoption.

5.8 THE ORGANIZATION CONTEXT

- **Top Management Support**

Organizational context refers to the availability of resources facilitating innovation adoption, that is, organizational characteristics that promote or limit a company's adoption and implementation of innovation. Many factors affect the relationship with the organizational structure and innovation adoption, such as centralization level, power and control distribution, information links, insufficient resource availability, lateral communication, company size, and senior management support. Senior management support plays a significant role in cloud IT adoption by supporting resource allocation, integrating resources, and re-engineering processes (Abdollahzadehgan et al., 2013).

So, **H6.** Top management support will have a positive influence on cloud adoption.

- **Firm Size**

Nevertheless, large companies have an advantage over small firms as they have more resources and can take more risks related to innovation adoption. Research has shown that small companies, although more flexible, do not embrace emerging technologies readily. Therefore, enterprise size is a determining factor in cloud computing adoption (Thiesse et al., 2011).

Hence **H7.** The firm size will have a positive influence on cloud adoption.

- **Competence and Awareness**

One of the cloud computing's main challenges is the lack of competent cloud profiles. Today, these problems are critical for organizations that want to stand out from the crowd to attract and retain the best applicants and meet the standards of the new generations. The university's role is crucial for continuing evolution and helping companies learn and train cloud computing concepts and applications (Abolfazli et al., 2015).

Hence, **H8.** The firm size will have a positive influence on cloud adoption.

5.9 THE ENVIRONMENTAL CONTEXT

- **The Competitive Pressure**

The environmental backdrop is the context in which a company operates and depends on the consumer dynamics, its competitors, and others' ability to access capital and government relations. Cloud adoption factors include market competitiveness and regulatory environment. Adopting new technologies is also a competitive market rivalry imperative. Cloud computing offers greater operational flexibility, increased consumer exposure, and more reliable access to real-time data to businesses (Hsu et al., 2014).

That is why **H9**. The competitive pressure will influence the adoption of cloud computing positively.

- **Data Sovereignty**

Data sovereignty is the respect of rights associated with data based on the entity's location that has control over it. Governments generally apply data sovereignty to limit the cross-border storage of (sensitive) data, limiting organizations to operating local data centers only when external services may be more efficient and affordable (Abolfazli et al., 2015).

Guaranteeing the ownership, security, and sovereignty of data has become a vital issue for companies, especially governments, which have decided to dematerialize their information systems in the cloud (Zhu, Kraemer, et al., 2006). Several organizations are still asking questions about the storage and sovereignty of data in the cloud. Answering these questions and clarifying misunderstandings around data sovereignty promote better cloud adoption.

H10. Data sovereignty has an impact on cloud adoption.

5.10 RESEARCH METHODOLOGY

5.10.1 Quantitative Methodology

This research uses a quantitative approach in which participants are not supposed to justify their reactions (Tashakkori & Creswell, 2007). Through this approach, researchers will explore participants' thoughts, assumptions, and strategies. There are numerous studies comparing quantitative performance. Such findings are grouped into technological, cultural, and efficiency measures. Such studies interpret organizational characteristics, user characteristics, technological features, and information need as rigid, autonomous, and objective constructs rather than dynamic and interacting.

Our study focuses on various aspects of cloud computing in information systems and their effect on IT agility. The quantitative analysis approach is presented in Figure 5.2.

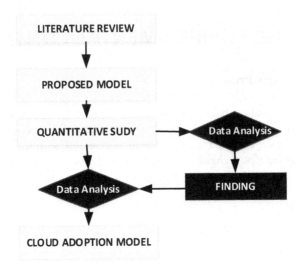

FIGURE 5.2   Research design.

5.10.2 Measurement Model

In the Middle East and North Africa (MENA) zone, 200 small and large organizations covering the manufacturing and service sectors were surveyed to determine theoretical constructions. These businesses work in the public and private sectors. Constructions (agility, protection concerns, cost savings, strategic benefit, difficulty, reliability, technical preparation, senior management support, competitive pressure, and regulatory support) were evaluated using the five-point Likert scale at intervals ranging from 'strongly disagree' to 'strongly accept'. The research was performed in different stages. The first edition was designed to understand the different scientific theories reviewed by managers and technical experts. A pre-test also made it easier to reformulate some questions to enhance the questionnaire's understanding and the quality of the answers. The questionnaire was formulated in the company's three common languages, such as English, French, and Arabic.

5.11 DATA COLLECTION

An online version of the questionnaire was e-mailed to the decision-makers and qualified individuals with an important position in the organization. Data were collected using a two-stage online questionnaire from mid-2018 to early 2019. These data were updated with responses from the first quarter of 2020. Table 5.3 presents the participants' demographics.

TABLE 5.3 Participants' Demographics

VARIABLES		FREQUENCY	PERCENTAGE
Organization size	100–500 employees	30	15
	500–1,000 employees	50	25
	1,000–2,000 employees	80	40
	More than 2,000 employees	40	20
Industry	Manufacturing	31	15.5
	Petrochemical	10	5
	Chemicals	22	11
	Engineering	33	16.5
	Energy	15	7.5
	Financial services	34	17
	IT	50	25
	Retail	2	1
	Other	3	1.5
Market scope	International	112	56
	Local	25	12.5
	National	63	31.5
Adoption stage	Yes	128	64
	No	72	36

The research used 'key informant' data collection approach (Benlian & Hess, 2011) to classify the organization's most active and competent cloud computing respondents. To target key informants, we provided clear descriptions of cloud computing and examples. To maximize content validity, we suggested that the most recognizable member of the organization would complete the survey. The final version of the questionnaire was written in English, comprising 34 questions, with multiple elements evaluating each factor. Table 5.5 shows the mean and standard deviation of full and subsamples.

5.12 RESULTS

This research aims to identify cloud acceptance determinants using a technique that integrates the revolutionary features of cloud computing with the company's technical, operational, and environmental insights. We found 9 factors influencing cloud adoption: agility, complexity, competitive pressure, technological readiness, top management support, regulatory, compatibility, firm size, and data sovereignty. Includes cloud-based computing with political, science, corporate, and environmental insights. The results show that five variables affect cloud adoption significantly: agility, cost saving, stability, privacy and confidence, and technical readiness and data sovereignty, as shown in Table 5.4.

TABLE 5.4   Quantitative Factors that Influence the Adoption of Cloud Computing

CONSTRUCTS	ITEMS	ADAPTED SOURCE
Agility	A1 – Cloud computing allows you to manage your business activities efficiently.	(Yang et al., 2013)
	A2 – Cloud computing services improve the quality of operations.	
	A3 – Using cloud computing helps you get the job done faster at specific locations.	
	A4 – The use of cloud computing offers new opportunities.	
Security, privacy, and trust concerns	S1 – Degree of company's concern with data security on the cloud computing	(Zhu, Dong, et al., 2006), (Luo et al., 2010), (Wu, 2011)
	S2 – Degree of concern for customers with data security in cloud computing	
	S3 – Degree of concern about privacy in cloud computing	
Cost savings	CS1 – Enterprise-level concerns about data security in cloud computing	(Thiesse et al., 2011), (Sangle, 2011)
	CS2 – Level of customer concern about data security in cloud computing	
	CS3 – Level of concern about privacy in cloud computing	
Complexity	CP1 – Using cloud computing requires lots of mental effort	(Ifinedo, 2011), (Thiesse et al., 2011)
	CP2 – Using cloud computing is frustrating	
	CP3 – Using cloud computing is too complicated for business operations	
	CP4 – For firm employees, the skills required to adopt cloud computing are too complicated	
Compatibility	CT1 – Cloud computing can accommodate a company's work style	(Ifinedo, 2011), (Thiesse et al., 2011)
	CT2 – Cloud computing is fully compatible with today's business operations	
	CT3 – Cloud computing is compatible with your company's culture and value system	

CONSTRUCTS	ITEMS	ADAPTED SOURCE
	CT4 – Cloud computing will be compatible with existing company hardware and software	
Technology readiness	TR1 – Percentage of employees with Internet access	(Ifinedo, 2011)
	TR2 – The company knows how IT can be used to support operations	
	TR3 – In the enterprise, there are the skills needed to implement cloud computing	
Top management support	TS1 – Enterprise management supports the implementation of cloud computing	(Shah Alam et al., 2011)
	TS2 – Company management demonstrates strong leadership and commitment to the process when it comes to information systems	
	TS3 – Business leaders are prepared to take risks (financial and organizational) in adopting cloud computing	
Firm size	FS1 – The number of company employees	(Zhu et al., 2003), (Premkumar & Roberts, 1999)
	FS2 – Annual business volume	
Competence and awareness	CA1 – The competencies needed to manage and adopt cloud computing	(Abolfazli et al., 2015), (Cragg et al., 2011)
	CA2 – The level of awareness and adoption of cloud computing by the organization staff	
Competitive pressure	CP1 – The company believes that cloud computing can influence competition in their industry	(Ifinedo, 2011)
	CP2 – Competition is putting pressure on our site firm to adopt cloud computing	
	CP3 – Some competitors have already started using cloud computing	
Data sovereignty	DS1 – There is legal protection in the use of cloud computing	(Shah Alam et al., 2011), (Abolfazli et al., 2015)
	DS2 – As regulations become more stringent, companies storing data in the public cloud must ensure that they comply with data sovereignty laws.	

(Continued)

TABLE 5.4   (Continued)

CONSTRUCTS	ITEMS	ADAPTED SOURCE
Cloud computing adoption	CA1 – In terms of cloud adoption, at what stage is your organization currently engaged in cloud adoption. I do not think about it; being evaluated (e.g., as part of a pre-pilot study); evaluating this technology, but not planning to adopt it; evaluating and planning for the adoption of this technology; already adopted cloud computing services, infrastructure, or platforms. CCA2 – If you think in future you will embrace cloud computing. How do you think that will happen? Do not consider; more than 5 years; between 2 and 5 years; between 1 and 2 years; less than 1 year; already-adopted cloud computing services, infrastructure, or platforms.	(Thiesse et al., 2011)

Note: All questions are based on a five-point scale unless otherwise indicated.

TABLE 5.5   The Mean and Standard Deviation of Full and Subsamples

FACTORS	MEAN	SD
Agility	3.33	0.87
Security, privacy, and trust concerns	3.76	1.11
Cost savings	3.14	0.79
Complexity	2.26	0.80
Compatibility	2.90	0.80
Technology readiness	4.27	1.19
Top management support	2.89	0.96
Firm size	2.54	0.86
Competence and awareness	2.72	1.02
Competitive pressure	2.30	0.86
Regulatory support	2.58	0.85
Data sovereignty	3.81	0.81
Cloud computing adoption	2.40	1.61

5.13 FINDING

- **Innovation Characteristics**

Of the four innovation functions, Agility (H1) positively affects cloud-computing adoption. This finding reflects similar literature studies (Hsu et al., 2014). The survey confirms that cloud computing agility benefits organizations. The benefits found by the report include improved service efficiency, faster task execution, increased profitability, and new market opportunities.

Due to recent advances in privacy technology, monitoring, and encryption systems, security issues (H2a) do not preclude cloud adoption ensuring confidentiality, integrity, and data protection in the cloud (Ifinedo, 2011). Current federal guidelines and legislation like GDPR (Tankard & Pathways, 2016) and FedRampt (Montalbano, 2012) act helps create trust and organizational control over data while implementing cloud-based technologies that can clarify why security and privacy are not a concern while considering cloud computing.

Cost reduction (H2b) is verified as an integral factor illustrating cloud computing's relative advantage. This finding is consistent with studies showing that cost savings are a powerful driver of cloud-based solutions in sectors such as technology, manufacturing, finance, logistics, services, and education (Adamson et al., 2017).

Compatibility (H4) is considered to encourage the adoption of cloud computing for the business industry, but not essential for manufacturing. The work-style preferences and Internet business transactions prevalent among companies in this sector may explain their significance in the service industry. The lack of consistency in manufacturing may be attributed to the complexity of applications (e.g., the vital position of in-house software systems such as resource planning software and computer-controlled machining) and restricted market standards for Internet solutions (Ramdani et al., 2009). Compatibility findings are therefore still inconsistent compared to previous studies, and further research is needed to draw a definitive conclusion.

The complexity factor (H3) is also an obstacle to cloud computing in the service sector. Cloud computing's concept of complexity is no different from other disruptive technologies and appears to be an essential deterrent to cloud computing. Results suggest that uncertainty is not a limiting factor for manufacturing firms. Some researchers found complexity insignificant (Skafi et al., 2020), while others said the opposite (Borgman et al., 2013). Consequently, previous studies are not explicit on the position of complexity, suggesting that more work is required before a definite conclusion.

Technology Readiness

Technology readiness (H5) is a cloud adoption catalyst. According to the study, companies with established technology infrastructure and technically skilled workforce will be better suited to cloud computing integration. However, our study shows that cloud computing can disrupt services and create management challenges in IT and non-IT organizations. The finding suggests that companies must ensure that IT professionals' technology resources and availability are sufficient to incorporate cloud applications into business operations under limited downtime. Unlike previous studies that suggested technological readiness doesn't necessarily influence cloud adoption (Skafi et al., 2020). Therefore, technical readiness does not apply to technology companies, and cloud computing is less appropriate for organizations with more information processing power.

5.14 ORGANIZATIONAL CONTEXT

Our research empirically found that top-management support (H6) is important to understand cloud-computing adoption. According to the study results, senior management influences adoption by demonstrating support through financial and organizational resources commitment and engaging in the process. Such results are consistent with previous technology adoption and usage work (IFINEDO, 2011).

Enterprise size factor (H7) is a cloud adoption predictive. This conclusion is consistent with the literature that large firms have the resources needed to address investment risk and costs associated with emerging technology. Small businesses generally lack the resources to build knowledge, implement, and test cloud computing (Thiesse et al., 2011).

Competence and understanding (H8) is a key factor in cloud adoption in various organizations. Organizations are embracing the cloud worldwide (Abolfazli et al., 2015). The pattern will continue with talent acquisition, retention, and performance management. Today, these problems are critical for businesses that want to stand out from the crowd to attract and retain the best applicants and meet new generations' standards.

5.15 ENVIRONMENTAL CONTEXT

Few kinds of research have discussed cloud computing's environmental significance. According to competitive pressure pushed high-tech firms to adopt cloud computing faster, Ifinedo (2011) also determined that competitive pressure positively impacts the adoption of e-commerce technologies. While customer pressures, business partners, and government support played no significant role.

Data sovereignty (H10) is a crucial factor in cloud adoption. The challenge for companies to handle data sovereignty is heightened by various approaches that governments are taking to ensure citizens' data privacy (Abolfazli et al., 2015).

5.16 DISCUSSION AND INTERPRETATIONS

Survey results indicate that market pressure will not decide cloud adoption. Companies are probably aware of cloud benefits, but specific technology factors and organizational contexts prevent cloud benefits from translating to a competitive advantage. Also, regulatory support for cloud computing adoption was not significant. Regulatory processes are important to instill trust in companies to transform creativity into business opportunities. Our study findings suggest that agility, cost saving, security, privacy, and trust, technological readiness, and data sovereignty influences cloud computing adoption.

5.17 THE PROPOSED CLOUD GOVERNANCE FRAMEWORK

A key success factor for governance is not simply managing cloud impacts on the business but also governing the use of the cloud. By defining enterprise architecture (EA), you must have defined how it will be managed, including using a governance framework in which accountability controls are established to ensure appropriate adoption and use of EA. In this case, the next step is to incorporate cloud governance considerations as illustrated in Figure 5.3.

The Computing Cloud Governance Framework is intended to support the organization's cloud adoption strategy. Five core components of the framework include:

- Policies and principles;
- Organization;
- Finance;
- Process;
- Tools and metrics.

5.18 POLICIES AND PRINCIPLES

Policies and principles are the company's rules and laws for cloud adoption. A principle is a belief statement that serves as the basis for establishing decision-making policies. In contrast, a policy outlines the underlying rules that an organization must consider when making decisions about cloud adoption.

Usually, policies are defined at the strategy level. For example, they may relate to decisions about cloud service vendor selection (e.g., contractual restrictions, who is and isn't allowed, processes for managing required services, and specification of what business applications and data can be moved in the cloud). Policies define management's direction to support the company's business purposes and needs, ensure the company's compliance with applicable legislation, reflect management's commitment, and clarify responsibilities. As such, you may have a data encryption or separation policy that must apply to all clouds, whether private, public, hybrid, or community.

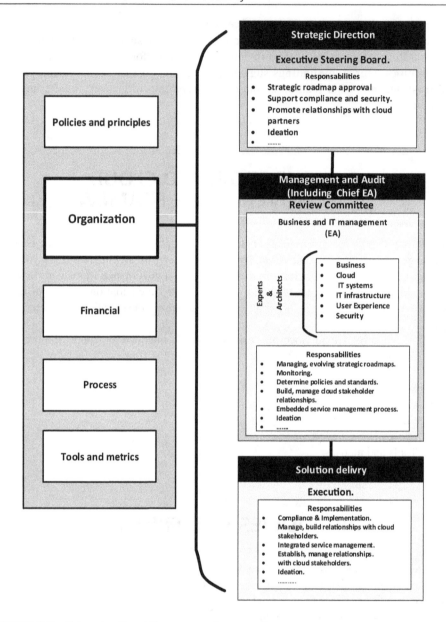

FIGURE 5.3   Enterprise Cloud Governance Framework.

In many cases, policies reflect the law and the principles that must be followed – this is particularly true of security and privacy policies. Guidelines can also exist, which are general statements of direction, a wanted future outcome that is not necessarily imposed. Guidelines are similar in content to principles, except that they lack the motivations and benefits them. The governance model should reflect the combination of principles, policies, and guidelines for IT services, whether provided from your IT service center or the cloud. Cloud governance requires policy management considering the complex relationships between user groups, cloud vendors, and consumers.

5.19 ORGANIZATION

The 'Organizational Structure' section illustrates the leadership and the key roles, responsibilities, and levels of accountability necessary for effective decision-making around cloud adoption. Examples include creating an executive steering board (ESB) to authorize and approve cloud-related acquisitions and a review board (RB) responsible for the effective integration of cloud into the environment. These committees are critical to the creation, execution, and integration of the cloud into the company.

The chief enterprise architect will need to communicate to senior executives the benefits of the cloud and develop and execute the strategy without getting into the details of cloud infrastructure and implementation. Clarify the value and impacts of cloud adoption on the business and opportunities that positively impact the organization's strategy.

This responsibility applies to both small and large enterprises that, for example, want to expand their market share or are on the verge of adopting a solution but are hesitant due to high-profile outages. In turn, the chief enterprise architect can suggest innovative strategies, such as partnering with aggregated cloud providers, to ensure that in the event of a primary provider's service unavailability, partner services are executed in a way that preserves service levels and the end-customer experience.

If you're an enterprise architect, it's highly recommended that you have at least some cloud business skills and the ability to guide decisions. This is because you will face situations such as service management asking you what the guidelines are for commissioning and decommissioning cloud environments in your organization. Traditionally, this has not been the case; however, given that it is possible to offload key dimensions of your EA to the cloud (e.g., you can offload a large majority of your IT infrastructure assets and services), you need to have the skills necessary to make the appropriate business decisions to ensure interoperability within your organization and across different business lines.

The cloud architect has been added to the review committee (RC). The expertise and talents of this role from a technology and business perspective should not be ignored. A cloud architect role can assist in standardizing virtualization strategies and associated business efficiencies.

Included is the UX architect, who is critical in determining the appropriate service interfaces presented to cloud end-users and consumers. For instance, many consumers want their portal to be the entry point to the cloud, which implies that the vendor's services are accessed through application programming interfaces (APIs) or web services. The review committee should also include a test and security architect, and both should be tailored to support the integration of cloud solutions into the enterprise through the development of testing strategies and the implementation of proper processes, procedures, and tools that validate that any proposed cloud adoption is secure to mitigate vulnerability risks.

Indeed, security is a fundamental component of your organization's cloud adoption strategy. The more we know security requirements and factor them into the cloud decision-making process, the less likely projects will face costly downstream project or vendor issues once the move to the cloud begins.

Various organizations have created a cloud center of excellence to drive cloud-based transformation (CCoE), composed of resources with deep cloud technology and business skills. This may not be necessary for organizations that are interested in the public cloud. But in the case where your strategy depends on the 'on-premises' private cloud, more in-depth skills are required. You should also expect a CCoE or similar organization to exist in your cloud provider's domain and consider this as a key part of your vendor selection criteria in areas such as product viability.

Important strategic-level responsibilities include the following:

- Strategic roadmap approval;
- Support compliance and security;
- Promote relationships with cloud partners.

The company's executive steering board authorizes and supports strategic roadmaps, ensuring that budget and funding activities are prioritized and that roadmaps are aligned with the overall company strategy. The more executive leadership is engaged during the development of your enterprise cloud adoption strategy (typically led by a dedicated strategy team), the more effective it is, because a key outcome is a strategic cloud roadmap, and because the same stakeholders who make up your strategy team could very well become members of your executive steering committee.

As illustrated, the executive steering committee is an advocate and speaker to comply with industry regulations and company policies. They emphasize the validity of building relationships with partners in advance by leveraging their networks to facilitate the process. Each of the responsibilities described is critical and should not be overlooked given the direct impacts on service excellence.

Management and control responsibilities, particularly those of the Architectural Review Board, include the following:

- Manage evolving strategic roadmaps;
- Monitor;
- Determine policies and standards;
- Build and manage cloud stakeholder relationships;
- Embedded service management process.

The Architecture Review Board includes IT and business leaders and includes architects and subject matter experts or specialists. Working closely with the steering committees and solution delivery teams, the review committee manages and monitors cloud adoption across the enterprise, ensuring that the cloud adoption strategy continues to evolve and remain accurate as your business environment changes. In other words, an agile strategy.

The solution delivery team is responsible for executing the company's cloud adoption strategy and applying the standards to specific projects. Communication occurs both downstream for specific projects and upstream in the form of feedback to the review board and executive steering board, typically in the form of practical experiences and lessons learned. The responsibilities of the executive steering board include ensuring that projects:

- Compliance and Implementation;
- Manage and build relationships with cloud stakeholders;
- Integrate service management;
- Establish and manage the relationship with cloud stakeholders.

Delivery experiences, where best practices are captured as part of your EA, keep your organization's cloud adoption strategy viable and relevant. They adhere to and implement cloud project standards, policies, and principles, resulting in a resilient and agile cloud adoption strategy. The team is responsible for ultimately selecting cloud providers and managing relationships to benefit the projects they support. The team can build relationships with cloud partners based on partners suggested by the ESB and review board and integrates and implements service management policies and principles across vendor channels to ensure Delivery Excellence.

5.20 FINANCIALS

Financial governance is a key factor in the adoption of cloud and enterprise technologies as a whole. It includes financial stewardship, funding models, financial management, and building acceptable business models for cloud investments.

Financial management may seem less complex for the cloud because of the pay-per-use pricing model and bundling of services, which minimizes the number of contracts your company needs to manage and prepares for a hybrid environment of traditional and cloud-based services and contracts, at least initially.

Therefore, how should cloud services be governed, manage renewals, and maintain only those subscriptions that provide business value?

One example of a financial area that needs to be governed is the revenue generated by the cloud adoption benefits. As the transition to the cloud helps organizations improve services to customers (as well as business entities with private adoption) thanks to, for instance, a faster time to value and reduced costs as IT support personnel are rationalized or no longer have to deal with customer issues, the cloud adoption strategy may require re-budgeting and reallocating earned revenue to strategic and related business imperatives, such as implementing executive education programs that enable employees to more effectively oversee and govern cloud service providers.

In this example, financial governance ensures that monetary goals are identified and achieved through stakeholder accountability, budget allocations, auditing of financial activities, tracking revenue and expenses, and allocating funds related to cloud adoption.

Assessing the financial viability and impact of cloud adoption on the organization, in both the short and long terms, is key.

5.21 PROCESS

Process governance is organized around four main categories, listed and illustrated in Figure 5.4.

- Management;
- Vitality;
- Compliance;
- Communication.

Process management ensures management's involvement and monitoring of cloud adoption strategy and execution. Risk management is no longer a new addition to management processes, but it is still critical when considering cloud adoption. It should be addressed at an early stage of strategy development and considered at every phase of the enterprise cloud adoption lifecycle.

As for service management, it involves more comprehensive principles, which we discussed in Figure 5.4. Then, there is performance management. Among the key questions that stakeholders ask about performance management are the following:

- What are the opportunities to improve business performance?
- Where should IT resources be allocated to support the enterprise cloud adoption strategy?

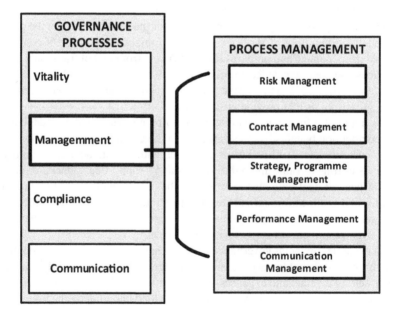

FIGURE 5.4   Management processes framework.

- When is it appropriate to use cloud-sourcing for your core business applications?
- Who will update the EA to ensure that cloud adoption and enablement models are standardized?

Either of the identified processes can be harder to implement and maintain in a cloud environment, as you have no real visibility into the provider's operations. That's why the joint development of contracts, service level agreements (SLAs), precise service requirements, such as identifying when and how you want to be notified when an SLA is in threat, as well as business controls, is critical and will help mitigate business risk.

The vitality processes will ensure that your adoption strategy is maintained and communicated as the organization evolves and as new business and IT components are integrated into the EA.

Standards are specifications that provide authority and value. Standards are what the organization perceives as valuable and chooses to adhere to facilitate business performance. As mentioned in the previous section, 'Organizational Structure', Delivery Solution's execution of its enterprise cloud adoption strategy is an example of how it measures vitality (Sahid et al., 2020).

Compliance processes provide a formalized approach to reviewing and approving cloud adoption decisions. They include formal reviews at key checkpoints before and during project implementation. The ability and convenience of a monthly expense of IT capabilities using a cloud business model can allow a business unit to introduce new technology without giving IT staff and other executives the opportunity to review solutions for reuse or to ensure that any candidate cloud selection complies with your company's information management standards and security policies.

Exception handling and appeals are other examples of a compliance process. Exception handling is critical to managing risk and complexity as well as tracking cloud and other business technologies.

Industry-specific and regulatory compliance policies and processes should be addressed as early as possible in the decision lifecycle, such as the implications of data privacy on the decision to adopt clouds. The company's cloud adoption strategy should contain compliance processes tailored to common business scenarios and serve as a baseline for those seeking guidance on compliance procedures.

Effective exception management is necessary to ensure the agility of your strategy and its value if applied appropriately. It does not change with the introduction of the cloud into the enterprise; however, experts in the field should be part of the exception and appeal process to ensure that requests are interpreted appropriately. It is essential to ensure that justifiable exceptions are approved to prevent the exception handling process from being misused and requests from being approved by default, which would defeat the value of the process. The exception handling process is typically initiated by a project manager making an exception request.

Communication processes ensure that all stakeholders remain informed of the company's cloud adoption strategy.

Tools and metrics enable effective governance, management, and performance monitoring of local and extended environments that incorporate the cloud. They are an essential part of the governance framework. Metrics ensure that processes are properly controlled and deliver the expected results.

Indicators should have a solid correlation to targeted objectives and can be collected in a consistent manner and without high costs. Factors for selecting indicators should be included, such as data collection frequency, reporting frequency, indicator recipients, and tools.

For example, tools that support information gathering (e.g., cloud portfolio and application inventory), metrics databases, and dashboards for self-service cloud entry and exit with traceability, e-learning, invoicing and metering, application development, benchmarking, quality assurance (QA) and tests, and communication tools.

Cloud users require assurance that security and privacy policies are consistently enforced. Thus, processes and tools are needed to monitor and report compliance or violate privacy or security policies on remote clouds. The governance framework must identify an appropriate set of tools for managing data and the organization's internal and external cloud environments.

The key to measurement and tracking capability is using performance dashboards that anticipate and monitor the organization's progress. For example, what percentage does the organization leverage a cloud-powered learning effectiveness system for executive advancement?

After learning initiatives are completed, are leaders performing better, the same, or worse at work?

Looking at this same example and more specific to the enterprise cloud adoption strategy, the organization can more effectively anticipate who should benefit from using the cloud's performance dashboard and learning efficiency systems.

5.22 SUMMARY

In the era of digitalization and uncertainty, cloud computing constitutes an important IS evolution. It provides attractive characteristics such as mobility, scalability, pay-per-use, and profitability. This study aimed to define the determinants of cloud computing adoption based on innovation characteristics and organizations' technical, organizational, and environmental contexts and determine how agility is evolving in cloud computing and proposing a conceptual model that incorporates DOI theory and TOE structure. The model was evaluated through a quantitative study from 200 different MENA region medium and large enterprises.

Results showed that agility, cost savings, security, privacy and confidence, technology readiness, and data sovereignty directly affect a company's cloud computing adoption. Results analysis confirmed agility's direct effect on cloud adoption.

REFERENCES

Abdollahzadehgan, A., Che Hussin, A. R., Gohary, M. M., & Amini, M. (2013). The organizational critical success factors for adopting cloud computing in SMEs. *Journal of Information Systems Research and Innovation*, 4(1), 67–74. https://ssrn.com/abstract=2333028

Abolfazli, S., Sanaei, Z., Tabassi, A., Rosen, S., Gani, A., & Khan, S. U. (2015). Cloud adoption in Malaysia: Trends, opportunities, and challenges. *IEEE Cloud Computing, 2*(1), 60–68. https://doi.org/10.1109/MCC.2015.1

Adamson, G., Wang, L., Holm, M., & Moore, P. (2017). Cloud manufacturing – a critical review of recent development and future trends. *International Journal of Computer Integrated Manufacturing, 30*(4–5), 347–380. https://doi.org/10.1080/0951192X.2015.1031704

Alam, S. S. (2009). Adoption of internet in Malaysian SMEs. *Journal of Small Business and Enterprise Development, 16*(2), 240–255. https://doi.org/10.1108/14626000910956038

Amini, M., &Bakri, A. (2015). Cloud computing adoption by SMEs in the Malaysia: A multiperspective framework based on DOI theory and TOE framework. *Journal of Information Technology & Information Systems Research (JITISR), 9*(2), 121–135.

Amron, M. T., Ibrahim, R., Abu Bakar, N. A., & Chuprat, S. (2019). Determining factors influencing the acceptance of cloud computing implementation. *Procedia Computer Science, 161*, 1055–1063. https://doi.org/10.1016/j.procs.2019.11.216

Azadegan, A., & Teich, J. (2010). Effective benchmarking of innovation adoptions: A theoretical framework for e-procurement technologies. *Benchmarking: An International Journal, 17*(4), 472–490. https://doi.org/10.1108/14635771011060558

Benlian, A., & Hess, T. (2011). Opportunities and risks of software-as-a-service: Findings from a survey of IT executives. *Decision Support Systems, 52*(1), 232–246. https://doi.org/10.1016/j.dss.2011.07.007

Bishop, M. (2002). *Lorica segmentata volume I: A handbook of articulated roman plate armour* (Vol. 1). The Armatura Press.

Borgman, H. P., Bahli, B., Heier, H., & Schewski, F. (2013). Cloudrise: Exploring cloud computing adoption and governance with the TOE framework. *Proceedings of the Annual Hawaii International Conference on System Sciences*, 4425–4435. https://doi.org/10.1109/HICSS.2013.132

Butt, S. A., Tariq, M. I., Jamal, T., Ali, A., Martinez, J. L. D., & De-La-Hoz-Franco, E. (2019). Predictive variables for agile development merging cloud computing services. *IEEE Access, 7*, 99273–99282. https://doi.org/10.1109/ACCESS.2019.2929169

Cervone, H. F. (2010). An overview of virtual and cloud computing. *OCLC Systems & Services: International Digital Library Perspectives, 26*(3), 162–165.

Chemjor, E. M., & Lagat, C. (2017). Determinants of level of cloud computing adoption in small and medium enterprises in Nairobi County. *International Journal of Economics, Commerce and Management, 5*(4).

Cragg, P., Caldeira, M., & Ward, J. (2011). Organizational information systems competences in small and medium-sized enterprises. *Information & Management, 48*(8), 353–363. https://doi.org/10.1016/j.im.2011.08.003

Hemlata, G., Hema, D., & Ramaswamy, R. (2015). Understanding determinants of cloud computing adoption using an integrated TAM-TOE model. *Journal of Enterprise Information Management, 28*(1), 107–130. https://doi.org/10.1108/JEIM-08-2013-0065

Hsu, P.F., Ray, S., & Li-Hsieh, Y.-Y. (2014). Examining cloud computing adoption intention, pricing mechanism, and deployment model. *International Journal of Information Management, 34*(4), 474–488. https://doi.org/10.1016/j.ijinfomgt.2014.04.006

Ifinedo, P. (2011a). Internet/e-business technologies acceptance in Canada's SMEs: An exploratory investigation. *Internet Research, 21*(3), 255–281. https://doi.org/10.1108/10662241111139309

Ifinedo, P. (2011b). An empirical analysis of factors influencing internet/e-business technologies adoption by SMES in Canada. *International Journal of Information Technology & Decision Making, 10*(4), 731–766. https://doi.org/10.1142/S0219622011004543

Klein, R. (2012). Assimilation of internet-based purchasing applications within medical practices. *Information & Management, 49*(3), 135–141. https://doi.org/10.1016/j.im.2012.02.001

Kshetri, N. (2013). Privacy and security issues in cloud computing: The role of institutions and institutional evolution. *Telecommunications Policy, 37*(4), 372–386. https://doi.org/10.1016/j.telpol.2012.04.011

Kunio, T. (2010). NEC cloud computing system. *NEC Technical Journal*, 5(2), 10–15.

Lin, A., & Chen, N. C. (2012). Cloud computing as an innovation: Perception, attitude, and adoption. *International Journal of Information Management*, 32(6), 533–540. https://doi.org/10.1016/j.ijinfomgt.2012.04.001

Low, C., Wu, M., & Chen, Y. (2011). Understanding the determinants of cloud computing adoption. *Industrial Management & Data Systems*, 111(7), 1006–1023. https://doi.org/10.1108/02635571111161262

Luo, X., Gurung, A., & Shim, J. P. (2010). Understanding the determinants of user acceptance of enterprise instant messaging: An empirical study. *Journal of Organizational Computing and Electronic Commerce*, 20(2), 155–181. https://doi.org/10.1080/10919391003709179

Lynn, T., Liang, X., Gourinovitch, A., Morrison, J. P., Fox, G., & Rosati, P. (2018). Understanding the determinants of cloud computing adoption for high performance computing. *51st Hawaii International Conference on System Sciences (HICSS-51)*, 3894–3903.

Mazhelis, O., & Tyrväinen, P. (2012). Economic aspects of hybrid cloud infrastructure: User organization perspective. *Information Systems Frontiers*, 14(4), 845–869. https://doi.org/10.1007/s10796-011-9326-9

Montalbano, E. (2012). Feds refine cloud security standards. *InformationWeek*.

Nasir, U. (2017). *An assessment model for enterprise clouds adoption*. http://eprints.keele.ac.uk/4281/

Nkhoma, M. Z., Dang, D. P. T., & De Souza-Daw, A. (2013). Contributing factors of cloud computing adoption: A technology-organisation-environment framework approach. *Proceedings of the European Conference on Information Management & Evaluation*, 180–189.

Noor, T. H., Zeadally, S., Alfazi, A., & Sheng, Q. Z. (2018). Mobile cloud computing: Challenges and future research directions. *Journal of Network and Computer Applications*, 115, 70–85. https://doi.org/10.1016/J.JNCA.2018.04.018

Oliveira, T., Thomas, M., & Espadanal, M. (2014). Assessing the determinants of cloud computing adoption: An analysis of the manufacturing and services sectors. *Information and Management*, 51(5), 497–510. https://doi.org/10.1016/j.im.2014.03.006

Premkumar, G., & Roberts, M. (1999). Adoption of new information technologies in rural small businesses. *Omega*, 27(4), 467–484. https://doi.org/10.1016/S0305-0483(98)00071-1

Ramdani, B., Kawalek, P., & Lorenzo, O. (2009). Predicting SMEs' adoption of enterprise systems. *Journal of Enterprise Information Management*, 22, 10–24. https://doi.org/10.1108/17410390910922796

Rogers, E. M. (2003). *Diffusion of innovations* (5th ed.). A Division of Macmillan Publishing Co Inc., Free Press.

Sahid, A., Maleh, Y., & Belaissaoui, M. (2020). Cloud computing as a drive for strategic agility in organizations. In *Strategic information system agility: From theory to practices* (pp. 117–151). Emerald Publishing Limited. https://doi.org/10.1108/978-1-80043-810-120211007

Sandu, R., & Gide, E. (2018). Technological, organisational and environmental (TOE) factors that influence the adoption of cloud based service SMEs in India. *2018 IEEE 11th International Conference on Cloud Computing (CLOUD)*, 866–870. https://doi.org/10.1109/CLOUD.2018.00123

Sangle, S. (2011). Adoption of cleaner technology for climate proactivity: A technology – firm – stakeholder framework. *Business Strategy and the Environment*, 20(6), 365–378.

Schneiderman, R. (2011). For cloud computing, the sky is the limit [special reports]. *IEEE Signal Processing Magazine*, 28(1), 15–144.

Senarathna, I., Wilkin, C., Warren, M., Yeoh, W., & Salzman, S. (2018). Factors that influence adoption of cloud computing: An empirical study of Australian SMEs. *Australasian Journal of Information Systems*, 22.

Senarathna, R. (2016). *Cloud computing adoption by SMEs in Australia* [PhD thesis, Deakin University].

Shah Alam, S., Ali, M. Y., & Jani, M. (2011). An empirical study of factors affecting electronic commerce adoption among SMEs in Malaysia. *Journal of Business Economics and Management*, 12(2), 375–399. https://doi.org/10.3846/16111699.2011.576749

Sharma, M., Gupta, R., & Acharya, P. (2017). Prioritizing the critical factors of cloud computing adoption using multi-criteria decision-making techniques. *Global Business Review*, *21*(1), 142–161. https://doi.org/10.1177/0972150917741187

Sitaram, D., & Manjunath, G. (2012). Moving to the cloud. *Moving To The Cloud*, *2*(1), 1–10. https://doi.org/10.1016/C2010-0-66389-9

Skafi, M., Yunis, M. M., & Zekri, A. (2020). Factors influencing SMEs' adoption of cloud computing services in Lebanon: An empirical analysis using TOE and contextual theory. *IEEE Access*, *8*, 79169–79181. https://doi.org/10.1109/ACCESS.2020.2987331

Tankard, C., & Pathways, D. (2016). What the GDPR means for. *Network Security*, *6*, 5–8. https://doi.org/10.1016/S1353-4858(16)30056-3

Tashakkori, A., & Creswell, J. W. (2007). *Exploring the nature of research questions in mixed methods research*. Sage Publications.

Thiesse, F., Staake, T., Schmitt, P., & Fleisch, E. (2011). The rise of the "next-generation bar code": An international RFID adoption study. *Supply Chain Management*, *16*(5), 328–345. https://doi.org/10.1108/13598541111155848

Tornatzky, L. G., Fleischer, M., & Chakrabarti, A. K. (1990). *The processes of technological innovation*. Issues in organization and management series. Lexington Books. Retrieved June 10, 2013, from http://www.Amazon.Com/Processes-Technological-Innovation-Organization/Management/Dp/0669203483

Trigueros-Preciado, S., Pérez-González, D., & Solana-González, P. (2013). Cloud computing in industrial SMEs: Identification of the barriers to its adoption and effects of its application. *Electronic Markets*, *23*(2), 105–114. https://doi.org/10.1007/s12525-012-0120-4

Trisha, G., Glenn, R., Fraser, M., Paul, B., & Olivia, K. (2004). Diffusion of innovations in service organizations: Systematic review and recommendations. *The Milbank Quarterly*, *82*(4), 581–629. https://doi.org/10.1111/j.0887-378X.2004.00325.x

Tsai, M.C., Lee, W., & Wu, H.C. (2010). Determinants of RFID adoption intention: Evidence from Taiwanese retail chains. *Information & Management*, *47*(5), 255–261. https://doi.org/10.1016/j.im.2010.05.001

Wu, W.W. (2011). Mining significant factors affecting the adoption of SaaS using the rough set approach. *Journal of Systems and Software*, *84*(3), 435–441.

Wu, Y., Cegielski, C. G., Hazen, B. T., & Hall, D. J. (2013). Cloud computing in support of supply chain information system infrastructure: Understanding when to go to the cloud. *Journal of Supply Chain Management*, *49*(3), 25–41.

Yang, H., Huff, S. L., & Tate, M. (2013). Managing the cloud for information systems agility. In A. Bento & A. K. Aggarwal (Eds.), *Cloud computing service and deployment models: Layers and management* (pp. 70–93). IGI Global. https://doi.org/10.4018/978-1-4666-2187-9.ch004

Yang, H., & Tate, M. (2012). A descriptive literature review and classification of cloud computing research. *Communications of the Association of Information Systems*, *31*(2), 35–60. https://doi.org/10.1.1.261.3070

Zhang, G., Fu, L., & Liang, Y. (2020). The impact of cloud computing infrastructure capability on enterprise agility: Based on the perspective of IT business alignment. *Proceedings of the 2020 3rd International Conference on Signal Processing and Machine Learning*, 48–55. https://doi.org/10.1145/3432291.3433642

Zhu, K., Dong, S., Xu, S. X., & Kraemer, K. L. (2006). Innovation diffusion in global contexts: Determinants of post-adoption digital transformation of European companies. *European Journal of Information Systems*, *15*(6), 601–616.

Zhu, K., Kraemer, K. L., & Xu, S. (2003). Electronic business adoption by European firms: A cross-country assessment of the facilitators and inhibitors. *European Journal of Information Systems*, *12*(4), 251–268.

Zhu, K., Kraemer, K. L., & Xu, S. (2006). The process of innovation assimilation by firms in different countries: A technology diffusion perspective on e-business. *Management Science*, *52*(10), 1557–1576.

SECTION 3

Maturity Frameworks for Information Security Governance

Information Security Governance

6

Best Practices in Organizations

6.1 INTRODUCTION

The threat to technology-based information assets is greater today than in the past (Maleh et al., 2018). The evolution of technology has also reflected in the tools and methods used by those attempting to gain unauthorized access to the data or disrupt business processes (Goodhue & Straub, 1991). Attacks are inevitable, whatever the organization ('Information Security Governance: Guidance for Boards of Directors and Executive Management Guidance for Boards of Directors and Executive Management', 2006). However, the degree of sophistication and persistence of these attacks depend on the attractiveness of this organization as a target (Rockart & Crescenzi, 1984), mainly regarding its role and assets. Today, the threats posed by some misguided individuals have been replaced by international organized criminal groups highly specialized or by foreign states that have the skills, personnel, and tools necessary to conduct secret and sophisticated cyber espionage attacks. These attacks are not only targeted at government entities. In recent years, several large companies have infiltrated, and their data have been 'consulted' for several years without their knowledge. Improving cybersecurity has emerged as one of the top IT priorities across all business lines. So, while companies (von Solms & van Niekerk, 2013; Bowen et al., 2007) and areas such as the aerospace industry and strategic resources are ideal targets for cyber espionage by nation-states, others managing financial assets or large-scale credit card information are equally attractive to international criminal groups (Posthumus & von Solms, 2004; Humphreys, 2008).

These malicious actors no longer content themselves with thwarting the means of technical protection. Instead, they survey and exploit various weaknesses detected in the targeted environment (Galliers & Leidner, 2014). These shortcomings are technological and result from failures in protection procedures or gaps in vulnerability management practices. If misused, the best technology in the world will not provide an adequate defense against such threats (von Solms & van Niekerk, 2013).

Ensuring IS security in a large organization is a real challenge (Sohrabi Safa et al., 2016). Only good governance can reassure the general management, customers and partners, shareholders, and ultimately the public at large (Mark Duffield, 2014).

The problem is that the security governance framework is designed to guide organizations in their IS security governance strategy but does not define the practical framework for the engagement in this strategy.

Some best practices and international standards (NIST, ISACA, ISO 27000 suite, etc.) now include chapters on security governance to address these concerns. The first reports or articles in academic journals that evoke the governance of information security date back to the early 2000s.

The proposed referential and best practices are designed to guide organizations in their IT security governance strategy. However, it does not define the practical framework to implement or measure the organization's engagement in IT security governance.

This chapter studies the practices and commitments of organizations in IS security governance. A survey of 836 medium and large companies at the international level (USA, UK, France, Morocco, China, Russia, etc.) was set up to define the best practices of these organizations regarding information security governance (ISG). This study allowed us to propose a practical framework to evaluate the organization's maturity state and improve its level of information security governance according to its needs and resources.

This chapter is structured as follows. Section 6.2 presents the previous work on information security governance proposed in the literature. Section 6.3 describes the research methodology. Section 6.4 presents the survey carried out among 836 medium and large international companies and gave an accurate picture of their practices in ISG through statistical analysis. Section 6.5 describes the proposed capability maturity framework for ISG. Finally, Section 6.6 presents the summary of this chapter.

6.2 LITERATURE REVIEW AND BACKGROUND

In management sciences, several authors put forward the responsibilities and roles of management and general management. Thereby, Straub & Welke (1998) argued that the security risk for IT could be reduced when managers are aware of the extent of existing controls and implement the most efficient controls based on the identified risks. P. Williams (2001) then the president of ISACA and co-founder of the IT Governance Institute recalled that directors of organizations are responsible for protecting shareholder value and that this responsibility applies to valued information assets. F. Rockart & D. Crescenzi (1984), Markus (1983), and Knapp et al. (2009) confirmed that security must take into account at the general management level of the organization.

Several authors have studied the added value, the strategic, or competitive advantage provided by implementing an ISG. In this sense, Schou & Shoemaker (2006) found that to provide a more significant benefit to the organization, the ISG can eventually coordinate with strategic approaches to economic intelligence, social responsibility, or communication. Huang et al. (2006) relied on a balanced dashboard to establish performance indicators for information security management in organizations and strengthen the link between these indicators and the institutional strategy. Williams (2007) outlined the roles of management and the board of directors in the area of information security. Dhillon et al. (2007) presented the results of an empirical study to understand the dimensions of IS security governance better. Kraemer et al. (2009) showed that human and organizational factors play a significant role in developing vulnerabilities related to IS and suggest a multilevel approach to improve security performance. Johnston & Hale (2009) examined the strategic aspects of information security and tried to assess the added value to the organization through the security governance approach. The authors proposed an information security roadmap based on a survey conducted among security professionals and suggest programs for its implementation. For Kryukov & Strauss (2009), the added value and performance are crucial ISG elements.

In his thesis on ISG, Brotby (2009) devoted several chapters to the roles and responsibilities of managers, the strategic measures and benefits of the approach, the development and implementation of a strategy for ISG and incident management. Klaic (2010) discussed the need to define a level of governance in the organization and clarify the link between that level and security programs.

Da Veiga & Eloff (2010) provided a framework to develop a culture of information security within an organization and illustrated how to use it. An empirical study was conducted to validate the proposed culture of information security. Michael E. Whitman (2011) proposed value to the executive by first defining governance as it is applied to information security and exploring three specific governance issues. He first inspected how government can be used to the critical aspect of planning for both formal and contingency operations. The next issue describes the need for program measurement and how it can develop an information security assessment and a continuous improvement.

Finally, aspects of effective communication between and among the general security and information managers are presented. Williams et al. (2013) illustrate the malleability and heterogeneity of ISG across different organizations involving intra- and inter-organizational trust mechanisms. They identified the need to reframe ISG, adopting the new label information to protecting governance (IPG), to present a more multifaceted vision of the information protection integrating a vast range of technical and social aspects that constitute and are constituted by governance arrangements. The objective of Yaokumah (2014) is to assess the implementation of ISG in the main sectors of the Ghanaian industry. The purpose is to compare the implementation of the ISG of the inter-industry sector and identify areas requiring improvement.

In their study, Horne et al. (2016) argued for a paradigm shift from internal information protection across the organization with a strategic vision that considers the inter-organizational level. In their paper, Soomro et al. (2016), using a systematic approach to the literature review, synthesized the research on management roles in information security to explore management activities and improve information security management. They found that many management activities, particularly the development and implementation of information security policy, awareness-raising, compliance training, development of efficient commercial information architecture, IT infrastructure management, IT alignment, business, and human resource management, have a significant impact on the quality of ISG. They argued that a more holistic approach to information security is needed and suggest how managers can play a valuable role in information security.

In a recent work, Carcary et al. (2016) proposed a maturity framework that helps organizations assess their ISG maturity and identify problems. It addresses the technical, procedural, and human aspects of information security and provides guidelines for implementing information security management and related business processes.

6.3 RESEARCH METHODOLOGY

Our literature review suggests that information security has gradually moved from an operational to a strategic dimension. Past contributions have proposed various models for ISG, discussed the role of management, and the added value of this approach. But it appears that the involvement of organizations in the ISG process has not yet been studied.

Moreover, within the academic community, difficulties are regularly reported by security researchers, both in the development of theories (Dlamini et al., 2009) and in empirical research (low participation rates in studies attest to this); apart from a few case studies, surveys identifying the detailed practices of a significant sample of organizations in ISG are rare. It seems that a state of current organizational practices, based on new data, would update knowledge in this area of research. Therefore, we propose to answer two questions here:

- What are the factors that determine the commitment of organizations to ISG?
- How to define a conceptual maturity framework based on best practices and commitments in organizations?

6.3.1 Data Collection

Our data are collected from large and medium companies on an international scale. There are several justifications for this choice. Governance first implemented by large firms (Waddock & Graves, 1997) demonstrated that organizations with significant financial resources could invest more in strategic activities (Archibugi & Michie, 1995). Cohen (2006) stated that organizations must consider the security dimension in their strategy when operating in a competitive environment, which is often the case for large enterprises. Moreover, small- and medium-sized enterprises (SMEs) have always shown an overall lack of security awareness (Mitchell et al., 1999). They faced more severe problems than those encountered by large companies regarding security difficulties and a realistic assessment of the risks involved (Siponen & Willison, 2009; Goodhue & Straub, 1991; Peltier, 2013).

Hong et al. (2006) investigated the dominant factors for an organization to build an information security policy (ISP), and whether an ISP may elevate an organization's security level in Taiwan. De Haes & Van Grembergen (2006) interpreted some important existing practices and models in the IT governance field and derived open research questions and some research suggestions from it. They form the basis of the pilot case research in Belgian organizations. Lomas (2010) argued that by integrating ISO 27001, the international information security standard, in co-occurrence with the ISO 15489 document management standard, holistic information governance strategies will provide a responsive response to changes in the UK context. Bahl & Wali (2014) examined, as a case, the perceptions of the ISP's (service providers) in India regarding ISG and its impact on the security service quality. Ula et al. (2011) proposed an initial framework for governing information security in the banking system. The framework is classified into three levels: tactical, strategic, operational, and technical. This proposed framework is implemented in a banking environment. Mohamed & Singh (2012) proposed a conceptual framework that examines information technology governance effectiveness, its determinants, and its impacts on private organizations.

Lee et al. (2013) proposed an ISG maturity model to search for relevant maturity characteristics of ISG. According to the information security assessment and maturity assessment tool, this study found that schools with a little maturity rate occupied 59.8%, 31.7% average and 8.5%. With correlation analysis, this study concludes that 33 elements have a significant correlation with ISG maturity. With ANOVA, post hoc scoping test, and ANOVA multiple comparative differences, this study finds significant differences between the ISG maturity components. This study also finds that the maturity of schools is basic. They can improve their ISG maturity according to this model.

Lunardi et al. (2014) attempted to study and measure the improvement in the financial performance of firms that have adopted IT management and governance strategies through pre- and post-adoption measures. They found that the organizational activities of improved IT governance practices boost their performance compared to the control group, particularly about profitability. They also concluded that adopting IT management and governance mechanisms on financial performance was more pronounced in the year following the adoption than in the year in which they took. Da Veiga & Martins (2015) discussed through a case study of an international financial institution in which ISCA conducted at four intervals over 8 years in 12 countries. Multivariate and comparative analyses were performed to determine whether the culture of information security has improved from one evaluation to another depending on the development actions implemented. One of the primary measures performed was training and awareness-raising on the critical dimensions identified by ISCA. The culture of information security has improved from one evaluation to another, with the most favorable results in the fourth assessment.

Dhillon et al. (2017) evaluate disturbances in the security culture following a merger. They conducted an exhaustive case study of a company in the telecom sector. The data were collected during the merger, allowing us to evaluate the changing structures in real-time. The results of this analysis help researchers and practitioners to theorize on the formulation of security culture during a merger. On the practical side, decision-makers will find this analysis helpful in engaging in strategic security planning.

Eroğlu and Çakmak (2016) measured information systems regarding information security and risk. On the other hand, it also aims to describe the potential effects of evaluation techniques and tools for state organizations to manage their critical assets. The information systems of one of the major healthcare organizations in Turkey have been evaluated through an international assessment tool adapted to Turkish specificities and conditions in certain parts of the legal regulations. The results obtained through an evaluation tool provide the current level of maturity of the organization and point out areas that should improve the security of information systems and essential components such as risks, processes, people, IT dependence, and technology.

6.3.2 Demography Characteristics

The target organizations belong to almost all sectors of activity: telecommunications and information technology, construction, transport, industry, commerce, services, and finance. This sectoral breakdown is in line with the International Standard Industrial Classification of All Economic Activities (Revision 4) (Nations, 2008) commonly used in community surveys.

The questionnaire was carried out in several stages. A first version has been developed to take into account the different theoretical assumptions. This first version has been tested with security managers and consultants. This pre-test allowed rephrasing specific questions to improve the questionnaire's comprehension and improve the quality of the given answers. In the end, the questionnaire consists of 45 questions divided into five topics: knowledge of the governance of information security and its strategic issues, its implementation conditions, its organization, its maturity level, and the economic characteristics of the responding organizations. The questionnaire was written in the three most widely spoken languages, namely English, French, and Spanish.

Data collection was conducted during the last quarter of 2016. It took place in two steps. First, 1,000 questionnaires were transmitted by e-mail to participants, using Google's facilities, giving 890 responses. A total of 54 questionnaires were not considered mainly for confidential reasons (65%), informal organization or outsourcing (20%), contact not interested (15%). Finally, 836 final questionnaires were examined for data analysis, with a response rate of 83.6%. Table 6.1 shows the demographics of participants in a concise form.

TABLE 6.1   Participants' Demographics

VARIABLES		FREQUENCY	PERCENT
Gender	Male	480	57.42
	Female	356	42.58
Age (years)	21–30	185	22.13
	31–40	290	34.69
	41–50	240	28.71
	51 and above	121	14.47
Position	Top manager personnel	99	11.84
	IT manager/risk manager/security officer	266	31.82
	Security consultant/engineer/analyst	471	56.34

VARIABLES		FREQUENCY	PERCENT
Number of	Retail/wholesale	162	19.38
participants	TelComs/IT	257	30.74
	Financial services	183	21.89
	Education	95	11.36
	Government	139	16.63
Size of the company	Fewer than 500	263	31.46
(# of employees)	500–999	227	27.15
	1,000–4,999	155	18.54
	5,000–10,000	118	14.11
	More than 10,000	73	8.73
Geography	North-America	116	13.88
	Asia-Oceania	156	18.66
	Europe/Middle-East/Africa	343	41.03
	Central and South America	114	13.64
	Global	107	12.80
Evolution of	Less than 1 million	216	25.84
turnover and	1–5 million	243	29.07
revenue of the	6 –10 million	166	19.86
company in $	10–50 million	93	11.12
	50–100 million	65	7.78
	100–500 million	38	4.55
	More than 500 million	15	1.79

6.3.3 Measurement Survey Model

In this study, we confronted qualitative data to model the organization engagement or not in an approach to ISG. We note the lack of continuity in the modalities of the variable explained. We have chosen to implement a multivariate analysis. This choice finds its motivation because we will be able to isolate the influence of the variation of a characteristic, to the exclusion of any other factor (analysis of other things being equal) on the probability of engagement or not in an IS security governance. Engaging or not in such an approach is a binary variable that takes the value 1 for a positive response and the value 0 for a negative response. This characteristic of the explained variable requires using specific methods, in this case, simple Logit and Probit dichotomous models.

We consider the sample of our population of 836 organizations of indices ($i = 1, \ldots, n$, where $n = 836$). For each organization, it observed whether an individual event had taken place and:

- $(Y_i = 0)$, if the organization i engages in a governance approach to information security;
- $(Yi = 1)$, if the organization i do not engage in such an approach.

We note here the choice of the coding (0,1), which is traditionally retained for dichotomous models. Indeed, it allows defining the probability of occurrence of the event as the expectation of the variable yi, since dichotomous models admit for variable explained that the probability of occurrence of this event is conditional on the exogenous variables. The model takes the following form:

$$pi = Prob\ (yi=1 \mid xi) = F(xi\beta)$$

where the function $F(.)$ denotes a distribution function, xi denotes the explanatory variables, and β is the vector of the parameters to be estimated.

If $yi*$ is a latent (unobservable) variable that depends on the explanatory variables xi, the vector of the parameters to be determined (noted β) and the error term (noted εi), and then the probabilistic decision rule is written as:

$$Prob(yi = 1) = Prob(yi* > 0) = 1 - F(-\beta xi) = F(\beta xi)$$

$$Prob(yi = 0) = Prob(yi* \leq 0) = F(-\beta xi) = 1 - F(\beta xi)$$

where β is the vector of the estimated coefficients and $F(.)$ is the distribution function.

The distribution function $F(.)$ can be of two types: either a logistic law (Logit model) or a regular centered reduced law (Probit model). The results obtained from the Logit and Probit models are relatively similar (Kahn & Morimune, 1979; Davidson & MacKinnon, 1984). For our estimates, we will retain a Logit model where the estimation of the model's parameters is carried out by the method of maximum likelihood.

Since the analysis population is medium in size (836 organizations), the number of explanatory variables introduced into our models should be limited. To remove this constraint, we have aggregated the modalities of individual variables. To take advantage of the richness of the questionnaire, we have created variables that synthesize the available information and make several estimates where all available information is introduced alternately. The sectors of activity are grouped into three areas: industry, service, and finance (variables IND, SRV, and FINA). The results obtained with this specification show that membership in the banking sector does not affect the probability of engaging in ISG.

To consider the change in turnover for each organization, we will focus on the impact of a growing turnover variable (TURNOVER). So that's how the variables constructed do not affect our estimates. Specific characteristics are taken into account using different variables.

Thus, knowledge of the environment and structures engaged in a security governance approach will be taken into account in four ways:

- Using the number of structures involved in a security governance strategy that the organization knows, between 0 and 3 (variable NB_INVOLVED);

  Using a variable knowing other organizations involved in a security governance strategy, implemented locally, regionally, or internationally (variable INVOLVED);

  Using a variable to identify competitors involved in a security governance approach (variable COMPETITORS).
- Using a variable: Identifying organizations that promoting the security governance approach (variable ORGANIZATION).

To consider the benefits, obstacles, and priority areas taken from an approach to ISG, we will introduce each benefit, barrier, and focus area in turn. We also constructed three variables that take into account the number of benefits derived from an ISG approach (NB_BENEF), the number of obstacles and challenges encountered (NB_CHALL), and the number of priority areas (NB_ PRIORITY). The set of variables introduced in our model is presented in Appendix 1 (Table A.2).

6.4 SURVEY RESULTS

This section shows the detailed practices of organizations interviewed in ISG using descriptive statistics, thus answering our second research question.

6.4.1 IT Security Governance Knowledge

The survey reveals that 78% of organizations are familiar with ISG practices, mainly through the Internet, vocational training, and technology watch. As shown in Figure 6.1, 75% of these organizations are involved in an approach to ISG; 80% of organizations are aware of other organizations involved in ISG, of which 34% are clients, 59% are suppliers, and 41% are competitors. Eighty of these organizations (78%) are involved in the governance of information security.

6.4.2 Conditions for Implementing Information Security Governance

Before embarking on an approach to ISG, practicing organizations took stock of actions already carried out internally (81%) as well as possible envisaged measures (87%), knowledge of standards, and certifications (80%). The collected information from specialized security agencies and organizations (73%), evaluated security budget and costs (75%), and reviewed actions by other organizations (39%). These results are illustrated in Figure 6.2.

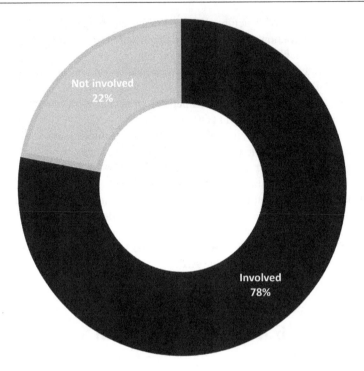

FIGURE 6.1   Involvement of organizations in governance approach to the security of the information system.

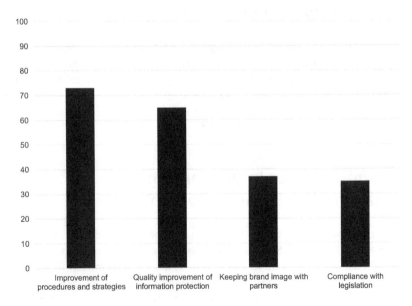

FIGURE 6.2   Key benefits of ISG.

On average, five persons per organization assigned to the ISG process, including two managers, two members of the IT team, one external consultant. Almost one out of every two organizations (59%) has a budget dedicated to information security. The implementation of ISG is described and valued by 38% of organizations in their activity report, by 27% on their website, by 63% in their internal documents (intranet, Procedures, and IT charts), nowhere for 23% of them. Similarly, 71% of the organizations have plans to communicate their commitments internally, 22% to the outside, and 29% have not talked about these commitments.

6.4.3 Strategic Issues in Information Security Governance

In organizations that practice ISG, its implementation is primarily the result of satisfying customers (79%). It is intended to satisfy shareholders and management (48%), employees (40%), legislation in force (36%), suppliers (17%), and local authorities or non-governmental organizations (12%). About 95% of organizations believe they can gain a competitive advantage (very significant or significant benefits) from ISG, and 75% are committed to the process. Among the benefits of an approach to ISG, which are considered very important, organizations mainly focus on improving security procedures and strategies (73%), quality improvement of information protection (65%), compliance with legislation (35%), and Trust for partners (31%). These results are illustrated in Figure 6.2.

Conversely, 93% of organizations interviewed perceive difficulties (very significant or significant obstacles) in implementing ISG, yet 74% are involved in the process. Examination of the obstacles considered very important by the organizations shows, in descending order of citation; the lack of time (27%), the lack of internal talent (24%), the lack of top management interest (19), and the cost of implementation (17%). These results are illustrated in Figure 6.3. Within organizations practicing ISG, the responsibility

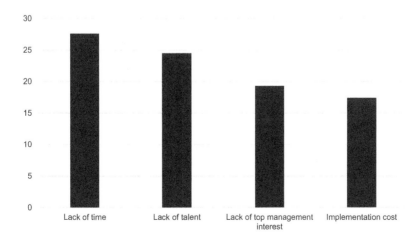

FIGURE 6.3 Key obstacles to the implementation of ISG.

for this process is entrusted to 53% of IS/IT (CIO), 14% of risk manager, 13% of chief executive officer (CEO), 12% of a quality/compliance manager, and only 8% of a Chief Information Security Officer (CISO).

6.4.4 IT Security Governance Strategy and Metrics

According to the responding organizations, 70% of the organizations confirm that the definition of a strategy and policy plays the main role of adopting a governance approach to information security. Strategic alignment of security (68%), communication and training (63%), evaluation of performance by monitoring security indicators (73%), and value through optimization of security investments (75%). These results are illustrated in Figure 6.4.

6.4.5 IT Service and Asset Security Management

Among the organizations practicing ISG, 66% set measurable targets, such as reducing security incidents, reducing operational risk, implementing incidents management tools and procedures Security, and others. In terms of information security classes and data classification, 66% of the organizations take no interest in this axis, 78% of the organizations confirm the mastery of the technical architecture of their IS security, and 83% implement measures to manage their IT assets (servers, networks, storage devices, printers, and smartphones). About 68% have a management and a return on investment concerning the hard and soft resources deployed for the security of the IS organization. About 66%

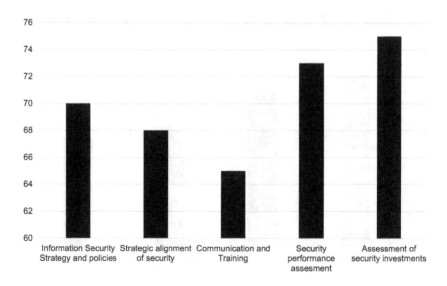

FIGURE 6.4 Information security governance: strategy and metrics.

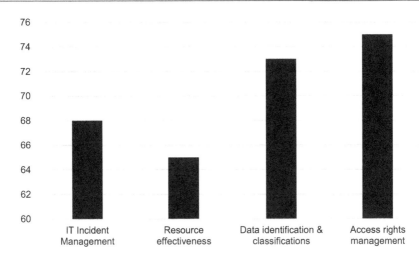

FIGURE 6.5 IT service and asset security management practices in organizations.

have access to management tools and policies that enable them to identify and trace the various SI access operations, including granting, denying, and revoking access privileges. Figure 6.5 illustrates the results.

6.4.6 Vulnerability and Risk Management

According to the responding organizations, the priority areas (or values) of an ISG approach is vulnerability and risk management. In terms of the security threats profile, 70% of organizations are adopting a process to gather information on computer security threats and vulnerabilities to understand better the landscape of the IT security threat in which the organization operates. About 68% assess safety risks and quantify their probability and potential impact, 65% adopts a process of prioritizing risks according to their impact on the organization, and 73% adopt tools and processes for risk monitoring and management and information security control options. These results are illustrated in Figure 6.6.

6.4.7 Information Security Compliance, Control, and Verification

To avoid any infringement of the intellectual property, legal, regulatory and contractual provisions and security requirements of the organization. The organization must adopt an approach to Compliance. Verification is focused on the processes and activities related to how an organization checks, and tests artifacts produced throughout software development. This typically includes quality assurance work such as testing, but it can also include other review and evaluation activities.

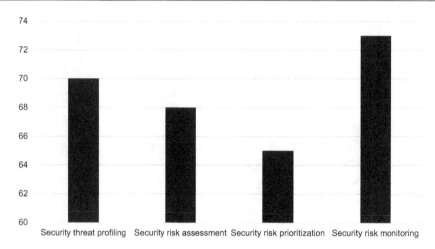

FIGURE 6.6   Vulnerability and risk management practices in organizations.

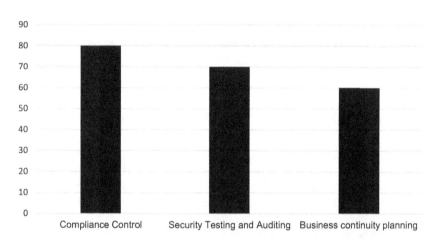

FIGURE 6.7   Security compliance, control, and verification practices in organizations.

Among the organizations practicing ISG, 80% adopted compliance repositories such as ISO 2700x and PCI DSS, 70% have conducted at least one IT security audit in the last 3 years. 60% have developed action plans, either current or future, within the framework of ISG, such as the implementation of a business continuity plan, staff training, Network redundancy, data centralization, server virtualization, improved traceability, etc.

6.4.8 Organizational Maturity of Information Security Governance

In total, 51% of the organizations interviewed to confirm that ISG is indispensable, 40% consider it necessary, 6% unhelpful, and 3% useless. About 87% of those surveyed perceive ISG as a significant value for the organization; 78% of these organizations are engaged in an ISG approach. By analyzing the maturity of organizations in the governance of information security according to a typology proposed by the ('Information Security Governance: Guidance for Boards of Directors and Executive Management Guidance for Boards of Directors and Executive Management', 2006), it appears that:

- For 7%, no procedure is applied. The organization does not recognize any need for information security. No obligation or liability is established. This corresponds to the basic level (level 0);
- 14% of procedures exist but remain disorganized. IT risks are assessed ad hoc per project. The organization recognizes the need to secure its information resources but reactively. Responsibilities are informal. This corresponds to level 1;
- For 19%, the procedures follow a defined model. IT risks are considered significant. Security policies are developed. The report is incomplete or inadequate. This corresponds to level 2;
- For 25%, the procedures are formalized, documented, and communicated by an organizational policy. The report remains focused on IT rather than on the organization. This corresponds to level 3;
- For 17%, the procedures are monitored and measured. A senior manager provides the security function. Responsibilities are applied. The report is linked to the objectives of the organization. This corresponds to level 4;
- For 18%, procedures, safety technologies, and contingency plans are integrated into the organization's activity, optimized and automated. The report makes it possible to anticipate the risks. This corresponds to level 5.

These results are illustrated in Figure 6.8.

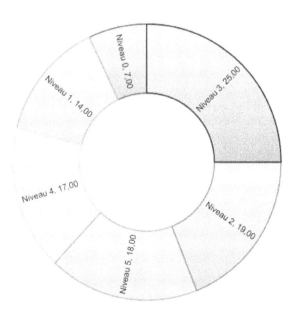

FIGURE 6.8 Information security maturity according to the IT Governance Institute (2006).

The project's portfolio of ISG does not include any projects for 23% of organizations surveyed. Projects are envisaged for 43% of them (on average two projects per organization); in progress for 67% of the organizations (on average three projects per organization), and have closed during the last 3 years for 43% of them (on average four projects per organization). About 87% of organizations have embarked on an ISG approach to report organizational changes: recruitment of external management profiles (31%), changes in internal business for 59% (e.g., changes in the technical profiles specialization), and implementing specific training for 63%.

6.5 DISCUSSION AND INTERPRETATION

To answer our first research question, we present the different determinants of the organizational engagement process in an ISG approach, using the Logit model specifications described in the research methodology section. We define several models to introduce the determinant variables to ensure the quality of the effects obtained. Table A.3 (Appendix 2) describes the results of the five models used. Model 1 highlights the positive impact of the expected benefits of an ISG approach on the likelihood of adopting it. It is also noted that the number of organizations known to have adopted an ISG approach has a positive effect on the probability of adopting such an approach. On the other hand, the economic characteristics of the organization (its sector of activity, the growth of its turnover, membership of a group) do not affect results.

To refine this last result, we have introduced successively different obstacles encountered by the organizations. We note that only two obstacles have a significant effect: the difficulty of translating concepts into concrete actions is a brake on the adoption of ISG (model 2); the low interest of top management for issues related to information security also has a negative impact (model 3). The simultaneous consideration of these two obstacles confirms only the negative effect of translating the concepts into concrete actions (model 4).

The set of models 1 to 5 shows that the number of values shared by the organization under the governance of ISP does not affect its adoption. When the values considered necessary by the organization are taken into account successively, this result persists.

A detailed analysis of the impact of the organization's environment (knowing an organization with an ISG approach, recognizing an organization that seeks to promote it) shows that the organization's environment has a positive effect on the probability of adopting such an approach, regardless of how this dimension is taken into consideration. Generally speaking, on models 4 and 5, the effects obtained in the model that could be qualified as model 1 are summarized: the growth of turnover and the number of values of the 'organization do not affect'. Knowledge of other competing organizations at the regional or international level has a positive effect on adopting governance information security (Model 5).

Given that the benefits derived from security governance approaches have a positive effect on the probability of adopting models 1 to 5, we have successively introduced each profit considered necessary by the organization to identify the profits having a positive impact. The variables not having a significant effect on the probability of adopting an ISG approach have not been reported in the corresponding results in Table A.3 of Appendix 2. This result shows that it is the accumulation of different benefits deemed essential that prompts organizations to embrace such an approach and not impact a particular benefit.

In summary, the probability of adopting an ISG approach is positively affected by the number of benefits derived from such an approach, by the knowledge of structures involved in this process (organizations that have implemented this approach and organizations to promote it). The difficulty of translating concepts into concrete actions is the only one that adversely affects the likelihood of adopting an ISG approach. Belonging to the industry sector, as compared to the service sector, negatively impacts this probability. Other characteristics of the organizations (group membership, growth turnover) and their values do not affect them. Figure 6.9 summarizes the proposals suggested by our research on the determinants of organizational engagement in ISG.

Note that the proposed determinants of the organizational engagement process in ISG are very close to the four determinants identified by Venkatesh et al. (2003) and Venkatesh (2012) in their Unified Technology Adoption Unified Theory of Acceptance and Use of Technology UTAUT model (Figure 6.10). This model synthesizes eight previous models into four main determinants; (PE) Performance Expectancy of the governance approach (added value, benefits, and competitive advantage), (EX) Effort Expectancy deployed for

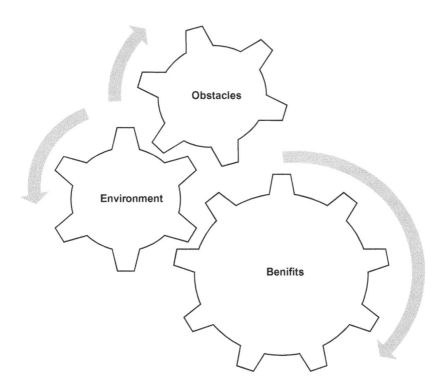

FIGURE 6.9 Proposed determinants process of the engagement in information security governance.

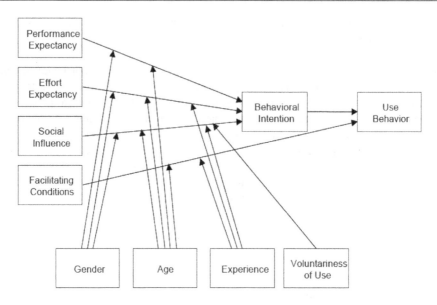

FIGURE 6.10 Unified Technology Adoption Unified Theory of Acceptance and Use of Technology.

its implementation (overcoming brakes, obstacles), (FC) Facilitating Conditions (knowledge of organizations likely to help the organization in its approach), and (SI) Social Influence (subjective norms, image, values). The proximity of our results to this model would suggest that organizations' commitment to the governance process could be compared to the commitment that organizations could make to innovation, in other words to the adoption of innovation.

However, all the conditions of the UTAUT model are collected in our survey. In particular, the four moderating variables (gender, age, education level, and experience) that have significant influence in the model have not been taken into account. Aware of this limit, we can base on the survey conducted that the adoption of the unified theory of Venkatesh et al. (2003) can be a relevant model for analyzing the phenomenon of engagement in ISG.

The responses to our survey confirm that ISG is an integral subset of IS/IT governance, as the organizations involved in both approaches are the same. The responsibility for security governance is attributed, according to the organizations, to various players ranging from the IT manager, risk manager, quality and compliance manager, chief information security officer CISO to the general manager. The sample studied the affiliation of the governance and the information system division concerns organizations with weak or moderately exposed information risks, where the security function is more operational than strategic and managerial aspects. The relationship between governance and risk management, audit, or internal control is rather typical of organizations exposed to information risks (tertiary and quaternary sectors). The linkage of governance to the organization's general manager is preferred when information is the organization's product, and the risk of the organization and that of the information are almost confused. It is also interesting to note another result of the survey: 31% of organizations surveyed practicing security governance did not value this approach either internally or externally, and 33% have not communicated at all about their engagements. Evidence that ISG is not necessarily considered an asset in the communication plan of the organization with its various partners and collaborators.

Given the results of the survey, it seemed interesting to test whether the perception of the stakes of the governance of the information security was the same or not, for the organizations involved in the process and for those having no practical experience, given the distinction made in the questionnaire about the organizations involved in the governance of information security. We observe 100% similarity in ranking the first three profits by comparing each type of information security response. The ranking then differs from only a few organizations (fewer than 30) for the following benefits. Regarding the perceived obstacles of the approach, we observe 100% of similarity in all the classification results. Therefore, the perceived strategic issues of ISG are very similar, whether or not the organization is involved in this process.

On the practical aspect, this research provides managers a detailed information on the engagement of organizations in ISG. The survey suggests that knowledge of organizations engaged in or promoting the process, expected performance, effort to overcome difficulties, and sharing of positive values associated with ISG promote the organization's involvement in this process. It also describes and updates medium and large companies of different sectors involved in the ISG in terms of knowledge and strategic challenges, implementation conditions, and governance organization. Finally, we addressed the maturity challenge of the organizations interviewed regarding ISG.

Based on the return of experience of this empirical study and different maturity models in the literature (ISACA, ISO 2700x), we suggest a practical IT security management and governance framework in the next part of this chapter.

6.6 SUMMARY

Today, protecting ourselves against IT risks through the establishment of good governance has become an important activity to maintain the operational capacity of any organization.

This chapter proposes an exploration of the determinants of organizations best practices in ISG. The survey conducted among 200 large organizations proposes a model consisting of seven determinants of the commitment of organizations in the ISG process: it suggests that the knowledge of organizations engaged in the governance of security Information or promotion, the performance expected, and the effort deployed to encourage the commitment of organizations in the process. The responses to the questionnaire also increase awareness of current practices of ISG implemented by organizations.

By this empirical study and the results of our survey, a framework for measuring the maturity of information security was proposed to provide a practical tool for measuring and improving governance of information security in the organization. To show the effectiveness of the proposed framework, we implemented the resultant maturity framework in a large organization. The results will be presented in the next chapter.

REFERENCES

Archibugi, D., & Michie, J. (1995). Technology and innovation: An introduction. *Cambridge Journal of Economics, 19.* https://doi.org/10.1093/oxfordjournals.cje.a035298

Bahl, S., & Wali, O. P. (2014). Perceived significance of information security governance to predict the information security service quality in software service industry: An empirical analysis. *Information Management & Computer Security, 22*(1), 2–23.

Bowen, P., Chew, E., & Hash, J. (2007). Information security guide for government executives information security guide for government executives. *National Institute of Standards and Technology NIST,* 3–9. http://csrc.nist.gov/publications/nistir/ir7359/NISTIR-7359.pdf

Brotby, K. (2009). *Information security governance: A practical development and implementation approach.* John Wiley & Sons.

Carcary, M., Renaud, K., McLaughlin, S., & O'Brien, C. (2016). A framework for information security governance and management. *It Professional, 18*(2), 22–30.

Cohen, F. (2006). *IT security governance guidebook with security program metrics.* Auerbach Publishers Inc.

Da Veiga, A., & Eloff, J. H. P. (2010). A framework and assessment instrument for information security culture. *Computers & Security, 29*(2), 196–207. http://doi.org/10.1016/j.cose.2009.09.002

Da Veiga, A., & Martins, N. (2015). Improving the information security culture through monitoring and implementation actions illustrated through a case study. *Computers & Security, 49,* 162–176.

Davidson, R., & MacKinnon, J. G. (1984). Convenient specification tests for logit and probit models. *Journal of Econometrics, 25*(3), 241–262.

De Haes, S., & Van Grembergen, W. (2006, February). Information technology governance best practices in Belgian organisations. *Proceedings of the Annual Hawaii International Conference on System Sciences, 8.* https://doi.org/10.1109/HICSS.2006.222

Dhillon, G., Syed, R., & de Sá-Soares, F. (2017). Information security concerns in IT outsourcing: Identifying (in) congruence between clients and vendors. *Information & Management, 54*(4), 452–464.

Dhillon, G., Tejay, G., & Hong, W. (2007). *Identifying governance dimensions to evaluate information systems security in organizations.* https://doi.org/10.1109/HICSS.2007.257

Dlamini, M. T., Eloff, J. H. P., & Eloff, M. M. (2009). Information security: The moving target. *Computers & Security, 28*(3), 189–198. https://doi.org/10.1016/j.cose.2008.11.007

Duffield, M. (2014). *Global governance and the new wars: The merging of development and security.* Zed Books.

Eroğlu, Ş., & Çakmak, T. (2016). Enterprise information systems within the context of information security: A risk assessment for a health organization in Turkey. *Procedia Computer Science, 100,* 979–986.

Galliers, R. D., & Leidner, D. E. (2014). Strategic information management: Challenges and strategies in managing information systems. *Information Strategy, 625.* www.worldcat.org/isbn/0750656190

Goodhue, D. L., & Straub, D. (1991). Security concerns of system users: A study of perceptions of the adequacy of security. *Information & Management, 20.* https://doi.org/10.1016/0378-7206(91)90024-V

Hong, K., Chi, Y., Chao, L. R., & Tang, J. (2006). An empirical study of information security policy on information security elevation in Taiwan. *Information Management & Computer Security, 14*(2), 104–115. https://doi.org/10.1108/09685220610655861

Horne, C. A., Ahmad, A., & Maynard, S. B. (2016). *A theory on information security.* Australasian Conference on Information Systems.

Huang, S., Lee, C.L., & Kao, A.C. (2006). Balancing performance measures for information security management: A balanced scorecard framework. *Industrial Management and Data Systems, 106*. https://doi.org/10.1108/02635570610649880

Humphreys, E. (2008). Information security management standards: Compliance, governance and risk management. *Information Security Technical Report, 13*(4), 247–255. http://doi.org/10.1016/j.istr.2008.10.010

Information Security Governance: Guidance for Boards of Directors and Executive Management Guidance for Boards of Directors and Executive Management, (2006). *IT Governance Institute*, 1–52. www.itgi.org

Johnston, A., & Hale, R. (2009). Improved security through information security governance. *Communications of the ACM, 52*. https://doi.org/10.1145/1435417.1435446

Kahn, L. M., & Morimune, K. (1979). Unions and employment stability: A sequential logit approach. *International Economic Review, 20*(1), 217–235.

Klaic, A. (2010). *Overview of the state and trends in the contemporary information security policy and information security management methodologies*. International Convention on Information and Communication Technology, Electronics and Microelectronics MIPRO.

Knapp, K., Morris, R., Marshall, T. E., & Byrd, T. (2009). Information security policy: An organizational-level process model. *Computers & Security, 28*. https://doi.org/10.1016/j.cose.2009.07.001

Kraemer, S., Carayon, P., & Clem, J. (2009). Human and organizational factors in computer and information security: Pathways to vulnerabilities. *Computers & Security, 28*. https://doi.org/10.1016/j.cose.2009.04.006

Kryukov, D., & Strauss, R. (2009). Information security governance as key performance indicator for financial institutions. *Journal Riga Technical University, 38*. https://doi.org/10.2478/v10143-009-0014-x

Lee, Y. H., Huang, Y. L., Hsu, S. S., & Hung, C. H. (2013). Measuring the efficiency and the effect of corporate governance on the biotechnology and medical equipment industries in Taiwan. *International Journal of Economics and Financial Issues, 3*(3), 662

Lomas, E. (2010). Information governance: information security and access within a UK context. *Records Management Journal, 20*(2), 182–198. https://doi.org/10.1108/09565691011064322

Lunardi, G. L., Becker, J. L., Maçada, A. C. G., & Dolci, P. C. (2014). The impact of adopting IT governance on financial performance: An empirical analysis among Brazilian firms. *International Journal of Accounting Information Systems, 15*(1), 66–81.

Maleh, Y., Sahid, A., Ezzati, A., & Belaissaoui, M. (2018). A capability maturity framework for IT security governance in organizations. In A. Abraham, A. Haqiq, A. K. Muda, & N. Gandhi (Eds.), *Innovations in bio-inspired computing and applications* (pp. 221–233). Springer.

Markus, M. (1983). Power, Politics, and MIS Implementation. In *Communications of the ACM* (Vol. 26). https://doi.org/10.1145/358141.358148

Michael, E., & Whitman, H. J. M. (2011). *Roadmap to information security: For IT and Infosec managers*. Delmar Learning.

Mitchell, R. C., Marcella, R., & Baxter, G. (1999). Corporate information security management. *New Library World, 100*. https://doi.org/10.1108/03074809910285888

Mohamed, N., & Singh, J. K. a/p. G. (2012). A conceptual framework for information technology governance effectiveness in private organizations. *Information Management & Computer Security, 20*(2), 88–106. https://doi.org/10.1108/09685221211235616

Nations, U. (2008). *International standard industrial classification of all economic activities (revision 4)*. United Nations Publication.

Peltier, T. R. (2013). *Information security fundamentals* (2nd ed.). CRC Press, Taylor & Francis.

Posthumus, S., & von Solms, R. (2004). A framework for the governance of information security. *Computers & Security, 23*(8), 638–646. http://doi.org/10.1016/j.cose.2004.10.006

Rockart, J. F., & D. Crescenzi, A. (1984). Engaging top management in information technology. *Sloan Management Review, 25*, 3–16.

Schou, C., & Shoemaker, D. P. (2006). *Information assurance for the enterprise: A roadmap to information security*. McGraw-Hill, Inc.

Siponen, M., & Willison, R. (2009). Information security management standards: Problems and solutions. *Information & Management, 46*(5), 267–270. http://doi.org/10.1016/j.im.2008.12.007

Sohrabi Safa, N., Von Solms, R., & Furnell, S. (2016). Information security policy compliance model in organizations. *Computers and Security, 56*, 1–13. https://doi.org/10.1016/j.cose.2015.10.006

Soomro, Z. A., Shah, M. H., & Ahmed, J. (2016). Information security management needs more holistic approach: A literature review. *International Journal of Information Management, 36*(2), 215–225.

Straub, D., & Welke, R. (1998). Coping with systems risk: Security planning models for management decision making. *MIS Quarterly, 22*(4), 441–469. www.jstor.org/stable/249551

Ula, M., Ismail, Z., & Sidek, Z. (2011). A framework for the governance of information security in banking system. *Journal of Information Assurance & Cybersecurity, 23*(8), 1–12. https://doi.org/10.5171/2011.726196

Venkatesh, V. (2012). Consumer acceptance and use of information technology: Extending the unified theory. *MIS Quarterly, 36*(1), 157–178.

Venkatesh, V., Morris, M. G., Davis, G. B., & Davis, F. D. (2003). User acceptance of information technology: Toward a unified view. *Source: MIS Quarterly, 27*(3), 425–478. https://doi.org/10.2307/30036540

von Solms, R., & van Niekerk, J. (2013). From information security to cyber security. *Computers & Security, 38*, 97–102. http://doi.org/10.1016/j.cose.2013.04.004

Waddock, S. A., & Graves, S. B. (1997). The corporate social performance-financial performance link. *Strategic Management Journal, 18*(4), 303–319. https://doi.org/10.1002/(SICI)1097-0266(199704)18:4<303::AID-SMJ869>3.0.CO;2-G

Williams, P. (2001). Information security governance. *Information Security Technical Report, 6*(3), 60–70. http://doi.org/10.1016/S1363-4127(01)00309-0

Williams, P. (2007). Executive and board roles in information security. *Network Security*. https://doi.org/10.1016/S1353-4858(07)70073-9

Williams, S. P., Hardy, C. A., & Holgate, J. A. (2013). Information security governance practices in critical infrastructure organizations: A socio-technical and institutional logic perspective. *Electronic Markets, 23*(4), 341–354. https://doi.org/10.1007/s12525-013-0137-3

Yaokumah, W. (2014). Information security governance implementation within Ghanaian industry sectors: An empirical study. *Information Management & Computer Security, 22*(3), 235–250.

Appendix 1

TABLE A.2 List of Variables Introduced in the Measurement Model

VARIABLE	LABEL
GEN	Gender of participants
Ag	Age (years)
NB_ORG	Number of participants organization
SIZE	Size of the company (# of employees)
INDUS	Belonging to industry
SERV	Belong to other sectors
FINA	Be part of a finance sector
TURNOVER	Evolution of Turnover and Revenue of the Company in $
ORGANISME	Knowledge of an organization promoting the governance of information security
NB_BENEF	Number of benefits derived from an information security governance approach
IMAGE	Improving the image of the organization
ATTRACT	Attract new customers/employees
DIFFER	Differentiating from the competition
ESTABLISH	Building confidence
CONFORME	Compliance with legislation
CERTIF	Get certification
IMPROVE	Improve safety procedures
ENSURE	Ensure decisions and activities at risk
CONTROL	Guarantee the mastery of the computer tool
VAL	Increase the value of the organization
INCREASE	Increase predictability and reduce uncertainty in management operations
RESP	Do not incur civil/legal liability
RESOURCE	Optimize security resources
NB_CHALL	Number of barriers to implement an information security governance approach
COST	Cost of implementation
TEMPS	Lack of time
HOUSERES	Lack of in-house resources
SKILLS	Lack of in-house skills
INFO	Difficulty in finding relevant information
CHANGE	Resistance to change
MANAGEMENT	Low level of management interest

VARIABLE	LABEL
ACTIONS	Translation of the concept into concrete actions
NB_PRIORITY	Number of priority areas for engagement in a governance approach to information security
TECHNO	Safety-related technology choices
ALIGN	Aligning information security with organizational strategy
RISQUE	Risk management and reduction of potential impacts to an acceptable level
RESSOURCE	Management of information resources
PERF	Evaluation of performance through the monitoring of safety indicators
CREAT	Creating value through optimization of security investments

Appendix 2

TABLE A.3 The Determinants of the Adoption of Information Security Governance (Logit Model)

VARIABLE	MODEL 1	MODEL 2	MODEL 3	MODEL 4	MODEL 5
Constante	−0.6983	−1.0383	−0.8540	−0.8863	**−1.3922***
	(0.7184)	(0.7556)	(0.7376)	(0.7183)	**(0.8330)**
INDUS	−0.7934	−0.8387	−0.8684	−0.9198	**−0.9606***
	(0.6134)	(0.6465)	(0.5454)	(0.5674)	**(0.5735)**
SERV	Référence	Référence	Référence	Référence	Référence
FINA	0.5037	0.5275	0.4239	0.4853	0.5987
	(0.6239)	(0.6538)	(0.6636)	(0.6848)	(0.7237)
TURNOVER	0.3165	0.3389	0.3490	0.3156	0.2554
	(0.5239)	(0.5330)	(0.5373)	(0.5333)	(0.5479)
NB_INVOLVED	**0.5983*****	**0.6254*****	**0.5867*****	**0.5993*****	X
	(0.1736)	**(0.1773)**	**(0.1717)**	**(0.1739)**	
INVOLDED	X	X	X	X	**1.5375*****
					(0.5569)
COMPETITORS	X	X	X	X	**1.1348****
					(0.5654)
ORGANISME	X	X	X	X	X
NB_BENEF	**0.3875****	**0.3397****	**0.3935****	**0.3098****	**0.2548****
	(0.1350)	**(0.1336)**	**(0.1440)**	**(0.1335)**	**(0.1203)**
NB_CHALL	−0.3223	X	X	X	X
	(0.2129)				
MANAGEMENT	X	X	**−1.2745***	−1.2004	X
			(0.6843)	(0.7198)	
ACTIONS	X	**−1.9048****	X	**−1.8055***	**−2.1347****
		(0.8938)		**(0.9912)**	**(0.9564)**
NB_PRIORITY	0.1763	0.1117	−0.1153	0.1346	0.1734
	(0.2763)	(0.2579)	(0.2530)	(0.2534)	(0.2634)
Number of observations	836	836	836	836	836
% concordance	87.4	87.6	87.4	88.4	87.7

Significance threshold: ***1%; **5%; *10%.

Coefficient, the standard deviation in parentheses.

Information Security Governance

7

A Maturity Framework Based on ISO/IEC 27001

7.1 INTRODUCTION

Many organizations today face a global governance revolution that could directly impact their information management practices. Information security has become an integral part of daily life, and organizations must ensure that their information security systems are an integral part of everyday life.

In a distributed and dynamic services environment, security must not be limited to providing technological solutions but finding a strategy taking into account business, organizational, and technical dimensions (Nassar et al., 2009). Besides, security must be seen as an ongoing process that aims to optimize security investments and ensure the sustainability of the security measures implemented (Lomas, 2010). However, reference service domain models and architectures have underestimated the definition of security needs, the assets to be protected, and the identification of risks to these assets (Huang et al., 2006; Williams, 2007). We propose approaching the problem of security by a practical approach of governance, allowing us to identify the various axes of my IT security and propose adequate security measures to the context. However, IT security governance is a real challenge in an open collaborative service environment (Maleh et al., 2018). Improving security has emerged as one of the top IT priorities across all business lines.

Areas such as the aerospace industry and strategic resources can be ideal targets for cyber espionage by nation-states. Others managing financial assets or large-scale credit card information are equally attractive to international criminal groups (Posthumus &

DOI: 10.1201/9781003161998- 11

von Solms, 2004; Humphreys, 2008). These malicious actors no longer content themselves with thwarting the means of technical protection. Instead, they survey and exploit various weaknesses detected in the targeted environment (Galliers & Leidner, 2014). These shortcomings are technological and result from failures in protection procedures or gaps in vulnerability management practices. If misused, the best technology in the world will not provide an adequate defense against such threats (von Solms & van Niekerk, 2013).

IT and security executives have to make complex calculations and decisions about security with limited information (Dhillon et al., 2016). They need to make decisions that are based on analyzing opportunities, risks, and security. In such an environment, information security governance (ISG) issues are at the forefront of any discussions for security organization's information assets, which includes considerations for managing risks, data, and costs. Organizations worldwide have adopted practical and applied approaches for mitigating risks and managing information security programs (Maleh et al., 2018; Yassine Maleh, 2018).

The problem is that the security governance framework is designed to guide organizations in their IS security governance strategy but does not define the practical framework for the engagement in this strategy. Some practice repositories (NIST, Cobit, ISACA, and RiskIT) and international standards (ISO 27000 suite and ISO 15408) now include paragraphs on security governance to address these concerns. The first reports or articles in academic journals that evoke the governance of information security date back to the early 2000s. The proposed referential and best practices are designed to guide organizations in their IT security governance strategy. However, it does not define the practical framework to implement or measure the organization's engagement in IS security governance (Yassine Maleh et al., 2021). The main contributions of the proposed frameworks are as follows:

- It includes standards, methodologies, procedures, and processes that align policy, business, and technological approaches to address information security governance;
- It provides a prioritized, flexible, repeatable, performance-based, and cost-effective approach, including information security measures and controls, to help owners and operators of critical infrastructure identify, assess, and manage information security;
- It identifies areas for improvement to be addressed through future collaboration with particular sectors and standard-developing organizations;
- It is consistent with voluntary international standards (IS2700, NIST, COBIT, ISACA).

This chapter proposes a practical maturity framework to evaluate the organization's maturity state and improve the IS security governance level according to their needs and resources. This chapter is structured as follows. Section 2 presents the theoretical framework and describes the proposed capability maturity framework for information security governance. Section 3 discusses the results of the implementation through a practical use case. Finally, section 4 presents the summary of this chapter.

7.2 THEORETICAL FRAMEWORK

ISG frameworks can be successfully implemented by adopting best practices (Williams, 2001). Von Solms (2005) indicated that companies realize that instead of establishing an information security governance environment on an ad hoc basis, it is preferable to follow an internationally recognized framework. Several resources can be used as a guide for information security governance, for example:

- Control Objectives for Information Technology and Related Technologies (COBIT) that help mitigate risk, assess the maturity of strategic alignment and value of IT delivery (Mataracioglu & Ozkan, 2011; Raup-Kounovsky et al., 2010; Saetang & Haider, 2011; Simonsson et al., 2008);
- National Institute of Standards and Technology (NIST) (IT Governance) 2008 (Dlamini et al., 2009);
- International Organization for Standardization (ISO)/International Electrotechnical Commission (IEC) 27000 family of safety standards (ITG, 2008) such as ISO17799 (Spafford, 2003) and ISO27001 (Mataracioglu & Ozkan, 2011);
- Certified Information Systems Security Professional (CISSP) (Harris, 2007).

Von Solms (2005) discussed the advantages and disadvantages of using COBIT and ISO17799 and stated that both are good choices for information security governance and are complementary and therefore, when used together, can bring benefits to the organization. COBIT allows information security to be integrated into a broader IT framework, which means that it is available if the company decides to implement the rest of the framework. COBIT focuses on what needs to be done but does not provide detailed guidelines on how to do it. ISO17799, on the other hand, provides more detailed guidance on how things should be done, but only addresses information security and is not integrated into a broader IT governance framework. It is the only framework that allows an organization to obtain third-party audit certification (Saint-Germain, 2005).

The IT Governance Institute (ITG, 2008) recommended that a framework be established and maintained by the management to guide the development and maintenance of an information security program to achieve effective information security governance (Spafford, 2003). Several compelling reasons why organizations should instead adopt existing standards, such as a well-defined structure, have been developed and evaluated over many years by many individuals and organizations. They provide a platform for knowledge sharing among organizations, and they also facilitate the certification of organizations against a basic standard from which improvements can be recommended.

The following section presents a capacity maturity framework focused on practitioners that integrate the technical, process, and human dimensions. The framework is based on the fact that the pace and manner in which an organization can respond proactively to new and emerging security threats depend on the maturity of its ISG capacity. The fundamental pillars of the framework must be fluid and responsive to the changing landscape of information security; by developing their capabilities to detect, assess, and respond to new and emerging security threats, organizations can position themselves more proactively to efficiently and continuously secure information resources.

7.2.1 Framework Overview

We propose a global maturity framework to achieve an effective information security governance and governance approach, as shown in Figure 7.1. The path to security maturity requires a diversified range of layered endpoint protection, management, and capabilities, all integrated and fully automated. The only practical and survivable defensive strategy is moving to a more mature security model that incorporates multiple layers of protective technology.

The proposed framework focuses on determining the capacity of an organization to directly oversee and monitor the actions and processes necessary to protect documented and digitized information and information systems and to ensure protection against access, unauthorized use, disclosure, disruption, alteration, or destruction, and to guarantee confidentiality, integrity, availability, accessibility, and usability of the data (Kenneally et al., 2012). The framework extends the triad confidentiality, integrity, and availability of commonly cited with accessibility and usability concepts. Concerning accessibility, a failure to support and understand how security can change work practices can impede how data and information are accessed, shared, and acted on in an increasingly dynamic, competitive

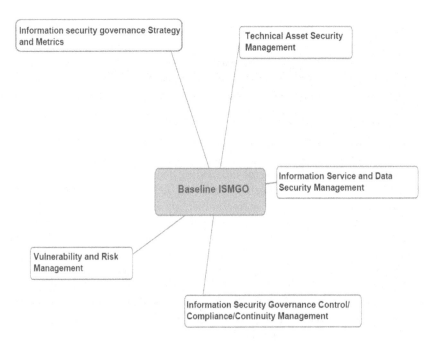

FIGURE 7.1   The proposed maturity framework for information security governance.

environment. Similarly, usability is one of the main key factors to engaging stakeholders in the business processes, independently of the availability of technology to support work practices. If the technology is difficult to interact and engage with, users might adopt other locally developed, less-secure methods of access. The proposed information capability maturity framework is a comprehensive suite of proven management practices, assessment approaches, and improvement strategies covering 5 governance capabilities, 21 objectives, and 80 controls.

7.2.2 Framework Core

The ISG framework classifies the information security activities across the following five high-level function categories:

- Information security strategy and governance provide the oversight structures for supporting ISG; it implements information security strategy, policies, and controls; assigns; defines roles and responsibilities for ISG activities; provides communication and training; reports on ISG activities' effectiveness; manages supplier security requirements; and plans and tests the security of business continuity measures;
- Technical asset security management establishes a security architecture and implements measures to control IT components and physical infrastructure security;
- Information services, system, and data management provide security budgets, tools, and resources; measure the resource efficiency of security investments; define data security classifications; and guides managing access rights and data throughout its lifecycle;
- Vulnerability and risk management control profiles security threats and assess priorities, handles, and monitors security-related risks;
- Information security compliance, control, and verification.

As Table 7.1 shows, these high-level function categories are decomposed into 21 security practice objectives (SPOs).

TABLE 7.1   ISG Framework Functions and Objectives

GOVERNANCE FUNCTIONS	SECURITY PRACTICE OBJECTIVE	DESCRIPTION
Information security governance strategy and metrics	Information security strategy and policies	Develop, communicate, and support the organization's information security objectives. Establish and maintain security policies and controls, considering relevant security standards, regulatory and legislative security requirements, and the organization's security goals.

(Continued)

TABLE 7.1   (Continued)

GOVERNANCE FUNCTIONS	SECURITY PRACTICE OBJECTIVE	DESCRIPTION
	Strategic alignment of security	From risk analysis to the actual deployment of global policy, security must be aligned with the business priorities of the company while respecting regulatory and legal constraints
	Communication and training	Disseminate security approaches, policies, and other relevant information to develop security awareness and skills.
	People's roles and responsibilities	Document and define the responsibilities and roles for the security of employees, contractors, and users, by the organization's information security strategy.
	Security performance assessment	Report on the efficiency of information security policies and activities, and the level of compliance with them.
	Assessment of security budget and investments	Provide security-related investment and budget criteria.
Technical asset security management	Security architecture	Build security measures into the design of IT solutions – for example, by defining coding protocols, depth of the defense, the configuration of security features, and so on.
	IT component security	Implement measures to protect all IT components, physical and virtual, such as client computing devices, servers, networks, storage devices, printers, and smartphones.
	Physical infrastructure security	Establish and maintain measures to safeguard the IT physical infrastructure from harm. Threats to be addressed include extremes of temperature, malicious intent, and utility supply disruptions.
Information service/ system/data security management	Incident management	Manage security-related incidents and near incidents. Develop and train incident response teams to identify and limit exposure, manage communications, and coordinate with regulatory bodies as appropriate.
	Resource effectiveness	Measure 'value for money' from security investments; capture feedback from stakeholders on the effectiveness of security resource management.

GOVERNANCE FUNCTIONS	SECURITY PRACTICE OBJECTIVE	DESCRIPTION
	Data identification and classifications	Define information security classes, and guide protection and access control appropriate to each level.
	Access management	Manage user access rights to information throughout its lifecycle, including granting, denying, and revoking access privileges.
	System acquisition, development, and maintenance security policy	Ensure the management of security throughout the life cycle of information systems. Reduce risks related to exploiting technical vulnerabilities and applications.
Vulnerability and risk management	Security threat profiling	Gather intelligence on IT security threats and vulnerabilities to better understand the IT security threat landscape within which the organization operates, including the actors, scenarios, and campaigns that might pose a threat.
	Security risk assessment	Identify exposures to security-related risks and quantify their likelihood and potential impact.
	Security risk prioritization	Prioritize information security risks and risk-handling strategies based on residual risks and the organization's risk appetite.
	Security monitoring	Manage the ongoing efficacy of information security risk-handling strategies and control options.
Information security governance control/ compliance/ continuity management	Compliance control	Identify applicable law, statutory and contractual obligations that might impact the organization. Establish security and compliance baseline and understand per-system risks.
	Security testing and auditing	Adopt a solution for an information security audit. Establish project audit practice. Derive test cases from known security requirements
	Business continuity planning	Continuity management Business continuity planning Provide stakeholders throughout the organization with security advice to assist in analyzing incidents and ensuring that data is secure before, during, and after the execution of the business continuity plan.

7.2.3 Framework Maturity Profile

The bottom line on information security is that the threat environment of today is simply too dynamic. The only practical and survivable defense strategy is to move to a more mature security model that integrates multiple layers of protection technology.

We propose a mature and systematic approach to information security governance. Adopting a security maturity strategy requires a full range of protection, management, and defensive features that must be integrated and capable of fully automated operation.

Concerning each security practice objectives SPO outlined in Table 7.1, the framework defines a five-level maturity that serves as the basis for understanding an organization's ISG capability and provides a foundation for capability improvement planning.

Level 0 – None: No process or documentation in place;

Level 1 – Initial: Maturity is characterized by the ad hoc definition of an information security strategy, policies, and standards. Physical environment and IT component security are only locally addressed. There is no explicit consideration of budget requirements for information security activities and no systematic management of security risks. Access rights and the security of data throughout its lifecycle are managed at best using informal procedures. Similarly, security incidents are managed on an ad hoc basis;

Level 2 – Basic: Maturity reflects the linking of a basic information security strategy to business and IT strategies and risk appetite in response to individual needs. It also involves the development and review of information security policies and standards, typically after significant incidents. IT component and physical environment security guidelines are emerging. There is some consideration of security budget requirements within IT, and requirements for high-level security features are specified for major software and hardware purchases. A basic risk and vulnerability management process are established within IT according to the perceived risk. The access rights control and management depend on the solutions provided by the provider. Processes for managing the security of data throughout its life cycle are emerging. Major security incidents are tracked and recorded within IT;

Level 3 – Defined: Maturity reflects a detailed information security strategy that's regularly aligned to business and IT strategies and risk appetite across IT and some other business units.

Information security policies and standards are developed and revised based on a defined process and regular feedback. IT and some other business units have agreed on IT component and physical environment security measures. IT budget processes acknowledge and provide the most important information security budget requests in IT and some other business units. The security risk management process is proactive and is jointly shared with corporate collaboration. Access rights are granted on the basis of a formal and audited authorization process. Detailed methods for managing data security throughout its life cycle are implemented. Security incidents are handled based on the urgency to restore services, as agreed on by IT and some other business units;

Level 4 – Managed: Maturity is characterized by regular, enterprise-wide improvement in the alignment of the information security strategy, policies, and standards with business and IT strategies and compliance requirements. IT component security measures on IT systems are implemented and tested enterprise-wide for threat detection and mitigation. Physical environment security is integrated with access controls and surveillance systems across the enterprise. Detailed security budget requirements are incorporated into enterprise-wide business planning and budgeting activities. A standardized security risk-management process is aligned with a firm risk-management process. Access rights are implemented and audited across the company. Data are adequately preserved throughout its life cycle, and data availability is an effective requirement. Recurring incidents are systematically addressed enterprise-wide through problem-management processes that are based on the root cause analysis;

Level 5 – Optimized: Maturity reflects an information security strategy regularly aligned to business and IT strategies and risk appetite across the business ecosystem. Information security policies and standards are periodically reviewed and revised on the basis of the input from the business ecosystem. The management of IT component security is optimized across the security framework layers. Physical access and environmental controls are regularly improved. Security budget requirements are adjusted to provide adequate funding for the current and future security purposes. The security risk management process is agile and adaptable, and tools can address the business ecosystem's requirements. The control and management of access rights are dynamic and can effectively deal with the organizational restructuring of acquisitions and divestitures. Processes for managing data security throughout its life cycle are continuously improved. Automated incident prediction systems are in place, and security incidents are effectively managed.

7.3 USE CASE

The pre-established questionnaire took into account the realities of the organization. At the end of this survey, and following a metric, we evaluated the deviations from the norm and assessed the level of maturity regarding security concerning the different axes of our framework. The audit questionnaire consists of 100 questions divided into different objectives and control of the information security governance inspired by best practice guides ISO 27001 (Johnson, 2014) and OWASP (Deleersnyder et al., 2009). Each item is assigned a weighting coefficient on the effectiveness of the rule of the reference system to which the question relates regarding risk reduction. After the validation of the questionnaire, the chosen answers were introduced into the software maturity framework used to allow the automation of the processing and to determine the maturity score. The treatment consists of calculating a weighted average of the scores obtained according to the chosen responses and the efficiency coefficient. The result is a numerical result (0–5 or expressed as a percentage), representing the audited IS level of security (maturity).

7.3.1 Data Collection

The questionnaire was carried out in several stages. A first version has been developed to take into account the different theoretical assumptions. This first version has been tested with IT service managers and consultants. This pre-test allowed rephrasing some questions to improve the questionnaire's comprehension and improve the quality of the given answers. In the end, the questionnaire consists of 100 questions divided into different security objectives and controls. Table 7.2 shows the organization background, and Table 7.3 presents the participants' demographics.

TABLE 7.2 Organization Background

	YEAR	FREQUENCY
Size of the company (no. of employees)	2019	More than 1,200
Position	Senior executives	460
	Executives	95
	Lower management	420
	Qualified non-supervisory	146
	Non-supervisory	79
Evolution of turnover and revenue of the company for the last 5 years in dollars	2012	More than 1.5 million
	2013	Fewer than 3 million
	2014	More than 1.7 million
	2015	More than 1.5 million
	2016	Fewer than 1.7 million
	2017	More than 1.8 million
	2018	More than 1.8 million
	2019	More than 2 million

TABLE 7.3 Participants' Demographics

PARTICIPANTS	FREQUENCY	%
Male	68	68.42
Female	36	31.58
Top manager personnel	17	14.91
Senior manager	23	20.18
IT manager	7	6.14
Consultant/engineer/analyst	13	11.40
IT technical staff	19	16.67
Helpdesk technician	7	6.14
Quality assurance/quality control	15	13.16
Other entities staff	13	14.91

7.3.2 Data Analysis

The pre-established questionnaire took into account the realities of the organization. At the end of this survey, and following a metric, the authors evaluated the deviations from the norm and assessed the level of ISG maturity regarding the different axes of the framework. The audit questionnaire consists of 110 questions divided into different ITSG objectives and controls inspired by best practice guides ISO 27000 (Johnson, 2014) and COBIT (Deleersnyder et al., 2009). Each item is assigned a weighting coefficient on the effectiveness of the rule of the reference system to which the question relates regarding risk reduction. After the validation of the questionnaire, the chosen answers were introduced into the software maturity framework used to allow the automation of the processing and to determine the ISG maturity score. The treatment consists of calculating a weighted average of the scores obtained according to the chosen responses and the efficiency coefficient. The result is a numerical result (0–5 or expressed as a percentage) representing the level of maturity of the audited ISG.

7.3.3 Conducting Assessments

A comprehensive picture of integrated security assurance activities is created by measuring an organization based on defined security practices. This type of evaluation is helpful in understanding the extent of the security activities currently in place in an organization. Also, it allows the organization to use the maturity framework to create a future roadmap for continuous improvement.

An important first step of the assessment is to define the assessment scope. An assessment can be carried out for a complete organization or selected business units. This scope should be agreed upon with the key stakeholders involved (Figure 7.2).

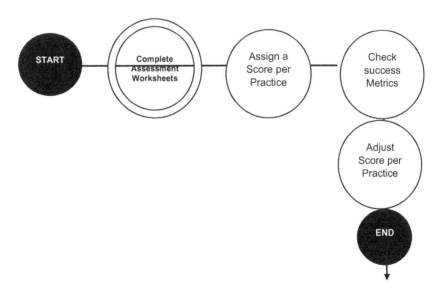

FIGURE 7.2   Conducting assessment model.

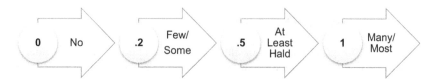

FIGURE 7.3   Assessment score.

Scoring an organization using the evaluation spreadsheets is simple. After answering questions, the answer column is assessed to determine the score. Insurance programs may not always consist of activities that fall carefully over a limit between maturity levels.

An organization will receive credit for the different levels of works it has performed in practice. The score is fractional to two decimal places for each practice and one decimal for a response. Questions were also changed from yes/no to five options related to maturity levels. Anyone who completed the assessment discussed whether to report a yes or no answer when it is honestly something in between.

The toolbox worksheet contains contextual answers for each question in the assessment. The formulas in the toolbox will average the answers to calculate the score for each practice, a loop average for each business function and an overall rating. The toolkit also features dashboard graphics that help to represent the current score and can help show program improvements when the answers to the questions change (Figure 7.3). An example of an evaluation calculation can be found in Appendix 2 (Table 7.8).

7.3.4 Assessing Capability Maturity

The framework's assessment tool provides a granular and focused view of an organization's current maturity state for each SPO, desired or target maturity state for each SPO, and importance attributed to each SPO. These maturity and significance scores are primarily determined by an online survey undertaken by the organization's key IT and business stakeholders, as shown in Appendix 1 (Table 7.7). The survey typically takes each assessment participant 30–45 minutes to complete. The data collected can be augmented by qualitative interview insights that focus on issues such as key information security-related business priorities, successes achieved, and initiatives taken or planned. The assessment provides valuable insight into the similarities and differences in how key stakeholders view both the importance and maturity of individual SPOs and the overall vision for success. Figure 7.4 shows the organization's ISG capability maturity assessment results, outlining its current and target SPO maturity across all 21 SPOs. For each SPO, the maturity results are automatically generated by the proposed assessment tool based on averaging the survey participants' scores across all questions about that SPO. Based on this average score achieved, the organization highlighted in Figure 7.4 reflects a level 1.4 (initial) current maturity status for ISG overall. Still, it is less mature in some SPOs, such as security budgeting, resource effectiveness, security threat profiling, and security risk handling. Based on the average across all SPOs, its desired target ISG maturity state is maturity level 2.4 (Basic) for the first 6 months after the first organization assessment.

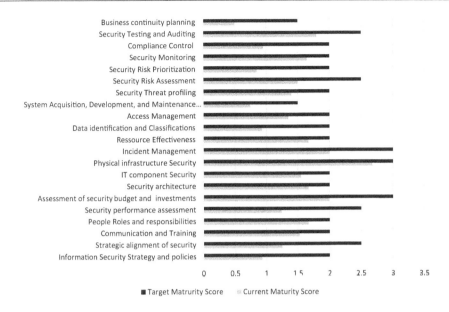

FIGURE 7.4   The proposed information security governance assessment results.

7.3.5 Developing Improvement Action Plans

The output from the framework's assessment supports understanding the actions necessary to drive improvement and enables the organization to transition from its current to target maturity state systematically. This is achieved by implementing a series of industry-validated practices that allow organizations to improve incrementally and monitor and track progress over time using a number of industry-validated metrics. Table 7.4 includes sample practices and metrics for the five SPOs highlighted for prioritized improvement in . For each of these SPOs, the figure outlines the currently reported maturity and the practices required to transition to the next maturity state. Note that additional practices are available to support transitioning to the desired maturity state.

To reach the target maturity levels score, the organization adopted an action plan planned over three phases in 2 years, as presented in Table 7.5.

To reach the desired level of maturity, the organization implemented some programs during each phase of the rollout. The following initiatives were adopted in the first phase (months 0–6):

- Construct a white paper of technical guidance for application security on the technologies used within the organization;
- Create a risk process and conduct high-level business risk assessments for application platforms and review the business risk;
- Prepare initial guidelines and technical standards for developers;
- Conduct short implementation reviews on application platforms that pose a significant risk to the organization;

TABLE 7.4   Example Practices and Metrics to Drive Improvement in Specific Security Practice Blocks (CSPBs)

GOVERNANCE FUNCTIONS	CONTROL OBJECTIVE	CURRENT MATURITY SCORE	TARGET MATURITY SCORE	TARGET OBJECTIVES TO INCREASE MATURITY SCORE	METRICS
Information security governance strategy and metrics	Information security strategy and policies	0.93	2	Develop basic information security strategies that consider IT and business strategies and risk appetite. Build and maintain technical guidelines.	Existence and availability of security strategies that include business and IT strategies and risk appetite, number and percent of stakeholders aware of and using information security strategies.
	Strategic alignment of security	1.25	2.5	Align the governance strategy of security with the organization's overall IS governance strategy.	Control objectives tied to specific strategic and business objectives.
	Communication and training	1	2	Conduct technical security awareness training	Employee satisfaction surveys. Percent of staff trained within the past year. Percent of analyst/management staff trained within the previous year.
	People roles and responsibilities	1.67	2.8	A clear assignment of responsibilities for information security	System accounts-to-employees ratio. Security awareness level. Psychometrics.
	Security performance assessment	1.24	2.5	Develop a measurement dashboard and regular monitoring of the organization's security performance in terms of availability, integrity, confidentiality, and nonrepudiation.	A number of controls meeting defined control criteria/objectives. Percent of controls that are ossified or redundant.

Assessment of security budget and investments	2	3	Estimate overall business risk profile	Internal rate of return. The annual cost of information security controls. Return on investment. Return on security investment.
Technical asset security management				
Security architecture	1.67	2.4	Identify and promote security services and design patterns from architecture	Percent of project report, model, platform, and pattern usage feedback. Percent of project teams informed about appropriate security standards.
Information service/system/data security management				
IT component security	1.55	2.4	Identify, inventory, and classify all assets needed for information management. For each of them, a manager must be determined. It is responsible for enforcing the security policy for its assets.	Discrepancies between logical access location and physical location. A number of unacceptable physical risks on-premises. Percent of IT devices not securely configured.
Physical infrastructure security	2.67	3.5	Ensure the protection and availability of sensitive equipment. Ensure that only authorized persons have access to the buildings, technical premises, and archives of the organization and that access is traced	Number IT assets without an owner. Percent of information assets not (correctly) classified.

(Continued)

TABLE 7.4   (Continued)

GOVERNANCE FUNCTIONS	CONTROL OBJECTIVE	CURRENT MATURITY SCORE	TARGET MATURITY SCORE	TARGET OBJECTIVES TO INCREASE MATURITY SCORE	METRICS
Information service/ system/data security management	Incident management	2	3	Prioritize and manage security incidents based on the urgency to restore services. Identify indicators and establish security incidents dashboards.	A number of information security events and incidents, major and minor. IT security incidents cumulative cost to date. Nonfinancial impacts and effect of IT incidents.
	Resource effectiveness	1.5	2	Identify and classify data based on criticality, business risk, etc.	Percent of data by the degree of criticality.
	Data identification and classifications	0.93	2	Establish a process to withdraw employee access rights if abused. Discourage sharing of credentials. Provide employees with access to a password management package.	A number of access rights audit exceptions. A number of grant/revoke of access rights by the department.
	Access management	1.35	2	Conduct basic intelligence gathering and create basic threat profiles.	Percent of inactive user accounts disabled by policy.
	System acquisition, development, and maintenance security policy	0.75	1.5	Access control to applications/ programs source code. Restrictions on modifications to software packages.	Percent of controls tested practically. Percent of technical security checks.
Vulnerability and risk management	Security threat profiling	1.4	2	Create and conduct high-level risk assessments for application platforms and review business risk.	A number of unpatched vulnerabilities. IT security risk scores.

				Description	Metric
	Security risk assessment	1.5	2.5	Develop an application prioritization approach that identifies 'static' risks and 'relative' risk of each application.	A number of small, medium and high/risks currently untreated/unresolved. Number of attacks.
	Security risk prioritization	0.85	2	Implement security monitoring and analytics tool to quickly detect, analyze, and correct the widest range of threats to the organization's IT resources.	Application availability rates. IT application total downtime. Average response time of IT components.
Information security governance control/compliance/ continuity management	Security monitoring	1.65	2.2	Avoid violation of intellectual property, legal, regulatory, contractual, and organizational security requirements.	Historical consequences of noncompliance. Status of compliance with internally mandated (corporate) information security requirements. Number or rate of security policy noncompliance infractions detected.
	Compliance control	0.95	2	Derive test cases from known security requirements Conduct audit and penetration testing on software releases	Number and severity of findings in audit reports, reviews, assessments, etc.
	Security testing and auditing	1.8	2.5	Following a minor incident (failure of equipment), ensuring the IT back depending on business needs Following a major incident impacting the whole of a machine room, ensure a continuity of computer activity of the sensitive goods in the shortest time and according to the needs of the trades	Disaster recovery test results Business continuity plan for maintenance status

TABLE 7.5   Governance Maturity Assessment Roadmap

SECURITY PRACTICES	START	PHASE 1	PHASE 2	PHASE 3
Information security strategy and policies	0.93	1.25	1.75	2
Strategic alignment of security	1.25	1.75	2	2.5
Communication and training	1	1.50	1.75	2
People roles and responsibilities	1.67	1.85	2.5	2.8
Security performance assessment	1.67	1.85	2.5	2.8
Assessment of security budget and investments	1.24	1.75	2	2.5

SECURITY PRACTICES	START	PHASE 1	PHASE 2	PHASE 3

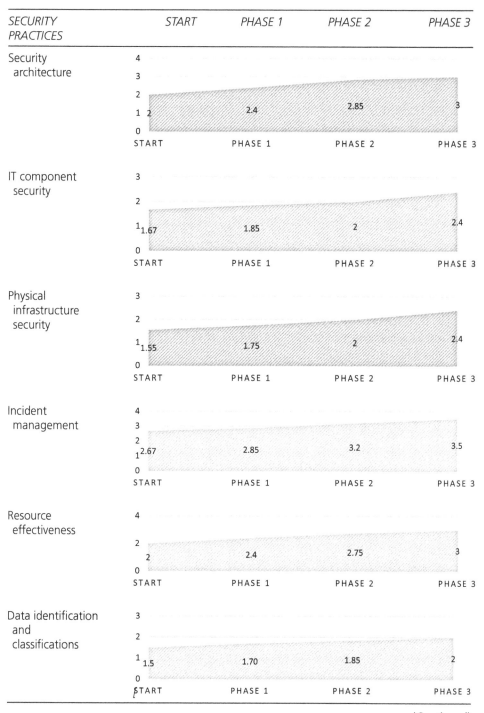

Security architecture: START 2, PHASE 1 2.4, PHASE 2 2.85, PHASE 3 3

IT component security: START 1.67, PHASE 1 1.85, PHASE 2 2, PHASE 3 2.4

Physical infrastructure security: START 1.55, PHASE 1 1.75, PHASE 2 2, PHASE 3 2.4

Incident management: START 2.67, PHASE 1 2.85, PHASE 2 3.2, PHASE 3 3.5

Resource effectiveness: START 2, PHASE 1 2.4, PHASE 2 2.75, PHASE 3 3

Data identification and classifications: START 1.5, PHASE 1 1.70, PHASE 2 1.85, PHASE 3 2

(Continued)

TABLE 7.5   (Continued)

SECURITY PRACTICES	START	PHASE 1	PHASE 2	PHASE 3

Access management

START	PHASE 1	PHASE 2	PHASE 3
0.93	1.25	1.75	2

Security threat profiling

START	PHASE 1	PHASE 2	PHASE 3
1.35	1.55	1.8	2

System acquisition, development, and maintenance security policy

START	PHASE 1	PHASE 2	PHASE 3
1.4	1.6	1.8	2

Security risk assessment

START	PHASE 1	PHASE 2	PHASE 3
0.75	1.00	1.25	1.5

Security risk prioritization

START	PHASE 1	PHASE 2	PHASE 3
1.4	1.6	1.8	2

Security monitoring

START	PHASE 1	PHASE 2	PHASE 3
1.5	1.85	2.10	2.5

SECURITY PRACTICES	START	PHASE 1	PHASE 2	PHASE 3
Compliance control	0.85	1.25	1.70	2
Security testing and auditing	1.65	1.75	1.95	2.2
Business continuity planning	0.95	1.35	1.75	2

- Develop test cases and use cases for projects and evaluate arguments against applications;
- Created a role in application security initiatives;
- Generated a strategic roadmap for the next phase of the security program.

Due to limited expertise in the intern, the company partnered with a third-party safety consulting group to assist in the creation of the training program. It helped to elaborate a threat modeling and a strategic security road map.

The organization was aware that they had applications with vulnerabilities and no real strategy to identify existing vulnerabilities or resolve risks within a reasonable timeframe. A methodology based on risk assessment was adopted, and the organization undertook a review of existing application platforms.

This phase also included implementing a number of concepts for the IT team to improve their security tools. IT teams already had a number of tools in place for quality assessments. An additional survey of code review and security testing tools was conducted. During this phase of the project, the organization will implement the following security maturity practices and activities as presented in Table 7.6.

TABLE 7.6   Target Objectives of Phase 1 (Months 0–6) to Achieve the Target Maturity Level

GOVERNANCE FUNCTIONS	TARGET GOALS (MONTHS 0–6)
Information security governance strategy and metrics	– Establish and maintain assurance and protection program roadmap – Classify applications and information based on business risk – Ensure data owners and appropriate security levels are defined
Technical asset security management	– Derive security requirements from business functionality – Ensure asset management system and process for hardware and software
Information service and data security management	– Identify, inventory, and classify all assets needed for data management – Define and maintain appropriate security levels
Vulnerability and risk management	– Ensure that standards are implemented on all machines, have current definitions and appropriate settings – Ensure users are periodically informed of unit virus prevention policies
Information security governance control/compliance/continuity management	– Ensure documented control processes are used to ensure data integrity and accurate reporting – Ensure periodic system self-assessments/risk assessments, and audits are performed – Ensure identification and monitoring of external and internal compliance factors

7.4 SUMMARY

Compliance audits and reviews are the secret ingredients to ensuring that security policies and processes are strictly adhered to, in line with an organization's risk or security management strategy. They are also an integral component of all operations management programs, including ISO 27001, COBIT, Sarbanes Oxley, and ITIL. Without a compliance assurance process, it is impossible to ensure that risks are being managed as intended or to detect and correct potential problems when they are not.

This chapter proposes an ISG maturity framework to provide a practical tool for measuring and improving governance in organizations. ISG has been implemented in a medium organization to drive and improve ISG maturity. The results are satisfactory and prove that the model will provide great support to organizations in different sizes and various sectors of activity in their governance and management of information security. Nevertheless, it is suggested that the scientific community and organizations adopt this framework and test it in different case studies.

BIBLIOGRAPHY

Archibugi, D., & Michie, J. (1995). Technology and innovation: An introduction. *Cambridge Journal of Economics*, *19*(1), 1–4.

Cohen, F. (2006). *IT security governance guidebook with security program metrics*. Auerbach Publishers Inc.

Deleersnyder, S., Win, B. De, Glas, B., Arciniegas, F., Bartoldus, M., Carter, J., Challey, D., Clarke, J., Cornell, D., Craigue, M., Deleersnyder, S., Derry, J., & Fern, D. (2009). *Software assurance maturity model*. OWSAP.

Dhillon, G., Syed, R., & Pedron, C. (2016). Interpreting information security culture: An organizational transformation case study. *Computers & Security*, *56*, 63–69. http://doi.org/10.1016/j.cose.2015.10.001

Dhillon, G., Syed, R., & Sá-Soares, F. de. (2017). Information security concerns in IT outsourcing: Identifying (in) congruence between clients and vendors. *Information & Management*, *54*(4), 452–464. https://doi.org/10.1016/j.im.2016.10.002

Dlamini, M. T., Eloff, J. H. P., & Eloff, M. M. (2009). Information security: The moving target. *Computers & Security*, *28*(3), 189–198. https://doi.org/10.1016/j.cose.2008.11.007

Galliers, R. D., & Leidner, D. E. (2014). Strategic information management: Challenges and strategies in managing information systems. *Information Strategy*, *625*. www.worldcat.org/isbn/0750656190

Goodhue, D. L., & Straub, D. (1991). Security concerns of system users: A study of perceptions of the adequacy of security. *Information & Management*, *20*. https://doi.org/10.1016/0378-7206(91)90024-V

Gupta, A., & Hammond, R. (2005). Information systems security issues and decisions for small businesses: An empirical examination. *Information Management & Computer Security*, *13*(4), 297–310. https://doi.org/10.1108/09685220510614425

Harris, S. (2007). *CISSP certification all-in-one: Exam guide* (4th ed.). McGraw-Hill Publishing.

Huang, S., Lee, C. L., & Kao, A. C. (2006). Balancing performance measures for information security management: A balanced scorecard framework. *Industrial Management and Data Systems*, *106*. https://doi.org/10.1108/02635570610649880

Humphreys, E. (2008). Information security management standards: Compliance, governance and risk management. *Information Security Technical Report*, *13*(4), 247–255. http://doi.org/10.1016/j.istr.2008.10.010

ITG. (2008). *Information security governance: Guidance for information security managers*. Retrieved July 10, 2012, from http://www.Globalteksecurity.Com/SEGURIDAD_EN_LA_NUBE%20%20VIRTUALIZACION/INformation%20Security%20Governance

Johnson, B. G. (2014). *Measuring ISO 27001 ISMS processes* (pp. 1–20). IGI Global.

Kenneally, J., Curley, M., Wilson, B., & Porter, M. (2012, December). Enhancing benefits from healthcare IT adoption using design science research: Presenting a unified application of the IT capability maturity framework and the electronic medical record adoption model. In *European Design Science Symposium* (pp. 124–143). Springer.

Lomas, E. (2010). Information governance: Information security and access within a UK context. *Records Management Journal*, *20*(2), 182–198. https://doi.org/10.1108/09565691011064322

Maleh, Y. (2018). *Security and Privacy Management, Techniques, and Protocols* (Yassine Maleh (ed.); IGI Global). IGI Global. https://doi.org/10.4018/978-1-5225-5583-4

Maleh, Y., Sahid, A., & Belaissaoui, M. (2021). A maturity framework for cybersecurity governance in organizations. *EDPACS*, *64*(2), 1–22. https://doi.org/10.1080/07366981.2020.1815354

Maleh, Y., Sahid, A., Ezzati, A., & Belaissaoui, M. (2018). A capability maturity framework for IT security governance in organizations. *Advances in Intelligent Systems and Computing*, *735*. https://doi.org/10.1007/978-3-319-76354-5_20

Mataracioglu, T., & Ozkan, S. (2011). *Governing information security in conjunction with COBIT and ISO 27001*. ArXiv Preprint ArXiv:1108.2150. https://arxiv.org/abs/1108.2150

Mitchell, R. C., Marcella, R., & Baxter, G. (1999). Corporate information security management. *New Library World, 100*. https://doi.org/10.1108/03074809910285888

Moody, G. D., Siponen, M., & Pahnila, S. (2018). Toward a unified model of information security policy compliance. *MIS Quarterly, 42*(1).

Moulton, R., & Coles, R. S. (2003). Applying information security governance. *Computers & Security, 22*(7), 580–584. http://doi.org/10.1016/S0167-4048(03)00705-3

Nassar, P. B., Badr, Y., Barbar, K., & Biennier, F. (2009). Risk management and security in service-based architectures. *2009 International Conference on Advances in Computational Tools for Engineering Applications*, 214–218. https://doi.org/10.1109/ACTEA.2009.5227927

Peltier, T. R. (2013). *Information security fundamentals* (2nd ed.). CRC Press, Taylor & Francis.

Posthumus, S., & von Solms, R. (2004). A framework for the governance of information security. *Computers & Security, 23*(8), 638–646. http://doi.org/10.1016/j.cose.2004.10.006

Raup-Kounovsky, A., Canestraro, D. S., Pardo, T. A., & Hrdinová, J. (2010). IT governance to fit your context: Two U.S. case studies. *Proceedings of the 4th International Conference on Theory and Practice of Electronic Governance*, 211–215. https://doi.org/10.1145/1930321.1930365

Saetang, S., & Haider, A. (2011). Conceptual aspects of IT governance in enterprise environment. *Proceedings of the 49th SIGMIS Annual Conference on Computer Personnel Research*, 79–82. https://doi.org/10.1145/1982143.1982164

Saint-Germain, R. (2005). Information security management best practice based on ISO/IEC 17799. *The Information Management Journal, 39*(4), 60–66.

Simonsson, M., Lagerström, R., & Johnson, P. (2008). A Bayesian network for IT governance performance prediction. *Proceedings of the 10th International Conference on Electronic Commerce*, 1:1–1:8. https://doi.org/10.1145/1409540.1409542

Siponen, M., & Willison, R. (2009). Information security management standards: Problems and solutions. *Information & Management, 46*(5), 267–270. http://doi.org/10.1016/j.im.2008.12.007

Spafford, G. (2003). *The benefits of standard IT governance frameworks*. Retrieved April 4, 2012, from http://www.Itmanagementonline.Com/Resources/Articles/The_Benefits_of_Standard_IT_Gov Ernance_Frameworks.Pdf

Von Solms, B. (2005). Information security governance: COBIT or ISO 17799 or both? *Computers and Security, 24*(2), 99–104. https://doi.org/10.1016/j.cose.2005.02.002

Von Solms, R., & van Niekerk, J. (2013). From information security to cyber security. *Computers & Security, 38*, 97–102. http://doi.org/10.1016/j.cose.2013.04.004

Von Solms, S. H. (2005). Information security governance – compliance management vs operational management. *Computers and Security, 24*(6), 443–447. https://doi.org/10.1016/j.cose.2005.07.003

Waddock, S. A., & Graves, S. B. (1997). The corporate social performance-financial performance link. *Strategic Management Journal, 18*(4), 303–319. https://doi.org/10.1002/(SICI)1097-0266(199704)18:4

Williams, P. (2001). Information security governance. *Information Security Technical Report, 6*(3), 60–70. http://doi.org/10.1016/S1363-4127(01)00309-0

Williams, P. (2007). Executive and board roles in information security. *Network Security*. https://doi.org/10.1016/S1353-4858(07)70073-9

Appendix 1

TABLE 7.7 Governance Maturity Assessment Roadmap

SECURITY GOVERNANCE FUNCTION	AB	SECURITY PRACTICES	MATURITY SCORE	SIGNIFICANCE SCORE
Information security and cybersecurity governance strategy and metrics	SM1	Information security and cybersecurity strategy and policies	0.93	2
	SM2	Strategic alignment of cybersecurity	1.25	2.5
	SM3	Communication and training	1	2
	SM4	People roles and responsibilities	1.67	2.8
	SM5	Cybersecurity performance assessment	1.24	2.5
	SM6	Assessment of cybersecurity budget and investments	2	3
Technical asset security management	AS1	Information security architecture	1.67	2.4
	AS2	IT component	1.55	2.4
	AS3	Physical infrastructure	2.67	3.5
Information service and data security management	SD1	Incident management	2	3
	SD2	Resource effectiveness	1.5	2
	SD3	Data identification and classifications	0.93	2
	SD4	Access management	1.35	2
	SD5	System acquisition, development, and maintenance security policy	0.75	1.5
Vulnerability and risk management	RM1	Cybersecurity threat profiling	1.4	2
	RM2	Cybersecurity risk assessment	1.5	2.5

SECURITY GOVERNANCE FUNCTION	AB	SECURITY PRACTICES	MATURITY SCORE	SIGNIFICANCE SCORE
	RM3	Cybersecurity risk prioritization	0.85	2
	RM4	Cybersecurity monitoring	1.65	2.2
Information security governance control/ compliance/ continuity management	SC1	Compliance control	0.95	2
	SC2	Testing and auditing	1.8	2.5
	SC3	Business continuity planning	0.5	1.5

Appendix 2

TABLE 7.8 Governance Maturity Assessment Interview (Sample)

INFORMATION SECURITY GOVERNANCE STRATEGY AND METRICS		CURRENT STATE	
INFORMATION SECURITY AND CYBERSECURITY STRATEGY AND POLICIES		ANSWER	RATING
SP1	Is there an information security policy and program in place?	Yes, in ad hoc basis	0.93
	Do the security rules specify a clear definition of tasks, specific roles affecting information security officers?	Yes, a small percentage are/do	
	A plan ensures that the review is conducted in response to changes in the baseline of the initial assessment, such as major security incidents, new vulnerabilities, or changes to organizational or technical infrastructure?	Yes, there is a standard set	
	Is there a formal contract containing, or referring to all security requirements to ensure compliance with the organization's security policies and standards?	Yes, a small percentage are/do	
SP2	Management actively supports the organization's security policy through clear direction, demonstrated commitment, explicit function assignment, and recognition of information security responsibilities?	Yes, at least half of them are/do	
	Are risk ratings used to adopt security and insurance required?	No	
	Does the organization know what's required based on risk ratings?	Yes, at least half of them are/do	

(Continued)

STRATEGIC ALIGNMENT OF CYBERSECURITY		*ANSWER*	*RATING*
SA1	Does the organization measure the contribution of IT security to its performance?	Yes, a small percentage are/do	1.25
	Does the organization define and manage the role of information security in the face of business and technological change?	Yes, but on an ad hoc basis	
SA2	Are there formal processes in place that emphasize strengthening the partnership relationships between IT security and business (e.g., cross-functional teams, training, risk sharing/ recognition)?	Yes, there is a standard set	
	What is the degree of IT control of security or business changes (implementation of new technology, business process, and merger/acquisition)?	Yes, a small percentage are/do	
SA3	What is the degree of perception of IT security by the organization?	Yes, a small percentage are/do	
	Does the organization periodically use audits to collect and control compliance conformity?	Yes, localized to business areas	

COMMUNICATION AND TRAINING		*ANSWER*	*RATING*
CT1	Have IT staff been given high-level security awareness training?	Yes, we do it every few years	1
	Are system security items included with employee orientation?	Yes, at least half of them are/do	
CT2	Are those involved and engaged in the IT process, given specific guidance and training on security roles and responsibilities?	Yes, at least half of them are/do	

COMMUNICATION AND TRAINING		ANSWER	RATING
	Are users aware and equipped to comply with IS principles, policies, and procedures	Yes, a small percentage are/do	
CT3	Is ongoing security education of users planned and managed?	Yes, teams write/run their own	
	There is any regular communication process with unit personnel (unit security newsletter/web page)	Yes, a small percentage are/do	

PEOPLE ROLES AND RESPONSIBILITIES		ANSWER	RATING
PR1	Do the security rules specify a clear definition of tasks, specific roles affecting information security officers?	Yes, we do it every few years	1.67
	Are the roles and responsibilities for the safety of employees, contractors, and third-party users defined and documented by the organization's information security policy?	Yes, at least half of them are/do	
PR2	Are users, IT staff, and providers given roles and responsibilities for throughout the organization?	Yes, at least half of them are/do	
	Are information security responsibilities allocated to ensure accountability and responsibility for the implementation of IS initiatives?	Yes, a small percentage are/do	
PR3	Is security-related guidance centrally controlled and consistently distributed throughout the organization?	Yes, teams write/run their own	
	Are responsibilities identified at the unit and at the division or enterprise level?	Yes, we did it once	

(Continued)

CYBERSECURITY PERFORMANCE ASSESSMENT		ANSWER	RATING
PA1	Is management oversight performed to ensure security measures in line with business requirements?	Yes, we do it every few years	1.24
	Does the organization use any tools or proprietary methods for conducting risk assessments and keeping the IT contingency plans up-to-date?	Yes, at least half of them are/do	
PA2	Has a risk assessment been conducted?	Yes, at least half of them are/do	
	Is there an overall coordination plan for implementation, including damage assessment, emergency response salvage, etc.?	Yes, a small percentage are/do	
PA3	Are reports concerning risk assessments and risk mitigation measures produced regularly?	No	
	Are standard reports concerning performance produced on a regular basis?	Yes, we did it once	

ASSESSMENT OF CYBERSECURITY BUDGET AND INVESTMENTS		ANSWER	RATING
BI1	Does financial management for IT security provide information concerning forecasts for IT service delivery expenditure?	Yes, we do it every few years	2
	Does financial management of IT security offer information about the actual costs of providing services and resources against planned costs?	Yes, at least half of them are/do	
BI2	Does financial management for IT security provide information concerning the performance of managing service costs against the financial target?	Yes, at least half of them are/do	

ASSESSMENT OF CYBERSECURITY BUDGET AND INVESTMENTS		ANSWER	RATING
	Does financial management for IT security provide information concerning actions necessary to achieve financial targets?	Yes, a small percentage are/do	
BI3	Does financial management for IT security provide information concerning the analysis of deviations from plans?	Yes, teams write/run their own	
	Does financial management for IT security provide information concerning the current charging policies and IT accounting methods?	Yes, we did it once	

Information Security Policy

8

A Maturity Framework Based on ISO/IEC 27002

8.1 INTRODUCTION

Information systems (IS) is an integral part of the functioning of public administrations and bodies, the activity of businesses, and the way of life of citizens. The security of these information systems has become a significant issue for all public or private sectors, which would be very strongly affected in the event of serious malfunctions (Paliszkiewicz, 2019).

Information security policy is the general term used to describe any document that transmits an element of the security program to ensure compliance with the organization's security goals and objectives. Since this definition covers a wide range of security policy documents, it is helpful to describe the various types of information security policies that an organization may use. The terms used later to describe these types of information security policies are generally used in the information security industry and will be used consistently throughout this chapter (Ifinedo, 2014). However, it is not unusual for a government organization or agency to have different names for the same types of information security policies. For example, in many organizations and certainly in government departments, the word 'policy' is closely associated with laws and regulations (Rees et al., 2003). In these cases, a limited number of individuals (e.g., the legislature) have the power to create a policy, so that an information security policy is generally referred to by other names such as 'information security statement', or 'information security document' or other terms avoiding the use of the word 'policy'. The term used by an organization to describe these documents is irrelevant. The overall organization and completeness of these documents are important (Hong et al., 2006).

DOI: 10.1201/9781003161998- 12

The security policy is primarily implemented to communicate with system users and administrators, which must be taken into account when security decisions are made. It defines the explicit expectations and responsibilities of users and administrators and allows both groups to know what to expect (Knapp et al., 2009). It should explain why certain decisions have been made and why they are important, to help all users understand how the policy is designed to benefit them (Flowerday & Tuyikeze, 2016).

The security policy should specifically state the types of data that are considered important enough to warrant protection. This would include the user's files in the form of programs, text documents like a thesis or an email message, and system-specific configuration files (Yassine et al., 2017). This helps users better understand why security measures are in place, and why certain insecure services have been restricted.

A password policy is already in place. However, it should most definitely be mentioned in the security policy. This is one of many things the user could do to help keep the system secure, but it is probably one of the most important. Other ways that a user could contribute to system security would be properly managing its file and directory permissions or using other software designed with the security-conscious person in mind (Knapp et al., 2009).

Should a security incident occur, the security policy should state who is responsible for restoring the system to a certain state and any procedures that should be followed throughout the repair. If the person in charge of system security detects a break-in, who should be notified and what should be done with the compromised machine? Issues like these must be addressed to ensure that any disrupted services are restored promptly and second, so that proof of the incident can be obtained should the legal need arise (Maleh, 2018). The source of the security breach should be determined and fixed so that the incident doesn't repeat itself. Once the problem has been adequately documented, the system administration team should be aware of what happened (Gwebu et al., 2020).

The Information Systems Security Policy (ISSP) reflects the expectations and requirements of the executive management concerning the information system (Canavan, 2003; Höne & Eloff, 2002b). It must take into account the needs in terms of availability, confidentiality, and integrity of applications and data used and transiting on networks and systems. It consolidates a set of technical, organizational, legal, and human security rules and principles to ensure an efficient and uniform level of security (Fomin, 2008). The ISSP is the counterpart of the Information Systems Master Plan for security. It can lead to an ISSP action plan that prioritizes projects to meet ISSP objectives. The objectives of the ISSP are described in Figure 8.1.

There are several standards and best practice guidelines to assist organizations in implementing an information systems security policy such as ISO 27000, ISACA, and NIST. ISO 27001 (ISECT, 2012) is an international standard that is part of the ISO 27000 family of standards (Von Solms, 2005). It refers to a set of standards relating to the ISMS. The ISO 27001 standard is a British standard that came into being in October 2005, succeeding the BS 7799–2 standard. It describes the requirements for the implementation of ISMS. This standard allows companies to choose security measures to protect sensitive assets within a well-defined perimeter by implementing a systematic and proactive approach to security risk management. Figure 8.2 presents a brief history of ISO/IEC 27001.

Best practice guides such as ISO 27000, COBIT, and ISACA do not provide the practical framework for implementing an IS security policy (Höne & Eloff, 2002a). The

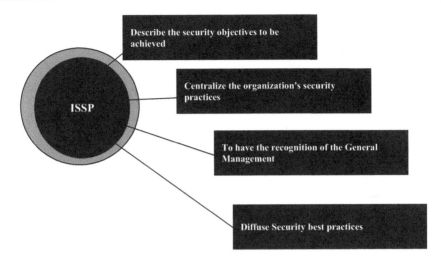

FIGURE 8.1   Information System Security Policy objectives.

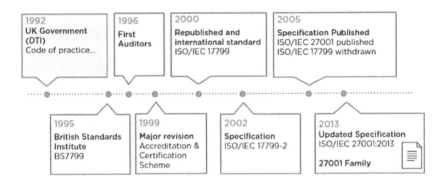

FIGURE 8.2   A brief history of ISO/IEC 27001.

objective is to guide organizations in implementing an IS security policy through a practical guide to implementing an IS security policy.

8.1.1 Problem Statement

Many prescriptive approaches to ISO 27002 already exist, for example, ISO 27003, which is the official standard with guidelines for ISO 27001 (Talib et al., 2012). Several steps to implement the management framework provided in ISO 27001, called ISMS, are presented. However, a practical methodology for implementing an information security policy does not exist.

Many organizations do not have the resources or expertise to conduct a risk analysis and implement an ISMS (Mintzberg et al., 2003). Therefore, they could now know what aspects of security might be relevant to them. Instead of doing a comprehensive risk analysis, an organization could also look to its peers. What are they doing? Although it is not as good to follow your peers as it is to do an extensive risk analysis, it is certainly better than setting up controls for no reason.

Modern times require different approaches to problems. Nowadays, mobile phones and tablets are common products. Employees are supposed to work everywhere. Information is quickly shared via social media. How do companies manage these new issues – what controls do they put in place and how do they select them?

To date, there was no literature on practical research using ISO 27000, using Google Scholar and SCOPUS. Almost all results had a very limited number of references. However, some were still useful. The following paragraphs describe the documentation used for the research.

There are very few scientific papers on ISO 27002, and none found that research practice uses ISO 27002 controls as described in the background section. This chapter can be considered exploratory: The data collected in this research may well be used to formulate hypotheses for other research projects.

8.1.2 Research Question/Approach

The research question in this chapter is: What relevant ISO 27002 controls and good practices do corporate information security managers choose to implement, and why are they chosen?

The approach taken in this research is qualitative research, using interviews with experts. Expert interviews are a good way to explore an area of research. Experts often know a lot about the research topic. It is possible to know whether there is a consensus or whether there is still much debate on certain subjects by talking to several of them. Both results could be used in future research.

Unlike quantitative research, qualitative research focuses more on 'why' and 'how' questions. As a result, qualitative research generally takes smaller, but more focused samples than quantitative research. Qualitative research often does not have a clear hypothesis in advance. Instead, we need an open question. The selection is not made by statistical chance, but according to what is available. When interviewing information security officials, the objective is to get an overview of the controls they choose and why they have been chosen over others.

8.1.3 Purpose

As there is very little scientific literature on the practical use of ISO 27002, this research can be exploratory. The purpose of this chapter is to investigate what controls are commonly used and how they are selected for the implementation of information security in large public organizations in the Middle East and North Africa MENA through ISO27002 (Calder & Watkins, 2010), with a specific focus on a practical framework for the implementation of an effective information security policy through ISO27002 (Calder & Watkins, 2010).

8.2 BACKGROUND

The business policy has been conceptualized as a form of strategic management (Mintzberg, 1983). Two perspectives make up how strategy is made: deliberate formulation and emergent formation (Mintzberg, 1983). The classical approach advocated by Quinn is the approach to strategy grounded in the military strategy used for thousands of years. This type of strategy advocates the use of deliberate plans to win battles and wars. Prominent historical figures in military strategies such as Sun Tzu, Napoleon, Lenin, and Machiavelli have contributed to advancing the classical strategy to its modern form. Rees et al. (2003) stepped away from this rigid approach to business strategy and policy by advocating an emergent approach. In this, an organization's realized strategy is a combination of the organization's deliberate strategy with the evolving emergent strategy. This emergent strategy is identified by a stream of actions that can represent a pattern.

These two perspectives of strategic management can be used to investigate the research behind IS security policy. One stream is grounded in the classical approach, while the other in the emergent approach. The following section will utilize each of these perspectives in examining the literature behind IS security policy.

From the classical, planned strategic perspective, research has aimed to provide information security professionals and top management a framework through which useable security strategy and policy for applications can be created and maintained in line with the standard information technology life cycle (Glasgow et al., 1992). This framework was cyclical and consisted of four stages: plan, access, operate, and deliver. At the theoretical level, Kühnhauser (1999) created a formal framework for specifying security policies. This framework, called security logic, defines what a subject knows, what information a subject has permission to know, and what information a subject is obligated to know. The paper has been presented on this via a logical approach based on modal logic formalism.

Continuing with the classical perspective, Kühnhauser (1999) expounded on planning out a multi-policy system rationally. These are defined as systems that support a multitude of independent security domains in which an individual IS security policy is enforced on the applications. Joshi et al. (2001) performed a logical analysis to introduce a formal model of policy groups. Research has also examined the issue of multi-policy systems by investigating the emerging 'digital government' (Knapp et al., 2007). A sequence of solutions to the issues of multi-domain environments are presented, including ad hoc approaches, formal approaches, model-based methods, agent-based methods, architectural methods, and the database federation approach. However, policy enforcement does not highly correlate with policy effectiveness (Baskerville & Siponen, 2002).

The classical perspective has also witnessed a call for a security meta-policy (Willison, 2002). It is noted that existing IS security policy approaches do not pay much attention to policy formulation itself. In other words, the actual creation of the policy is done in an ad hoc manner. Calling for a meta-policy implies that the way to the best strategy or policy is through concise rational planning.

On the emergent side of the strategic paradigm, researchers have examined how problems are dealt with after creating an IS security policy. It has been noted that 52% of all logistical and physical security breaches arose from the activities of personnel within the organization (Ahmad & Ruighaver, 2003). Research has sought to determine the most optimal control method to handle these breaches. IS security policy formally defines security requirements, outlines the main security objectives, and allocates responsibilities. To maximize the probability of compliance, the enlightenment of staff to their responsibilities as outlined in the IS security policy is one potential solution.

Also, from the emergent perspective, there has been a call for the improvement of audit management technology to allow administrators to configure the software to reflect an organization's security needs as defined in the IS security policy. This demonstrates a dynamic approach to the policy in that it can be reactive to how an audit trail affects an information system. Changing the configuration from the status quo bottom-up approach to a policy-centric top-down approach would help the configuration more closely match an organization's security goals (Coyne & Kluksdahl, 1994).

While not explicitly approaching the issue from an emergent perspective (Coyne & Kluksdahl, 1994), examining a failed IS security policy implementation demonstrates an analysis from an emergent perspective. The implication resides in how the implementers could have adapted to how the actual scenario was different from the rational plan. They found that compliance-based approaches are more prone to failure than risk-based approaches. A de facto compliance-based policy led to the reaction of all security-related matters being adversarial (Walsham, 1993).

This research was conducted via an interpretive case study in the Information Technology Department of a large state university in the south-eastern portion of the United States. The interpretive tradition perceives that the knowledge of reality is a social construction by human actors (Howcroft, 2005). In contrast to the assumptions of positivist science, this knowledge of reality applies equally to researchers. It leads to the perception that there is no objective reality that researchers can discover. This perspective is also described whereby 'interpretive research provides in-depth insights into social, cultural and historical contexts within which particular events and actions are described and interpreted as grounded in the authentic experiences of the people studied' (Reich & Benbasat, 2000).

Approximately 45 employees worked for the department under study. Of these, 20 participated in the interviews. The subjects who participated were the stakeholders involved in the formulation and implementation of the IS security policy. They included the Chief Information Officer, Security Officer, and a group of operational level employees who were members of a Security Planning Team (SPT). SPT members included systems analysts, web developers, a database administrator, two school administrators, and three faculty members. The employees within the department who did not participate in the study included those who were not stakeholders in the IS security policy formulation and implementation process.

The previously discussed conceptual framework grounded the interviews. Although the interview questions were grounded in the theoretical framework, they were conducted in a semi-structured manner. Many IS researchers have utilized semi-structured interviewing techniques (Walsham, 1993). The semi-structured nature of the interview questions helped facilitate effective aspects. As discussed in the framework, affective aspects refer to subjective value judgments. Immediately after each of the interviews, the investigator debriefed. This immediate 'debriefing' process helped clarify the researcher's interpretations and deepen his level of understanding (Walsham, 1993).

Besides gathering data, the interviews served as subject recruitment opportunities. The process of building the network of interviewees was done in a 'referral' manner. This means that the interviewees themselves will point the researcher to the next best contacts to continue the interview process. The point of saturation became apparent when the same names began to appear. At this point, the totality of who the stakeholders were involved in the IS Security policy process became clear (Walsham, 1993).

Once the interview process was complete, the researcher interpreted the data (Fomin, 2008). This process involved systematic analysis and categorization of the data by emergent themes that the researcher identified. These themes were not known a priori but emerged as thematic principles categorized the data. These thematic principles, which included such topics as security awareness, deterrence, and resistance, emerged in part from existing themes in the security literature and by the data gathered in the study.

Gikas (2010) is trying to find the reasons for the low adoption of the international ISO/IEC 2700 standard on information security management. The author compares ISO/IEC 27001 with the other two widely applied management system standards – ISO 9001 for quality management and ISO 14001 for environmental management – and shows that in addition to low adoption rates, ISO/IEC 27001 has attracted much less academic interest, as evidenced by the number of scholarly publications on the subject. The author compares the reasons for applying ISO/IEC 27001 with those of ISO 9001 and concludes by listing possible factors and obstacles for the dissemination of standards and suggesting a roadmap for future research on the subject.

Gillies (2011) discusses two pieces of legislation (HIPAA and FISMA) that focus on information security for US government agencies and two private sector standards (PCI-DSS and ISO 27000) that address the information security needs of a broader range of institutional users of information technology (IT). It will provide a brief description of the four entities, a high-level comparison of suggested and/or prescribed guidelines to identify gaps and overlaps, and suggest a possible threshold model that could incorporate safety parameters that meet the requirements of the four entities.

ISO & Std (2005) is looking at global adoption of the ISO27000 series of standards and compared them with ISO9000 and ISO14000 adoption rates. They compare the barriers to the adoption of different standards. Adopting ISO27001 has been slower than ISO9001 and ISO14001 management system standards, with about half of ISO14001 certifications. In response to the questions raised in this analysis, the paper examines how a maturity model approach can help overcome these barriers, particularly in small businesses. The 2008 survey of ISO27001 certified companies found that 50% of the certified organizations that responded had fewer than 200 employees and therefore fell into the SME category. The framework used the ISO code of practice 27002 to define the elements that should be taken into account in ISMS. Each element is then developed through a maturity model life cycle to develop processes where an ISO27001 compliant ISMS can be implemented.

8.2.1 The ISO/IEC 2700x Family

Several standards, methods, and repositories of good practices in information systems security are available. They constitute methodological guides and the means to guarantee a coherent security approach.

ISO has undertaken a significant effort to streamline existing work, resulting in the ISO/IEC 27000 series of standards. This number corresponds to the reservation of a series of safety standards. To date, only standards 27000, 27001, 27002, and 27006 are published. Some are mandatory to obtain certification, and others are mere guides:

- ISO/IEC 27000 presents the vocabulary and definitions of the security field, applicable to each of the standards;
- ISO/IEC 27001 describes the information systems security management policy within a company that serves as a reference for certification;
- ISO/IEC 27002 is the good practice guide for IS security;
- ISO/IEC 27003 is intended to be an implementation guide;
- ISO/IEC 27004 will be a new standard for steering indicators and measurements in the field of IS security;
- ISO/IEC 27005 will be a new standard on risk management for IS security;
- ISO/IEC 27006 summarizes the requirements applicable to external auditors in their ISO 27001 certification assignment.

As shown in Figure 8.3, ISO/IEC 27001 is the center of gravity of the ISMS referential.

FIGURE 8.3 The ISO 2700x series.

8.2.1.1 ISO/IEC 27001

The ISO/IEC 27001 standard, published in November 2005, defines the IS security management policy within a company (Johnson, 2014). It is derived from the BS 7799–2:1999 specification (Specification for Information Security Management Systems), which defines the requirements to be met to create an ISMS (PRGL, 2011). It specifies in the annex specific safety controls, taken from the ISO/IEC 17799 standard, the mandatory implementation. ISO 27001 comprises six process areas.

- Define an information security policy;
- Define the scope of the ISMS;
- Conduct a safety risk assessment;
- Manage identified risks;
- Select and implement controls;
- Prepare SoA (statement of applicability).

ISO 27001 specifies the processes that enable a company to build, manage, and maintain ISMS. It integrates the process approach and the PDCA (Plan-Do-Check-Act) cycle of continuous improvement already contained in ISO 9001 and ISO 14001 standards (Figure 8.4):

- Plan: Organize the implementation of the ISMS;
- Do: Set up and operate the system;
- Check: Monitor system effectiveness through internal audits and risk assessments;
- Act: Improve the system through appropriate corrective and preventive actions and maintain it through communication and training actions.

In terms of security, the improvement loop is synonymous with a risk reduction loop. In practice, procedures should be put in place for:

- Quickly detect processing errors;
- Immediately identify any noncompliance with safety rules and organize the immediate reporting of incidents;

FIGURE 8.4 PDCA cycle.

- Verify that all safety-related tasks are performed, whether by men or automatons;
- Identify the actions to be taken to correct noncompliance with safety rules.

Regarding control, regular reviews of the system's effectiveness should be carried out based on audit results, incident reports, and suggestions and comments received from the parties concerned. On the other hand, acceptable residual risk levels must be continuously reviewed and adapted in the light of organizational, technological, legal, and regulatory developments or public opinion.

Measurement requirements are explicitly contained in the standard in risk assessments, audits, incident data collection, and noncompliance. However, the standard lacks metrics that would make it easier to compare certified entities with a single repository.

8.2.1.2 ISO/IEC 27002:2005 (Revised by ISO/IEC 27002:2013)

ISO/IEC 27002:2005 is another generic standard applied to health information systems to ensure security. It establishes general principles and guidelines for effective initialization, implementation, maintenance, and improvement of information security management. The objectives outlined therein provide general guidance on the commonly accepted goals of information security management. Thus, any organization seeking to adopt a comprehensive information security management program or improve its existing information security practices can use the standard. The ISO standard asserts that information can be protected using a wide variety of controls. Such controls include hardware and software functions, procedures, policies, processes, and organizational structures. Organizations including healthcare organizations must develop, implement, monitor, evaluate, and improve these security controls (PRGL, 2011).

8.2.1.3 ISO/IEC 27002:2005

ISO/IEC 27002 2005 is entitled Information technology – Security techniques – Code of practice for information security management. It is published by the International Organization for Standardization (ISO) and International Electrotechnical Commission (IEC).

ISO/IEC 27002:2005 was developed from BS7799, a British standard that was published in the 1990s. ISO/IEC adopted this standard as ISO/IEC 17799:2000 in December 2000. In June 2005, the standard was revised and officially published as ISO/IEC 17799:2005. On July 1, 2007, it was renumbered ISO/IEC 27002:2005 to align with the other ISO/IEC 27000-series standards (ISO/IEC, 2013). On the other hand, ISO/IEC 27002:2005 has been revised by ISO/IEC 27002:2013 (ISECT, 2012).

In this research, ISO 27002 serves as the framework for measuring information security in organizations. It is surprisingly well suited for this work, as the idea behind ISO 27002 is to have a list of controls that should mitigate all possible information security risks.

8.2.1.4 ISO/IEC 27002:2005

The 39 main security categories of the standard are specified under 11 security control clauses. Each main security category contains one control objective stating what is to be achieved. In addition, one or more controls are specified to help achieve the control objective. The standard also has one introductory clause that discusses the risk assessment and treatment. The control clauses include the following:

1. Risk assessment and treatment;
2. Security policy;
3. Organization of information security;
4. Asset management;
5. Human resources security;
6. Physical and environmental security;
7. Communications and operations management;
8. Access control;
9. Information systems acquisition, development, and maintenance;
10. Information security incident management;
11. Business continuity management;
12. Compliance.

Although ISO/IEC recommends a complete consideration of the practices, organizations do not have to implement every recommended security practice stated therein. The important thing is to know what works best for the unique information security risks and requirements (ISO/IEC, 2013).

ISO/IEC 27001: 2013 now contains 114 controls for 14 domain areas as shown in Table 8.1 (ISO/IEC, 2013):

1. Information Security Policies

Objectives: To establish an Information Systems Security Policy published, regularly updated, and supported by general management, to provide information security guidance in line with business requirements and regulations in force.

TABLE 8.1 ISO/IEC 27001: 2013 Controls and Domains

#	DOMAIN	NUMBER OF CONTROLS
1	Information Security Policies	2
2	Organization of Information Security	7
3	Human Resource Security	6
4	Asset Management	10
5	Access Control	14
6	Cryptography	2
7	Physical & Environmental Security	15
8	Operations Security	14
9	Communications Security	7
10	System Acquisition, Development & Maintenance	13
11	Supplier Relationships	5
12	Information Security Incident Management	7
13	Information Security Aspects of Business Continuity	4
14	Compliance	8

The ISSP centralizes the organization's information protection strategy. It is validated by the COSI and approved by the General Management and is available to all the organization's agents and transmitted to the third parties concerned.

2. Organization of Information Security

Objectives: To manage, monitor, and guarantee the security of information within the organization in a transversal way, and to define the responsibilities and roles of the various security actors.

The organization of the information security clause addresses the need to define and allocate the necessary roles and responsibilities for information security management processes and activities. This includes controls related to the definition of information security roles and responsibilities, segregation of duties, contact with authorities, contact with special interest groups, information security in project management, and mobile devices and teleworking.

3. Human Resource Security

Objectives: To ensure that employees and contractors understand their responsibilities and are suitable for the roles for which they are considered. To ensure that employees and contractors are aware of and fulfill their information security responsibilities. To protect the organization's interests as part of the process of changing or terminating employment.

The Human Resource Security clause addresses the required controls for processes related to staff recruiting, their job during employment, and after the termination of their contracts. These considerations should include information security coordination, allocation of information security responsibilities, authorization processes for information processing facilities, confidentiality agreements, contact with authorities, contact with special interest groups, independent review of information security, identification of risks related to external parties, addressing security when dealing with customers, addressing security on contractors' agreements, etc.

4. Asset Management

Objectives: To identify, inventory, and classify all assets required for information management. For each of them, a person in charge must be identified. The latter is responsible for enforcing the security policy for its assets.

The asset management clause addresses the responsibilities that need to be defined and assigned for asset management processes and procedures. The owner of the assets and other parties involved in this issue should be identified to be held responsible for the security of the assets, including classification, labeling, and information processing, and the information processing facilities should be identified and maintained. In addition, this clause addresses the control of removable media management, media disposal, and physical media transfer.

5. Access Control

Objectives: To ensure that users are aware of security responsibilities. To reduce the risk of accidents, errors, and/or malicious acts by integrating safety principles into human resources management, from recruitment to the end of the collaboration.

The access control clause addresses the requirements for controlling access to information assets and information processing facilities. Controls focus on protection against accidental damage or loss, overheating, threats, etc. This requires documented control policies and procedures, registration, removal, and review of user access rights, including physical access, access to the network and control of privileged utilities, and restriction of access to program source code.

6. Cryptography

Objectives: To ensure proper and effective use of cryptography to protect the confidentiality, authenticity, and/or integrity of information.

The cryptography clause addresses policies on cryptographic controls for the protection of information to ensure proper and effective use of cryptography to protect the confidentiality, authenticity, integrity, nonrepudiation, and authentication of the information. It also includes the need for digital signatures and message authentication codes and cryptographic key management.

7. Physical and Environmental Security

Objectives: To ensure the protection and availability of sensitive equipment. To ensure that only authorized persons have access to the organization's buildings, technical, and archive premises, access is traced.

The physical and environmental security clause addresses the need to prevent unauthorized physical access, damage, and interference to the organization's information and information-processing facilities.

8. Operations Security

Objectives: To ensure correct and secure operations of information processing facilities. To ensure that information and information processing facilities are protected against malware. To protect against loss of data. To record events and generate evidence. To ensure the integrity of operational systems. To prevent exploitation of technical vulnerabilities. To minimize the impact of audit activities on operational systems.

The Operations Security clause addresses the organization's ability to ensure correct and secure operations. The controls cover the need for operational procedures and responsibilities, protection from malware, backup, logging and monitoring, control of operational software, technical vulnerability management, and information systems audit considerations.

9. Communication Security

Objectives: To ensure the protection of information in networks and its supporting information processing facilities. To maintain the security of information transferred within an organization and with any external entity.

The Communications Security clause addresses the organization's ability to protect the information in systems and applications of supporting networks and information-processing facilities. Controls cover information security in connected networks and services against unauthorized access, transfer policies and procedures, secure transfer of business information between the organization and external parties, the information involved in e-mail, and the need for confidentiality or nondisclosure agreements.

10. System Acquisition, Development, and Maintenance

Objectives: To guarantee security management throughout the lifecycle of information systems. To reduce the risks associated with exploiting technical and application vulnerabilities.

The System Acquisition, Development, and Maintenance clause covers controls for identifying, analyzing, and specifying information security requirements, securing application services in development and support processes, technical review restrictions on changes to software packages, secure system engineering principles, secure development environment, outsourced development, system security testing, system acceptance testing, and test data protection.

11. Supplier Relationships

Objectives: To ensure the protection of the organization's assets that are accessible by suppliers. To maintain an agreed level of information security and service delivery in line with supplier agreements.

The Supplier Relationships clause addresses controls for supplier's relationship issues, including information security policies and procedures, addressing security within supplier agreements, communication, and awareness about technology supply chain and service delivery management.

12. Information Security Incident Management

Objectives: To ensure a consistent and effective policy for the management of information security incidents. To guarantee the reporting of security events and vulnerabilities. To identify indicators and report on security incidents.

The information security incident management clause covers controls over responsibilities and procedures, reporting information and security weaknesses, assessing and deciding on information security events, responding to information security incidents, learning from information security incidents, and gathering evidence.

13. Information Security Aspects of Business Continuity Management

Objectives: After a minor incident (equipment failure), provide computer backup according to business needs. After a major incident affecting an entire engine room, ensure continuity of IT activity for sensitive assets as quickly as possible and according to business needs.

The business continuity management clause addresses the organization's ability to counter normal business interruptions, including the availability of information processing facilities, verifying, reviewing, and assessing information security continuity, implementing information security continuity, and planning information security continuity.

14. Compliance

Objectives: To avoid any violation of intellectual property, legal, regulatory and contractual provisions, and security requirements of the organization.

The compliance clause addresses the organization's ability to comply with regulatory, statutory, contractual, and security requirements, including identification of applicable laws and contractual requirements, intellectual property rights, record protection, confidentiality and protection of personally identifiable information, regulation of cryptographic controls, independent review of information security, compliance with security policies and standards, and review of technical compliance.

8.2.1.5 Other ISO 27000 Standards

In addition to ISO 27001 and 27002, there are several other ISO standards in the 27000 range. These other standards guide and support ISO 27001/27002 for both organizations and auditors.

8.2.1.5.1 ISO 27003
ISO 27003 is used as the implementation standard for ISO 27001. This standard is intended to obtain management approval, define CMSS, conduct an organizational analysis and a risk analysis.

8.2.1.5.2 ISO 27004
ISO 27004 is a standard that helps measure the effectiveness of ISMS. ISO 27004 includes the following chapters:

- Overview of Information Security Measurement; Management Responsibilities;
- Measurement and measurement development;
- Measurement operation;
- Data analysis and reporting on measurement results;
- Evaluation and improvement of the information security measurement program.

8.2.1.5.3 ISO 27005
ISO 27005 is a standard that guides the implementation of ISO 27001. ISO 27005's approach begins by setting the context – defining the scope (primary processes and related assets) and boundaries of the organization. When defining the scope, a risk analysis will be carried out. Risk analysis consists of identifying the assets and the threats they face. In addition, the impact of a successful exploitation of a certain threat must be analyzed. When this is done, for each threat, an estimate of the likelihood that the threat will be successfully exploited will be multiplied by the costs of the impact of that exploitation. Based on this list, each risk should be mitigated by implementing controls, risk acceptance, risk avoidance, or risk transfer.

8.2.1.5.4 ISO 27006 and Certification

An organization can be certified in ISO 27001. Accredited auditors can only do this. The organization can only be certified if the ISMS and a number of controls are correctly implemented. ISO 27002 defines how an auditor can evaluate an organization to accredit it. ISO 27002 defines two steps for the accreditation of an organization.

8.3 RESEARCH METHODOLOGY

8.3.1 Data Collection

As part of this research, MENA large organizations experts are interviewed. These experts hold the title of a security officer, or what most closely resembles their organization. We chose the large public sector organizations because there are interesting problems specific to this sector. For example, government organizations usually possess a lot of privacy-sensitive data – for example, information about citizens. In addition, it appears that data leaks from public bodies are often well exposed in the media.

In the first round, we mailed a letter with details of the research content, what they would be asked for, and their benefits. Before sending the final question, wish is an optimized version of the ISO 27002 questionnaire presented in Appendix 1 (Table 8.4). A total of 20 organizations were selected, 6 organizations agreed to give us interviews to answer our questions, that is, 30%, a percentage too credible for this research.

In the second round, we validate the first study results with a qualitative methodology through a case study in a large public organization in Morocco.

As we conducted interviews by e-mail, we did not need to go to the locations of the interviewees. Therefore, the interviews did not require travel expenses. When participants sent me answers that we could not understand, we could then ask them to give me more details or explanations on previous comments. The e-mail interviews allowed us to interview several participants at the same time. They were also easy to transcribe. At the same time, there was a lack of richness in the responses we received from participants. It was also not easy for participants to get clarification on the meaning of the questions, so we sent them a brief explanation of the theories by email. These explanations would improve their possibilities if they gave appropriate answers. Table 8.2 shows the summary of key attributes of participating organizations.

TABLE 8.2 Summary of Key Attributes of MENA Organizations

Organizations	A	B	C	D	E	F
No. of employees	1,125	2,400	7,000	12,000	2,400	1,700
No. of IT staff	80	190	220	420	44	35
No. of IT Security staff	5	12	9	10	3	5
Government (Gov.)/Multinational (multi.)	Gov.	Gov.	Gov.	Gov.	Gov.	Gov.
ISO 27002 Version	V4	V4	V4	V5	V5	V4
Certified ISO 27002 Load auditor staff	6%	5%	3%	3%	7%	0%

8.3.2 Data Analysis

For each interview, a report was written. The size was limited to about one page. The following section contains the reports from each interview. For reasons of anonymity, organizations are indicated by alphabets from A to F. The questionnaire results for each organization are presented in the following section. For each organization, the scores for each sub-theme are displayed.

The quotation is based on ISO/IEC 27002:2013 (Peltier, 2013). Each question is waiting for an answer in the form according to the maturity model described in Table 8.3.

TABLE 8.3   The Maturity Level Model

VALUE	SHORT NAME	DESCRIPTION	DETAILS
0	Nonexistent	Nonexistent; process does not exist or is not applied	Nonexistent – complete lack of any recognizable processes. The enterprise has not even recognized that there is an issue to be addressed.
1	Initial/ad hoc	Initial/ad hoc; process is ad hoc and disorganized	Initial/ad hoc – There is evidence that the enterprise has recognized that the issues exist and need to be addressed. There are, however, no standardized processes; instead, there are ad hoc approaches that tend to be applied on an individual or case-by-case basis. The overall approach to management is disorganized.
2	Repeatable	Repeatable but intuitive; processes follow a regular pattern	Repeatable but intuitive – processes have developed to the stage where similar procedures are followed by different people undertaking the same task. There is no formal training or communication of standard procedures, and responsibility is left to the individual. There is a high degree of reliance on the knowledge of individuals, and therefore, errors are likely.
3	Defined	Defined; processes are documented and communicated	Defined process – procedures have been standardized and documented and communicated through training. It is mandated that these processes be followed; however, it is unlikely that deviations will be detected. The procedures themselves are not sophisticated but are the formalization of existing practices.

(Continued)

VALUE	SHORT NAME	DESCRIPTION	DETAILS
4	Managed and measured	Managed and measured; processes are monitored and measured	Managed and measurable – Management monitors and measures compliance with procedures and takes action where processes appear not to be working effectively. Processes are under constant improvement and provide good practice. Automation and tools are used in a limited or fragmented way.
5	Optimized	Optimized; good practices are followed and automated	Optimized – processes have been refined to a level of good practice, based on continuous improvement and maturity modeling with other enterprises. IT is used in an integrated way to automate the workflow, providing tools to improve quality and effectiveness, making the enterprise quick to adapt.

8.3.3 Results and Discussion

Figure 8.5 provides an overview of how the six organizations ranked for each of the sub-themes.

For organizations A, E, and F, there is no specific security agent. However, one group of people is responsible for information security. The Information Security Policy was created in 2012 and is approved by management. However, the IT security policy is not signed by management.

For these organizations, the most important controls are those related to information security, for example, high-level policies, risk assessment. This means that the following two documents must exist and be signed by the management:

• Information Security Policy;
• Classification of information sources.

Security awareness should also be emphasized. In these organizations, awareness training is organized so that employees are knowingly incompetent in information security, rather than unconsciously incompetent.

Management should become more aware of safety issues themselves to play an exemplary role vis-à-vis other employees. An example of this is: According to the information security policy, identification badges must be displayed at all times. Management does not do it.

Organization E: One of the major problems within the organization is that information security is not an integral part of the organization, but something that is considered an IT problem. This results in several problems for the security guard, for example:

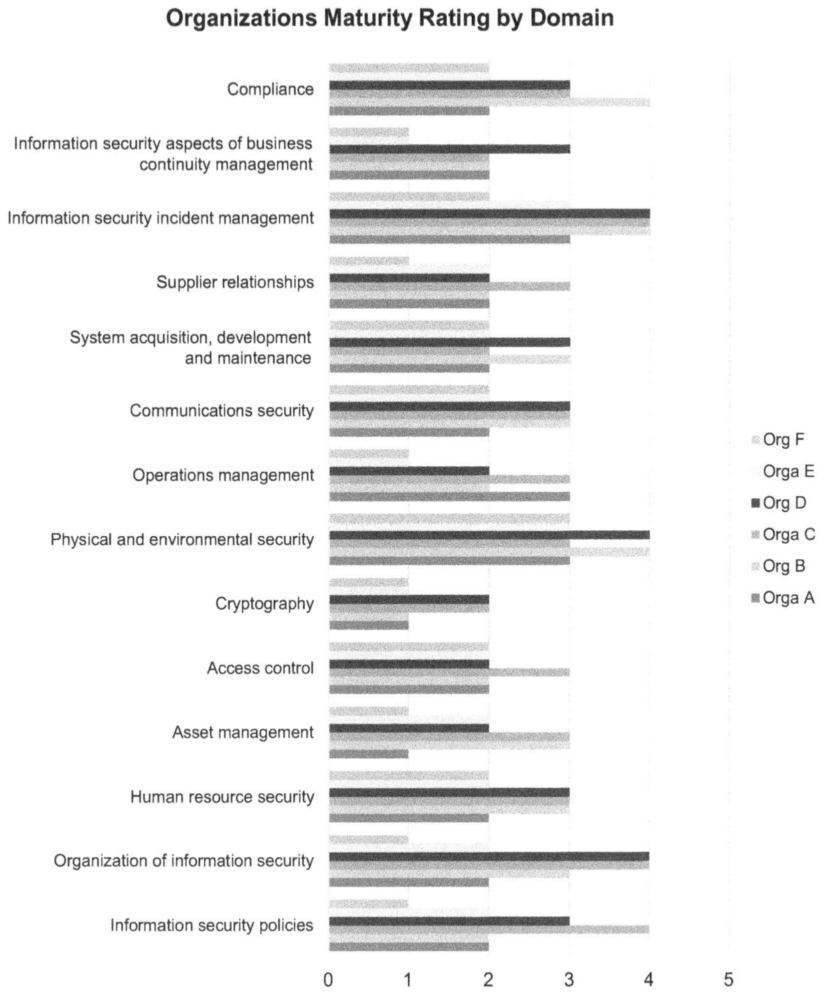

Organizations Maturity Rating by Domain

FIGURE 8.5 Organizations maturity rating through ISO/IEC 27001:2013.

- Lack of management commitment – information security policy has not been approved/signed by management;
- Not all information security issues are technical. For example, in the past, employees did not need a nondisclosure agreement. This situation changed in the spring of 2014, requiring all new employees to sign a nondisclosure agreement;
- There is no confidentiality classification for the information;
- There is no list of processes within the organization;
- There are several courses for employees, for example, a LinkedIn course or an Office course.

However, information security is little or not taken into account in these courses. Employees know little about how their actions (online) could harm the organization's image.

All contracts with third parties contain information security clauses. This includes cleaners. An outside company disposes of used paper and hard drives.

There are employment procedures, both for new employees and for dismissals. However, these procedures are not always followed correctly – employees only get more access rights and almost never less, even if their work no longer requires it. Employees can work from home. Authentication works with an SMS token, giving user access similar to what is possible in the office.

For organization F: For the moment, there is still no information security policy. However, interviews were conducted with experts within the organization to develop a list of ISO 27002 controls that should be implemented.

The systems used are shared with other organizations in a shared service center. This center also includes a service desk for incidents. For high-priority incidents, a process is in place that includes management and impacts analysis. Physical access is regulated by the use of tokens, where access is distributed according to the need. Utility offices have emergency buttons that can be used in the event of a disturbance in freely accessible areas. At night, the inner courtyard is locked with fences by the security team.

The organization has undergone intrusion tests, for example, using a mystery guest. A mystery guest is hired by the organization to pose as a stranger trying to access critical information. This mystery guest made a video about how to get in. This video was shown to management to raise awareness.

It is possible to bring a mobile phone or a tablet computer. There are three different wireless networks – a public network, one for guests, and one for employees. These use a ticket system, which allows only one device for a certain time. After that, a new ticket must be requested.

Information security is always a secondary issue, and the level of maturity switches between levels 1 (ad hoc) and 2 (repeatable). Efforts must be made to complete levels 3 (defined) and 4 (managed), especially in the areas of asset management, operation management, supplier relationships, business continuity, and compliance.

For organizations B–D: Within these organizations, ISO 27002 is used as a guideline for information security. Currently, a baseline is applied across these organizations.

On third parties: Paper waste is disposed of by a company specializing in organizations C and D. For as much software as possible, a SaaS solution is used. However, the change management is always done within the organization. Backups are performed regularly and tested. Physical security has three different zones: public areas, employee areas, and specific areas, such as server rooms. Organizations support telework through a VPN virtual private network.

For organizations C and D: In these two organizations, a difference is made between the information security policy and the information security plan. The policy is higher than the plan. The plan is based on ISO 27002 controls. Controls are selected using a risk analysis: A matrix of estimated risks and impacts is established and serves as the basis for selecting controls.

Employees of these organizations were not sworn in, except temporary staff. Instead, they must sign a nondisclosure agreement. Employees are informed of information security through intranet bulletins, but there is no policy for security awareness training.

For third parties, for example, application hosting, information security clauses are either included in service or included in the contract.

A third party takes care of all the equipment that needs to be disposed of, including paper, old computers, printers, etc. When it comes to new applications, ready-to-use solutions are preferred to custom software. If necessary, they can be modified to meet additional needs. For large requests, a tendering procedure is organized. There is a formal change management process, which has improved considerably in recent years.

There are several networks within this organization, and they are physically or virtually separate, for example, a network on which employees are connected, one for servers, a public wireless network, a wireless network for employees. Both can be used for mobile devices and are therefore not connected to other networks.

Each week, a list of terminated employees is generated and used to ensure that these employees no longer have access to the applications. There is an employee transfer procedure. However, since a transfer may take some time during which the employee may still need their former access rights, it is more complex than hiring and termination.

It is possible to work from home. A virtual office system is used, giving a virtual workplace at home. In the future, the computers in the office will use the same system. In the office, all office spaces are flexible: no fixed rooms for employees.

For incidents, a form exists on the Intranet for organization E. Depending on the incident, it is assigned either to facilities management or to IT. Priority is given depending on the impact of the incident. There is an escalation procedure: the more important an incident is, the more critical the follow-up of an incident is. This may be management or a subsequent evaluation.

In general, the three organizations are at level 3 (defined). At least efforts must be made in cryptography and information security aspects of business continuity management.

8.4 CASE STUDY

A qualitative methodology was used and semi-structured interviews were conducted in the study (Creswell & Creswell, 2017). An interview guide was developed containing open questions. The interview questions were based on ISO 27002. The interview guide is presented in Appendix 1 (Table 8.4). We organized a meeting with the interviewees to explain the control objectives, and we also sent a short explanation of the theories by email (Burns, 2010). Accordingly, those explanations would enhance their possibility if giving adequate answers. The next step was to send the interview questions to the security coordinator, the employees from other departments of the public organization in Morocco.

The second part of this document deals with developing an information systems security policy in a large organization (for confidentiality reasons, we will not be able to disclose the organization's name). The objective of this policy will be to provide a coherent, recognized, and shared security framework between all the organization's stakeholders, enable the implementation and ensure the long-term security of their information systems, and define a coordinated action plan enabling each entity to better address its challenges.

The case study took place at a large organization in Morocco. The extended time required for the study resulted from difficult access to the subjects and multiple visits to subjects. The security officer was interviewed four times, and the CIO was interviewed three times. During the study, both the CIO and security officer have been removed from their positions and new employees replaced them. This required yet more follow-up interviews.

The objective is to draw up a macroscopic inventory of the level of security of all information systems, assets, and people at the organizational and technological levels. For this purpose, we have developed a questionnaire whose analysis of the responses recorded in it will make it possible to evaluate the levels of maturity of the IS. In this context, we refer, for this exhaustive questionnaire, to the standard ISO/IEC 27002:2013 as defined in Appendix 1 (Table 8.4).

The study found that the organization has an information security policy and helps the organization successfully manage information security. The organization's security maturity is at level 2 (initial). The organization agrees that the information security policy is an important tool that organizations should have to manage the proper implementation of information security.

The information security policy is deployed during an awareness session and is explained to senior management and the heads of each section. Following the session, each section head is responsible for communicating and disseminating all information regarding the information security policy to end-users within each section.

The organization uses a type of information security policy, which helps to protect the information in general.

The organization's information security policy document is understandable, which means that employees can understand the content of the policy. One interviewee explained that 'Our organization's information security policy is written to be understood by all to follow the meaning of the policy'. It is also placed on a very easy access place on the net, internal (Intranet) and external (website).

The person responsible for creating the information security policy is the security manager with the support of the IT department. The municipality uses ISO 27001 and ISO 27002 as a guide in its work. The organization places a high priority on information security policy, starting with senior management and reaching end users.

The information security policy is the main document that was intended for the organization. Organizations should have a structure and procedures on which policies should exist and how they are developed, and the organization should take this into account. What do you call politics? For example, operational policy (which probably includes elements other than information security), security policy (which addresses security issues) or information security policy is the responsibility of each organization. The important thing is that management must show its intentions regarding information security.

The policy should not contain concrete rules of conduct without expressing management's intentions and frame other documents that govern it. A policy should be brief and accessible to all. More information and explanations can be presented on the internal web, for example. The policy expresses the general intentions of management. When it comes to information security policy, it can be called information security policy or security policy to all security work. The policy should be developed at an early stage, before or at the same time as activities determine security design and security processes. It is important to identify all existing policy documents to know what material you need to work with. This gives an idea of the work required to prepare regulatory documents and to put policy documents in order. The working group can then update and draft policy documents to correspond to the organization's information security needs.

The scheme of declination of the PSSI is shown in Figure 8.6.

8.4.1 ISSP Global Plan

The Information Systems Security Policy is generally composed of two parts (Figure 8.7):

- The Security Policy Framework;
- Security principles and rules.

8.4.2 Preamble

For confidentiality reasons, we are not authorized to disclose the corporate name of the organization. For this reason, we use the name PUBLIC_ORG to indicate the name of the

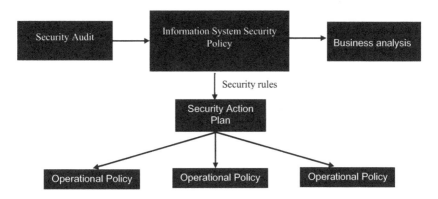

FIGURE 8.6 The scheme of declination of the PSSI.

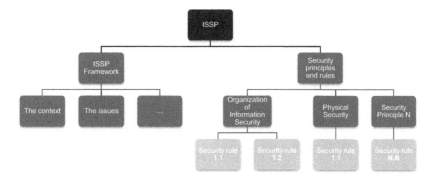

FIGURE 8.7 ISSP global plan.

organization. This document constitutes the reference, also called 'Information Systems Security Policy' (ISSP) of the PUBLIC_ORG. It is based on the ISO 27002 standard (good practice guide for information security). It translates into applicable terms the will and requirements of the PUBLIC_ORG to implement the means to protect in the most effective way the heritage represented by Information Systems, with all its resources (information and their various means of sharing, processing, exchange, and storage), and to preserve its operation as a production tool for users.

8.4.3 Context

The PUBLIC_ORG has an inheritance of sensitive information constituting one of its most important assets, on which its image and its capacity to maintain and develop its activities are based:

- The information heritage, composed of all the information contributing to its knowledge and know-how;
- Information contributing to the functioning of the union such as financial data;
- Information relating to personnel, such as administrative files, payslips, etc.;
- Information relating to its user-customers and third parties with whom it has a relationship.

8.4.4 Perimeter

The ISSP applies to all the Information Systems (IS) of the PUBLIC_ORG. This includes all the human, technical, and organizational means enabling, in support of the activity, to create, store, exchange, and share information between the internal and external actors of the organization, whatever the form in which it is used (electronic, printed, handwritten, voice, images, etc.). It applies:

- To all personnel authorized to access, use, or process information or information system resources of the PUBLIC_ORG;
- On a contractual basis, to all third parties, as soon as they use the IS of PUBLIC_ORG or their IS is connected to the IT network of PUBLIC_ORG;
- All hardware and software components of the IS.

8.4.5 ISSP Issues in the PUBLIC_ORG

Information Systems Security (ISS) is an essential component of protecting the PUBLIC_ORG in its interests and those related to the issues related to its activity. This requires, as a priority, the definition and implementation within the PUBLIC_SECT of ISSP to manage the:

- Risk of unavailability of information and the systems processing it (intrusion, theft, destruction, breakdown, denial of service);

- Risk of disclosure – loss of accidental or voluntary confidentiality of sensitive information such as personal data, remote management data, strategic documents, financial data, etc.;
- Risk of alteration – loss of integrity, particularly in institutional site data, video protection, etc.

Its objectives are as follows:

- Define the target in terms of Information Systems Security management;
- Organize security;
- Comply with the regulations in force;
- Federating around the theme of security;
- Monitor and improve security on a daily basis;
- The security rules set out in the PSSI are supplemented by operational policies (rules for using the information system, internal rules, password policy, backup, etc.).

8.4.6 Security Requirements

The Information Systems Security needs of the PUBLIC_ORG are based on four criteria (AICD):

- Availability: Guarantee that the elements considered (files, messages, applications, services) are accessible at the desired time by the authorized persons;
- Integrity: Ensure that the elements considered (data, messages, etc.) are accurate and complete and that they have not been modified;
- Confidentiality: Guarantee that only authorized persons have access to the elements considered (applications, files);
- Data recovery point: Ensure that data are restored following a loss according to its criticality.

8.4.7 Security Clauses

8.4.7.1 Organization of Information Security

8.4.7.1.1 Internal Organization

To manage, monitor, and guarantee the security of information within the PUBLIC_ORG in a transversal way, the following organization is implemented as shown in Figure 8.8.

The Information Security Committee (ISC), composed of the Information System Security Officer (ISSO), the Information System Officer (CIO), and the security referents and guests as appropriate (agent, third parties, etc.), has the following objectives:

- Guarantee the same level of information to the different referents;
- To provide feedback and exchange on each other's good practices in the field of information security;

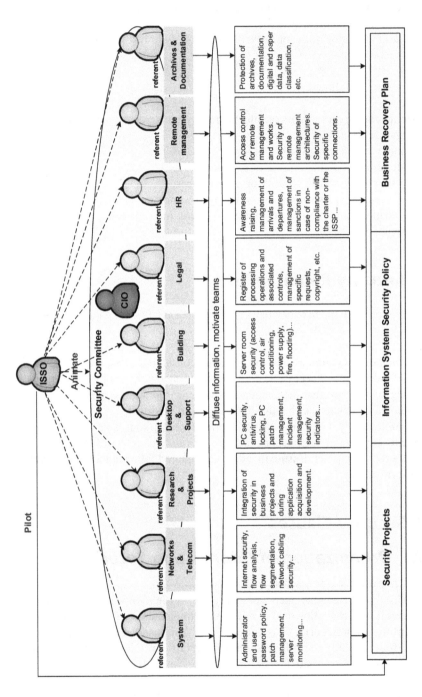

FIGURE 8.8 Organization of security diagram.

- Define operational policies;
- Prioritize and distribute the different projects among the referents;
- Propose and arbitrate the training plan for the referents;
- Coordinate safety awareness and communication actions;
- Organize safety/compliance audits;
- Report on security incidents;
- Integrate and share technical, legal, and regulatory intelligence;
- Manage exceptions (event not taken into account in the PSSI) impacting the security of the Information Systems of the PUBLIC_ORG.

The Information Systems Security Officer (ISSO) has a coordinating role in implementing and applying the PSSI of the PUBLIC_ORG. It does not intervene directly at the operational level as prime contractor for security projects, but

- Leads the ISC;
- Manages the Information Systems Security Policy and controls its application;
- Coordinates the day-to-day management of the security function;
- Ensures the management of transversal safety projects;
- Participates in the homogenization of the security level;
- Ensures the perenniality of security;
- Defines, implements, analyses, and monitors major security indicators in coordination with the ISC;
- Keeps abreast of state of the art in the field of information systems.

The security referents are responsible for security watch (legal, regulatory, technical) according to their scope of intervention.

8.4.7.1.2 Third-Party Management
When PUBLIC_ORG entrusts third parties with the management and control of all or part of its Information Systems (outsourcing, outsourcing, etc.), it integrates its security requirements into the contracts with them.

8.4.7.2 Information System Security Policy

The information security policy constitutes the reference framework for information security within PUBLIC_ORG. It, therefore, defines the various rules to be observed and the work methodology to be implemented to understand the security issues of the information system.

8.4.7.2.1 Objectives
PUBLIC_ORG's information system security policy aims to ensure:

- Compliance with any legislation or regulatory obligation in Morocco and with any internal Bank policy and regulations, in particular laws 07–03, 53–05, and 09–08 governing information security at the national level;

- The protection of the information assets essential to the performance of its activities;
- Minimize the risk of information unavailability or alteration;
- Ensure and guarantee the brand image.

8.4.7.2.2 *The Scope of the IS Security Policy*
The IS Security Policy applies to the following assets:

- Computer, network, and telecom equipment;
- Software and computer data;
- Information system services;
- Bank premises at the central and regional level;
- Human resources.

8.4.7.2.3 *Review and Evaluation*
The security policy must be reviewed regularly. Regular reassessment (at least once a year) ensures its relevance and effectiveness. The organization of this revision is the responsibility of the PUBLIC_ORG ISSR.

8.4.7.2.4 *Compliance with Policy*
PUBLIC_ORG requires any natural or legal person who accesses its information to respect the information security policy and the procedures, charters, and measures that result from it.

8.4.7.3 Asset Management

8.4.7.3.1 *Property Inventory*
An inventory of all assets (activities, data, applications, and infrastructures) of the information system must be carried out. This inventory should not be limited to physical assets. Inventory monitoring and updating must also be ensured. An owner must be designated for each asset (activities, data, applications, and infrastructure). The IS security officer must be responsible for updating the inventory.

8.4.7.3.2 *Classification of Information and Assets*
Assets (activities, data, applications, and infrastructures) must be classified in terms of values, legal or regulatory requirements, sensitivity, or criticality concerning availability, integrity, confidentiality, and traceability (DICT) criteria.

Such classification makes it possible to better fight against threats that could harm PUBLIC_ORG. The impact analysis conducted by the process owner, assisted by the safety manager, enables the value of the IS asset, and therefore, its sensitivity level to be assessed.

8.4.7.4 Human Resources Security

8.4.7.4.1 *Transfer and Departure of Staff*
Any transfer or departure of an employee automatically entails updating or suppressing all his access rights. The line manager decides the new access rights according to the employee's new tasks. The departments and services concerned must notify the Information System Department, by a note, of any change in the status of an employee.

8.4.7.4.2 Information Security Awareness and Training

The IS Security Policy must be assimilated, implemented, and maintained at all levels of the organization. The involvement of all employees is necessary for this policy to be a success and for the defined level of safety to be achieved.

Users must be made aware of information security issues, threats, and good practices. They must thus be able to support PUBLIC_ORG's security policy within the regular and daily framework of their work.

8.4.7.5 Physical and Environmental Safety

8.4.7.5.1 Access to Buildings

PUBLIC_ORG has taken measures to restrict access to its buildings. All visitors and external speakers must identify themselves and visibly wear a badge throughout their visit on the PUBLIC_ORG site.

8.4.7.5.2 Security Service

A security service (from 7 am to 7 pm) ensures the physical security and operation of the PUBLIC_ORG building. An external company provides the security service.

In this sense, the security service must record the CIN number of visitors in the access register.

A remote monitoring system must be put in place.

8.4.7.5.3 Datacenter Security

Security zones must be located and protected to reduce the risks posed by environmental threats and hazards (fire, flood, earthquake, explosion, or other types of natural disasters). The following measures may be required to enhance physical security:

- Automatic fire detection and suppression systems;
- Protection against water damage;
- Air conditioning safety;
- Protection against electrical incidents;
- Surveillance cameras;
- False floors;
- Protection against physical access.

8.4.7.5.4 Disposal of Such Sensitive Assets

Equipment used to store sensitive information (data) for disposal must be destroyed effectively to prevent recovery attempts.

8.4.7.6 Operations Management

8.4.7.6.1 Development of Operating Procedures

Operational procedures related to the management and operation of information processing facilities shall be documented and maintained. The management and the use of information processing resources must be formalized through operational procedures. These procedures shall include the measures necessary to address the security needs expressed.

8.4.7.6.2 Backup Procedures

A backup policy must be defined for sensitive or critical PUBLIC_ORG information, applications, and systems based on the analysis of business impacts carried out in collaboration with information owners and business departments.

Backups must be performed regularly, tested, and protected appropriately. Regular recovery tests ensure that backups have been performed correctly and that backup media is readable. To ensure the protection of backup media, the following steps can be taken:

- Conservation at a remote site;
- Storage in a secure location (fireproof box, locked cabinet).

8.4.7.6.3 Management of Traceability of Operations

Traceability of safety-related operations and events must be ensured. Traces of these events must also be kept secure. Regular analyses and reviews of trace files should be performed by the CISO.

8.4.7.6.4 Use of Communication Tools (Internet, Intranet, Messaging)

Information technologies, such as the Internet or email, are necessary tools for business activities. However, their advantageous features may present risks related to the PUBLIC_ORG environment.

The use of communication tools must be regulated and integrated into PUBLIC_ORG's information resources use charter.

Particular attention should be paid to the presence of wireless networks that could compromise the access control devices envisaged.

8.4.7.6.5 Maintenance of IT Assets and Environmental Equipment

IT assets (servers, databases, network, workstations, etc.) and environmental equipment (inverters, fire detection systems, etc.) must be adequately maintained to ensure their proper operation.

This maintenance must be carried out regularly to avoid incidents related to equipment obsolescence and poor maintenance.

8.4.7.6.6 External IT Service Providers

Suppliers, external consultants, and subcontractors working for PUBLIC_ORG are subject to PUBLIC_ORG's information security policy. External providers who access the information system must sign a confidentiality agreement that defines the roles, rights, and obligations that the provider must comply with to guarantee.

8.4.7.7 Access Controls

8.4.7.7.1 System Access Control Standard

All users of the IT system must have an identifier to ensure optimal management of access controls, individual accountability, and the creation of complete audit reports. The user ID linked to a user must not be shared. Shared identifiers must be limited and restricted in use.

8.4.7.7.2 Workstation and Equipment
It is a question of controlling allocations for strictly professional needs through:

* The deactivation of the administrator account;
* Internet filtering;
* Disabling USB flash drives;
* Standardization of positions.

8.4.7.7.3 Password Management
Users should follow good security practices when selecting and using passwords. Following the password policy defined by PUBLIC_ORG, rules must be defined to ensure proper password management.

8.4.7.7.4 Network Partitioning
The implementation of control measures within the network to isolate information services, users, and information systems should be considered.

8.4.7.8 Cryptography

8.4.7.8.1 Cryptographic Controls
Confidential information within PUBLIC_ORG must be encrypted using valid encryption processes for data at rest and in motion, as required by state or federal laws or regulations. This includes but is not limited to sensitive information stored on mobile devices, removable disks, and laptops.

8.4.7.8.2 Cryptographic Authentication
Public Sec Information system must obtain and issue public key and Transport Layer Security (TLS) certificates from an approved service provider. This control focuses on certificates with visibility external to the information system and does not include certificates related to internal system operations, for example, application-specific time services. Secure Socket Layer (SSL) protocol must be disabled on all devices.

8.4.7.9 System Acquisition, Development, and Maintenance of Information Security

8.4.7.9.1 Separation of Development and Production Facilities
As far as possible, development, test, and production environments should be separated according to the risks involved. The transfer of programs and information must be controlled. The development and testing environment must be independent and separate from the production environment. The production environment must be installed on machines that will not be used simultaneously in development or test environments. A developer must not access production.

8.4.7.9.2 Integrating Security into Projects Development
PUBLIC_ORG's statements of requirements for acquiring new systems or for improvements to existing systems shall specify the requirements for security measures.

8.4.7.10 *Supplier Relationships*

8.4.7.10.1 Information Security Incident Management

A procedure to ensure the recording and reporting of any security incident must be defined. Users (bank staff, contractors, and third-party users with access to the information system) must be informed of their obligation to report any security incident (loss/theft of PUBLIC_ORG information, documents, or material) as soon as possible.

PUBLIC_ORG's incident management procedure includes reporting mechanisms for these incidents and a specific organization for handling security alerts.

8.4.7.10.2 Information Security Aspects of Business Continuity Management

Business continuity and business resumption plans must be developed to maintain or restore PUBLIC_ORG's critical activities within the required timeframe after an interruption or failure of their critical processes.

The continuity plan integrates preventive and curative measures enabling business management to overcome a major incident by reducing the impact on its activities to an acceptable level.

These continuity plans must indicate the conditions under which they are triggered, the organization of the implementation, the crisis management measures, the detailed planning of the actions to be carried out, the communication plans, and the means used for crisis management.

A disaster scenario approach is preferred to consider the various scenarios (e.g., fire, destruction of the computer room, and unavailability of premises) and to plan appropriate corrective measures (e.g., regular extraction of vital information on paper, redundancy of sensitive environments).

The emergency site in Tangier must meet international standards in terms of physical security.

8.4.7.11 *Compliance*

8.4.7.11.1 Identification and Communication of Applicable Legislation

All legal, regulatory, and contractual requirements must be identified and documented for each information system. These regulatory requirements may include the following:

- Protection of personal data;
- Respect for intellectual property (e.g., keeping proof of software purchase, maximum number of users allowed on a system, information to staff on legal issues).

8.4.7.11.2 IS Security Audit

Information security should be audited and monitored periodically. The audit should focus on compliance with security policies and procedures and the effectiveness of the security measures in place and their adequacy to the potential risks identified.

Access to security audit tools and reports must be protected to prevent possible misuse or compromise.

8.5 SUMMARY

The objective of this study was to establish a practical framework for the formulation and implementation of the IS security policy. The problem arising from this situation is an ineffective IS security policy and therefore a vulnerable system. To achieve this objective, we reviewed the ISO 20002 security policy frameworks and put them in place.

During this part, the document called ISSP was set up, which reflects PUBLIC_ORG and requirements to implement the means to protect in the most effective way the heritage represented by Information Systems, with all its resources (information and their various means of sharing, processing, exchange, and storage), and to preserve its operation as a production tool for users.

Further research is needed to determine situations within more controlled environments, such as commercial or private organizations. Being a state educational entity may have distorted the results to a degree and having additional, more diverse data would validate the framework to a greater level. Also, this study focused on the relatively small subset of those most directly involved in policy. A quantitative examination of a wide base of users might shed some additional light on policy implementation.

REFERENCES

Ahmad, A., & Ruighaver, A. (2003, January). *Improved event logging for security and forensics: Developing audit management infrastructure requirements*. Proceedings of the ISOneWorld.

Baskerville, R., & Siponen, M. (2002). An information security meta-policy for emergent organizations. *Logistics Information Management*, 15(5–6), 337–346. https://doi.org/10.1108/09576050210447019

Burns, E. (2010). Developing email interview practices in qualitative research. *Sociological Research Online*, 15(4), 1–12. https://doi.org/10.5153/sro.2232

Calder, A., & Watkins, S. G. (2010). *Information security risk management for ISO27001/ISO27002*. IT Governa.

Canavan, S. (2003). *An information security policy development guide for large companies*. SANS Institute.

Coyne, J. W., & Kluksdahl, N. C. (1994). Automated information systems security engineering (a case study in security Run Amok). *Proceedings of the 2Nd ACM Conference on Computer and Communications Security*, 251–257. https://doi.org/10.1145/191177.191241

Creswell, J. W., & Creswell, J. D. (2017). *Research design: Qualitative, quantitative, and mixed methods approaches*. Sage Publications.

Flowerday, S. V., & Tuyikeze, T. (2016). Information security policy development and implementation: The what, how and who. *Computers & Security*, 61, 169–183. https://doi.org/10.1016/j.cose.2016.06.002

Fomin, V. V. (2008). *Iso/Iec 27001 information systems security management standard: Exploring the reasons for low adoption, February 2016* (pp. 1–13). https://www.researchgate.net/publication/228898807_ISOIEC_27001_Information_Systems_Security_Management_Standard_Exploring_the_reasons_for_low_adoption

Gikas, C. (2010). A general comparison of FISMA, HIPAA, ISO 27000 and PCI-DSS standards. *Information Security Journal: A Global Perspective, 19*(3), 132–141. https://doi.org/10.1080/19393551003657019

Gillies, A. (2011). Improving the quality of information security management systems with ISO27000. *The TQM Journal, 23*(4), 367–376. https://doi.org/10.1108/17542731111139455

Glasgow, J., Macewen, G., & Panangaden, P. (1992). A logic for reasoning about security. *ACM Transactions on Computer Systems, 10*(3), 226–264. https://doi.org/10.1145/146937.146940

Gwebu, K. L., Wang, J., & Hu, M. Y. (2020). Information security policy noncompliance: An integrative social influence model. *Information Systems Journal, 30*(2), 220–269. https://doi.org/10.1111/isj.12257

Höne, K., & Eloff, J. H. P. (2002a). What makes an effective information security policy? *Network Security, 6*, 14–16. https://doi.org/10.1016/S1353-4858(02)06011-7

Höne, K., & Eloff, J. H. P. (2002b). Information security policy – what do international information security standards say? *Computers & Security, 21*(5), 402–409. https://doi.org/10.1016/S0167-4048(02)00504-7

Hong, K., Chi, Y., Chao, L. R., & Tang, J. (2006). An empirical study of information security policy on information security elevation in Taiwan. *Information Management & Computer Security, 14*(2), 104–115. https://doi.org/10.1108/09685220610655861

Howcroft, T. (2005). *Handbook of critical information systems research.* Edward Elgar Publishing, Inc.

Ifinedo, P. (2014). Information systems security policy compliance: An empirical study of the effects of socialisation, influence, and cognition. *Information & Management, 51*(1), 69–79. https://doi.org/10.1016/j.im.2013.10.001

ISECT. (2012). *ISO 27001 security.* Retrieved September 2012, from http://www.Iso27001security.Com/Html 27002.Html#HistoryOfISO17799

ISO, I., & Std, I. E. C. (2005). *ISO 27002: 2005.* Information Technology-Security Techniques-Code of Practice for Information Security Management.

ISO/IEC. (2013). *ISO/IEC 27002:2013.* Retrieved March 24, 2014, from http://www.Iso.Org/Iso/Home/StoreCatalogue_ics/Catalogue_detail_ics.Htm?Csnumber=54533

Johnson, B. G. (2014). *Measuring ISO 27001 ISMS processes* (pp. 1–20). ISO.

Joshi, J., Ghafoor, A., Aref, W. G., & Spafford, E. H. (2001). Digital government security infrastructure design challenges. *Computer, 34*(2), 66–72. https://doi.org/10.1109/2.901169

Knapp, K. J., Marshall, T. E., Rainer, R. K., & Ford, F. N. (2007). Information security effectiveness: Conceptualization and Validation of a Theory. *International Journal of Information Security and Privacy, 1*(2), 88–112. https://doi.org/10.4018/978-1-60566-196-4.ch006

Knapp, K. J., Morris, R., E. Marshall, T., & Byrd, T. (2009). Information security policy: An organizational-level process model. *Computers & Security, 28.* https://doi.org/10.1016/j.cose.2009.07.001

Kühnhauser, W. E. (1999). Policy groups. *Computers & Security, 18*(4), 351–363. https://doi.org/10.1016/S0167-4048(99)80081-9

Maleh, Y. (2018). *Security and privacy management, techniques, and protocols.* IGI Global. https://doi.org/10.4018/978-1-5225-5583-4

Mintzberg, H. (1983). *Structures in fives: Designing effective organizations.* Prentice Hall.

Mintzberg, H., Lampel, J., & Quinn, J. B. (2003). *The strategy process: Concepts, context, cases, global* (4th ed.). Pearson Education, Prentice Hall.

Paliszkiewicz, J. (2019). Information security policy compliance: Leadership and trust. *Journal of Computer Information Systems, 59*(3), 211–217. https://doi.org/10.1080/08874417.2019.1571459

Peltier, T. R. (2013). *Information security fundamentals* (2nd ed.). CRC Press, Taylor & Francis.

PRGL. (2011). *Praxiom research group limited.* Retrieved March 4, 2012, from www.praxiom.com/iso-17799-intro.htm

Rees, J., Bandyopadhyay, S., & Spafford, E. H. (2003). PFIRES: A policy framework for information security. *Communications of the ACM, 46*(7), 101–106. https://doi.org/10.1145/792704.792706

Reich, B. H., & Benbasat, I. (2000). Factors that influence the social dimension of alignment between business and information technology objectives. *MIS Quarterly*, *24*(1), 81–113. https://doi.org/10.2307/3250980

Talib, M. A., El Barachi, M., Khelifi, A., & Ormandjieva, O. (2012). Guide to ISO 27001: UAE case study. *Issues in Informing Science and Information Technology*, *7*, 331–349.

Von Solms, B. (2005). Information security governance: COBIT or ISO 17799 or both? *Computers and Security*, *24*(2), 99–104. https://doi.org/10.1016/j.cose.2005.02.002

Walsham, G. (1993). *Interpreting information systems in organizations.* John Wiley & Sons, Inc.

Willison, R. A. (2002, August). *Opportunities for computer abuse: Assessing a crime specific approach in the case of Barings Bank* [PhD thesis, London School of Economics and Political Science].

Yassine, M., Abdelkebir, S., & Abdellah, E. (2017). *A capability maturity framework for IT security governance in organizations.* 13th International Symposium on Information Assurance and Security (IAS 17).

Appendix 1

TABLE 8.4 ISO 27002 Domains and Questions

DOMAIN	*NO.*	*ISO SECTION QUESTION*	*PROCESS SELF-ASSESSMENT RATING (FROM 0 TO 5)*
Information Security Policies		**Management Direction for Information Security**	
	1	Is there an information security policy that has been approved by management, communicated to appropriate constituents and an owner to maintain and review the policy? (as specified in ISO/IEC 27001 section 5.2.)	
	2	Periodic review of policies and feedback (e.g., every 12 months?)	
	3	Thoroughness and completeness of policies and standards (see comments).	
Organization of Information Security		**Internal Organization**	
	4	Is there an information security function responsible for security initiatives within the organization?	
	5	Contacts with relevant external authorities (such as CERTs and special interest groups) on information security matters.	
	6	Do external parties have access to Scoped Systems and Data or processing facilities? If so, rate the maturity of the controls around reviewing third-party contracts, active controls, and monitoring/auditing.	

(Continued)

TABLE 8.4   (Continued)

DOMAIN	NO.	ISO SECTION QUESTION	PROCESS SELF-ASSESSMENT RATING (FROM 0 TO 5)
Organization of Information Security		**Mobile Devices and Teleworking**	
	7	Policy/standard and guidelines specific for mobile devices (laptops, mobile phones, tablets, etc.).	
	8	Policy/standard and guidelines for remote work locations, and remote virtual conferencing.	
Human Resource Security		**Prior to Employment**	
	9	Are security roles and responsibilities of constituents defined and documented in accordance with the organization's information security policy?	
	10	Is a background screening performed prior to allowing constituent access to Scoped Systems and Data?	
	11	Are new hires required to sign any agreements upon hire?	
Human Resource Security		**During Employment**	
	12	Is there a disciplinary process for noncompliance with information security policies? (employees and contractors)	
	13	Security Awareness Training Program	
Human Resource Security		**Termination and Change of Employment**	
	14	Is there a constituent termination or change of status process? A person's exit from the organization or significant changes of roles should be managed; returning corporate information and equipment, updating access rights.	
Asset Management		**Responsibility for Assets**	
	15	Is there an asset management policy or program that has been approved by management, communicated to appropriate constituents, and an owner to maintain and review the policy? (See comment)	

DOMAIN	NO.	ISO SECTION QUESTION	PROCESS SELF-ASSESSMENT RATING (FROM 0 TO 5)
	16	Information assets should be inventoried and owners should be identified to be held accountable for their security.	
	17	Is there insurance coverage for business interruptions or general services interruption?	
Asset Management		**Information Classification**	
	18	Information should be classified and labeled by its owners according to the security protection needed, and handled appropriately (see comment).	
Asset Management		**Media Handling**	
	19	Asset decommissioning, reuse, disposal, and physical media security. Information storage media should be managed, controlled, moved, and disposed of in such a way that the information content is not compromised.	
Access Control		**Business Requirements of Access Control**	
	20	The organization's requirements to control access to information assets should be clearly documented in an access control policy and procedures.	
	21	Electronic systems; adherence to the principle of least privilege, separation of duties, role-based access controls.	
	22	Multifactor authentication for critical services.	
	23	Isolation of environments and assets within those environments (e.g., production, development, staging).	
	24	Remote access, access controls, and auditing.	
Access Control		**User Access Management**	
	25	Processes and procedures regarding account creation, modification, and revocation.	

(Continued)

TABLE 8.4   (Continued)

DOMAIN	NO.	ISO SECTION QUESTION	PROCESS SELF-ASSESSMENT RATING (FROM 0 TO 5)
	26	Special restrictions for privileged access rights and the management of passwords.	
	27	Review and audit of access controls, accounts, and entitlements.	
Access Control		**User Responsibilities**	
	28	Internal Security Training (aside from security awareness).	
Access Control		**System and Application Access Control**	
	29	Information access should be restricted in accordance with the access control policy, for example, through secure log-on, password management, control over privileged utilities, and restricted access to program source code.	
Cryptography		**Cryptographic Controls**	
	30	Are there standards in place to dictate cryptographic best practices? (the use of encryption, cryptographic authentication, and integrity controls such as digital signatures and message authentication codes, key management)	
	31	Utilization of cryptographic controls following best practices, providing confidentiality and integrity with respect to scope systems and data.	
Physical and Environmental Security		**Secure Areas**	
	32	Is there a physical security program for scoped systems and environments where scoped data are stored and processed?	
	33	Are reasonable physical security and environmental controls present in the building/data center that contains Scoped Systems and Data? Have these controls been audited and/or certified by an independent third party?	

DOMAIN	NO.	ISO SECTION QUESTION	PROCESS SELF-ASSESSMENT RATING (FROM 0 TO 5)
Physical and Environmental Security		**Equipment Security**	
	34	Equipment should not be taken off-site unless authorized and must be adequately protected both on and off-site	
	35	Information must be destroyed prior to storage media being disposed of or reused. Unattended equipment must be secured.	
Operations Management		**Operational Procedures and Responsibilities**	
	36	IT operating responsibilities and procedures should be documented. Changes to IT facilities and systems should be controlled. Capacity and performance should be managed. Development, test, and operational systems should be separated.	
Operations Management		**Protection from Malware**	
	37	For all scoped systems and networks, malware controls are required, including user awareness.	
Operations Management		**Backup**	
	38	Appropriate backups should be taken and retained in accordance with a backup policy.	
Operations Management		**Logging and Monitoring**	
	39	For all scoped systems and systems containing scoped data, system user and administrator/operator activities, exceptions, faults, and information security events should be logged and protected. Clocks should be synchronized.	
Operations Management		**Control of Operational Software**	
	40	Software installation on scoped operational systems should be controlled.	

(Continued)

TABLE 8.4   (Continued)

DOMAIN	NO.	ISO SECTION QUESTION	PROCESS SELF-ASSESSMENT RATING (FROM 0 TO 5)
Operations Management		**Technical Vulnerability Management**	
	41	For scoped systems, vulnerabilities should be actively identified and patched.	
Operations Management		**Information Systems Audit Considerations**	
	42	IT audits should be planned and controlled to minimize adverse effects on production systems or inappropriate data access.	
Communications Security		**Network Security Management**	
	43	Networks and network services should be secured and hardened.	
Communications Security		**Information Transfer**	
	44	There should be policies, procedures, and agreements (e.g., nondisclosure agreements and security control clauses) concerning information transfer to/from third parties, including electronic messaging.	
System Acquisition, Development, and Maintenance		**Security Requirements of Information Systems**	
	45	Security control requirements should be analyzed and specified, including web applications and transactions.	
	46	Are systems and applications patched?	
	47	Are vulnerability tests (internal/external) performed on all applications at least annually?	
System Acquisition, Development, and Maintenance		**Security in Development and Support Processes**	
	48	Rules governing secure software/systems development should be defined as policy. Changes to systems (both applications and operating systems) should be controlled.	

DOMAIN	NO.	ISO SECTION QUESTION	PROCESS SELF-ASSESSMENT RATING (FROM 0 TO 5)
	49	Software packages should ideally not be modified, and secure system engineering principles should be followed. The development environment should be secured, and outsourced development should be controlled.	
	50	System security should be tested and acceptance criteria defined to include security aspects.	
System Acquisition, Development, and Maintenance		**Test Data**	
	51	Test data should be carefully selected/generated and controlled.	
Supplier Relationships		**Information Security in Supplier Relationships**	
	52	There should be policies, procedures, awareness, etc. to protect the organization's information that is accessible to IT outsourcers and other external suppliers throughout the supply chain, agreed within the contracts or agreements.	
Supplier Relationships		**Supplier Service Delivery Management**	
	53	Service delivery by external suppliers should be monitored and reviewed/audited against the contracts/agreements. Service changes should be controlled.	
Information Security Incident Management		**Management of Information Security Incidents and Improvements**	
	54	Responsibilities and procedures exist to manage (report, assess, respond to, and learn from) information security events, incidents, and weaknesses consistently and effectively, and to collect forensic evidence.	

(Continued)

TABLE 8.4   (Continued)

DOMAIN	NO.	ISO SECTION QUESTION	PROCESS SELF-ASSESSMENT RATING (FROM 0 TO 5)
Information Security Aspects of Business Continuity Management		**Information Security Continuity**	
	55	The continuity of information security should be planned, implemented, and reviewed as an integral part of the organization's business continuity management systems.	
Information Security Aspects of Business Continuity Management		**Redundancies**	
	56	Is there a documented policy for business continuity and disaster recovery that has been approved by management, communicated to appropriate constituents, and an owner to maintain and review the policy?	
	57	Is there an annual schedule of required tests and testing occurs?	
	58	Is a business impact analysis conducted at least annually? (to confirm SLA commitments)	
Compliance		**Compliance with Legal and Contractual Requirements**	
	59	The organization must identify and document its obligations to external authorities and other third parties in relation to information security, including intellectual property, records, privacy/personally identifiable information, and cryptography.	
Compliance		**Information Security Reviews**	
	60	There an internal audit, risk management, or compliance department with responsibility for identifying and tracking resolution of outstanding regulatory issues	

DOMAIN	NO.	ISO SECTION QUESTION	PROCESS SELF-ASSESSMENT RATING (FROM 0 TO 5)
	61	The organization's information security arrangements are independently reviewed (audited) and reported to management.	
	62	Managers routinely review employees' and systems' compliance with security policies, procedures, etc. and initiate corrective actions where necessary.	

Conclusion

This chapter presents a summarized review of the book. The IT governance evolutions and standards are described in Chapters 1 and 2. These included material on different Information Technology Governance evolution, definitions, issues, and standards. Chapter 3 provided a practical framework to evaluate Information Technology governance through COBIT 5. This chapter presented a review of related theories and an applied discussion of IT Governance aspects, including use, strategy, and adoption by large organizations. Chapter 4 investigated IT service management and proposed a practical maturity framework based on ITIL. Chapter 5 discussed cloud computing adoption for IT governance agility. The last three chapters described Information Security Governance by exploring the engagement processes, and the practices of organizations involved in a strategy of information security governance are presented in Chapter 7. A capability maturity framework for information security governance is presented in Chapter 8. Finally, Chapter 9 aimed to guide organizations in implementing an effective Information Security Policy through ISO 27002.

Organizations are becoming more and more dependent on IT to manage their business processes. The IT domain is a dynamic and fast-changing environment that is directly beneficial to organizations. However, the constant evolution of this environment implies new challenges for information security and management of critical IT infrastructures of organizations while maintaining the performance of primary processes, including business continuity.

Discussions on governance deal with all the processes involved in managing the information system, from the budgetary approach and strategic alignment (CMMI, COBIT, etc.) to SOA (urbanization, service catalog, versions, etc.), data administration, and production assets (ITIL, CMDB, etc.). In the end, if you look closely, these practices simply formalize historical management concerns that are now being reclassified under the term 'governance'. This at least has the merit of promoting mutualized practices, which are usually the best. However, there is a severe problem with the current discourse on governance: it claims to govern existing assets, but too rarely the evolution of the information system. The risk is to implement governance processes that are more rigid than the agility of the systems, especially the new service-oriented systems.

Security governance brings together all the essential elements of cyber defense and effective risk management. Without this governance, dangerous gaps remain and assets are inevitably compromised. By taking the steps outlined in this book, an organization will be better prepared to implement an agile IT governance and manage risks as they arise and become sufficiently security resilient to counter today's threats.

It has been suggested in this book to address the issue of IT governance and information through guides, practices, and maturity frameworks. This book explores the characteristics of IT governance and information security to give a theoretical and practical basis for understanding IT governance and to provide decision-makers the necessary tools to succeed in their IT governance strategy in the organization.

DOI: 10.1201/9781003161998- 13

References

Aasi, P., Rusu, L., & Han, S. (2014). Culture influence on IT governance: What we have learned? *International Journal of IT/Business Alignment and Governance (IJITBAG)*, *5*(1), 34–49.

Abdelkebir, S., Maleh, Y., & Belaissaoui, M. (2017). An agile framework for ITS management in organizations: A case study based on DevOps. *Proceedings of the 2nd International Conference on Computing and Wireless Communication Systems*, 67:1–67:8. https://doi.org/10.1145/3167486.3167556

Abdollahzadehgan, A., Che Hussin, A. R., Gohary, M. M., & Amini, M. (2013). The organizational critical success factors for adopting cloud computing in SMEs. *Journal of Information Systems Research and Innovation*, *4*(1), 67–74. https://ssrn.com/abstract=2333028

Abolfazli, S., Sanaei, Z., Tabassi, A., Rosen, S., Gani, A., & Khan, S. U. (2015). Cloud adoption in Malaysia: Trends, opportunities, and challenges. *IEEE Cloud Computing*, *2*(1), 60–68. https://doi.org/10.1109/MCC.2015.1

Adams, D. A., Nelson, R. R., Todd, P. A., Ahmi, A., Kent, S., Al-Ansi, A. A., Ismail, N. A. Bin, Al-Swidi, A. K., Banker, R. D., Chang, H., Kao, Y., Bedard, J. C., Jackson, C., Ettredge, M. L., Johnstone, K. M., Bierstaker, J. L., Burnaby, P., Thibodeau, J., Bierstaker, J. L., . . . Willborn, W. W. (2009). Factors affecting the adoption of open systems: An exploratory study. *MIS Quarterly*, *16*(2), 1521–1552. https://doi.org/10.1108/02686900510606092

Adamson, G., Wang, L., Holm, M., & Moore, P. (2017). Cloud manufacturing – a critical review of recent development and future trends. *International Journal of Computer Integrated Manufacturing*, *30*(4–5), 347–380. https://doi.org/10.1080/0951192X.2015.1031704

Ahmad, A., & Ruighaver, A. (2003, January). *Improved event logging for security and forensics: Developing audit management infrastructure requirements*. Proceedings of the ISOneWorld.

Aiken, M. W., Liu Sheng, O. R., & Vogel, D. R. (1991). Integrating expert systems with group decision support systems. *ACM Transactions on Information Systems (TOIS)*, *9*(1), 75–95.

Alaceva, C., & Rusu, L. (2015). Barriers in achieving business/IT alignment in a large Swedish company: What we have learned? *Computers in Human Behavior*, *51*, 715–728. https://doi.org/10.1016/j.chb.2014.12.007

Alam, S. S. (2009). Adoption of internet in Malaysian SMEs. *Journal of Small Business and Enterprise Development*, *16*(2), 240–255. https://doi.org/10.1108/14626000910956038

Alavi, M., & Leidner, D. E. (2001). Knowledge management and knowledge management systems: Conceptual foundations and research issues. *MIS Quarterly*, 107–136.

Albrecht, C. C., Dean, D. L., & Hansen, J. V. (2005). Marketplace and technology standards for B2B e-commerce: Progress, challenges, and the state of the art. *Information & Management*, *42*(6), 865–875.

Alewine, N., Ruback, H., & Deligne, S. (2004). Pervasive speech recognition. *IEEE Pervasive Computing*, *3*(4), 78–81.

Ali, S., Green, P., & Robb, A. (2015). Information technology investment governance: What is it and does it matter? *International Journal of Accounting Information Systems*, *18*, 1–25. https://doi.org/10.1016/j.accinf.2015.04.002

Al-Khazrajy, M. (2011). *Risk based assessment of IT control frameworks: A case study* [Master of philosophy thesis, Auckland University of Technology].

Allen, J. P. (2003). The evolution of new mobile applications: A sociotechnical perspective. *International Journal of Electronic Commerce*, *8*(1), 23–36.

Alonso, G., Agrawal, D., El Abbadi, A., & Mohan, C. (1997). Functionality and limitations of current workflow management systems. *IEEE Expert, 12*(5), 105–111.

Amini, M., & Bakri, A. (2015). Cloud computing adoption by SMEs in the Malaysia: A multi-perspective framework based on DOI theory and TOE framework. *Journal of Information Technology & Information Systems Research (JITISR), 9*(2), 121–135.

Amron, M. T., Ibrahim, R., Abu Bakar, N. A., & Chuprat, S. (2019). Determining factors influencing the acceptance of cloud computing implementation. *Procedia Computer Science, 161*, 1055–1063. https://doi.org/10.1016/j.procs.2019.11.216

Anthony Byrd, T., Lewis, B. R., & Bryan, R. W. (2006). The leveraging influence of strategic alignment on IT investment: An empirical examination. *Information and Management, 43*(3), 308–321. https://doi.org/10.1016/j.im.2005.07.002

Aprilinda, Y., Puspa, A. K., & Affandy, F. N. (2019). The use of ISO and COBIT for IT governance audit. *Journal of Physics: Conference Series, 1381*, 12028. https://doi.org/10.1088/1742-6596/1381/1/012028

Archibugi, D., & Michie, J. (1995). Technology and innovation: An introduction. *Cambridge Journal of Economics, 19*. https://doi.org/10.1093/oxfordjournals.cje.a035298

Arteta, B. M., & Giachetti, R. E. (2004). A measure of agility as the complexity of the enterprise system. *Robotics and Computer-Integrated Manufacturing, 20*(6 special issue), 495–503. https://doi.org/10.1016/J.rcim.2004.05.008

Ashrafi, A., Ravasan, A. Z., Trkman, P., & Afshari, S. (2019). The role of business analytics capabilities in bolstering firms' agility and performance. *International Journal of Information Management, 47*, 1–15.

Azadegan, A., & Teich, J. (2010). Effective benchmarking of innovation adoptions: A theoretical framework for e-procurement technologies. *Benchmarking: An International Journal, 17*(4), 472–490. https://doi.org/10.1108/14635771011060558

Azizi Ismail, N. (2008). Information technology governance, funding and structure: A case analysis of a public university in Malaysia. *Campus-Wide Information Systems, 25*(3), 145–160. https://doi.org/10.1108/10650740810886321

Bahl, S., & Wali, O. P. (2014). Perceived significance of information security governance to predict the information security service quality in software service industry: An empirical analysis. *Information Management & Computer Security, 22*(1), 2–23. https://doi.org/10.1108/IMCS-01-2013-0002

Bakos, Y., Lucas, H. C., Oh, W., Simon, G., Viswanathan, S., & Weber, B. W. (2005). The impact of e-commerce on competition in the retail brokerage industry. *Information Systems Research, 16*(4), 352–371.

Bamber, C. J., Sharp, J. M., & Hides, M. T. (2000). Developing management systems towards integrated manufacturing: A case study perspective. *Integrated Manufacturing Systems, 11*(7), 454–461.

Bart, C., & Turel, O. (2010). IT and the board of directors: An empirical investigation into the "governance questions" Canadian board members ask about IT. *Journal of Information Systems, 24*(2), 147–172. https://doi.org/10.2308/jis.2010.24.2.147

Baruch, Y., & Holtom, B. C. (2008). Survey response rate levels and trends in organizational research. *Human Relations, 61*(8), 1139–1160. https://doi.org/10.1177/0018726708094863

Baskerville, R., & Pries-Heje, J. (2004). Short cycle time systems development. *Information Systems Journal, 14*(3), 237–264.

Baskerville, R., & Siponen, M. (2002). An information security meta-policy for emergent organizations. *Logistics Information Management, 15*(5–6), 337–346. https://doi.org/10.1108/09576050210447019

Basson, G., Walker, A., McBride, T., & Oakley, R. (2012). ISO/IEC 15504 measurement applied to COBIT process maturity. *Benchmarking: An International Journal, 19*(2), 159–176. https://doi.org/10.1108/14635771211224518

Batra, D., Hoffer, J. A., & Bostrom, R. P. (1988). A comparison of user performance between the relational and the extended entity relationship models in the discovery phase of database design. *ICIS*, 43.

Bauer, M. J., Poirier, C. C., Lapide, L., & Bermudez, J. (2001). *E-business: The strategic impact on supply chain and logistics*. Council of Logistics Management.

Beatty, S. E., & Smith, S. M. (1987). External search effort: An investigation across several product categories. *Journal of Consumer Research, 14*(1), 83–95.

Beloglazov, A., Banerjee, D., Hartman, A., & Buyya, R. (2014). Improving productivity in design and development of information technology (IT) service delivery simulation models. *Journal of Service Research, 18*(1), 75–89. https://doi.org/10.1177/1094670514541002

Benamati, J., & Lederer, A. L. (2001). Coping with rapid changes in IT. *Communications of the ACM, 44*(8), 83–88.

Benaroch, M., & Chernobai, A. (2017). Operational IT failures, IT value destruction, and board-level IT governance changes. *MIS Quarterly, 41*(3), 729–762. https://doi.org/10.25300/MISQ/2017/41.3.04

Benlian, A., & Hess, T. (2011). Opportunities and risks of software-as-a-service: Findings from a survey of IT executives. *Decision Support Systems, 52*(1), 232–246. https://doi.org/10.1016/j.dss.2011.07.007

Benlian, A., Kettingaer, W. J., Sunyaev, A., Winkler, T. J., & EDITORS, G. (2018). The transformative value of cloud computing: A decoupling, platformization, and recombination theoretical framework. *Journal of Management Information Systems, 35*(3), 719–739.

Berger, H., & Beynon-Davies, P. (2009). The utility of rapid application development in large-scale, complex projects. *Information Systems Journal, 19*(6), 549–570.

Bergner, J., Witherspoon, C. L., Cockrell, C., & Stone, D. N. (2013). Antecedents of organizational knowledge sharing: A meta-analysis and critique. *Journal of Knowledge Management, 17*(2), 250–277. https://doi.org/10.1108/13673271311315204

Bermejo, P. H. de S., Tonelli, A. O., Zambalde, A. L., Santos, P. A. dos, & Zuppo, L. (2014). Evaluating IT governance practices and business and IT outcomes: A quantitative exploratory study in Brazilian companies. *Procedia Technology, 16*, 849–857. https://doi.org/10.1016/j.protcy.2014.10.035

Bhattacharjya, J., & Chang, V. (2010). Adoption and implementation of IT governance: Cases from Australian higher education. *Strategic Information Systems: Concepts, Methodologies, Tools, and Applications. IGI Global*, 1308–1326.

Bishop, M. (2002). *Lorica segmentata volume I: A handbook of articulated roman plate armour* (Vol. 1). The Armatura Press.

Booch, G., Rumbaugh, J., & Jacobson, I. (1999). *The unified modeling language user guide*. Rational Software Corporation.

Borgman, H. P., Bahli, B., Heier, H., & Schewski, F. (2013). Cloudrise: Exploring cloud computing adoption and governance with the TOE framework. *Proceedings of the Annual Hawaii International Conference on System Sciences*, 4425–4435. https://doi.org/10.1109/HICSS.2013.132

Bowen, P., Chew, E., & Hash, J. (2007). Information security guide for government executives information security guide for government executives. *National Institute of Standards and Technology NIST*, 3–9. http://csrc.nist.gov/publications/nistir/ir7359/NISTIR-7359.pdf

Braga, G. (2015). COBIT 5 applied to the Argentine digital accounting system. *COBIT Focus*, 1–4.

Briol, P. (2008). *BPMN, the business process modeling notation pocket handbook*. LuLu.com.

Broadbent, M., & Weill, P. (1997). Management by maxim: How business and IT managers can create IT infrastructures. *Sloan Management Review, 38*, 77–92.

Brotby, K. (2009). *Information security governance: A practical development and implementation approach*. John Wiley & Sons.

Brown, A. E., Grant, G. G., & Sprott, E. (2005a). Framing the frameworks: A review of IT governance research. *Communications of the Association for Information Systems, 15*, 696–712. https://doi.org/Article

Brown, A. E., Grant, G. G., & Sprott, E. (2005b, May). Framing the frameworks: A review of IT governance research. *Communications of the Association for Information Systems, 15*, 696–712. https://doi.org/Article

Brown, W. A., Laird, R., Gee, C., & Mitra, T. (2008). *SOA governance: Achieving and sustaining business and IT agility.* Pearson Education.

Bruce, K. (1998). Can you align IT with business strategy? *Strategy & Leadership, 26*(5), 16–20. https://doi.org/10.1108/eb054620

Brustbauer, J. (2016). Enterprise risk management in SMEs: Towards a structural model. *International Small Business Journal, 34*(1), 70–85. https://doi.org/10.1177/0266242614542853

Buhalis, D. (2004). eAirlines: Strategic and tactical use of ICTs in the airline industry. *Information & Management, 41*(7), 805–825.

Burns, E. (2010). Developing email interview practices in qualitative research. *Sociological Research Online, 15*(4), 1–12. https://doi.org/10.5153/sro.2232

Butler, B. S., & Gray, P. H. (2006). Reliability, mindfulness, and information systems. *MIS Quarterly*, 211–224.

Butt, S. A., Tariq, M. I., Jamal, T., Ali, A., Martinez, J. L. D., & De-La-Hoz-Franco, E. (2019). Predictive variables for agile development merging cloud computing services. *IEEE Access, 7*, 99273–99282. https://doi.org/10.1109/ACCESS.2019.2929169

Byrd, T. A., & Turner, D. E. (2000). Measuring the flexibility of information technology infrastructure: Exploratory analysis of a construct. *Journal of Management Information Systems, 17*(1), 167–208. https://doi.org/10.1080/07421222.2000.11045632

Cadete, G. R., & da Silva, M. M. (2017). *Assessing IT governance processes using a COBIT5 model BT – information systems* (M. Themistocleous & V. Morabito, Eds., pp. 447–460). Springer International Publishing.

Calder, A., & Watkins, S. G. (2010). *Information security risk management for ISO27001/ISO27002.* IT Governa.

Canavan, S. (2003). *An information security policy development guide for large companies.* SANS Institute.

Cao, L., Mohan, K., Xu, P., & Ramesh, B. (2009). A framework for adapting agile development methodologies. *European Journal of Information Systems, 18*(4), 332–343.

Cervone, H. F. (2010). An overview of virtual and cloud computing. *OCLC Systems & Services: International Digital Library Perspectives, 26*(3), 162–165.

CESIN. (2019). *Club des Experts de la Sécurité de l' Information et du Numérique Baromètre de la cyber- sécurité des entreprises Sommaire.* Barometre CESIN.

Chamanifard, R., Nikpour, A., Chamanifard, S., & Nobarieidishe, S. (2015). Impact of organizational agility dimensions on employee's organizational commitment in foreign exchange offices of Tejarat Bank, Iran. *European Online Journal of Natural and Social Science, 4*(1), 199–207.

Charles, T., & Tashakkori, A. (2009). *Foundations of mixed methods research: Integrating quantitative and qualitative approaches in the social and behavioral sciences.* Sage.

Chatterjee, S., Kar, A. K., & Gupta, M. P. (2018). Alignment of IT authority and citizens of proposed smart cities in India: System security and privacy perspective. *Global Journal of Flexible Systems Management, 19*(1), 95–107. https://doi.org/10.1007/s40171-017-0173-5

Chemjor, E. M., & Lagat, C. (2017). Determinants of level of cloud computing adoption in small and medium enterprises in Nairobi County. *International Journal of Economics, Commerce and Management, 5*(4).

Chen, R. S., Sun, C. M., Helms, M. M., & (Kenny) Jih, W.-J. (2008). Aligning information technology and business strategy with a dynamic capabilities perspective: A longitudinal study of a Taiwanese semiconductor company. *International Journal of Information Management, 28*(5), 366–378. https://doi.org/10.1016/j.ijinfomgt.2008.01.015

Chenoweth, T., Corral, K., & Demirkan, H. (2006). Seven key interventions for data warehouse success. *Communications of the ACM, 49*(1), 114–119.

Chiang, R. H. L., Grover, V., Liang, T.-P., & Zhang, D. (2018). *Special issue: Strategic value of big data and business analytics.* Taylor & Francis.

Chin, W. W., Marcolin, B. L., & Newsted, P. R. (2003). A partial least squares latent variable modeling approach for measuring interaction effects: Results from a Monte Carlo simulation study and an electronic-mail emotion/ adoption study. *Information Systems Research, 14*(2), 189–217. https://doi.org/10.1287/isre.14.2.189.16018

Chiu, T., & Wang, T. (David). (2019). The COSO framework in emerging technology environments: An effective in-class exercise on internal control. *Journal of Emerging Technologies in Accounting*, *16*(2), 89–98. https://doi.org/10.2308/jeta-52500

Chung, S. H., Rainer, Jr., R. K., & Lewis, B. R. (2003). The impact of information technology infrastructure flexibility on strategic alignment and application implementations. *Communications of the Association for Information Systems*, *11*(1), 11.

Ciborra, C. U. (2009). From thinking to tinkering: The grassroots of strategic information systems. *Bricolage, Care and Information*, 206–220. https://doi.org/10.1057/9780230250611_10

Clark, C. E., Cavanaugh, N. C., Brown, C. V, & Sambamurthy, V. (1997). Building change-readiness capabilities in the IS organization: Insights from the Bell Atlantic experience. *MIS Quarterly*, 425–455.

Claudepierre, B., & Nurcan, S. (2007). A framework for analysing IT governance approaches. *ICEIS 2007–9th International Conference on Enterprise Information Systems, Proceedings*, 512–516. www.scopus.com/inward/record.url?eid=2-s2.0-70349560477&partnerID=40&md5=2b2b4447a92d4202094243103e916a44

Cohen, F. (2006). *IT security governance guidebook with security program metrics*. Auerbach Publishers Inc.

Conboy, K. (2009). Agility from first principles: Reconstructing the concept of agility in information systems development. *Information Systems Research*, *20*(3), 329–354. https://doi.org/10.1287/isre.1090.0236

Conboy, K., & Fitzgerald, B. (2004). Toward a conceptual framework of agile methods: A study of agility in different disciplines. *Proceedings of the 2004 ACM Workshop on Interdisciplinary Software Engineering Research*, 37–44. https://doi.org/10.1145/1029997.1030005

Couger, J. D., Zawacki, R. A., & Oppermann, E. B. (1979). Motivation levels of MIS managers versus those of their employees. *MIS Quarterly*, 47–56.

Coyne, J. W., & Kluksdahl, N. C. (1994). Automated information systems security engineering (a case study in security Run Amok). *Proceedings of the 2Nd ACM Conference on Computer and Communications Security*, 251–257. https://doi.org/10.1145/191177.191241

Cragg, P., Caldeira, M., & Ward, J. (2011). Organizational information systems competences in small and medium-sized enterprises. *Information & Management*, *48*(8), 353–363. https://doi.org/10.1016/j.im.2011.08.003

Creswell, J. W., & Creswell, J. D. (2017). *Research design: Qualitative, quantitative, and mixed methods approaches*. Sage Publications.

Cronin, C. (2014). Using case study research as a rigorous form of inquiry. *Nurse Researcher*, *21*(5), 19.

Cumps, B., Viaene, S., Dedene, G., & Vandenbulcke, J. (2006). An empirical study on business/ICT alignment in European organisations. *Proceedings of the Annual Hawaii International Conference on System Sciences*, *8*(C), 1–10. https://doi.org/10.1109/HICSS.2006.53

Currie, A. R., Mcconnell, A., Parr, G. P., McClean, S. I., & Khan, K. (2014). Truesource: A true performance for hierarchical cloud monitoring. *Proceedings of the 2014 IEEE/ACM 7th International Conference on Utility and Cloud Computing*, 980–985. https://doi.org/10.1109/UCC.2014.161

Dahlberg, T., & Kivijärvi, H. (2006). An integrated framework for IT governance and the development and validation of an assessment instrument. *39th Hawaii International Conference on System Sciences*, *C*, 1–10. https://doi.org/10.1109/HICSS.2006.57

Dahlberg, T., & Lahdelma, P. (2007). IT governance maturity and IT outsourcing degree: An exploratory study. *Proceedings of the Annual Hawaii International Conference on System Sciences*, 1–10. https://doi.org/10.1109/HICSS.2007.306

Daniel, E. M., & White, A. (2005). The future of inter-organisational system linkages: Findings of an international Delphi study. *European Journal of Information Systems*, *14*(2), 188–203.

Darke, P., Shanks, G., & Broadbent, M. (1998). Successfully completing case study research: Combining rigour, relevance and pragmatism. *Information Systems Journal*, *8*(4), 273–289. https://doi.org/10.1046/j.1365-2575.1998.00040.x

Da Veiga, A., & Eloff, J. H. P. (2010). A framework and assessment instrument for information security culture. *Computers & Security*, *29*(2), 196–207. http://doi.org/10.1016/j.cose.2009.09.002

Davenport, T. H. (1993). *Process innovation: Reengineering work through information technology.* Harvard Business Press.

De Haes, S., & Van Grembergen, W. (2005). IT governance structures, processes and relational mechanisms: Achieving IT/business alignment in a major Belgian financial group. *Proceedings of the 38th Annual Hawaii International Conference on System Sciences*, 237b. https://doi.org/10.1109/HICSS.2005.362

De Haes, S., & Van Grembergen, W. (2006, February). Information technology governance best practices in Belgian organisations. *Proceedings of the Annual Hawaii International Conference on System Sciences*, 8. https://doi.org/10.1109/HICSS.2006.222

De Haes, S., Van Grembergen, W., & Debreceny, R. S. (2013). COBIT 5 and enterprise governance of information technology: Building blocks and research opportunities. *Journal of Information Systems*, *27*(1), 307–324. https://doi.org/10.2308/isys-50422

De Haes, S., Van Grembergen, W., Joshi, A., & Huygh, T. (2020). *COBIT as a framework for enterprise governance of IT BT – enterprise governance of information technology: Achieving alignment and value in digital organizations* (S. De Haes, W. Van Grembergen, A. Joshi, & T. Huygh, Eds. pp. 125–162). Springer International Publishing. https://doi.org/10.1007/978-3-030-25918-1_5

Deleersnyder, S., Win, B. De, Glas, B., Arciniegas, F., Bartoldus, M., Carter, J., Challey, D., Clarke, J., Cornell, D., Craigue, M., Deleersnyder, S., Derry, J., Win, B. De, Fern, D., & Glas, B. (2009). *Software assurance maturity model.* OWSAP.

Dennis, A. R., George, J. F., Jessup, L. M., Nunamaker Jr, J. F., & Vogel, D. R. (1988). Information technology to support electronic meetings. *MIS Quarterly*, 591–624.

Denscombe, M. (2014). *The good research guide: For small-scale social research projects* (5th ed.). McGraw-Hill Education.

Dhillon, G., Syed, R., & Pedron, C. (2016). Interpreting information security culture: An organizational transformation case study. *Computers & Security*, *56*, 63–69. http://doi.org/10.1016/j.cose.2015.10.001

Dhillon, G., Tejay, G., & Hong, W. (2007). *Identifying governance dimensions to evaluate information systems security in organizations.* https://doi.org/10.1109/HICSS.2007.257

Dlamini, M. T., Eloff, J. H. P., & Eloff, M. M. (2009). Information security: The moving target. *Computers & Security*, *28*(3), 189–198. https://doi.org/10.1016/j.cose.2008.11.007

Dove, R. (1995). *Rick Dove agility forum best agile practice reference base – 1994: Challenge models and benchmarks Rick Dove, director strategic analysis, agility forum, Bethlehem, PA.* 4th Annual Agility Conference.

Drucker, P. F. (1995). The new productivity challenge. *Quality in Higher Education*, *37*, 45–53.

Duncan, N. B. (1995). Capturing flexibility of information technology infrastructure: A study of resource characteristics and their measure. *Journal of Management Information Systems*, *12*(2), 37–57. www.jstor.org/stable/40398165

Elhasnaoui, S., Medromi, H., Chakir, A., & Sayouti, A. (2015). A new IT governance architecture based on multi agents system to support project management. *2015 International Conference on Electrical and Information Technologies (ICEIT)*, 43–46. https://doi.org/10.1109/EITech.2015.7162957

El-Mekawy, M., Rusu, L., & Perjons, E. (2015). An evaluation framework for comparing business-IT alignment models: A tool for supporting collaborative learning in organizations. *Computers in Human Behavior*, *51*, 1229–1247. https://doi.org/10.1016/j.chb.2014.12.016

Eroğlu, Ş., & Çakmak, T. (2016, January). Enterprise information systems within the context of information security: A risk assessment for a health organization in Turkey. *Procedia Computer Science*, *100*, 979–986. https://doi.org/10.1016/j.procs.2016.09.262

Felix, R., Rauschnabel, P. A., & Hinsch, C. (2017). Elements of strategic social media marketing: A holistic framework. *Journal of Business Research*, *70*, 118–126. https://doi.org/10.1016/j.jbusres.2016.05.001

Fink, L., & Neumann, S. (2009). Taking the high road to web services implementation: An exploratory investigation of the organizational impacts. *ACM SIGMIS Database: The DATABASE for Advances in Information Systems, 40*(3), 84–108.

Flowerday, S. V., & Tuyikeze, T. (2016). Information security policy development and implementation: The what, how and who. *Computers & Security, 61*, 169–183. https://doi.org/10.1016/j.cose.2016.06.002

Fomin, V. V. (2008). *Iso/Iec 27001 information systems security management standard: Exploring the reasons for low adoption, February 2016* (pp. 1–13). https://www.researchgate.net/publication/228898807_ISOIEC_27001_Information_Systems_Security_Management_Standard_Exploring_the_reasons_for_low_adoption

Galliers, R. D. (2006). Strategizing for agility: Confronting information. *Agile Information Systems, 1.*

Galliers, R. D., & Leidner, D. E. (2014). Strategic information management: Challenges and strategies in managing information systems. *Information Strategy, 625.* www.worldcat.org/isbn/0750656190

Gallupe, R. B., DeSanctis, G., & Dickson, G. W. (1988). Computer-based support for group problem-finding: An experimental investigation. *MIS Quarterly*, 277–296.

Gerth, A. B., & Rothman, S. (2007). The future IS organization in a flat world. *Information Systems Management, 24*(2), 103–111.

Gikas, C. (2010). A general comparison of FISMA, HIPAA, ISO 27000 and PCI-DSS standards. *Information Security Journal: A Global Perspective, 19*(3), 132–141. https://doi.org/10.1080/19393551003657019

Gillies, A. (2011). Improving the quality of information security management systems with ISO27000. *The TQM Journal, 23*(4), 367–376. https://doi.org/10.1108/17542731111139455

Glasgow, J., Macewen, G., & Panangaden, P. (1992). A logic for reasoning about security. *ACM Transactions on Computer Systems, 10*(3), 226–264. https://doi.org/10.1145/146937.146940

Goldman, S. L., & Nagel, R. N. (1993). Management, technology and agility: The emergence of a new era in manufacturing. *International Journal of Technology Management, 8*, 18–38. https://doi.org/10.1504/IJTM.1993.025758

Goodhue, D. L., Quillard, J. A., & Rockart, J. F. (1988). Managing the data resource: A contingency perspective. *MIS Quarterly*, 373–392.

Goodhue, D. L., & Straub, D. (1991). Security concerns of system users: A study of perceptions of the adequacy of security. *Information & Management, 20.* https://doi.org/10.1016/0378-7206(91)90024-V

Goranson, H. T., & Goranson, T. (1999). *The agile virtual enterprise: Cases, metrics, tools.* Greenwood Publishing Group.

Grant, G., Brown, A., Uruthirapathy, A., Mcknight, S., & Grant, G. G. (2007). Association for information systems AIS electronic library (AISeL): An extended model of IT governance: A conceptual proposal. *AMCIS 2007 Proceedings, 215.* http://aisel.aisnet.org/amcis2007/215

Grant, G., & Tan, F. B. (2013). Governing IT in inter-organizational relationships: Issues and future research. *European Journal of Information Systems, 22*(5), 493–497. https://doi.org/10.1057/ejis.2013.21

Gregor, S., & Benbasat, I. (1999). Explanations from intelligent systems: Theoretical foundations and implications for practice. *MIS Quarterly*, 497–530.

Grembergen, W. V. (2004). *Strategies for information technology governance.* IGI Global.

Group, O. M. (1997, February). *The common object request broker: Architecture and specification, revision 2.0.* O. M. Group.

Grover, V., & Kohli, R. (2012). Cocreating IT value: New capabilities and metrics for multifirm environments. *MIS Quarterly, 36*(1), 225–232.

Grunwel, D., & Sahama, T. (2016, February). Delegation of access in an information accountability framework for eHealth. *Proceedings of the Australasian Computer Science Week Multiconference on – ACSW'16*, 1–8. https://doi.org/10.1145/2843043.2843383

Guldentops, E. (2002). *Governing information technology through CobiT BT – integrity, internal control and security in information systems: Connecting governance and technology* (pp. 115–159). Springer. https://doi.org/10.1007/978-0-387-35583-2_8

Guldentops, E., Van Grembergen, W., & De Haes, S. (2002). Control and governance maturity survey: Establishing a reference benchmark and a self assessment tool. *Information Systems Control Journal*, *6*, 32–35.

Gwebu, K. L., Wang, J., & Hu, M. Y. (2020). Information security policy noncompliance: An integrative social influence model. *Information Systems Journal*, *30*(2), 220–269. https://doi.org/10.1111/isj.12257

Halawi, L. A., Aronson, J. E., & McCarthy, R. V. (2005). Resource-based view of knowledge management for competitive advantage. *The Electronic Journal of Knowledge Management*, *3*(2), 75.

Hancock, D. R., & Algozzine, B. (2016). *Doing case study research: A practical guide for beginning researchers*. Teachers College Press.

Harris, S. (2007). *CISSP certification all-in-one: Exam guide* (4th ed.). McGraw-Hill Publishing.

Hasselbring, W. (2000). Information system integration. *Communications of the ACM*, *43*(6), 32–38. https://doi.org/10.1145/336460.336472

Hayes, D. C., Hunton, J. E., & Reck, J. L. (2001). Market reaction to ERP implementation announcements. *Journal of Information Systems*, *15*(1), 3–18.

Heier, H., Borgman, H. P., & Mervyn, G. M. (2007). *Examining the relationship between IT governance software and business value of IT: Evidence from four case studies*. Proceedings of the 40th Hawaii International Conference on System Sciences.

Hemlata, G., Hema, D., & Ramaswamy, R. (2015). Understanding determinants of cloud computing adoption using an integrated TAM-TOE model. *Journal of Enterprise Information Management*, *28*(1), 107–130. https://doi.org/10.1108/JEIM-08-2013-0065

Henderson, J. C., & Venkatraman, H. (1999). Strategic alignment : Leveraging information technology for transforming organizations. *IBM Systems Journal*, *32*(1), 472–484.

Herath, T., & Rao, H. R. (2009). Encouraging information security behaviors in organizations: Role of penalties, pressures and perceived effectiveness. *Decision Support Systems*, *47*(2), 154–165. http://doi.org/10.1016/j.dss.2009.02.005

Hiererra, S. E. (2012). *Assessment of IT governance using COBIT 4.1 framework methodology: Case study university IS development in IT directorate* [Master's thesis, BINUS University].

Hobbs, B., & Petit, Y. (2017). Agile methods on large projects in large organizations. *Project Management Journal*, *48*(3), 3–19.

Hohpe, G., & Woolf, B. (2004). *Enterprise integration patterns: Designing, building, and deploying messaging solutions*. Addison-Wesley Professional.

Höne, K., & Eloff, J. H. P. (2002a). What makes an effective information security policy? *Network Security*, *6*, 14–16. https://doi.org/10.1016/S1353-4858(02)06011-7

Höne, K., & Eloff, J. H. P. (2002b). Information security policy – what do international information security standards say? *Computers & Security*, *21*(5), 402–409. https://doi.org/10.1016/S0167-4048(02)00504-7

Hong, K., Chi, Y., Chao, L. R., & Tang, J. (2006). An empirical study of information security policy on information security elevation in Taiwan. *Information Management & Computer Security*, *14*(2), 104–115. https://doi.org/10.1108/09685220610655861

Howcroft, & T. (2005). *Handbook of critical information systems research*. Edward Elgar Publishing, Inc.

Hsu, P. F., Ray, S., & Li-Hsieh, Y. Y. (2014). Examining cloud computing adoption intention, pricing mechanism, and deployment model. *International Journal of Information Management*, *34*(4), 474–488. https://doi.org/10.1016/j.ijinfomgt.2014.04.006

Huang, S., Lee, C. L., & Kao, A. C. (2006). Balancing performance measures for information security management: A balanced scorecard framework. *Industrial Management and Data Systems*, *106*. https://doi.org/10.1108/02635570610649880

Huissoud, M. (2005). *IT self-assessment project, current results and next steps*. Presentation to EUROSAI IT Working Group, Cypress, 14.

Humphreys, E. (2008). Information security management standards: Compliance, governance and risk management. *Information Security Technical Report*, *13*(4), 247–255. http://doi.org/10.1016/j.istr.2008.10.010

Hunton, J. E., Bryant, S. M., & Bagranoff, N. A. (2004). *Core concepts of information technology auditing*. Wiley.

Hyett, N., Kenny, A., & Dickson-Swift, V. (2014). Methodology or method? A critical review of qualitative case study reports. *International Journal of Qualitative Studies on Health and Well-Being, 9*(1), 23606. https://doi.org/10.3402/qhw.v9.23606

Ifinedo, P. (2011). An empirical analysis of factors influencing internet/e-business technologies adoption by SMES in Canada. *International Journal of Information Technology & Decision Making, 10*(4), 731–766. https://doi.org/10.1142/S0219622011004543

Ifinedo, P. (2011). Internet/e-business technologies acceptance in Canada's SMEs: An exploratory investigation. *Internet Research, 21*(3), 255–281. https://doi.org/10.1108/10662241111139309

Ifinedo, P. (2014). Information systems security policy compliance: An empirical study of the effects of socialisation, influence, and cognition. *Information & Management, 51*(1), 69–79. https://doi.org/10.1016/j.im.2013.10.001

Imache, R., Izza, S., & Ahmed-Nacer, M. (2012). An enterprise information system agility assessment model. *Computer Science and Information Systems, 9*(1), 107–133. https://doi.org/10.2298/CSIS101110041I

Information Security Governance: Guidance for Boards of Directors and Executive Management Guidance for Boards of Directors and Executive Management. (2006). *IT governance institute*, 1–52. www.itgi.org

ISACA. (2012). *COBIT 5: A business framework for the governance and management of enterprise IT*. Information Systems Audit and Control Association.

ISACA. (2013). *Self-assessment guide: Using COBIT 5*. Information Systems Audit and Control Association.

Isakowitz, T., Stohr, E. A., & Balasubramanian, P. (1995). RMM: A methodology for structured hypermedia design. *Communications of the ACM, 38*(8), 34–44.

ISECT. (2012). *ISO 27001 security*. Retrieved September 2012, from http://www.Iso27001security.Com/Html 27002.Html#HistoryOfISO17799

ISO, I., & Std, I. E. C. (2005). *ISO 27002: 2005*. Information Technology-Security Techniques-Code of Practice for Information Security Management.

ISO. (2013). *ISO home: Standards*. Retrieved March 24, 2013, from http://www.Iso.Org/Iso/Home/Standards.Htm

ISO/IEC. (2013). *ISO/IEC 27002:2013*. Retrieved March 24, 2014, from http://www.Iso.Org/Iso/Home/StoreCatalogue_ics/Catalogue_detail_ics.Htm?Csnumber=54533

ITG. (2008). *Information security governance: Guidance for information security managers*. Retrieved July 10, 2012, from http://www.Globalteksecurity.Com/SEGURIDAD_EN_LA_NUBE%20%20VIRTUALIZACION/INformation%20Security%20Governanc

ITGI. (2003). *Board briefing on IT governance*. ITGI.

ITGI. (2007). *COBIT mapping overview of international IT guidance* (2nd ed.). IT Governance Institute.

Izza, S., & Imache, R. (2010). An approach to achieve IT agility by combining SOA with ITSM. *International Journal of Information Technology and Management, 9*(4), 423–445.

Jarke, M., Mylopoulos, J., Schmidt, J. W., & Vassiliou, Y. (1992). DAIDA: An environment for evolving information systems. *ACM Transactions on Information Systems (TOIS), 10*(1), 1–50.

Jarke, M., & Pohl, K. (1993). Establishing visions in context: Towards a model of requirements processes. *International Conference on Information Systems (ICIS)*, 23–24.

Johnston, A., & Hale, R. (2009). Improved security through information security governance. *Communications of the ACM, 52.* https://doi.org/10.1145/1435417.1435446

Johnson, B. G. (2014). *Measuring ISO 27001 ISMS processes* (pp. 1–20). ISO.

Joshi, A., Bollen, L., Hassink, H., De Haes, S., & Van Grembergen, W. (2018). Explaining IT governance disclosure through the constructs of IT governance maturity and IT strategic role. *Information and Management, 55*(3), 368–380. https://doi.org/10.1016/j.im.2017.09.003

Joshi, J., Ghafoor, A., Aref, W. G., & Spafford, E. H. (2001). Digital government security infrastructure design challenges. *Computer, 34*(2), 66–72. https://doi.org/10.1109/2.901169

Kale, E., Aknar, A., & Başar, Ö. (2018). Absorptive capacity and firm performance: The mediating role of strategic agility. *International Journal of Hospitality Management, 78.*

Kalle, L., & Rose, M. G. (2003). Disruptive information system innovation: The case of internet computing. *Information Systems Journal, 13*(4), 301–330. https://doi.org/doi:10.1046/j.1365-2575.2003.00155.x

Kaplan, R. S., & Norton, D. P. (1996). *The balanced scorecard: Translating strategy into action.* Harvard Business Press.

Kasper, G. M. (1996). A theory of decision support system design for user calibration. *Information Systems Research, 7*(2), 215–232.

Kaur, S. P., Kumar, J., & Kumar, R. (2017). The relationship between flexibility of manufacturing system components, competitiveness of SMEs and business performance: A study of manufacturing SMEs in Northern India. *Global Journal of Flexible Systems Management, 18*(2), 123–137. https://doi.org/10.1007/s40171-016-0149-x

Keen, P. G. W. (1978). *Decision support systems; an organizational perspective.* Springer.

Klaic, A. (2010). *Overview of the state and trends in the contemporary information security policy and information security management methodologies.* International Convention on Information and Communication Technology, Electronics and Microelectronics MIPRO.

Klein, R. (2012). Assimilation of Internet-based purchasing applications within medical practices. *Information & Management, 49*(3), 135–141. https://doi.org/10.1016/j.im.2012.02.001

Knapp, K. J., Marshall, T. E., Rainer, R. K., & Ford, F. N. (2007). Information security effectiveness: Conceptualization and validation of a theory. *International Journal of Information Security and Privacy, 1*(2), 88–112. https://doi.org/10.4018/978-1-60566-196-4.ch006

Knapp, K., Morris, R., Marshall, T. E., & Byrd, T. (2009). Information security policy: An organizational-level process model. *Computers & Security, 28.* https://doi.org/10.1016/j.cose.2009.07.001

Korac-Kakabadse, N., & Kakabadse, A. (2001). IS/IT governance: Need for an integrated model. *Corporate Governance: The International Journal of Business in Society, 1*(4), 9–11. https://doi.org/10.1108/EUM0000000005974

Kraemer, S., Carayon, P., & Clem, J. (2009). Human and organizational factors in computer and information security: Pathways to vulnerabilities. *Computers & Security, 28.* https://doi.org/10.1016/j.cose.2009.04.006

Kryukov, D., & Strauss, R. (2009). Information security governance as key performance indicator for financial institutions. *Journal Riga Technical University, 38.* https://doi.org/10.2478/v10143-009-0014-x

Kshetri, N. (2013). Privacy and security issues in cloud computing: The role of institutions and institutional evolution. *Telecommunications Policy, 37*(4), 372–386. https://doi.org/10.1016/j.telpol.2012.04.011

Kühnhauser, W. E. (1999). Policy groups. *Computers & Security, 18*(4), 351–363. https://doi.org/10.1016/S0167-4048(99)80081-9

Kumar, R. L., & Stylianou, A. C. (2014). A process model for analyzing and managing flexibility in information systems. *European Journal of Information Systems, 23*(2), 151–184. https://doi.org/10.1057/ejis.2012.53

Kunio, T. (2010). NEC cloud computing system. *NEC Technical Journal, 5*(2), 10–15.

Lee, G., & Xia, W. (2005). The ability of information systems development project teams to respond to business and technology changes: A study of flexibility measures. *European Journal of Information Systems, 14*(1), 75–92.

Le Moigne, J. L. (1994). *La théorie du système général: Théorie de la modélisation.* Jeanlouis le moigne-ae mcx.

Lengnick-Hall, C. A., Beck, T. E., & Lengnick-Hall, M. L. (2011a). Developing a capacity for organizational resilience through strategic human resource management. *Human Resource Management Review, 21*(3), 243–255. https://doi.org/10.1016/j.hrmr.2010.07.001

Lengnick-Hall, C. A., Beck, T. E., & Lengnick-Hall, M. L. (2011b). Developing a capacity for organizational resilience through strategic human resource management. *Human Resource Management Review, 21*(3), 243–255. https://doi.org/10.1016/j.hrmr.2010.07.001

Lewis, S. (2015). Qualitative inquiry and research design: Choosing among five approaches. *Health Promotion Practice*, *16*(4), 473–475. https://doi.org/10.1177/1524839915580941

Lewis-Beck, M., Bryman, A. E., & Liao, T. F. (2003). *The Sage encyclopedia of social science research methods*. Sage Publications.

Lim, S. (2014). Impact of information technology infrastructure flexibility on the competitive advantage of small and medium sized-enterprises. *Journal of Business & Management*, *3*(1), 1–12. https://doi.org/10.12735/jbm.v3i1p1

Lin, A., & Chen, N. C. (2012). Cloud computing as an innovation: Perception, attitude, and adoption. *International Journal of Information Management*, *32*(6), 533–540. https://doi.org/10.1016/j.ijinfomgt.2012.04.001

Lomas, E. (2010). Information governance: Information security and access within a UK context. *Records Management Journal*, *20*(2), 182–198. https://doi.org/10.1108/09565691011064322

Low, C., Wu, M., & Chen, Y. (2011). Understanding the determinants of cloud computing adoption. *Industrial Management & Data Systems*, *111*(7), 1006–1023. https://doi.org/10.1108/02635571111161262

Luftman, J., Papp, R., & Brier, T. (1999). Enablers and Inhibitors of business-IT alignment. *Commun. AIS*, *1*(3es). http://dl.acm.org/citation.cfm?id=374122.374123

Luna-Reyes, L., Juiz, C., Gutierrez-Martinez, I., & Duhamel, F. B. (2020). Exploring the relationships between dynamic capabilities and IT governance. *Transforming Government: People, Process and Policy*, *14*(2), 149–169. https://doi.org/10.1108/TG-09-2019-0092

Luo, X., Gurung, A., & Shim, J. P. (2010). Understanding the determinants of user acceptance of enterprise instant messaging: An empirical study. *Journal of Organizational Computing and Electronic Commerce*, *20*(2), 155–181. https://doi.org/10.1080/10919391003709179

Lynn, T., Liang, X., Gourinovitch, A., Morrison, J. P., Fox, G., & Rosati, P. (2018). Understanding the determinants of cloud computing adoption for high performance computing. *51st Hawaii International Conference on System Sciences (HICSS-51)*, 3894–3903.

Lyytinen, K., & Rose, G. M. (2003). The disruptive nature of information technology innovations: The case of internet computing in systems development organizations. *MIS Quarterly*, 557–596.

Ma, Q., Pearson, J. M., & Tadisina, S. (2005). An exploratory study into factors of service quality for application service providers. *Information & Management*, *42*(8), 1067–1080.

Maas, J. (1998). Leveraging the new infrastructure: How market leaders capitalize on information technology. *MIT Sloan Management Review*, *40*(1), 104.

Maes, K., De Haes, S., & Van Grembergen, W. (2012). IT value management as a vehicle to unleash the business value from IT enabled investments. *International Journal of IT/Business Alignment and Governance*, *3*(1), 47–62. https://doi.org/10.4018/jitbag.2012010103

Maes, K., De Haes, S., & Van Grembergen, W. (2013). Investigating a process approach on business cases: An exploratory case study at Barco. *International Journal of IT/Business Alignment and Governance (IJITBAG)*, *4*(2), 37–53.

Maleh, Y. (2018a). *Security and privacy management, techniques, and protocols* (Y. Maleh, Ed.). IGI Global. https://doi.org/10.4018/978-1-5225-5583-4

Maleh, Y. (2018b). *Security and privacy management, techniques, and protocols*. IGI Global. https://doi.org/10.4018/978-1-5225-5583-4

Maleh, Y., Sahid, A., & Belaissaoui, M. (2019). *Strategic IT governance and performance frameworks in large organizations*. IGI Global. https://doi.org/10.4018/978-1-5225-7826-0

Maleh, Y., Sahid, A., & Belaissaoui, M. (2021). A maturity framework for cybersecurity governance in organizations. *EDPACS*, *64*(), 1–22. https://doi.org/10.1080/07366981.2020.1815354

Maleh, Y., Sahid, A., Ezzati, A., & Belaissaoui, M. (2018a). A capability maturity framework for IT security governance in organizations. *Advances in Intelligent Systems and Computing*, *735*. https://doi.org/10.1007/978-3-319-76354-5_20

Maleh, Y., Sahid, A., Ezzati, A., & Belaissaoui, M. (2018b). A capability maturity framework for IT security governance in organizations. In A. Abraham, A. Haqiq, A. K. Muda, & N. Gandhi (Eds.), *Innovations in bio-inspired computing and applications* (pp. 221–233). Springer International Publishing.

Maleh, Y., Zaydi, M., Sahid, A., & Ezzati, A. (2018). Building a maturity framework for information security governance through an empirical study in organizations. In Y. Maleh (Ed.), *Security and privacy management, techniques, and protocols* (pp. 96–127). IGI Global. https://doi.org/10.4018/978-1-5225-5583-4.ch004

Mark, D. (2014). *Global governance and the new wars: The merging of development and security.* Zed Books.

Markus, M. (1983). Power, politics, and MIS implementation. *Communication of ACM, 26.* https://doi.org/10.1145/358141.358148

Markus, M. L., & Benjamin, R. I. (1996). Change agentry-the next IS frontier. *MIS Quarterly,* 385–407.

Marrone, M., & Kolbe, L. M. (2011). Uncovering ITIL claims: IT executives' perception on benefits and business-IT alignment. *Information Systems and E-Business Management, 9*(3), 363–380. https://doi.org/10.1007/s10257-010-0131-7

Marrone, M., Gacenga, F., Cater-Steel, A., & Kolbe, L. (2014). IT service management: A cross-national study of ITIL adoption. *Communications of the Association for Information Systems, 34*(1), 865–892.

Mason, R. O., & Mitroff, I. I. (1973). A program for research on management information systems. *Management Science, 19*(5), 475–487. https://doi.org/10.1287/mnsc.19.5.475

Mataracioglu, T., & Ozkan, S. (2011). Governing information security in conjunction with COBIT and ISO 27001. *ArXiv Preprint ArXiv:1108.2150.*

Mazhelis, O., & Tyrväinen, P. (2012). Economic aspects of hybrid cloud infrastructure: User organization perspective. *Information Systems Frontiers, 14*(4), 845–869. https://doi.org/10.1007/s10796-011-9326-9

McEvoy, P., & Richards, D. (2006). A critical realist rationale for using a combination of quantitative and qualitative methods. *Journal of Research in Nursing, 11*(1), 66–78. https://doi.org/10.1177/1744987106060192

McGuire, M. (2016, February). The impact of performance management on performance in public organizations: A meta-analysis. *Public Administration Review, 76,* 48–66. https://doi.org/10.1111/puar.12433.48

McKay, J., Marshall, P., & Smith, L. (2003, July). Steps towards effective IT governance: Strategic IT planning, evaluation and benefits management. *Pacific Asia Conference on Information Systems,* 956–970. www.pacis-net.org/file/2003/papers/is-strategy/214.pdf

Michael E. Whitman, H. J. M. (2011). *Roadmap to information security: For IT and Infosec managers.* Delmar Learning.

Mintzberg, H. (1973). *The nature of managerial work.* Springer.

Mintzberg, H. (1983). *Structures in fives: Designing effective organizations.* Prentice Hall.

Mintzberg, H., Lampel, J., & Quinn, J. B. (2003). *The strategy process: Concepts, context, cases, global* (4th ed.). Pearson Education, Prentice Hall.

Mitchell, R. C., Marcella, R., & Baxter, G. (1999). Corporate information security management. *New Library World, 100.* https://doi.org/10.1108/03074809910285888

Moeller, R. R. (2011). *COSO enterprise risk management: Establishing effective governance, risk, and compliance (GRC) processes* (2nd ed.). John Wiley & Sons.

Moen, R., & Norman, C. (2006). *Evolution of the PDCA cycle.* API Organization.

Mohamed, N., & Singh, J. K. a/p G. (2012). A conceptual framework for information technology governance effectiveness in private organizations. *Information Management & Computer Security, 20*(2), 88–106. https://doi.org/10.1108/09685221211235616

Montalbano, E. (2012). Feds refine cloud security standards. *InformationWeek.*

Morse, J. M., & Niehaus, L. (2009). *Mixed method design: Principles and procedures* (4th ed.). Left Coast Press.

Morton, J., Stacey, P., & Mohn, M. (2018). Building and maintaining strategic agility: An agenda and framework for executive IT leaders. *California Management Review, 61*(1), 94–113.

Moy, B. (2018). PROGame: A process framework for serious game development for motor rehabilitation therapy. *PloS One*, 1–18.

Murphy, K., Lyytinen, K., & Somers, T. (2018). A socio-technical model for project-based executive IT governance. *Proceedings of the 51st Hawaii International Conference on System Sciences | 2018 A, 9*, 4825–4834.

Nasir, U. (2017). *An assessment model for enterprise clouds adoption.* http://eprints.keele. ac.uk/4281/

Nassar, P. B., Badr, Y., Barbar, K., & Biennier, F. (2009). Risk management and security in service-based architectures. *2009 International Conference on Advances in Computational Tools for Engineering Applications*, 214–218. https://doi.org/10.1109/ACTEA.2009.5227927

Nations, U. (2008). *International standard industrial classification of all economic activities (revision 4).* United Nations Publication.

Nehan, Y. R., & Deneckere, R. (2007). Component-based situational methods: A framework for understanding SME. *IFIP International Federation for Information Processing, 244*, 161–175. https://doi.org/10.1007/978-0-387-73947-2_14

Neto, J. S., CGEIT, C., Assessor, C. C., & de Luca Ribeiro, C. H. (n.d.). Is COBIT 5 process implementation a wicked problem? *COBIT Focus, 2*, 8–10.

Newcomer, E. (2002). *Understanding web services: XML, WSDL, SOAP, and UDDI.* Addison-Wesley Professional.

Newkirk, H. E., & Lederer, A. L. (2006). The effectiveness of strategic information systems planning under environmental uncertainty. *Information & Management, 43*(4), 481–501.

Nfuka, E. N., & Rusu, L. (2011). The effect of critical success factors on IT governance performance. *Industrial Management & Data Systems, 111*(9), 1418–1448. https://doi.org/10.1108/02635571111182773

Nfuka, E., & Rusu, L. (2010). IT governance maturity in the public sector organizations in a developing country: The case of Tanzania. *AMCIS 2010 Proceedings, 2010*, 536. http://aisel.aisnet.org/ecis2010/128/

Nianxin, W., Xue, Y., Liang, H., & Ge, S. (2011). The road to business-IT alignment: A case study of two Chinese companies. *Communications of AIS, 2011*(28), 415–436. http://content.ebscohost.com/ContentServer.asp?T=P&P=AN&K=70400209&S=R&D=buh&EbscoContent=dGJyMNLe80Sep7A4yOvqOLCmr0qeprJSsai4TLSWxWXS&ContentCustomer=dGJyMPGnr0m0r7JJuePfgeyx44Dt6fIA%5Cnwww.redi-bw.de/db/ebsco.php/search.ebscohost.com/login.aspx?d

Nicho, M. (2017). Managing information security risk using integrated governance risk and compliance. *Computer and Applications (ICCA), 2017 International Conference On*, 56–66. https://doi.org/10.1109/COMAPP.2017.8079741

Nkhoma, M. Z., Dang, D. P. T., & De Souza-Daw, A. (2013). Contributing factors of cloud computing adoption: A technology-organisation-environment framework approach. *Proceedings of the European Conference on Information Management & Evaluation*, 180–189.

Noor, T. H., Zeadally, S., Alfazi, A., & Sheng, Q. Z. (2018). Mobile cloud computing: Challenges and future research directions. *Journal of Network and Computer Applications, 115*, 70–85. https://doi.org/10.1016/J.JNCA.2018.04.018

Nugroho, H. (2014). Conceptual model of IT governance for higher education based on COBIT 5 framework. *Journal of Theoretical and Applied Information Technology, 60*(2), 216–221. https://doi.org/ISSN: 1992–8645

Nurcan, S., & Rolland, C. (2003). A multi-method for defining the organizational change. *Information and Software Technology, 45*(2), 61–82. https://doi.org/10.1016/S0950-5849(02)00162-3

Oetzel, J. M. (2004). Differentiation advantages in the on-line brokerage industry. *International Journal of Electronic Commerce, 9*(1), 105–126.

Oliveira, T., Thomas, M., & Espadanal, M. (2014). Assessing the determinants of cloud computing adoption: An analysis of the manufacturing and services sectors. *Information and Management, 51*(5), 497–510. https://doi.org/10.1016/j.im.2014.03.006

Oliver, D., & Lainhart, J. (2012). COBIT 5: Adding value through effective geit. *EDPACS, 46*(3), 1–12. https://doi.org/10.1080/07366981.2012.706472

Olson, M. H. (1985). *Management information systems: Conceptual foundations, structure, and development.* McGraw-Hill.

Omari, L. Al, Barnes, P. H., & Pitman, G. (2012). *An exploratory study into audit challenges in IT governance: A Delphi approach.* Symposium on IT Governance, Management and Audit. https://eprints.qut.edu.au/53110/

Otto, B. (2010). IT governance and organizational transformation: Findings from an action research study. *AMCIS, 421.*

Paliszkiewicz, J. (2019). Information security policy compliance: Leadership and trust. *Journal of Computer Information Systems, 59*(3), 211–217. https://doi.org/10.1080/08874417.2019.1571459

Pat, J. D., & Piattini, M. (2011). Software process improvement and capability determination. *11th International Conference, SPICE, 155,* 143–155. https://doi.org/10.1007/978-3-642-21233-8

Peltier, T. R. (2013). *Information security fundamentals* (2nd ed.). CRC Press, Taylor & Francis.

Perry, C., Alizadeh, Y., & Riege, A. (1997). Qualitative methods in entrepreneurship research. *Proceedings of the Annual Conference of the Small Enterprise Association Australia and New Zealand,* 547–567.

Peterson, R. R. (2001). Configurations and coordination for global information technology governance: Complex designs in a transnational European context. *Proceedings of the Hawaii International Conference on System Sciences, C,* 217. https://doi.org/10.1109/HICSS.2001.927133

Peterson, R. R. (2004). Crafting information technology governance. *Information Systems Management, 21*(4), 7–22.

Peterson, R. R., Parker, M., Ribbers, P., Peterson, R. R., & Parker, M. M. (2002). Information technology governance processes under environmental dynamism: Investigating competing theories of decision making and knowledge sharing. *ICIS 2002 Proceedings,* 562–575.

Pinsonneault, A., & Rivard, S. (1998). Information technology and the nature of managerial work: From the productivity paradox to the Icarus paradox? *MIS Quarterly,* 287–311.

Ploesser, K., Recker, J., & Rosemann, M. (2008). Towards a classification and lifecycle of business process change: A classification and lifecycle of process change strategies. *BPMDS'08: Business Process Life-Cycle: Design, Deployment, Operation & Evaluation, 2008,* 10–18.

Posthumus, S., & Von Solms, R. (2004). A framework for the governance of information security. *Computers & Security, 23*(8), 638–646. http://doi.org/10.1016/j.cose.2004.10.006

Posthumus, S., Von Solms, R., & King, M. (2010). The board and IT governance: The what, who and how. *South African Journal of Business Management, 41*(3), 23–32. https://journals.co.za/content/busman/41/3/EJC22396

Prager, K. P. (1996). Managing for flexibility: The new role of the aligned IT organization. *Information Systems Management, 13*(4), 41–46.

Premkumar, G., & Roberts, M. (1999). Adoption of new information technologies in rural small businesses. *Omega, 27*(4), 467–484. https://doi.org/10.1016/S0305-0483(98)00071-1

PRGL. (2011). *Praxiom research group limited.* Retrieved March 4, 2012, from www.praxiom.com/iso-17799-intro.htm

Prieto-Diaz, R. (1991). Implementing faceted classification for software reuse. *Communications of the ACM, 34*(5), 88–97. https://doi.org/10.1145/103167.103176

Punch, K. F. (2013). *Introduction to social research: Quantitative and qualitative approaches* (3rd ed.). Sage Publications.

Queiroz, M., Tallon, P. P., Sharma, R., & Coltman, T. (2018). The role of IT application orchestration capability in improving agility and performance. *Journal of Strategic Information Systems, 27*(1), 4–21. https://doi.org/10.1016/j.jsis.2017.10.002

Raghupathi, W. (2007). Corporate governance of IT: A framework for development. *Communications of the ACM, 50*(8), 94–99. https://doi.org/10.1145/1278201.1278212

Ramdani, B., Kawalek, P., & Lorenzo, O. (2009). Predicting SMEs' adoption of enterprise systems. *Journal of Enterprise Information Management, 22*, 10–24. https://doi.org/10.1108/17410390910922796

Ramesh, J. V., Singh, S. K., & Sharma, M. (2011). Development of private cloud for educational institution using Aneka grid container. *Proceedings of the International Conference & Workshop on Emerging Trends in Technology*, 244–247. https://doi.org/10.1145/1980022.1980078

Ramírez-Mora, S. L., Oktaba, H., & Patlán Pérez, J. (2020). Group maturity, team efficiency, and team effectiveness in software development: A case study in a CMMI-DEV level 5 organization. *Journal of Software: Evolution and Process, 32*(4), e2232. https://doi.org/10.1002/smr.2232

Raup-Kounovsky, A., Canestraro, D. S., Pardo, T. A., & Hrdinová, J. (2010). IT governance to fit your context: Two U.S. case studies. *Proceedings of the 4th International Conference on Theory and Practice of Electronic Governance*, 211–215. https://doi.org/10.1145/1930321.1930365

Ravichandran, T., Lertwongsatien, C., & Lertwongsatien, C. (2005). Effect of information systems resources and capabilities on firm performance: A resource-based perspective. *Journal of Management Information Systems, 21*(4), 237–276. https://doi.org/10.1080/07421222.2005.11045820

Rees, J., Bandyopadhyay, S., & Spafford, E. H. (2003). PFIRES: A policy framework for information security. *Communication of ACM, 46*(7), 101 106. https://doi.org/10.1145/792704.792706

Reich, B. H., & Benbasat, I. (2000). Factors that influence the social dimension of alignment between business and information technology objectives. *MIS Quarterly, 24*(1), 81–113. https://doi.org/10.2307/3250980

Renaud, A., Walsh, I., & Kalika, M. (2016). Is SAM still alive? A bibliometric and interpretive mapping of the strategic alignment research field. *The Journal of Strategic Information Systems, 25*(2), 75–103. https://doi.org/10.1016/j.jsis.2016.01.002

Reyck, B. De, Grushka-Cockayne, Y., Lockett, M., Calderini, S. R., Moura, M., & Sloper, A. (2005). The impact of project portfolio management on information technology projects. *International Journal of Project Management, 23*(7), 524–537. https://doi.org/10.1016/j.ijproman.2005.02.003

Rezaee, Z., & Reinstein, A. (1998). The impact of emerging information technology on auditing. *Managerial Auditing Journal, 13*(8), 465–471. https://doi.org/10.1108/02686909810236271

Ribeiro, J., & Gomes, R. (2009, September). IT governance using COBIT implemented in a high public educational institution – a case study. *Proceedings of the 3rd International Conference on European Computing Conference*, 41–52. wseas.us/e-library/conferences/2009/georgia/CCI/CCI04.pdf

Rizal, R. A., Sarno, R., & Sungkono, K. R. (2020). COBIT 5 for analysing information technology governance maturity level on masterplan e-government. *2020 International Seminar on Application for Technology of Information and Communication (ISemantic)*, 517–522. https://doi.org/10.1109/iSemantic50169.2020.9234301

Robson, W. (1998). Strategic management and information systems: An integrated approach. *Systems Research and Behavioral Science, 15*(4), 347–350.

Rocha Flores, W., Antonsen, E., & Ekstedt, M. (2014). Information security knowledge sharing in organizations: Investigating the effect of behavioral information security governance and national culture. *Computers & Security, 43*, 90–110. https://doi.org/10.1016/j.cose.2014.03.004

Rockart, J. F., & Crescenzi, A. D. (1984). Engaging top management in information technology. *Sloan Management Review, 25*, 3–16.

Rogers, E. M. (2003). *Diffusion of innovations* (5th ed). A Division of Macmillan Publishing Co Inc., Free Press.

Rolland, C. (1998). A comprehensive view of process engineering. *International Conference on Advanced Information Systems Engineering*, 1–24.

Roman, D., Keller, U., Lausen, H., De Bruijn, J., Lara, R., Stollberg, M., Polleres, A., Feier, C., Bussler, C., & Fensel, D. (2005). Web service modeling ontology. *Applied Ontology, 1*(1), 77–106.

Rummler, G. A., & Brache, A. P. (2012). *Improving performance: How to manage the white space on the organization chart*. John Wiley & Sons.

Saetang, S., & Haider, A. (2011). Conceptual aspects of IT governance in enterprise environment. *Proceedings of the 49th SIGMIS Annual Conference on Computer Personnel Research*, 79–82. https://doi.org/10.1145/1982143.1982164

Saha, N., Gregar, A., Van der Heijden, B. I. J. M., & Sáha, P. (2019). The influence of SHRM and organizational agility: Do they really boost organizational performance? In *Handbook of research on contemporary approaches in management and organizational strategy* (pp. 62–83). IGI Global.

Sahid, A., Maleh, Y., & Belaissaoui, M. (2018). A practical agile framework for IT service and asset management ITSM/ITAM through a case study. *Journal of Cases on Information Technology, 20*(4), 71–92.

Sahid, A., Maleh, Y., & Belaissaoui, M. (2020a). Cloud computing as a drive for strategic agility in organizations. In *Strategic information system agility: From theory to practices* (pp. 117–151). Emerald Publishing Limited. https://doi.org/10.1108/978-1-80043-810-120211007

Sahid, A., Maleh, Y., & Belaissaoui, M. (2020b). Information system evolution. In *Strategic information system agility: From theory to practices* (pp. 29–66). Emerald Publishing Limited. https://doi.org/10.1108/978-1-80043-810-120211004

Sahid, A., Maleh, Y., & Belaissaoui, M. (2020c). Strategic agility for IT service management: A case study. In *Strategic information system agility: From theory to practices* (pp. 93–116). Emerald Publishing Limited. https://doi.org/10.1108/978-1-80043-810-120211006

Sahid, A., Maleh, Y., & Belaissaoui, M. (2020d). Strategic information system agility: From theory to practices. In *Strategic information system agility: From theory to practices*. Emerald Publishing Limited. https://doi.org/10.1108/978-1-80043-810-120211001

Saint-Germain, R. (2005). Information security management best practice based on ISO/IEC 17799. *The Information Management Journal, 39*(4), 60–66.

Sambamurthy, V., & Zmud, R. (1999). Arrangements for information technology governance: A theory of multiple contingencies. *Management Information Systems Quarterly, 23*(2), 261–290. https://doi.org/10.2307/249754

Sandu, R., & Gide, E. (2018). Technological, organisational and environmental (TOE) factors that influence the adoption of cloud based service SMEs in India. *2018 IEEE 11th International Conference on Cloud Computing (CLOUD)*, 866–870. https://doi.org/10.1109/CLOUD.2018.00123

Sangle, S. (2011). Adoption of cleaner technology for climate proactivity: A technology – firm – stakeholder framework. *Business Strategy and the Environment, 20*(6), 365–378.

Sarker, S., & Sarker, S. (2009). Exploring agility in distributed information systems development teams: An interpretive study in an offshoring context. *Information Systems Research, 20*(3), 440–461.

Sarkis, J. (2001). Benchmarking for agility. *Benchmarking: An International Journal, 8*(2), 88–107.

Sassone, P. G. (1988). A survey of cost-benefit methodologies for information systems. *Project Appraisal, 3*(2), 73–84.

Sawhney, N., & Schmandt, C. (2000). Nomadic radio: Speech and audio interaction for contextual messaging in nomadic environments. *ACM Transactions on Computer-Human Interaction (TOCHI), 7*(3), 353–383.

Scheer, A. W., & Habermann, F. (2000). Enterprise resource planning: Making ERP a success. *Communications of the ACM, 43*(4), 57–61.

Schneiderman, R. (2011). For cloud computing, the sky is the limit [special reports]. *IEEE Signal Processing Magazine, 28*(1), 15–144.

Scholl, H. J., Kubicek, H., & Cimander, R. (2011). Interoperability, enterprise architectures, and IT governance in government. *Lecture Notes in Computer Science (Including Subseries Lecture Notes in Artificial Intelligence and Lecture Notes in Bioinformatics)*, *6846 LNCS*, 345–354. https://doi.org/10.1007/978-3-642-22878-0_29

Schou, C., & Shoemaker, D. P. (2006). *Information assurance for the enterprise: A roadmap to information security*. McGraw-Hill, Inc.

Schubert, K. D. (2004). *CIO survival guide: The roles and responsibilities of the chief information officer*. John Wiley & Sons.

Selig, G. J. (2008). *Implementing IT governance-a practical guide to global best practices in IT management*. Van Haren Publishing.

Senarathna, I., Wilkin, C., Warren, M., Yeoh, W., & Salzman, S. (2018). Factors that influence adoption of cloud computing: An empirical study of Australian SMEs. *Australasian Journal of Information Systems*, *22*.

Senarathna, R. (2016). *Cloud computing adoption by SMEs in Australia* [PhD thesis, Deakin University].

Senn, J. A. (1978). Essential principles of information systems development. *MIS Quarterly*, 17–26.

Shah Alam, S., Ali, M. Y., & Mohd. Jani, M. (2011). An empirical study of factors affecting electronic commerce adoption among SMEs in Malaysia. *Journal of Business Economics and Management*, *12*(2), 375–399. https://doi.org/10.3846/16111699.2011.576749

Sharif, A. M., Irani, Z., & Love, P. E. D. (2005). Integrating ERP using EAI: A model for post hoc evaluation. *European Journal of Information Systems*, *14*(2), 162–174.

Sharifi, H., & Zhang, Z. (1999). Methodology for achieving agility in manufacturing organisations: An introduction. *International Journal of Production Economics*, *62*(1), 7–22. https://doi.org/10.1016/S0925-5273(98)00217-5

Sharma, M., Gupta, R., & Acharya, P. (2017). Prioritizing the critical factors of cloud computing adoption using multi-criteria decision-making techniques. *Global Business Review*, *21*(1), 142–161. https://doi.org/10.1177/0972150917741187

Sharp, J. M., Bamber, C. J., Desia, S., & Irani, Z. (1999, March 9). *An empirical analysis of lean & agile manufacturing*. Proceedings of the IMechE Conference on Lean & Agile for the Next Millennium.

Shein, C., Robinson, H. E., & Gutierrez, H. (2018). Agility in the archives: Translating agile methods to archival project management. *RBM: A Journal of Rare Books, Manuscripts, and Cultural Heritage*, *19*(2), 94.

Shekhar, G. (2020). Instructor led training and certification – ITIL V4 foundation. *Proceedings of the 21st Annual Conference on Information Technology Education*, 355. https://doi.org/10.1145/3368308.3415453

Shore, B. (2006). Enterprise integration across the globally disbursed service organization. *Communications of the ACM*, *49*(6), 102–106.

Siggelkow, N. (2007). Persuasion with case studies. *Academy of Management Journal*, *50*(1), 20–24. https://doi.org/10.5465/amj.2007.24160882

Simonsson, M., & Johnson, P. (2006). Defining IT governance – a consolidation of literature. *The 18th Conference on Advanced Information Systems Engineering*, 6.

Simonsson, M., & Johnson, P. (2006, December). *Assessment of IT governance – a prioritization of COBIT*. Proceedings of the Conference on Systems Engineering Research. http://sse.stevens.edu/fileadmin/cser/2006/papers/151-Simonsson-Assessment of IT Governance.pdf

Simonsson, M., Johnson, P., & Wijkström, H. (2007). Model-based IT governance maturity assessments with COBIT. *In ECIS*, 1276–1287.

Simonsson, Mårten, Lagerström, R., & Johnson, P. (2008). A Bayesian network for IT governance performance prediction. *Proceedings of the 10th International Conference on Electronic Commerce*, 1:1–1:8. https://doi.org/10.1145/1409540.1409542

Singh, M. P., Huhns, M. N., & Huhns, M. N. (2005). *Service-oriented computing: Semantics, processes, agents*. John Wiley & Sons.

Siponen, M., & Willison, R. (2009). Information security management standards: Problems and solutions. *Information & Management*, *46*(5), 267–270. http://doi.org/10.1016/j.im.2008.12.007

Sitaram, D., & Manjunath, G. (2012). Moving to the cloud. *Moving to the Cloud*, *2*(1), 1–10. https://doi.org/10.1016/C2010-0-66389-9

Skafi, M., Yunis, M. M., & Zekri, A. (2020). Factors influencing SMEs' adoption of cloud computing services in Lebanon: An empirical analysis using TOE and contextual theory. *IEEE Access*, *8*, 79169–79181. https://doi.org/10.1109/ACCESS.2020.2987331

Smits, D., & Hillegersberg, J. V. (2015). IT governance maturity: Developing a maturity model using the Delphi method. *2015 48th Hawaii International Conference on System Sciences*, 4534–4543. https://doi.org/10.1109/HICSS.2015.541

Sohrabi Safa, N., Von Solms, R., & Furnell, S. (2016). Information security policy compliance model in organizations. *Computers and Security*, *56*, 1–13. https://doi.org/10.1016/j.cose.2015.10.006

Soomro, Z. A., Shah, M. H., & Ahmed, J. (2016). Information security management needs more holistic approach: A literature review. *International Journal of Information Management*, *36*(2), 215–225. http://doi.org/10.1016/j.ijinfomgt.2015.11.009

Spafford, G. (2003). *The benefits of standard IT governance frameworks*. Retrieved April 4, 2012, from http://www.Itmanagementonline.Com/Resources/Articles/The_Benefits_of_Standard_IT_Gov Ernance_Frameworks.Pdf

Stein, M. K., Galliers, R. D., & Whitley, E. A. (2016). Twenty years of the European information systems academy at ECIS: Emergent trends and research topics. *European Journal of Information Systems*, *25*(1), 1–15. https://doi.org/10.1057/ejis.2014.25

Steuperaert, D. (2019). COBIT 2019: A significant update. *EDPACS*, *59*(1), 14–18. https://doi.org/10.1080/07366981.2019.1578474

Straub, D., & Welke, R. (1998). Coping with systems risk: Security planning models for management decision making. *MIS Quarterly*, *22*(4), 441–469. www.jstor.org/stable/249551

Susarla, A., Barua, A., & Whinston, A. B. (2006). Understanding the "service" component of application service provision: An empirical analysis of satisfaction with ASP services. In *Information systems outsourcing* (pp. 481–521). Springer.

Swafford, P. M., Ghosh, S., & Murthy, N. (2008). Achieving supply chain agility through IT integration and flexibility. *International Journal of Production Economics*, *116*(2), 288–297. https://doi.org/10.1016/j.ijpe.2008.09.002

Talib, M. A., El Barachi, M., Khelifi, A., & Ormandjieva, O. (2012). Guide to ISO 27001: UAE case study. *Issues in Informing Science and Information Technology*, *7*, 331–349.

Tankard, C., & Pathways, D. (2016). What the GDPR means for. *Network Security*, *2016*(6), 5–8. https://doi.org/10.1016/S1353-4858(16)30056-3

Tashakkori, A., & Creswell, J. W. (2007). *Exploring the nature of research questions in mixed methods research*. Sage Publications.

Tashi, I., & Ghernaouti-Hélie, S. (2007). Security metrics to improve information security management. *Proceedings of the 6th Annual Security Conference*, 47-1–47-13.

Thiesse, F., Staake, T., Schmitt, P., & Fleisch, E. (2011). The rise of the "next-generation bar code": An international RFID adoption study. *Supply Chain Management*, *16*(5), 328–345. https://doi.org/10.1108/13598541111155848

Tonelli, A. O., de Souza Bermejo, P. H., Aparecida dos Santos, P., Zuppo, L., & Zambalde, A. L. (2017). IT governance in the public sector: A conceptual model. *Information Systems Frontiers*, *19*(3), 593–610. https://doi.org/10.1007/s10796-015-9614-x

Tornatzky, L. G., Fleischer, M., & Chakrabarti, A. K. (1990). *The processes of technological innovation*. Issues in organization and management series. Lexington Books. Retrieved June 10, 2013, from http://www.Amazon. Com/Processes-Technological-Innovation-Organization/Management/Dp/0669203483

Trigueros-Preciado, S., Pérez-González, D., & Solana-González, P. (2013). Cloud computing in industrial SMEs: Identification of the barriers to its adoption and effects of its application. *Electronic Markets*, *23*(2), 105–114. https://doi.org/10.1007/s12525-012-0120-4

Trisha, G., Glenn, R., Fraser, M., Paul, B., & Olivia, K. (2004). Diffusion of innovations in service organizations: Systematic review and recommendations. *The Milbank Quarterly, 82*(4), 581–629. https://doi.org/10.1111/j.0887-378X.2004.00325.x

Tsai, M. C., Lee, W., & Wu, H. C. (2010). Determinants of RFID adoption intention: Evidence from Taiwanese retail chains. *Information & Management, 47*(5), 255–261. https://doi.org/10.1016/j.im.2010.05.001

Turban, E. (2007). *Information technology for management: Transforming organizations in the digital economy.* John Wiley & Sons, Inc.

Ula, M., Ismail, Z., & Sidek, Z. (2011). A framework for the governance of information security in banking system. *Journal of Information Assurance & Cybersecurity, 23*(8), 1–12. https://doi.org/10.5171/2011.726196

Valentine, E. L. H. (2016, January). *Enterprise technology governance: New information and technology core competencies for boards of directors* [Doctoral dissertation, Queensland University of Technology], 1–295. https://doi.org/10.13140/RG.2.2.34027.95529

Van Grembergen, W., & De Haes, S. (2009a). *Enterprise governance of information technology: Achieving strategic alignment and value.* Springer Science & Business Media.

Van Grembergen, W., & De Haes, S. (2009b). *COBIT as a framework for enterprise governance of IT BT – enterprise governance of information technology: Achieving strategic alignment and value* (S. De Haes & W. Van Grembergen (Eds., pp. 137–164). Springer. https://doi.org/10.1007/978-0-387-84882-2_5

Van Grembergen, W, & De Haes, S. (2009c). *The IT balanced scorecard as a framework for enterprise governance of IT BT – enterprise governance of information technology: Achieving strategic alignment and value* (S. De Haes & W. Van Grembergen (Eds.), pp. 111–136). Springer. https://doi.org/10.1007/978-0-387-84882-2_4

Van Wyk, J., & Rudman, R. (2019). COBIT 5 compliance: Best practices cognitive computing risk assessment and control checklist. *Meditari Accountancy Research, 27*(5), 761–788. https://doi.org/10.1108/MEDAR-04-2018-0325

Vaughan-Nichols, S. J. (2002). Web services: Beyond the hype. *Computer, 35*(2), 18–21.

Venkatesh, V. (2012). Consumer acceptance and use of information technology: Extending the unified theory. *MIS Quarterly, 36*(1), 157–178.

Venkatesh, V., Morris, M. G., Davis, G. B., & Davis, F. D. (2003). User acceptance of information technology: Toward a unified view. *Source: MIS Quarterly, 27*(3), 425–478. https://doi.org/10.2307/30036540

Verhoef, C. (2007). Quantifying the effects of IT-governance rules. *Science of Computer Programming, 67*(2–3), 247–277. https://doi.org/10.1016/j.scico.2007.01.010

Vlietland, J., van Solingen, R., & van Vliet, H. (2016). Aligning codependent scrum teams to enable fast business value delivery: A governance framework and set of intervention actions. *Journal of Systems and Software, 113*, 418–429. https://doi.org/10.1016/j.jss.2015.11.010

Von Solms, B. (2005). Information security governance: COBIT or ISO 17799 or both? *Computers and Security, 24*(2), 99–104. https://doi.org/10.1016/j.cose.2005.02.002

Von Solms, R., & van Niekerk, J. (2013). From information security to cyber security. *Computers & Security, 38*, 97–102. http://doi.org/10.1016/j.cose.2013.04.004

Von Solms, S. H. (2005). Information security governance – compliance management vs operational management. *Computers and Security, 24*(6), 443–447. https://doi.org/10.1016/j.cose.2005.07.003

Waddock, S. A., & Graves, S. B. (1997). The corporate social performance-financial performance link. *Strategic Management Journal, 18*(4), 303–319. https://doi.org/10.1002/(SICI)1097-0266(199704)18:4<303::AID-SMJ869>3.0.CO;2-G

Wallhoff, J. (2004). *Combining ITIL with COBIT and ISO/IEC 17799:2000.* Scillani Information AB.

Walls, J. G., Widmeyer, G. R., & El Sawy, O. A. (1992). Building an information system design theory for vigilant EIS. *Information Systems Research, 3*(1), 36–59.

Walsham, G. (1993). *Interpreting information systems in organizations.* John Wiley & Sons, Inc.

Walters, G. J. (2001). Privacy and security: An ethical analysis. *ACM SIGCAS Computers and Society, 31*(2), 8–23.

Wang, Z., Li, B., Sun, L., & Yang, S. (2012). Cloud-based social application deployment using local processing and global distribution. *Proceedings of the 8th International Conference on Emerging Networking Experiments and Technologies*, 301–312. https://doi.org/10.1145/2413176.2413211

Warland, C., & Ridley, G. (2005a). Awareness of IT control frameworks in an Australian state government: A qualitative case study. *Proceedings of the 38th Annual Hawaii International Conference on System Sciences, C*, 236b. https://doi.org/10.1109/HICSS.2005.116

Warland, C., & Ridley, G. (2005b). Awareness of IT control frameworks in an Australian state government: A qualitative case study. *Proceedings of the 38th Annual Hawaii International Conference on System Sciences, C*, 236b. https://doi.org/10.1109/HICSS.2005.116

Webb, P., Pollard, C., & Ridley, G. (2006). Attempting to define IT governance: Wisdom or folly? *Proceedings of the Annual Hawaii International Conference on System Sciences, 8*(C), 1–10. https://doi.org/10.1109/HICSS.2006.68

Weber, L. (2014). *Addressing the incremental risks associated with adopting a bring your own device program by using the COBIT 5 framework to identify keycontrols* [Doctoral dissertation, Stellenbosch University].

Weill, P., & Ross, J. (2005). A matrixed approach to designing IT governance. *MIT Sloan Management Review, 46*(2), 26–34. https://doi.org/10.1177/0275074007310556

Weill, P., & Ross, J. W. (2004). *How top performers manage IT decisions rights for superior results* (pp. 1–10). IT Governance, Harvard Business School Press. https://doi.org/10.2139/ssrn.664612

Weill, P., & Woodham, R. (2002). Don't just lead, govern: Implementing effective IT governance. *CISR Working Paper, 17*. https://doi.org/10.2139/ssrn.317319

West, L. A., & Hess, T. J. (2002). Metadata as a knowledge management tool: Supporting intelligent agent and end user access to spatial data. *Decision Support Systems, 32*(3), 247–264.

Wickramasinghe, N. (2003). Do we practise what we preach? Are knowledge management systems in practice truly reflective of knowledge management systems in theory? *Business Process Management Journal, 9*(3), 295–316.

Wiederhold, G. (1992). Mediators in the architecture of future information systems. *Computer, 25*(3), 38–49.

Willcocks, L. (2013). *Information management: The evaluation of information systems investments.* Springer. https://doi.org/10.1007/978-1-4899-3208-2

Williams, P. (2001). Information security governance. *Information Security Technical Report, 6*(3), 60–70. http://doi.org/10.1016/S1363-4127(01)00309-0

Williams, P. (2007). Executive and board roles in information security. *Network Security.* https://doi.org/10.1016/S1353-4858(07)70073-9

Williams, S. P., Hardy, C. A., & Holgate, J. A. (2013). Information security governance practices in critical infrastructure organizations: A socio-technical and institutional logic perspective. *Electronic Markets, 23*(4), 341–354. https://doi.org/10.1007/s12525-013-0137-3

Willison, R. A. (2002). *Opportunities for computer abuse: Assessing a crime specific approach in the case of Barings Bank* [PhD thesis, London School of Economics and Political Science].

Woo, H., Lee, S., Huh, J. H., & Jeong, S. (2020). Impact of ITSM military service quality and value on service trust. *Journal of Multimedia Information System, 7*(1), 55–72. https://doi.org/10.33851/JMIS.2020.7.1.55

Wood, D. J. (2010). *Assessing IT governance maturity: The case of San Marcos, Texas* [Master's thesis, Texas State University].

Wu, W. W. (2011). Mining significant factors affecting the adoption of SaaS using the rough set approach. *Journal of Systems and Software, 84*(3), 435–441.

Wu, Y., Cegielski, C. G., Hazen, B. T., & Hall, D. J. (2013). Cloud computing in support of supply chain information system infrastructure: Understanding when to go to the cloud. *Journal of Supply Chain Management*, *49*(3), 25–41.

Xiaoying, D., Qianqian, L., & Dezhi, Y. (2008). Business performance, business strategy, and information system strategic alignment: An empirical study on Chinese firms. *Tsinghua Science and Technology*, *13*(3), 348–354. https://doi.org/10.1016/S1007-0214(08)70056-7

Xue, Y., Liang, H., & Boulton, W. R. (2008). Information technology governance in information technology investment decision processes: The impact of investment characteristics, external environment, and internal context 1. *MIS Quarterly*, *32*(1), 67–96. www.jstor.org/stable/25148829

Yang, H., & Tate, M. (2012). A descriptive literature review and classification of cloud computing research. *Communications of the Association of Information Systems*, *31*(2), 35–60. https://doi.org/10.1.1.261.3070

Yang, H., Huff, S. L., & Tate, M. (2013). Managing the cloud for information systems agility. In A. Bento & A. K. Aggarwal (Eds.), *Cloud computing service and deployment models: Layers and management* (pp. 70–93). IGI Global. https://doi.org/10.4018/978-1-4666-2187-9.ch004

Yassine, M., Abdelkebir, S., & Abdellah, E. (2017). *A capability maturity framework for IT security governance in organizations*. 13th International Symposium on Information Assurance and Security (IAS 17).

Yoon, Y., Guimaraes, T., & O'Ncal, Q. (1995). Exploring the factors associated with expert systems success. *MIS Quarterly*, 83–106.

Zhang, G., Fu, L., & Liang, Y. (2020). The impact of cloud computing infrastructure capability on enterprise agility: Based on the perspective of IT business alignment. *Proceedings of the 2020, 3rd International Conference on Signal Processing and Machine Learning*, 48–55. https://doi.org/10.1145/3432291.3433642

Zhang, Z., & Sharifi, H. (2000). A methodology for achieving agility in manufacturing organizations. *International Journal of Operations & Production Management*, *20*(4), 496–512. https://doi.org/10.1108/01443570010314818

Zheng, J., Ng, T. S. E., & Sripanidkulchai, K. (2011). Workload-aware live storage migration for clouds. *Proceedings of the 7th ACM SIGPLAN/SIGOPS International Conference on Virtual Execution Environments*, 133–144. https://doi.org/10.1145/1952682.1952700

Zhu, K. (2004). The complementarity of information technology infrastructure and e-commerce capability: A resource-based assessment of their business value. *Journal of Management Information Systems*, *21*(1), 167–202. https://doi.org/10.1080/07421222.2004.11045794

Zhu, K., Dong, S., Xu, S. X., & Kraemer, K. L. (2006). Innovation diffusion in global contexts: Determinants of post-adoption digital transformation of European companies. *European Journal of Information Systems*, *15*(6), 601–616.

Zhu, K., Kraemer, K. L., & Xu, S. (2003). Electronic business adoption by European firms: A cross-country assessment of the facilitators and inhibitors. *European Journal of Information Systems*, *12*(4), 251–268.

Zhu, K., Kraemer, K. L., & Xu, S. (2006). The process of innovation assimilation by firms in different countries: A technology diffusion perspective on e-business. *Management Science*, *52*(10), 1557–1576.

Zviran, M. (1990). Relationships between organizational and information systems objectives: Some empirical evidence. *Journal of Management Information Systems*, *7*(1), 65–84.

Zwass, V. (1992). *Management information systems*. William C. Brown Publishers.

Acronyms

APO	Align, Plan and Organize
BAI	Build, Acquire, and Implement
BSC	Balanced Scorecard
ISO/IEC	International Standards Organization/International Electrotechnical Commission
CEO	Chief of Enterprise Officer
CG	Corporate Governance
CIA	Confidentiality, Integrity, and Availability
CIO	Chief of Information Officer
CMDB	Configuration Management Database
CMMI	Capability Maturity Model Integration
COBIT	Control Objectives for Information and related Technology
COSO	Committee of Sponsoring Organizations of the Treadway Commission
DOI	Diffusion of Innovation theory
DSS	Deliver, Service, and Support
EDA	Exploratory Data Analysis
EDM	Evaluate, Direct and Monitor
EUROSAI	European Organization of Supreme Audit Institutions
DSR	Design Science Research
EG	Enterprise Governance
IT	Information Technology
ITAM	Information Technology Asset Management
ITG	Information Technology Governance
ITGI	Information Technology Governance Institute
ITIL	Information Technology Infrastructure Library
ITSM	Information Technology Service Management
IS	Information Systems
SLA	Service Level Agreement
ISO	Information Security Officer
ISMS	Information Security Management System
ISG	Information Security Governance
ISSP	Information Systems Security Policy
ITIL	Information Technology Infrastructure Library
ISACA	Information Systems Audit and Control Association
KPI	Key Performance Indicator
MEA	Monitor, Evaluate and Assess
MENA	Middle East and North Africa
NIST	National Institute of Standards and Technology
OLA	Operational Level Agreement

PDCA	Plan-Do-Check-Act
PCM	Process Capability Model
PMBOK	Project Management Body of Knowledge
SLM	Service Level Management
SMEs	Small and medium-sized enterprises
SOX	Sarbanes-Oxley Act
SPOC	Single Point of Contact
UTAUT	Unified Theory of Acceptance and Use of Technology

Index